Alms

Alms
Charity, Reward, and Atonement in Early Christianity

David J. Downs

BAYLOR UNIVERSITY PRESS

Cover Design by AJB Design, Inc.
Cover image: St. Giles supports a beggar, south wall of the crypt (fresco), French School, (11th century) / Church of Saint-Aignan-sur-Cher, Loir et Cher, France / Hirmer Fotoarchiv / Bridgeman Images

Library of Congress Cataloging-in-Publication Data

Downs, David J., 1977–
  Alms : charity, reward, and atonement in early Christianity / David J. Downs.
  350 pages cm
  Includes bibliographical references and index.
  ISBN 978-1-60258-997-1 (hardback : alk. paper)
  1. Charity—History of doctrines. 2. Redemption—Christianity—History of doctrines. 3. Atonement—History of doctrines. 4. Charity—Biblical teaching. 5. Redemption—Biblical teaching. 6. Atonement—Biblical teaching. I. Title.
  BV4639.D69 2016
  248.4′6—dc23
                    2015027496

CONTENTS

v

ACKNOWLEDGMENTS

I am grateful for the support of many people who have encouraged me in the writing of this book.

Serving as a professor at Fuller Theological Seminary is one of the great joys of my life. Fuller's School of Theology, led during the period of this book's composition by Dean Howard Loewen and Dean Joel Green, has generously assisted this project in several ways, including the provision of funds to present at national and international conferences some of the ideas developed in this book and the granting of sabbaticals during the fall of 2009 and spring of 2012. Much of this book was written in Mwanza, Tanzania, where our family has lived for about six months a year since 2009. While there are good things about life in Tanzania, the lack of physical access to a research library makes academic writing difficult, and the completion of this book would not have been possible without the outstanding research assistance of Benjamin Lappenga, Brian Robinson, and Allison Quient, all of whom were funded by Fuller's Center for Advanced Theological Studies. Susan Wood kindly helped with the indexing.

Numerous colleagues graciously read or engaged with material in various parts of this book: Nathan Eubank, Steven Friesen and the other organizers and participants of the 2011 COMCAR trip to Greece, Gregg

Gardner, John Goldingay, Christopher M. Hays, Micah Kiel, Benjamin Lappenga, Bruce Longenecker, Oliver Crisp, Timothy Reardon, Helen Rhee, and Marianne Meye Thompson. In addition to various presentations at meetings of the Society of Biblical Literature, I am grateful to have had the opportunity to test some of the ideas developed in this book at the Nairobi Evangelical Graduate School of Theology in 2011 and at the Lausanne Movement Global Consultation on Prosperity Theology in Atibaia, Brazil, in 2014. I am also thankful for the comments from the anonymous readers from Baylor University Press and for Carey Newman and his excellent team at Baylor University Press for their preparation and publication of this manuscript.

On this, our thirteenth wedding anniversary, I would like to thank my wife and constant companion, Jennifer Alzos Downs, not only for encouraging me to write (and finish!) this book but also for modeling for me for more than twenty years a life full of merciful deeds. Your commitment to serving and working with the world's poor and powerless is an inspiration to me and to many. Our life together has always helped me to avoid the fate of those fallen angels in Milton's *Paradise Lost*, who "*apart* sat on a hill retired, / In thoughts more elevate, and reasoned high / Of providence, foreknowledge, will and fate, / Fixed fate, free will, foreknowledge absolute, / And found no end, in wandering mazes lost." With you I am never "apart," in life in general or in my theological studies in particular. If my scholarship is less aimless and fruitless than the discourse of Milton's fallen angels, it is largely because of your influence, for life with you daily reminds me of the real world of poverty and loss, justice and hope, to which all academic research is rightly directed.

This book is dedicated to our three beautiful children: Emily, Luke, and Elijah. As you grow in faith, hope, and love, may you come to know the joy of showing mercy to those in need, even as you joyfully receive when you are in need, and may you pursue all the rewards associated with almsgiving. As a wise father once instructed his child:

> Do not turn your face away from any poor person, and the face of God will not be turned away from you. When you have possessions, according to the abundance practice the merciful act of almsgiving from the possessions. If you have a little, do not be afraid to practice the merciful act of almsgiving according to the little that you have. For you will be storing up a good treasure for yourself against a day of necessity. Therefore, the merciful act of almsgiving delivers from death and keeps one from going into darkness. Indeed, the merciful act of almsgiving is a good gift, for all who practice it, in the sight of the Most High. . . .

Give some of your bread to the hungry and some of your clothing to the naked. Give whatever is an abundance for you as a merciful act of almsgiving, and do not let your eye be envious when you practice the merciful act of almsgiving. (Tob 4:7-11, 16-17)

May 11, 2015

INTRODUCTION
What Can Wash Away My Sin?

"What can wash away my sin?"

This personal and penetrating question opens Robert Lowry's (1826–1899) popular nineteenth-century hymn, "Nothing but the Blood." The title of the song portends the author's response to this query, an answer, spelled out in clear terms in the song's first and fourth stanzas, that offers a classic articulation of the doctrine of substitutionary atonement in early evangelical hymnody:

> What can wash away my sin?
> Nothing but the blood of Jesus.
> What can make me whole again?
> Nothing but the blood of Jesus.
>
> Nothing can for sin atone,
> Nothing but the blood of Jesus;
> Naught of good that I have done,
> Nothing but the blood of Jesus.[1]

---

[1] Robert Lowry, "Nothing but the Blood," in *Gospel Music* (ed. William Doane and Robert Lowry; New York: Biglow & Main, 1876); available online: http://hymn time.com/tch/htm/n/b/t/nbtblood.htm; on the theme of substitutionary atonement in

1

Writing some seventeen centuries earlier, in language no less lyrical, the anonymous author of the *Epistle to Diognetus* reflects a similar sentiment on the death of Christ as the only means of atonement for sin:

> In his mercy God took our sins upon himself. He himself handed over his own son as a ransom for us. . . . For what else but the righteousness of that Son could have covered our sins? In whom is it possible that we, lawless and ungodly, could be justified, except in the Son of God only? O, the sweet exchange! O, the incomprehensible creative act of God! O, the unexpected benefactions! That the sinfulness of many should be hidden in one righteous person, and the righteousness of one should justify many lawless people! (*Diogn.* 9.2-5)[2]

Given the extent to which these two poetic declarations of the belief that only Jesus' death can wash or cover sins capture a theological position reflected in various strands of contemporary Christian faith and practice, it may come as a surprise to some that many Christian authors in the second through the fourth centuries (and beyond) frequently advocated another means of cleansing sin: care for the poor. An example from the fourth century provides an interesting initial illustration of the close connection between care for the poor and the cleansing—or, in this case, destruction—of sin in patristic sources.

In the fall of 368 CE, the Roman province of Cappadocia was in the throes of a severe food shortage. Nestled in a mountainous region of modern-day Turkey, the region had experienced an extended drought during the previous winter and spring, leaving dried streams, parched fields, and hungry stomachs at what should have been harvest time. With the importation of grain difficult due to the lack of port access for the landlocked region, food prices rose sharply as supplies dwindled.[3] The destitute from the countryside flocked to the cities. Although the possibility of overstatement can be suspected, at least one eyewitness observer called the situation "the most severe famine ever recorded."[4]

During this crisis, a man called Basil—then a priest in the church of Caesarea, the capital city of Cappadocia—stepped to the forefront as an

---

Lowry's hymn, see William H. Brackney, *A Genetic History of Baptist Thought* (Macon, Ga.: Mercer University Press, 2004), 87.

   [2] Unless otherwise noted, all translations in this book are my own. On the soteriology of the *Epistle to Diognetus*, see Brandon D. Crowe, "'Oh, Sweet Exchange!' The Soteriological Significance of the Incarnation in the Epistle to Diognetus," *ZNW* 102 (2011): 96–109.

   [3] Gregory of Nazianzus, *Or. Bas.* 43.34.

   [4] Gregory of Nazianzus, *Or. Bas.* 43.34.

eloquent patron on behalf of the poor. Basil is lionized by his brother Gregory of Nyssa and his friend Gregory of Nazianzus for making food available to the starving, although precise details of Basil's actions are somewhat unclear. Probably, the aristocratic priest played the role of noble benefactor by redistributing some of his own wealth in order to provide sustenance for the hungry.

In addition, Basil also preached several sermons aimed at encouraging wealthy members of the church in Caesarea to make donations to the poor or at least to sell some of the grain that they held in storage to the church at below-market prices. In these sermons, Basil employs a number of rhetorical strategies and striking images in the attempt to promote φιλανθρωπία ("loving kindness") among the Christian community in Caesarea. In his homily "In Time of Famine and Drought," for example, Basil is concerned with the problem of sin, particularly the relationship between the present famine and various transgressions of Christians in Caesarea. According to Basil, the current distress had been caused not by God's neglect of the created order but by "the multitude of our sins," including the refusal of Christians to share with those in need. Other sins identified by Basil as causes of hunger include a lack of commitment to prayer, the practice of usury, and hoarding grain. In light of these offenses, Basil exhorts believers in Caesarea to mournful self-reflection, tearful repentance, and generosity. Even the poor are encouraged to trust in God and share what they have with those who are worse off. Near the end of this sermon, Basil offers his audience a bold theological challenge in the form of a remedy to the present problem of sin and a means of avoiding divine judgment in the future:

> Seize, therefore, and fulfill the commandment [i.e., the commandment to show pity on the hungry] as you would take hold of a fugitive, securing it from all sides with grasping hands and encircling arms. Give a little and gain much; destroy the original sin by freely distributing food. For as sin came through Adam's evil act of eating, so we ourselves blot out his treacherous consumption if we remedy the need and hunger of a brother.[5]

---

5 Basil, *In famem et siccitatem*, PG 31.303–28 [324]; trans. from Susan R. Holman, *The Hungry Are Dying: Beggars and Bishops in Roman Cappadocia* (Oxford Studies in Historical Theology; Oxford: Oxford University Press, 2001), 191. Excellent accounts of Basil's activities and preaching during the food shortage can be found in Holman, *Hungry*, 64–98; and Richard D. Finn, *Almsgiving in the Later Roman Empire: Christian Promotion and Practice (313–450)* (Oxford Classical Monographs; Oxford: Oxford University Press, 2006), 222–36.

Drawing a connection between two acts of eating, Basil suggests that giving material assistance to the hungry has the power to wipe out "original sin" (λῦσον τὴν πρωτότυπον ἁμαρτίαν): just as the first contagion came through Adam's illicit ingestion, feeding a hungry brother or sister can effectively erase (ἐξαλείφομεν) the infectious transgression of Adam.

Basil here promotes what has been called "redemptive almsgiving"— namely, the notion that providing material assistance to the needy does something to reckon with sin, whether charity is understood to cleanse, extinguish, redeem, cover, or destroy sin.[6] To be sure, Basil's declaration that the act of feeding the needy can destroy an original sin contracted in Adam's selfish consumption is highly original. It is not evident that any other early Christian writer before Basil draws upon the narrative of Genesis 3 in order to frame compassion for the hungry as an antidote to the contagious transgression of Adam. Indeed, Basil's creative establishment of an anti-typological link between these two instances of nourishment—one that led to death, the other that leads to life—seems rhetorically potent particularly in the context of the Cappadocian food shortage. Yet in his advocacy of the atoning potential of caring for the poor, Basil is by no means alone. The underlying logic of Basil's contention—that is, the idea that caring for the needy can erase or in some way reckon with human sin—is widely attested in the literature of early Christianity. Advocates of "redemptive almsgiving" include such early Christian documents and authors as 2 Clement (16.1–4), the Didache (4.5–8), the Epistle of Barnabas (19.8–11), Clement of Alexandria (Quis div.

[6] The nature of what merciful care for the poor is said to do to "sin" in biblical and patristic sources depends largely on the metaphor(s) employed to represent "sin." Is sin a burden, a stain, a debt, an illness, a stumble, a rebellion, a captivity, or a cosmic power? Does the response to sin take place through the action of lifting, cleansing, paying, healing, picking up, reconciling, releasing, or defeating? In the Bible, sin is imaged through all of these metaphors, some more common than others. A representative sample of these biblical metaphors would include the following: burden (Exod 10:17; Lev 24:15; 16:22; Ps 38:7); stain (Lev 16:30; Ps 51:2; Jer 2:22; Jas 3:6; 1 John 1:9); debt (Isa 40:1-2; 50:1; Matt 6:12); illness (Isa 57:17-19; 1 Pet 2:24); stumbling (Isa 8:14; Jer 6:21; Rom 11:11); rebelling (Exod 23:21; Isa 1:5; 30:1; Hos 9:15); captivity (Ps 111:9; Col 1:14; Titus 2:14); cosmic power (1 Cor 15:56; Gal 3:22; Rom 3:9; 6:12-20; 7:8-11). Paul's use of the term ἁμαρτία to characterize "Sin" as an enslaving, cosmic power may more accurately be described as "personification," but personification can also be considered a subset of metaphor; see Joseph R. Dodson, *The Powers of Personification: Rhetorical Purpose in the Book of Wisdom and the Letter to the Romans* (BZNW 161; Berlin: De Gruyter, 2008). On the use of various metaphors for sin and its solution in biblical literature, see Gary A. Anderson, *Sin: A History* (New Haven: Yale University Press, 2010); and Mark J. Boda, *A Severe Mercy: Sin and Its Remedy in the Old Testament* (Siphrut: Literature and Theology of the Hebrew Scriptures 1; Winona Lake, Ind.: Eisenbrauns, 2009).

31–32), ~~Origen~~ (*Hom. Lev.* 2.4), ~~Cyprian~~ (*Eleem.*), ~~Basil of Caesarea,~~ John ~~Chrysostom~~ (*Hom.* Jo. 73), ~~Ambrose~~ (*Hel.* 20, 76), and ~~Augustine~~ (*Enchir.* 67, 69, 70), among others. If Basil's claim sounds strange to some modern ears, it is perhaps because rhetorical appeals to almsgiving do not feature in (at least Protestant) Christian discourse to the extent that they did ~~in the earliest centuries of the Christian~~ movement, when ~~the giving of alms, along with prayer and fasting, was regarded as one of the customary expressions of penitential practice.~~[7]

This book aims to tell the story of the emergence of "atoning almsgiving" in the first two centuries of the Christian movement, roughly from the writings of the New Testament to Cyprian, the third-century bishop of Carthage. This story will trace the historical and theological development of this model for the cleansing of sin from its antecedents in the Old Testament and the literature of Second Temple Judaism, to statements that link almsgiving and reward in the New Testament, through patristic advocates of atoning almsgiving in the second and third centuries of the Common Era. The story will conclude with ~~Cyprian in the middle of the third century.~~ Cyprian marks a fitting endpoint not only because his treatise *De opere et eleemosynis* ("~~On Works and Alms~~") represents a bold and innovative attempt to hold together the confession that forgiveness, redemption, and healing are possible only through the suffering and death of Christ and the conviction that ~~sins after baptism can be washed away by deeds of mercy.~~ Cyprian also stands as an apt figure with whom to conclude because the practice of Christian almsgiving underwent a monumental change with the rise of episcopal power and the emergence of Christian monasticism in the fourth and fifth centuries.[8] In contrast to earlier assessments of atoning almsgiving, it shall be argued here that—~~far from compromising or contradicting the affirmation that salvation and forgiveness of sin come through the life, death, and resurrection~~

---

[7]   See, e.g., John Anthony McGuckin, "Almsgiving," in *The Westminster Handbook to Patristic Theology* (Louisville, Ky.: Westminster John Knox, 2004), 8; cf. H. B. Swete, "Penitential Discipline in the First Three Centuries," *JTS* 4 (1903): 249–65.

[8]   The narrative of almsgiving in the post-Constantinian church is admirably related in Finn, *Almsgiving*; see also Boniface Ramsey, "Almsgiving in the Latin Church: The Late Fourth and Early Fifth Centuries," *TS* 43 (1982): 226–59. See now also the magisterial study by Peter Brown, *Through the Eye of a Needle: Wealth, the Fall of Rome, and the Making of Christianity in the West, 350–550 AD* (Princeton: Princeton University Press, 2012). I regret that Professor Brown's *The Ransom of the Soul: Afterlife and Wealth in Early Western Christianity* (Cambridge, Mass.: Harvard University Press, 2015) appeared just as I was preparing the final manuscript of this book, leaving me unable to integrate his unparalleled wisdom on this topic with my own thinking. Even so, *The Ransom of the Soul* essentially begins, chronologically, where my book ends—namely, with Cyprian of Carthage.

of Jesus—patristic proponents of atoning almsgiving generally represent a faithful hermeneutical embodiment of the early church's inherited Scriptures, particularly since the biblical texts themselves present care for the poor as having the potential to secure future reward, and even the cleansing of sin, for those who practice mercy.[9] This study will demonstrate that the avowal of the unique, atoning death of Jesus, on one hand, and the conviction that the practice of merciful deeds for the needy in some way cleanses or covers sins, on the other, were not viewed as mutually exclusive by early Christian advocates of "atoning almsgiving," in part because Christian promotion of "atoning almsgiving" was itself shaped by scriptural traditions that connect charity, reward, and atonement. In order to advance this thesis, however, it will be helpful first to clarify some of the terms used throughout the study and then to register two fundamental convictions that affect the ensuing interpretation of the ancient evidence.

"Atoning Almsgiving" and "Meritorious Almsgiving"

Although it will be necessary to consider the definition and use of the term "almsgiving" by examining a number of particular biblical and early Christian texts, the English word "almsgiving" used here generally refers rather broadly to the merciful provision of material assistance to those in need, including monetary distributions, food, clothing, and shelter.[10] As will be

[9] The only other monograph on the subject of atoning almsgiving is Roman Garrison, *Redemptive Almsgiving in Early Christianity* (JSNTSup 77; Sheffield: JSOT Press, 1993). My thesis is intended to challenge Garrison's view that early Christian proponents of redemptive alms were willing "to *compromise* the view that after the death of Jesus there is no longer any offering for sin" (*Redemptive Almsgiving*, 60 [emphasis added]). See also Garrison's comments: "The early Christian tradition, from New Testament writings and from the *Doctrina* and the agrapha, allows for, even encourages, a doctrine of redemptive almsgiving. This implicit attitude towards the salvific power of charity *is in conflict with the view of Jesus' death as the unique and sufficient means of atonement.* This tension characterizes the early tradition but there is no attempt to resolve it. The eventual unhesitating endorsement of a doctrine *which seems utterly inconsistent* with the belief that Jesus died for sins once for all must be seen as more than an uncritical development of the idea of penance" (*Redemptive Almsgiving*, 75 [emphasis added]).

[10] This definition corresponds to the conventional use of the English word "charity," although as early as Thomas Aquinas there are debates about whether almsgiving (*eleemosyna*) counts as charity (*caritas*) (*Summa Theologiae*, vol. 3, II-II, Q. 32; see Stephen J. Pope, "Aquinas on Almsgiving, Justice and Charity: An Interpretation and Reassessment," *HeyJ* 32 [1991]: 167–91). In a discussion of Luke 11:41, Augustine offers a fairly expansive description of "almsgiving" that includes the one who "gives food to the hungry, drink to the thirsty, clothing to the naked, hospitality to the wayfarer, refuge to the fugitive, who visits the sick and the prisoner, redeems the captive, bears the burdens of the

seen, part of the difficulty involved in considering what kinds of human actions are understood to merit reward or atonement for sin is that the Greek word ἐλεημοσύνη, often translated as "alms" or "almsgiving," can denote monetary or other material contributions to the poor or, more broadly, ἐλεημοσύνη can refer to attitudes or actions of mercy, kindness, or compassion.[11]

Relatedly, it is helpful to make a clear and consistent distinction between meritorious almsgiving and atoning almsgiving. The former frames the provision of material assistance to those in need as a means of accumulating some reward or treasure, usually for the donor (e.g., Sir 17:22; 29:12; Matt 6:1-4; Luke 12:33) but sometimes as reward for someone else or a community associated with those who practice mercy; the latter frames charity as a means of canceling, cleansing, covering, extinguishing, lightening, or in some way atoning for human sin and/or its consequences. Atoning almsgiving is, of course, meritorious, but not all meritorious almsgiving is atoning because often rewards other than reckoning with sin are envisioned.[12] As will be seen, in early Christian sources the rewards for meritorious almsgiving are often framed in eschatological terms, although that is not the case in much Jewish literature of the Second Temple period. Occasionally, it will be useful to speak of "salvific almsgiving," if the reward for merciful deeds is framed as eschatological salvation.

Neither the term "meritorious almsgiving" nor the term "atoning almsgiving" is without difficulties, however. It is important, therefore, to be as clear as possible about the reasons that these terms will be used. The term "meritorious almsgiving" will be employed to refer to the provision of material

---

weak, leads the blind, comforts the sorrowful, heals the sick, shows the errant the right way, gives advice to the perplexed, and does whatever is needful for the needy" (*Enchir.* 19). The first definition of the word "alms" in the *Oxford English Dictionary* nicely captures how the noun "almsgiving" is commonly used in contemporary English: "Charitable relief given to the poor or needy, usu. (now only) in the form of material gifts, typically of money or food; (in later use esp.) the goods given in this way" ("Alms," *OED* [Oxford: Oxford University Press, 2014]).

[11] See the helpful discussion in Roman Heiligenthal, "Werke der Barmherzigkeit oder Almosen: Zur Bedeutung von ἐλεημοσύνη," *Novum Test.* 25, no. 4 (1983): 289–301; Fritz Mybes, ed., *Die Werke der Barmherzigkeit* (Dienst am Wort 81; Göttingen: Vandenhoeck & Ruprecht, 1998), esp. 33–40.

[12] Alyssa M. Gray, e.g., states that "redemptive almsgiving" is found in texts "in which the reward for *tzedakah* is said to be atonement for sin, prayer on behalf of the donor by the poor, or rescue from death in this world or from a severe divine decree and/ or the assurance of felicity in the next world" ("Redemptive Almsgiving and the Rabbis of Late Antiquity," *JSQ* 18 [2011]: 144–84 [147]). The problem with such a definition is that it does not clearly distinguish between rewards that are soteriological or atoning and those that reflect some other form of divine or human blessing.

assistance to those in need as a means of accumulating some reward or treasure in large part because there is not a suitable adjectival form of the word
"reward" in the English language. While it cannot be denied that "merit" has
played a crucial and contested role in soteriological debates from the time
of the Protestant Reformation until the present day, the term "meritorious
almsgiving" is not used in any technical soteriological sense here, not least
because, as will be seen, the rewards envisioned in some texts that describe
"meritorious almsgiving" are not soteriological at all, nor do the benefits of
almsgiving always come from God. Some texts frame "meritorious almsgiving" as this-worldly recompense for those who provide for the needy.[13] It
should be clear, therefore, that "meritorious almsgiving" as it is used in this
study is not connected to later developments of a system of "merit" and/or the
emergence of purgatory.[14]

The term "*atoning* almsgiving" represents a departure from "redemptive
almsgiving," the latter of which has become the most commonly used phrase
to describe texts that frame almsgiving as a means of canceling, cleansing,
covering, extinguishing, lightening, or in some way atoning for human sin
and/or its consequences.[15] The term "redemptive almsgiving" is problem-

---

[13] On "merit" in recent Catholic and Protestant dialogue, see Susan K. Wood, "Cath-
olic Reception of the Joint Declaration on the Doctrine of Justification," in *Rereading Paul
Together: Protestant and Catholic Perspectives on Justification* (ed. David E. Aune; Grand
Rapids: Baker, 2006), 43–59 [48–51]; Michael Root, "Aquinas, Merit, and Reformation
Theology after the Joint Declaration on the Doctrine of Justification," *Modern Theology*
20 (2004): 5–22. On the historical development of indulgences and merit in late medieval
Europe, see R. N. Swanson, ed., *Promissory Notes on the Treasury of Merits: Indulgences
in Late Medieval Europe* (BCCT 5; Leiden: Brill, 2006); cf. Emma Disley, "Degrees of
Glory: Protestant Doctrine and the Concept of Rewards Hereafter," *JTS* 42 (1991): 77–
105; Charles Raith II, "Calvin's Critique of Merit, and Why Aquinas (Mostly) Agrees,"
ProEccl 20 (2011): 135–66; Raith, "Aquinas and Calvin on Merit, Part II: Condignity and
Participation," *ProEccl* 21 (2012): 195–209.

[14] Issues of merit and purgatory are considered in Gary A. Anderson's wide-ranging
text: *Charity: The Place of the Poor in the Biblical Tradition* (New Haven: Yale University
Press, 2013).

[15] I myself have used the term "redemptive almsgiving" in several previous publications
(e.g., David J. Downs, "Redemptive Almsgiving and Economic Stratification in 2 *Clement*,"
JECS 19 [2011]: 493–517; idem, "'Love Covers a Multitude of Sins': Redemptive Almsgiving in 1 Peter 4:8 and Its Early Christian Reception," *JTS* 65 (2014): 489–514). As far as
I can tell, the English term "redemptive almsgiving" was popularized by the publication
of Roman Garrison's book *Redemptive Almsgiving in Early Christianity*. Garrison defines
"redemptive almsgiving" as the doctrine "that almsgiving not only wins favor with God,
earning the individual entrance into the kingdom of God, but even merits the forgiveness
of sin" (10). One obvious problem with Garrison's definition is that it conflates *meritorious*
almsgiving ("almsgiving not only wins favor with God") with *atoning* almsgiving ("even

atic, however, because it narrowly reflects one image ("redemption") for the treatment of sin while excluding other metaphors (e.g., covering, cleansing, destroying, extinguishing, lightening, washing, etc.).[16] Of course, it is impossible to speak about sin and its solution without employing metaphorical language.[17] The English word "atonement," however, can denote in the broadest possible terms "a reconciled state of 'at-one-ness' between parties formerly alienated in some manner."[18] In Christian theology the term "atonement" is usually focused on the reconciliation wrought through the Christ-event, with "atonement for sin" typically located in some connection with Jesus' death and/or resurrection.[19] It should be clear, however, that "atoning almsgiving" in this book does not refer to any particular theory or model of "the atonement" but instead refers to almsgiving as a means by which sin is dealt with in some way. For this reason, the term "atoning almsgiving" is preferable as a catchall for the variety of ways in which sin is counteracted by merciful deeds.[20]

---

merits the forgiveness of sin"). Moreover, Garrison's definition also assumes that *meritorious* and *atoning* almsgiving are both *salvific* and *individualistic* ("earning the individual entrance into the kingdom of God"), an assumption that is problematic on both points.

[16] In addition, according to the most common usage of the biblical image of redemption, it is *sinners* who are redeemed, not *sins*. This point is complicated, however, because Theodotion's Greek translation of Dan 4:24 does state that merciful deeds can redeem *sins*, and this image from Greek Daniel shapes both *Did.* 4.6 and *Barn.* 19.10 (see chaps. 2 and 8).

[17] So Anderson, *Sin*, 3–14.

[18] P. R. Eddy and J. Beilby, "Atonement," in *Global Dictionary of Theology: A Resource for the Worldwide Church* (ed. William A. Dyrness and Veli-Matti Kärkkäinen; Downers Grove, Ill.: InterVarsity, 2009), 84–92 [84]. Jay Sklar offers a similar definition: "By *atonement*, I mean the process or event that leads to repairing and restoring that relationship between the sinner and the Lord" ("Sin and Atonement: Lessons from the Pentateuch," *BBR* 22 [2012]: 467–91 [468]). Sklar is clear that his definition is focused on divine-human relations, even though atonement can address "the rupture and repair of human relationships" (486).

[19] Adam J. Johnson, e.g., defines the Christian doctrine of atonement broadly as "a conceptually unified account of how the life, death and resurrection of Jesus Christ are effective for the reconciliation of all things to God" (*Atonement: A Guide for the Perplexed* [London: T&T Clark, 2015], 37). According to Johnson, the fundamental reality of reconciliation is articulated in a variety of images and theories of atonement. One might argue that reconciliation itself is an image or metaphor for the relief of sin—and perhaps not even the dominant biblical metaphor—but, as was noted above, it is impossible to speak of sin and its solution without employing metaphorical language.

[20] Other possible alternatives to "redemptive almsgiving" are either too closely tied to a particular metaphor for reckoning with sin (e.g., "reparative almsgiving," "purgative almsgiving") or too closely tied to particular understandings of atonement (e.g., "satisfactory almsgiving"). I had considered the term "expiative almsgiving." After settling on the

Particular texts will employ a variety of metaphors to describe how sin is counteracted by charity under the broad category "atoning almsgiving," and those metaphors will include cleansing/purifying, covering, extinguishing, destroying, lightening the burden of, and (occasionally, due to the influence of Theodotion's translation of Dan 4:24) redeeming sin. It is important, as well, to emphasize that, while a variety of metaphors are employed in the biblical tradition and early Christian literature to describe something called "sin" and its remedy, sin itself must be understood as both an individual and a social phenomenon. The dominant lens through which sin has been viewed in the Western theological tradition—at least since the Reformation, if not since the time of Augustine—is that of the individual actor. This can be seen, for example, in the emphasis on the individual in Lowry's "Nothing but the Blood": "What can wash away *my* sin? What can make *me* whole again?" Yet recent developments in theological anthropology have emphasized that sin must be understood in communal as well as individualistic terms, especially given the manifestation of sin in human social structures and the notion that relationality is constitutive of the embodied self.[21] If sin is understood as something—either a state or an action—in opposition to the honor, will, commandments, or word of God, it is possible to name any number of "sins" that manifest themselves not in the actions of discrete individuals but in the collective actions of communities, social structures, and societies, including such sins as racism, sexism, crippling and inescapable global poverty, and environmental destruction.[22] Patristic advocates of the atoning power of almsgiving frequently have in mind sin as a socially and ecclesiologically embodied phenomenon. Modern commentators on, and critics of,

---

term "atoning almsgiving" for the reasons listed above, I noted that Peter Brown briefly introduces the term "expiatory almsgiving" in his *Ransom of the Soul*. "Expiatory almsgiving" would be suitably broad. But since, in common English usage, "to expiate" is essentially a less familiar synonym for "to atone," I prefer the more alliterative phrase "atoning almsgiving." I will occasionally use the verb "to expiate" as a synonym for "to atone."

[21] These points are made in Derek R. Nelson, *Sin: A Guide for the Perplexed* (London: Continuum, 2011), 78.

[22] Nelson writes, "Mysterious forces, learned behaviors, inherited sexist conceptual schemes and, quite simply, the social inertia of the status quo work together to condition humans both to construct and to comply with structures that perpetuate evil. The social dimension of sin thus involves not just the fact that sinful people emerge from contexts of distorted relationships, but that phenomena genuinely outside of human selves, like legal systems, theological concepts, and patterns of commerce and politics, can contribute to states of affairs that are profoundly contrary to God's intentions, and yet are not easily reduced to their constituent sinful actions. Thus a full notion of sin in its social dimensions would require attention both to the sin inherent in relational selfhood and to the sin implicit in structures that harm and oppress God's good creation" (*Sin*, 115).

the emergence of atoning almsgiving have frequently imposed individualistic conceptions of sin onto early Christian language concerning the reckoning of sin through care for the poor.

Gift-Giving and the Ancient Economy

The first conviction that frames this study is that the gift-giving practices of early Christians must be interpreted in light of the exchange of resources in the economies of classical antiquity. In contemporary parlance, the word "economy" typically refers to a system for the production, distribution, and consumption of scarce resources (i.e., goods and services), with the cognate "economics" denoting the study of economies and economic activity. The modern English word "economy" derives from the Greek οἰκονομία, a term that in the ancient world typically designated household management or, more generally, the activity of "organization" or "administration" (cf. Luke 16:1-4). The classical concept of *oikonomia* (οἰκονομία) is thus far more expansive than the modern understanding of an "economy," for ancient writers did not view economic activity as distinct from other aspects of estate and household management. Xenophon's fourth-century BCE work *Oeconomicus*, for example, is a Socratic dialogue that covers topics such as wealth, agriculture, household administration, and marital relations. For this reason, economic historians and anthropologists sometimes refer to the economic practices of Greco-Roman antiquity as "embedded," in the sense that activities and discourses that moderns would classify as "economic" were in the ancient world embedded in other social and political structures.[23]

Given the linkages between commodity- and gift-exchange and other sociopolitical relationships in the embedded economies of antiquity, the practice of sharing material resources with the needy regularly entailed far more than what many moderns would recognize as "charity," if by charitable giving one envisions an impersonal, unilateral contribution that does not establish any lasting social ties between donor and recipient.[24] But this

---

[23] The most influential articulation of this perspective is found in Karl Polanyi, *The Great Transformation: The Political and Economic Origins of Our Time* (Boston: Beacon, 1944). Polanyi's substantivist economic theory was subsequently applied to the ancient world in Moses I. Finley's seminal *The Ancient Economy* (2nd ed.; Sather Classical Lectures 43; Berkeley: University of California Press, 1999).

[24] In the United States, the Catholic Worker Movement, founded in 1933 by Dorothy Day and Peter Maurin, may be seen as a personalist response to the impersonal assistance offered by the state and other contemporary religious institutions; see, e.g., Rebecca Anne Allahyari, *Visions of Charity: Volunteer Workers and Moral Community* (Berkeley: University of California Press, 2000), 35–73.

only highlights problems inherent in the assumption that "charity" in modern English usage is a helpful term with reference to resource-sharing in the ancient world. Instead, in the world of Greco-Roman antiquity the act of giving generally created or reinforced social ties between those who gave and those who received. The practice of providing material assistance to the needy, therefore, would naturally result in the establishment or fortification of social bonds between donors and recipients. Thus, the promotion of almsgiving is deeply related to questions of community formation and identity. Atoning almsgiving in the Roman imperial period was as much an issue of ecclesiological identity as it was an economic transaction.

Similarly, discourse about and practices of gift-exchange in early Christianity cannot be separated from the larger issue of resource distribution in Greco-Roman antiquity. The identity of those who gave and those who received alms, as well as the nature and the number of the gifts distributed, would have been determined by the resources available to those involved in the exchange, and this fact raises the question of economic stratification as a possible heuristic tool for the examination of resource-sharing in early Christian communities.[25]

Elite authors in antiquity tend to paint economic stratification in binary terms, often as a distinction between the few privileged *honestiores* (including senatorial, equestrian, and curial orders) and the vast majority of the poor *humiliores* (cf. Tacitus, *Hist.* 1.3; Cicero, *Mur.* 1). Yet the binary division between "rich" and "poor" that is so deeply entrenched in the literature of the ancient world must be seen as an ideological conceit that often buttressed the power of the elite.[26] The image of an amorphous and faceless group known as "the poor" assisted the interests of elite authors through the construction of an undifferentiated mass against which wealth could be defended and, in

---

[25] Some material from the following section is adapted from Downs, "Redemptive Almsgiving," 493–517.

[26] Bruce W. Longenecker ("Exposing the Economic Middle: A Revised Economy Scale for the Study of Early Urban Christianity," *JSNT* 31 [2009]: 243–78 [248–49]) calls this ancient division between the rich and the poor "a rhetorical construct that served to reinforce the binary values and worldview of the elite, legitimating the accumulation of power by the elite over the masses." Though focusing on a later period, Christel Freu's study of the language of poverty used by Latin-speaking Christians in the fourth through the sixth centuries is helpful in this context. Freu shows that literary constructs of poverty are deeply related to the rhetorical aims of those authors who employ them; see Freu, *Les Figures du pauvre dans le sources italiennes de l'antiquité tardive* (Collections de l'Université Marc Bloch-Strasbourg / Études d'Archéologie et d'Histoire Ancienne; Paris: De Boccard, 2007).

some contexts, even critiqued (so Seneca, *Ep.* 17.3–5).[27] The second-century CE orator Aelius Aristides makes the point bluntly: "The existence of inferiors is an advantage to the superiors since they will be able to point out those over whom they are superior" (*Or.* 24.34). In the subsequent history of interpretation of biblical texts, sometimes the point has been reversed: the poor become the "pious poor," lauded for their humility before and dependence upon God, a spiritualization of the language of poverty that ignores the very real and often crushing material deprivation and diminished capabilities experienced by the poor.[28]

A binary economic division, with elites comprising 1 percent (or less) and "the poor" comprising 99 percent (or more) of the population, is not, however, a reliable description of economic stratification in the Roman imperial period.[29] A far more accurate picture of the Roman imperial economy is one that acknowledges a small but significant "middling" group of persons between the wealthy elite, on the one hand, and the great number of the poor, perhaps somewhere between 75–90 percent of the population, existing near, at, or below subsistence-level.[30] Yet at the same time, even this more stratified

[27] On this point, see Greg Woolf, "Writing Poverty in Rome," in *Poverty in the Roman World* (ed. Margaret Atkins and Robin Osborne; Cambridge: Cambridge University Press, 2006), 83–99; for a similar argument with regard to Rabbinic literature, see Gregg E. Gardner, "Who Is Rich? The Poor in Early Rabbinic Judaism," *JQR* 104 (2014): 515–36.

[28] On the problems of spiritualizing the language of poverty, see John S. Kloppenborg, "Poverty and Piety in Matthew, James, and the Didache," in *Matthew, James, and the Didache: Three Related Documents in Their Jewish and Christian Settings* (ed. Huub van de Sandt and Jürgen K. Zangenberg; SBLSymS 45; Atlanta: Society of Biblical Literature, 2008), 201–32.

[29] That is not to say that such a binary division between the 1 percent and the 99 percent is not rhetorically powerful, as the popularity of the "Occupy (Wall Street)" movement once demonstrated. For a relatively recent study that still insists on this binary construction, see Justin J. Meggitt, *Paul, Poverty and Survival* (Studies of the New Testament and Its World; Edinburgh: T&T Clark, 1998). On this point, however, Meggitt's work has received significant critique; see Dale B. Martin, "Review Essay: Justin J. Meggitt, *Paul, Poverty and Survival*," *JSNT* 24 (2001): 51–64; Gerd Theissen, "The Social Structure of Pauline Communities: Some Critical Remarks on J. J. Meggitt, *Paul, Poverty and Survival*," *JSNT* 24 (2001): 65–84; Meggitt, "Response to Martin and Theissen," *JSNT* 24 (2001): 85–94; and Theissen, "Social Conflicts in the Corinthian Community: Further Remarks on J. J. Meggitt, *Paul, Poverty and Survival*," *JSNT* 25 (2003): 371–91.

[30] Especially influential in the move toward a more highly stratified understanding of wealth distribution in the Roman imperial period has been the work of Steven J. Friesen. In an important article published in 2004, Friesen presented a seven-tiered "poverty scale" for cities in the Roman Empire, a scale that Friesen then used as a heuristic device to develop an economic profile of the individuals mentioned in Paul's letters ("Poverty

image of wealth distribution ought to serve as a reminder that poverty and subsistence living were ways of life (and death) for the vast majority of inhabitants of the Greco-Roman world, including believers in the first several generations of the Christian movement.[31]

If something like this model of distribution offers a helpful economic context for the literature of the early Christian period, then it must be assumed that the great majority of Christians in the first, second, and third centuries would have experienced "shallow" or "episodic" poverty.[32] To frame

---

in Pauline Studies: Beyond the So-Called New Consensus," *JSNT* 26 [2004]: 323–61; cf. Walter Scheidel, "Stratification, Deprivation, and Quality of Life," in *Poverty in the Roman World* [ed. Margaret Atkins and Robin Osborne; Cambridge: Cambridge University Press, 2006], 40–59). Friesen argued that the highest three levels of his "poverty scale" (i.e., PS1–3, representing imperial, regional/provincial, and municipal elites) comprised less than 3 percent of the population. A small group possessing "moderate surplus resources" (i.e., PS4) was estimated at 7 percent of the population. Those living near, at, or below subsistence level (i.e., PS5–7) made up the remaining 90 percent of the population. Subsequently, Scheidel and Friesen attempted to establish the Gross Domestic Product of the Roman Empire, and they employed this calculation as a means of outlining a model of income distribution and inequality. The numbers are slightly different, but the overall picture is quite similar: "We conclude that in the Roman Empire as a whole, a 'middling' sector of somewhere around 6 to 12 per cent of the population, defined by a real income of between 2.4 and 10 times 'bare bones' subsistence or 1 to 4 times 'respectable' consumption levels, would have occupied a fairly narrow middle ground between an élite segment of perhaps 1.5 percent of the population and a vast majority close to subsistence level of around 90 percent" ("The Size of the Economy and the Distribution of Income in the Roman Empire," *JRS* 99 [2009]: 61–91 [84–85]). A slightly more optimistic calculation of the size of the "middling" group (i.e., PS4) in an urban context is argued for in Bruce W. Longenecker, *Remember the Poor: Paul, Poverty, and the Greco-Roman World* (Grand Rapids: Eerdmans, 2010). Longenecker suggests that PS4 would have been around 15 percent in urban centers.

[31] What Peter Brown writes of a slightly later period is true of the first and second centuries of the Common Era as well: "We have found that late Roman society was not as drastically 'polarized' between the rich and the poor as we had been led to suppose. The class of 'middling' persons was more extensive and much more differentiated than we had thought. But such persons did not enjoy the autonomy and the protection that we associate with a modern 'middle class.' The powerful and the truly rich remained overbearing presences in a society where so many self-respecting persons lived uncomfortably close to the widespread 'shallow poverty' that had always characterized an ancient society" (*Poverty and Leadership in the Later Roman Empire: The Menahem Stern Jerusalem Lectures* [Hanover, N.H.: University Press of New England, 2002], 49; cf. Ekkehard W. Stegemann and Wolfgang Stegemann, *The Jesus Movement: A Social History of Its First Century* [trans. O. C. Dean Jr.; Minneapolis: Fortress, 1999], 53–94).

[32] The term "shallow poverty" is used by Peter Brown in *Poverty and Leadership in the Later Roman Empire*. For a discussion of "episodic" and "conjunctural" poverty, see Annelise Parkin, "Poverty in the Early Roman Empire: Ancient and Modern Conceptions

the issue in ancient terms, these were the *penētes* (πένητες, "needy") who eked out a modest living in agriculture or trade but who, for a variety of reasons (such as crop failure, famine, illness, unemployment, war, age, etc.), were vulnerable at any point to becoming *ptōchoi* (πτωχοί)—that is, "destitute" or "beggars." To say this is not to deny that in the second century a greater number of socially and economically elevated persons may have come to be associated with the Christian movement, nor is this claim intended to gloss over regional variations in the Roman economy. It is only to assert that, unless one is prepared to argue that all or a very high percentage of early believers were financially prosperous, it must be recognized that the vast majority of Christians in the Roman imperial period lived under the episodic threat of poverty.

The implications of this picture of wealth distribution for this study of the promotion and practice of atoning almsgiving are significant. For one thing, Christian "almsgiving"—both in ancient and in modern practice—is sometimes viewed as a form of resource distribution that establishes and reinforces relationships of hierarchy, dependence, and even economic and social abuse.[33] One view of atoning almsgiving in early Christianity frames this theological development in light of a sharp and growing social contrast between "the rich" and "the poor" in the nascent Christian movement.[34] Followers of Jesus are said to have struggled with two irreconcilably different views on the proper disposal of wealth in their scriptural traditions—namely, (1) Jesus' condemnation of wealth and demand for the renunciation of possessions (e.g., Matt 6:24; 19:21-24; Mark 10:21-23; Luke 6:24; 12:13-21; 14:33; 16:13; 18:22-25) and (2) the notion that wealth should be employed (and maintained) in order to support needy members of the community, including wandering charismatic teachers (Matt 5:42; 6:1-4; Luke 6:30-35; 12:32-34). The emergence of atoning almsgiving is seen as providing a tidy solution to this tension: the post-baptismal sins of wealthy Christians could be forgiven by the distribution of material resources to needy believers,

---

and Constructs" (Ph.D. diss., University of Cambridge, 2001); Neville Morley, "The Poor in the City of Rome," in *Poverty in the Roman World* (ed. Margaret Atkins and Robin Osborne; Cambridge: Cambridge University Press, 2006), 21–39; Finn, *Almsgiving*, 22–25; Evelyne Patlagean, *Pauvreté économique et pauvreté sociale à Byzance 4e–7e siècles* (Mouton: Paris, 1977).

[33] See, e.g., Albino Barrera, *Market Complicity and Christian Ethics* (New Studies in Christian Ethics 29; Cambridge: Cambridge University Press, 2011), 248–50. On the distinction between charity and social justice in modern Catholic social teaching, see Daniel G. Groody, *Globalization, Spirituality, and Justice* (Maryknoll, N.Y.: Orbis, 2007), esp. 91–121.

[34] This view is central to the thesis of Roman Garrison's *Redemptive Almsgiving*.

allowing "the rich" to maintain their possessions while providing a soteriological sanction for charity. Thus, a vertical model of financial redistribution channels resources from wealthy members of Christian communities down to poor believers with the aim of producing social harmony among these two fractious groups, the rich and the poor, and with the result of alleviating for the wealthy the problem of their property by providing a proper use for their possessions. If this soteriological exchange is not theologically compatible with the belief that sins are remitted through the death of Jesus, atoning almsgiving at least had the advantage of eliminating social conflict between rich and poor Christians (defined as a binary construct) and solving the problem of wealth posed by Jesus' rejection of it. So the argument goes.[35]

There can be no doubt that such a model of "top-down" charitable activity on behalf of impoverished believers is endorsed in some early Christian texts. As will be seen, examples may be found in the *Shepherd of Hermas* (*Sim.* 2.5–6) and in Clement of Alexandria's treatise *Salvation of the Rich* (or "Who Is the Rich Man That Is Being Saved?"), one of the earliest Christian texts devoted specifically to pecuniary matters. Both of these documents envision a reciprocal exchange between wealthy and poor believers: the rich serve as benefactors of the poor through the giving of material blessings, while the poor serve as benefactors of the rich through spiritual advocacy.[36]

Yet it should not be assumed that all early Christian appeals for financial support of those needing material assistance—including exhortations framed with reference to the atoning significance of alms—are directed solely at wealthy believers, with Christians of lesser means simply functioning as passive recipients of charity. Such an assumption, in fact, depends upon a binary construction of "the rich" and "the poor" that does not accurately describe the social reality of many early Christian communities, for scenarios in which impoverished (or relatively impoverished) believers are not merely objects but also active *agents* of almsgiving must be envisioned.[37] If it is true that the vast majority of Christians in the first through the third

---

[35] See Garrison, *Redemptive Almsgiving*, 103–4.

[36] The notion that almsgiving involved a two-way exchange with the recipients of alms offering prayers on behalf of donors became a major feature of Christian discourse on alms in late antiquity; see Finn, *Almsgiving*, 179–82; Helen Rhee, *Loving the Poor, Saving the Rich: Wealth, Poverty, and Early Christian Formation* (Grand Rapids: Baker, 2012), 58–64, 73–102.

[37] This point is helpfully articulated in Denise Kimber Buell, "'Be Not One Who Stretches Out Hands to Receive but Shuts Them When It Comes to Giving': Envisioning Christian Charity When Both Donors and Recipients Are Poor," in *Wealth and Poverty in Early Church and Society* (ed. Susan R. Holman; Holy Cross Studies in Patristic Theology and History; Grand Rapids: Baker, 2008), 37–47.

centuries in the Roman imperial period would have experienced the reality of episodic or conjunctural poverty, then constructions of static, binary
groups such as "the rich" and "the poor" do not sufficiently account for the
fluidity with which one might sometimes give to those with lesser means
and sometimes receive donations during times of financial distress. In the
following chapters, several texts—including 2 Corinthians, the *Didache*,
and *2 Clement*—will challenge the notion that early Christian authors who
advocate care for the poor direct their exhortations only to wealthy believers
and correspondingly present believers of lesser means as passive recipients of
charity. Instead, there is much evidence to suggest that boundaries separating donors and recipients of alms were often quite porous; in many instances,
an individual or community responsible for providing material assistance to
the needy might soon enough be among those requiring assistance. In fact,
there are two different models of almsgiving in early Christian texts: one
model, exemplified in Clement of Alexandria's *Salvation of the Rich*, might be
called "philanthropic"; the other, represented in Paul's appeals to the Corinthians, might be labeled "mutualism."[38] The former funnels funds along a
vertical axis from those with an abundance of assets to those with minimal
resources, while the latter involves a more horizontal exchange of resources
among those of lesser means.[39]

[38] The term "mutualism" comes from Justin Meggitt's book *Paul, Poverty and Survival*. I would differ from Meggitt, however, in asserting that "almsgiving" and "mutualism"
are not mutually exclusive. It is possible to find the rhetoric of ἐλεημοσύνη in contexts
where "alms" are exchanged among impoverished individuals or communities. Meggitt's
four "survival strategies" include αὐτάρκεια, almsgiving, hospitality, and "mutualism."

[39] It might be objected that—even in Christian communities where the vast majority
of members were characterized by relative resource scarcity—economic parity can never
obviate status difference and that there are sometimes marked status and economic differences even among the poorest communities. The observation is a fair one, yet we simply
do not possess enough data to offer the kind of fine-grained analysis needed to mark these
distinctions among early Christian communities. I share Friesen's skepticism about the
usefulness of a broad category like "status," given the fluidity of its definition and application, as well as the limitations of available evidence to assess it (Friesen, "Poverty," 333–
35). On the other hand, a work like Peter Oakes' *Reading Romans in Pompeii: Paul's Letter
at Ground Level* (Minneapolis: Fortress, 2009) masterfully employs literary and material
evidence from one local context in order to map issues of status-level and economic-level
among the readers of Paul's letter to the Romans, and Oakes generally maintains that
Paul's theology represents an attempt to undermine and transform conventional assessments of "status." My inclination (bias?) is to suspect that Oakes' perspective on Paul and
status in Romans would map well onto many, though not all, early Christian texts and
communities.

The Gift, Reciprocity, and Solidarity

A second conviction that animates this study is that it is a false assumption that all giving (or "true" giving) must be free and disinterested and that, conversely, giving with the expectation of return—a return from either the recipient or from God—invalidates the gift. Instead, Christian almsgiving in the ancient world, as a gift, generally involved both reciprocity and solidarity. This belief in the potentially "interested" nature of giving partly arises from the treatment of the ancient economy in the previous section, for if gift-giving takes place in an economic context in which the presentation of material assistance establishes or reinforces ties of social solidarity, then the act of almsgiving inevitably results in the receipt of something for the donor as well as the recipient, even if that "something" is simply the formation or tightening of a social bond. This conviction also emerges in conversation with recent anthropological, sociological, and philosophical discussions of gift-giving. The history of the gift from the Greco-Roman world to the post-Christendom West is one that can hardly be told in this introductory chapter. Several important points must suffice to summarize a complex phenomenon.

First, the act of gift-giving often involves a triple obligation to give, to receive, and to reciprocate. Cultural anthropologists and sociologists have regularly explored the ways in which gifts generate obligation in different societies.[40] In many contexts, and especially in traditional "embedded" economies, the exchange of resources is based not on the logic of the market but on the principle of reciprocity, or *do ut des* ("I give so that you give"). Gifts, or presentations, can appear to be "voluntary, disinterested and spontaneous,

---

[40] The seminal work on this subject is, of course, Marcel Mauss, *The Gift: Forms and Functions of Exchange in Archaic Societies* (trans. Ian Cunnison; London: Cohen & West, 1966); trans. of "Essai sur le don: Forme et raison de l'échange dans les sociétés archaïques," *Annee sociologique* 1 (1925): 30–186. Mauss' comparative analysis of the "gift economies" of Polynesian, Melanesian, and North American traditional groups suggested that exchange in "archaic" societies was based on the principle of reciprocity. Mauss begins his essay, in fact, by highlighting the embedded nature of the archaic social landscape, noting that the phenomenon of gift exchange involves ancient religious, legal, moral, and economic transactions in what Mauss calls "total social phenomena" (1). Gift exchange in primitive societies takes place not primarily among individuals through markets, according to Mauss, but among groups—tribes, clans, families—through the exchange of goods and property but also "courtesies, entertainments, ritual, military assistance, women, children, dances, and feasts," as well as "fairs that feature markets as but one aspect of social exchange" (2). An illuminating collection of essays on gift-giving in the ancient world that engages Mauss' work is Michael L. Satlow, ed., *The Gift in Antiquity* (Oxford: Wiley-Blackwell, 2013).

but are in fact obligatory and interested."[41] Among the three obligations of gift exchange—the obligation to give, to receive, and to reciprocate—it is the last of these that is potentially the most important in the formation of social relationships, since every gift can provoke a counter-gift, with the result that the practice of gift-giving forges social ties. At the same time, gift exchange is also potentially agonistic, sometimes leading to conflict, violence, and even the destruction of one's own property. The key point is that the gift involves a mixture of interest and disinterest, of obligation and freedom. Gift-giving is neither purely free (in the sense that no return is expected) nor purely utilitarian (in the sense that individuals act simply on the basis of rational self-interest).[42]

Second, an interested gift is nevertheless a gift. It has become something of a truism to insist that there are no free gifts, and this sentiment partly reflects the conviction that the problem with the "free gift" is that the one who offers a gift without expectation of return also rejects the mutual ties formed through gift exchange.[43] On the other hand, it is possible to point to examples of the exchange of goods or services in which the donor does not expect or receive recompense, including disinterested, altruistic giving in social institutions and practices ranging from the family, to anonymous gifts to strangers, to blood and organ donation.[44] In point of fact, not all gifts *actually* engender obligation, for some gifts (including anonymous charitable contributions) result in no obligation to reciprocate whatsoever. Some gifts (such as the dinner invitation of a friend) generate only the *feeling* of obligation, and some gifts (such as the patron of a church who donates money for the construction of a new stained-glass window) result in social but not legal obligation. Other presentations create varying degrees of liability: for example, *kula* exchange, modern rules of credit, and pre-colonial African

[41] Mauss, *The Gift*, 1.

[42] The anti-utilitarian implications of Mauss' theory have especially been associated with the members of MAUSS (Mouvement anti-utilitariste dans les sciences sociales); see, e.g., Alain Caillé, "Anti-utilitarianism, economics, and the gift-paradigm," http://www.revuedumauss.com.fr/media/ACstake.pdf.

[43] In her foreword to a 1990 edition of Mauss' book, Mary Douglas memorably declared that there are no free gifts: "What is wrong with the so-called free gift is the donor's intention to be exempt from return gifts coming from the recipient. Refusing requital puts the act of giving outside any mutual ties" ("Foreword: No Free Gifts," in Mauss, *The Gift*, ix–xxiii [ix]). Douglas notably opens the essay by declaring that even charity wounds: "Charity is meant to be a free gift, a voluntary, unrequited surrender of resources. Though we laud charity as a Christian virtue we know that it wounds."

[44] So Jacques T. Godbout and Alain Caillé, *The World of the Gift* (trans. Donald Winkler; Montreal: McGill-Queen's University Press, 1998).

debt practice all represent offerings for which there is a *legally obligated* right of return, which, if the return is not rendered, can result, respectively, in the seizure of a similar object, the recipient's property, or even the recipient.[45] Thus, it needs to be acknowledged that the relationship between gifts and obligation runs along something of a spectrum, ranging from entirely altruistic donations to presentations that explicitly create legal obligation.[46]

It is not necessary to enter the debate about the possibility of the free, disinterested gift. It can be granted that disinterested giving is theoretically possible and empirically demonstrable. Yet any interpretive or theological tradition that insists that gifts *must* be free and disinterested is a modern (especially capitalist) development.[47] In Christian theology, Immanuel Kant's

[45] See Alain Testart, "Uncertainties of the 'Obligation to Reciprocate': A Critique of Mauss," in *Marcel Mauss: A Centenary Tribute* (ed. Wendy James and N. J. Allen; Oxford: Berghahn, 1998), 97–110.

[46] From a philosophical perspective, Jacques Derrida points to the impossibility of the gift. According to Derrida, the very notion of the gift reflects an *aporia*: since a gift is to be defined as something that contains "no reciprocity, return, exchange, countergift, or debt," the moment a genuine gift is recognized as a gift by either the donor or the recipient, it ceases to be a gift (*Given Time: 1. Counterfeit Money* [trans. Peggy Kamuf; Chicago: University of Chicago Press, 1992], 11). As Derrida writes, "To tell the truth, the gift must not even appear or signify, consciously or unconsciously, as gift for the donors, whether individual or collective subjects. From the moment the gift would appear as gift, as such, as what it is, in its phenomenon, its sense, and its essence, it would be engaged in a symbolic, sacrificial, or economic structure that would annul the gift in the ritual circle of the debt" (23). Once the gift is recognized as gift, by either the giver or the receiver, something is taken from the recipient and added to the donor—namely, recognition of the gift's symbolic potential. Thus, Derrida represents a perspective that is the polar opposite of Mauss, which is why the postmodernist philosopher can suggest that Mauss' book *The Gift*, which details rules of exchange and obligation, nowhere actually discusses the gift. Indeed, according to Derrida, in order for a gift to function as true gift, the presentation must never appear as a gift and the giver and receiver must forget the event immediately. Far from creating social ties and bonds of obligation, as Mauss suggested, the gift must "untie itself from obligation, from debt, from contract, exchange, and thus from the bind" (27). Although Derrida's work on the gift reflects the philosopher's deconstructive aim of highlighting *différance*, his conviction regarding the nature of the gift as a gesture free from expectations of exchange or obligation creates its very impossibility.

[47] In a perceptive commentary on Mauss' essay, Jonathan Parry contends that one feature of *The Gift* often missed in the hagiography concerning the epochal volume is that Mauss' study of archaic gift exchange did not simply intend to identify gift economies as a *precursor* to modern market exchange. Mauss also aimed to analyze the rules of an altogether different understanding of the gift. Parry writes, "*Gift-exchange*—in which persons and things, interest and disinterest are merged— has been fractured, leaving gifts *opposed* to exchange, persons *opposed* to things and interest to disinterest. The ideology of a disinterested gift emerges in parallel with an ideology of a purely interested exchange" ("The

deontological ethics have been influential in shaping the notion that gifts must be disinterested, for Kant contended that only actions performed out of duty—those that conform to universal moral law—have moral worth and that deeds performed for some extrinsic end, such as heavenly reward, have no moral worth.[48] Yet, as will be seen in the analysis of early Christian almsgiving,

---

Gift, the Indian Gift and the 'Indian Gift,'" *Man* 21 [1986]: 453–73 [458] [emphasis in original]). Parry points to Mauss' concluding observation that it is "we" (by use of which pronoun Mauss means modern European society) who have set in opposition "the idea of the gift and disinterestedness" and "that of interest and the individual pursuit of utility" (Mauss, *The Gift*, 73). Parry avers, "[Mauss' goal] is not to suggest that there is no such thing as a pure gift in *any* society, but rather to show that for many the issue simply cannot arise since they do not make the kinds of distinction that we make. So while Mauss is generally represented as telling us how *in fact* the gift is *never* free, what I think he is really telling us is how *we* have acquired a *theory* that it should be. The interested exchange and the disinterested gift thus emerge as two sides of the same coin. Given a profound dislike of the first, mistrust of the second is only logical. The unreciprocated gift debases the recipient, and the charity of the 'rich almoner' is condemned—presumably because it denies obligation and replaces the reciprocal interdependence on which society is founded with an asymmetrical dependence" (458). In the field of biblical studies, John M. G. Barclay has recently published a stimulating study of gift and grace in Pauline theology (*Paul & the Gift* [Grand Rapids: Eerdmans, 2015]). I regret that Barclay's study was published after the present manuscript was sent to the press, but I was able to learn from some of Barclay's preliminary thinking on this subject, including his thoughts on the emergence of the concept of the unilateral gift in Reformation theology; see, e.g., "Paul, the Gift and the Battle over Gentile Circumcision: Revisiting the Logic of Galatians," *ABR* 58 (2010): 36–56.

[48] See the helpful discussion in Nathan Eubank, *Wages of Cross-Bearing and Debt of Sin: The Economy of Heaven in Matthew's Gospel* (BZNW 196; Berlin: De Gruyter, 2013), 4–11. The issue is complicated, however, and it is certainly possible to identify strands of Reformation theology that are inimical to any notion that charity might be motivated by the hope of reward (see Disley, "Degrees of Glory"). Klaus Koch, for example, declares the idea that heavenly treasure might be accumulated through almsgiving to be "an odious idea for Protestants" ("für den Protestanten eine abscheuliche Vorstellung"; "Der Schatz im Himmel," in *Leben angesichts des Todes: Beiträge zum theologischen Problem des Todes; Helmut Thielecke zum 60 Geburtstag* (ed. Bernhardt Lohse and H. P. Schmidt; Tübingen: Mohr Siebeck, 1968), 47–60 [52]). More recently, the explosive popularity of the so-called "prosperity gospel" in global Christianity has shaped discourse about self-interested giving. In prosperity teaching, which is found in many manifestations, material possessions can be exchanged for other blessings, particularly other material or financial blessings. Sometimes, prosperity teaching reflects a formulaic system of cosmic benefit exchange, a phenomenon that historian Kate Bowler calls "hard prosperity. More subtly and more commonly, however, the approach is to emphasize that giving provides blessing to givers"; see Bowler, *Blessed: A History of the American Prosperity Gospel* (Oxford: Oxford University Press, 2013). Not surprisingly, opponents of the prosperity gospel—whether in its hard or softer manifestations—regularly insist that giving must be altruistic, selfless, or

the concept of the interested gift is usually presupposed among biblical and
nascent Christian advocates of meritorious and atoning almsgiving, for alms
were not perceived by ancient authors to be unilateral, unreciprocated gifts.
The occasional modern distinction between charity and gift-giving does not
sufficiently account for the fact that early Christian advocates of atoning almsgiving consistently portray material donations to the needy as gifts that result
in reciprocity, whether the return comes from the recipients or from God,
whether the reciprocation is material or spiritual, or whether the recompense
is received in this world or in the next. Conversely, to the extent that recent
anthropological and sociological work on the gift has discussed the practice
of Christian almsgiving at all, this literature has tended to assume that almsgiving is distinct from gift exchange, sometimes even identifying almsgiving as
a "perversion" of the gift.[49] As will be shown in the following pages, however,
such assessments of the practice of almsgiving incorrectly assume that almsgiving is inherently unilateral, impersonal, and exclusionary.

---

dis-interested. In a recent and frequently reproduced article—"Errors of the Prosperity
Gospel," for example—Baptist ethicist David Jones tackles the "error" that "Christians
should give in order to gain material compensation from God," concluding that "the prosperity gospel's doctrine of giving is built upon faulty motives. Whereas Jesus taught his
disciples to 'give, hoping for nothing in return' (Luke 10:35 [sic: 6:35]), prosperity theologians teach their disciples to give because they will get a great return" (http://9marks.org/
article/journalerrors-prosperity-gospel/).

[49] See, e.g., the comment in Godbout and Caillé, World of the Gift, 224: "Alms, a
unilateral gift to an unknown recipient, is a curious phenomenon and will be dealt with
later. Logically, it is a gift that excludes, that asserts the giver's dominant position and
seems designed to expose the recipient's inability to reciprocate. With the giving of alms
in the street in aid of the Third World, we see the same perversion of the gift, except that it
is transposed into a religious system, as it will be 'returned to you a hundred times over' by
none other than God himself. The spiritual dimension can neutralize the perverse effects
of a unilateral gift to an unknown who cannot reciprocate (but it does not necessarily
happen)." For this perspective in the context of international humanitarian assistance,
see Diane Fairchild, "Don humanitaire, don pervers," Revue du Mauss 8 (1996): 294–
300. Similarly, betraying a lack of familiarity with the earliest Christian sources, David
Graeber writes, "True charity, in Christian doctrine, could not be based on any desire to
establish superiority, or gain anyone's favor, or indeed, from any egoistic motive whatever.
To the degree that the giver could be said to have gotten anything out of the deal, it wasn't
a real gift. But this in turn led to endless problems, since it was very difficult to conceive
of a gift that did not benefit the giver in any way. At the very least, doing a good deed put
one in better standing in the eyes of God and thus aided one's chance of eternal salvation.
In the end, some actually ended up arguing that the only person who can make a purely
benevolent act was one who had convinced himself that he was already condemned to
hell" (Toward an Anthropological Theory of Value: The False Coin of Our Own Dreams [New
York: Palgrave, 2001], 160–61).

A third point about the gift is that gift-giving engenders, solidifies, and in some cases threatens solidarity. Gift-exchange often functions as the glue that holds together social relationships.[50] Community is formed, symbolized, and reinforced through gift-exchange.[51] In this sense, there is a significant difference between the exchange of gifts and commodities, for "commodity exchange establishes objective quantitative relationships between the objects transacted, while gift exchange establishes personal qualitative relationships between the subjects transacting."[52]

Of course, it must be noted immediately that solidarity and exclusion are a two-edged sword, since strong bonds of in-group solidarity formed through gift-exchange can, at the same time, result in the definition of other individuals or groups as outsiders, with conflict as a potential result. Moreover, the act of reciprocal exchange is able not only to support but also to undermine social solidarity.[53] Sociological and anthropological research has suggested a variety of motivations for gift-giving: gifts symbolize and reflect community, especially in the context of family relationships; gifts instantiate relations of authority, power, and dependency; gifts are offered in response to other gifts, often with expectations of reciprocity and equality; and gifts occasionally mask market or professional relationships, as in bribes or gifts

[50] See especially Aafke Komter, *Social Solidarity and the Gift* (Cambridge: Cambridge University Press, 2005).

[51] Stephen Gudeman has argued that reciprocity *follows* rather than precedes solidarity; that is, "Communal allotment—contra the anthropological theorists—does not come 'after' reciprocity; rather, moments of reciprocity or the gift are tokens of existent community" ("Postmodern Gifts," in *Postmodernism, Economics and Knowledge* [ed. Stephen Cullenburg, Jack Amariglio, and David F. Ruccio; London: Routledge, 2001], 459–74 [467]; for a similar perspective, see Rodolphe Gasché, "Heliocentric Exchange," in *The Logic of the Gift: Toward an Ethic of Generosity* [ed. Alan D. Schrift; London: Routledge], 100–117). I disagree with Gudeman's claim that an initial gift *necessarily* distributes a community's base to those outside, with the implication that reciprocity is never contained within a community and reciprocity never exists without community. Yet Gudeman's perspective is a helpful reminder that gifts can extend already existing community to others.

[52] Chris A. Gregory, *Gifts and Commodities* (London: Academic, 1982), 41.

[53] See, e.g., Marshall Sahlins' influential perspective on various types of reciprocity in *Stone Age Economics* (New York: Aldine-Atherton, 1972). Sahlins describes three types of reciprocity: generalized reciprocity (i.e., altruistic giving, often in the context of kinship relations and often marked by delayed return; in this category, Sahlins includes the "pure gift"), balanced reciprocity (i.e., giving with the expectation of an equivalent and direct return, including trade, market activity, and some forms of gift-exchange), and negative reciprocity (unequal and impersonal exchange motivated by self-interest and profit, including haggling, theft, and gambling).

to physicians by pharmaceutical representatives.[54] To say that gift-giving *can* create and strengthen social ties is not to insist that gifts always have this positive effect. Gift-exchange is often a complicated, multidimensional phenomenon, with various actors perceiving and reacting to different actions in diverse ways. Gifts can exclude and/or include, sometimes accomplishing both at the same time.

This topic is pertinent to the present study of the emergence of atoning almsgiving because, as will be seen, the practice of providing material care for the poor was a key aspect of Christian—and even more specifically proto-Orthodox—identity in the second and third centuries.[55] On the one hand, there is no precise parallel to the Christian concept of atoning almsgiving in the literature of Greek and Roman pagans, primarily because wealthy pagans did not, by and large, direct their beneficence to the destitute of society and also because Hellenistic and Roman religions did not tend to emphasize systems of reward in the afterlife for generosity in the present. Instead, the concept of atoning almsgiving emerged as early Christian authors engaged their inherited Scriptures, texts that reflect the importance of care for the poor in the Jewish tradition. A commitment to the practice of almsgiving was a demonstration of solidarity with a community in which the poor were treated with dignity, value, and compassion—at least ideally.

At the same time, not all early Christian communities endorsed the practice of almsgiving; in fact, some texts, such as the *Gospel of Thomas*, explicitly reject almsgiving.[56] Thus, this study will also demonstrate that patristic advocates of atoning almsgiving present an understanding of sin and its cleansing that is socially and ecclesiologically embodied, a vision that frequently contrasts with Docetic disregard for the body, including disregard for the bodies of the poor. The practice of mercifully caring for the needy defined some forms of Christian community in opposition to others. Almsgiving, therefore, is an issue that stands at the heart of competing

---

[54] Komter, *Social Solidarity and the Gift*, 16–33. Komter draws upon Alan Paige Fiske's four psychological motives for social life, which are community sharing, authority ranking, equality matching, and market pricing; see Fiske, *Structures of Social Life: The Four Elementary Forms of Human Relations* (New York: Free Press, 1991).

[55] This point is masterfully explored in Rhee, *Loving the Poor*, 159–89.

[56] "Jesus said to them, 'If you fast, you will give rise to sin for yourselves; [2] and if you pray, you will be condemned; [3] and if you give alms, you will do harm to your spirits. [4] When you go into any land and walk about in the districts, if they receive you, eat what they will set before you, and heal the sick among them. [5] For what goes into your mouth will not defile you, but that which issues from your mouth—it is that which will defile you.'" (*Gos. Thom.* 14)

conceptions of Christian identity, solidarity, and community in the second and third centuries.

Conclusion

In telling the story of the development of atoning almsgiving in early Christianity through the middle of the third century, it will be shown that the emergence of the theology and practice of atoning almsgiving is deeply related to the question of Christian identity. Moreover, the historical development of atoning almsgiving cannot be disconnected from questions about the content and exegesis of Christian Scripture in the first through the third centuries of the Common Era. Quite often, when early Christian authors assert that offering material assistance to the destitute will result in the cleansing or covering of sin, these statements are rooted in appeals to scriptural texts. Yet given the fluidity of the concept of "scripture" in the period before the fixing of the canon in the fourth century—if it can even be assumed that there was a "fixed" canon in the fourth century—the scriptural texts and translations that early Christian authors frequently cite are often not those ultimately included in the Protestant canon in the sixteenth century. An examination of the concept of almsgiving in Second Temple Jewish literature, for example, will show movement in the direction of more explicit advocacy of the redemptive, cleansing, and atoning significance of material contributions to the needy in Second Temple literature, including texts such as the Septuagint versions of Daniel and Proverbs, as well as "apocryphal" texts like Tobit and Sirach—all writings that often served as "scripture" for at least some segments of the early church. Moreover, if support for atoning alms emerges in part from the *content* of the scriptural "canons" of early Christian authors, it also develops from and reflects the distinct hermeneutical approaches that patristic writers employ in the interpretation of these scriptural texts, including such strategies as allegorical reading and prosopological exegesis.

Thus, the story of the emergence and popularity of atoning almsgiving in early Christianity cannot be told without careful attention to larger canonical and hermeneutical questions. Economic, theological, and ethical convictions were (and still are) deeply intertwined in the literature and practices of early Christianity. Moreover, for those interested in the theological interpretation of Christian Scripture, this study also suggests that readings of the Bible by important voices from the church's tradition who advocate the power of almsgiving to atone for sin cannot simply and collectively be dismissed as theological aberrations. This book, then, also aims to raise questions about the nature and interpretation of the church's scriptural witness, about ecclesiological identity and praxis, and, ultimately, about the role of care for the poor among inheritors of the ancient theological tradition of atoning almsgiving.

CHAPTER I

REDEEM YOUR SINS WITH ACTS OF MERCY

Charity and Reward in the Hebrew-Aramaic Bible and Its Greek
Translation

Care for the poor is an integral component of Jewish religion—both past and present. The virtues and practices of Jewish charity are rooted in biblical traditions that emphasize God's special concern for the powerless and marginalized, coupled with the covenant community's responsibility to imitate God by demonstrating justice and refraining from oppression. Yet the mechanics of charity, as well as the symbolic and theological meanings attached to practices of benevolence, are rather fluid. The goal of this chapter and the two that follow is to examine meritorious and atoning almsgiving in Jewish literary sources from the writings of the Hebrew (and, in the case of Daniel, Aramaic) Scriptures and their Greek translation to the rabbinic literature of the Tannaitic period (ca. 70–225 CE). In telling the story of atoning almsgiving in early Judaism, this account will highlight both antecedents to Christian teaching about the meritorious and atoning value of alms (that is, antecedents in the sense that later Christian sources are explicitly informed by and draw upon these earlier Jewish traditions, especially scriptural texts) and (insofar as Jewish discourse about almsgiving in the first through third centuries of the Common Era develops at the same time as, and often in dialogue with, Christian reflection) a parallel, and sometimes overlapping, stream of reflection.

Given the nature of the available sources and the limitations of this project, it is not possible to construct a tightly organized chronology of the emerging concepts of meritorious and atoning almsgiving in biblical and postbiblical literature. Instead, this chapter and the next will focus on a number of texts that both imagine or exhort the provision of material assistance to the needy and promise some reward for such benevolent action. A primary question will be, In what contexts are appeals for beneficence combined with the promise of recompense—whether divine or human—for such charitable activity? Even more pointedly, Where and when is there evidence for the idea that caring for the poor leads to atonement for sin? Since one of the major contentions of this book is that early Christian advocacy of atoning almsgiving emerged, in part, on the basis of engagement with scriptural traditions, it will be helpful to concentrate on a cluster of texts from the Hebrew Bible and the Septuagint that feature prominently in later Christian discourse about the atoning value of almsgiving. To the extent that a chronology of atoning almsgiving emerges, it will be seen primarily in observations about how the translation of Hebrew Scriptures into Greek may have reflected and facilitated new theological perspectives on the relationship between charity and reward. The division between this chapter, which focuses on the Hebrew-Aramaic Bible and its Greek translation, and the following chapter, which looks at Jewish apocryphal and pseudepigraphical texts that were not included in the later rabbinic and Protestant canons, is admittedly artificial from a historical perspective, since, as will be seen, several texts later classified as "Apocryphal" or "Deuterocanonical" were important sources of *scriptural* engagement for early Christian proponents of atoning almsgiving.[1]

Care for the Poor and Reward in Deuteronomy

Israel's scriptural witness offers numerous prescriptions for communal support of the needy. Old Testament appeals for charitable action on behalf of the poor and powerless reveal and are rooted in a variety of ethical and

---

[1] Moreover, given this book's focus on early Christian promotion of meritorious and atoning almsgiving, I will tend to concentrate on the Greek translation of Old Testament Scriptures and Greek versions of apocryphal texts, even when earlier Hebrew traditions are available (e.g., Tobit, Sirach), for by and large it was the Greek versions of these documents that served as the basis for the received scriptural texts among Greek- and Latin-speaking Christians in the West in the first two and a half centuries of the Common Era. For a helpful introduction to the role of the Septuagint in the early church, see Timothy Michael Law, *When God Spoke Greek: The Septuagint and the Making of the Christian Bible* (Oxford: Oxford University Press, 2013).

theological warrants.[2] In the book of Deuteronomy, for example, caring for the poor reflects and imitates the character of the Maker, for God is a defender of orphans and widows, a lover of strangers who need food and clothing, and a protector of the poor (Deut 10:18; cf. 1 Sam 2:7-8; Pss 9:9, 18; 12:5; 14:6; 35:10; 68:5-6; 69:32-33; 82:3-4; 107:39-41; 113:7-9; 140:12; 146:5-9; Prov 15:25; 22:22-23; Isa 25:4; 41:17-20; Jer 20:13; cf. the vision in Isa 11:1-5 and 61:1-3).[3] Justice and compassion for resident aliens and orphans should stem from Israel's own experience and remembrance of living as aliens in a foreign land (Exod 23:9; Deut 24:17-18, 21-22). Similarly, liberation for Israelites from debt and indentured labor during the Year of Jubilee, which is stipulated in Leviticus 25, is grounded in the affirmation that all the land belongs to God (25:23) and that it was God who delivered the people from Egypt and brought them to the land of Canaan (25:38, 42, 55).

Both in legal and in prophetic traditions, oppression or abuse of the poor leads or may lead to starkly negative consequences, including God's wrath, judgment, or cursing (Exod 22:21-24; Deut 27:19; Isa 10:1-4; Jer 2:34-35; 5:27-29; cf. Prov 21:13; 22:16 [financial ruin]; 28:27; Ezek 16:49-50; 22:29-31; Amos 2:6-8; 4:1-3; 8:4-14; Zeph 7:8-14; Mal 3:5; cf. Eliphaz' account of Job's suffering in Job 22:6-13). Violence against or mistreatment of the poor is a sign of rebellion of the wicked against God (Job 24:1-25; Prov 17:5; 30:11-14; Isa 32:7-8). Conversely, refusing to oppress the alien, orphan, or widow secures God's presence with the people (Jer 7:5-7), and in the indictment leveled against Judah in Isa 1:2-20 (cf. 3:13-15), part of the remedy is for God's people to "seek justice, rescue the oppressed, defend the orphan, plead for the widow" (1:17, NRSV; cf. 58:6-10).

If failure to show justice to the poor brings negative retribution, the opposite scriptural motif is that those who care for and protect the oppressed

---

[2] Sometimes no explicit rationale is given other than that the command comes from the Lord (e.g., Exod 23:6, 10-11; Lev 19:10, 15-16; 23:22).

[3] Ps 72, a prayer for the king, asks for the ruler to be granted God's justice and righteousness in protecting the poor (e.g., Ps 72:1-4, 12-13; cf. Ps 112:9; Prov 29:7; 31:9; Jer 22:13-17; Ezek 18:5-9). Of course, the identity and definition of "the poor" in the Psalms are debated, and it has been argued that עניים is a socioreligious more than a socioeconomic descriptor; see Enrique Nardoni, *Rise Up, O Judge: A Study of Justice in the Biblical World* (trans. Sean Martin; Grand Rapids: Baker, 2001), 125–28; W. Dennis Tucker Jr., "A Polysemiotic Approach to the Poor in the Psalms," *PRSt* 31 (2004): 425–39. The notion that benevolence to the poor represents an imitation of the divine is occasionally found in pagan thought; cf. Seneca, *Ben.* 4.3, 25; Epictetus, *Diatr.* 2.14; Anneliese Parkin, "'You Do Him No Service': An Exploration of Pagan Almsgiving," in *Poverty in the Roman World* (ed. Margaret Atkins and Robin Osborne; Cambridge: Cambridge University Press, 2006), 60–82.

and destitute are often promised reward for obedience.[4] The theme of divine blessing for charitable action is particularly notable in the book of Deuteronomy. In Deut 14:22-29, for example, the law articulates a series of regulations regarding the practice of tithing (cf. Deut 12:17; 26:12-15). Although piecing together the various Old Testament legal traditions regarding the tithe is rather difficult, the prescription in Deuteronomy 14 is relatively straightforward.[5] The first section of the tithe law, found in verses 22-27, commands a yearly tithe consumed in a central sanctuary, the purpose of which is ostensibly "so that you may learn to fear the Lord your God always" (14:23, NRSV) and so that households may rejoice in God's presence together (14:26). The next section, however, describes a tithe offered every three years to provide for the Levites, resident aliens, orphans, and widows in local towns (14:28-29). Those with no allotment or inheritance, along with the marginalized and vulnerable, are provisioned by this triennial tithe "so that the Lord your God may bless you in all the work that you undertake" (14:29, NRSV). The motivation for this so-called poor tithe is that God will bless the Israelites and their work on account of their care for those in need. This point is reiterated in Deut 26:12-15, the other passage in the book of Deuteronomy that describes this triennial tithe given to Levites, resident aliens, orphans, and widows. According to the dictates in Deuteronomy 26, after those who pay the tithe articulate a series of affirmations regarding the purity and obedience with which they have adhered to the commandment (26:13-14), they are to offer the following prayer to God: "Look down from your holy habitation, from heaven, and bless your people Israel and the ground that you have given us, as you swore to our ancestors—a land flowing with milk and honey" (26:15, NRSV). While intercessory prayers for divine blessing are common in Deuteronomy and elsewhere in the Old Testament, the prayer in verses 13-15 assumes that God will recognize and reward the people of God for setting aside and distributing this tithe to the poor every third year (cf. Deut 24:19).[6]

---

[4] Reward for charitable action is, of course, only one aspect of divine blessing promised for Israel's covenant faithfulness.

[5] For a brief discussion, see David J. Downs, "Economics," in *DJG* (ed. J. B. Green and S. McKnight; Downers Grove, Ill.: InterVarsity, 2013), 219–26; D. L. Baker, *Tight Fists or Open Hands? Wealth and Poverty in Old Testament Law* (Grand Rapids: Eerdmans, 2009), 2519–2571 (kindle).

[6] Michael Widmer, *Moses, God, and the Dynamics of Intercessory Prayer: A Study of Exodus 32–34 and Numbers 13–14* (FAT II/8; Tübingen: Mohr Siebeck, 2004), 9–56; Christopher R. Seitz, "Prayer in the Old Testament or Hebrew Bible," in *Into God's Presence: Prayer in the New Testament* (ed. Richard N. Longenecker; Grand Rapids: Eerdmans, 2001), 3–22.

Similarly, Deuteronomy 15 provides instructions for the remission of debts every seventh year.[7] The legal requirements are presented in the first three verses, which offer a general directive (15:1), instructions regarding the manner by which creditors ought to remit (or possibly delay) the debts of their neighbors who are members of the community (15:2), and a statement indicating that foreigners (נכרי) are exempt from this remission of debts (15:3). The next several verses frame the issue of debt remission in the context of social inequity, as God insists that the obedience of the people to the commandments given them by God will result in God's blessing them in the land. The result of the people's obedience is that "there will be no one in need among you" and "you will lend to many nations, but you will not borrow" (15:4-6). The following textual unit then reckons with the pragmatic possibility that need might exist among members of the community and encourages openhanded lending toward a needy neighbor (15:7-8). This call for generosity in the bestowal of interest-free loans (cf. Deut 23:19-20) to fellow Israelites, however, raises the specter that potential lenders will be tight-fisted as the seventh year approaches, for a lender who provides a loan immediately before the sabbatical year runs the risk that the debt will not be repaid before the law prescribes its remission:

> [9]Be careful that you do not entertain a mean thought, thinking, "The seventh year, the year of remission, is near," and therefore view your needy neighbor with hostility and give nothing; your neighbor might cry to the LORD against you, and you would incur guilt. [10]Give liberally and be ungrudging when you do so, for on this account the LORD your God will bless you in all your work and in all that you undertake. [11]Since there will never cease to be some in need on the earth, I therefore command you, "Open your hand to the poor and needy neighbor in your land." (Deut 15:9-11, NRSV)

Deuteronomy 15 holds out both the threat that the stingy lender will incur guilt because of the needy neighbor's cries to God (15:9) and the promise that God will reward magnanimous giving by blessing generous lenders in their work and in all their undertakings (15:10). Participation in this divinely authorized economy by lending generously even when a loan may be quickly remitted by the sabbatical law may be unwise in terms of a purely

---

[7] On this passage, see Walter J. Houston, "'You Shall Open Your Hand to Your Needy Brother': Ideology and Moral Formation in Deut 15:1-18," in *The Bible in Ethics: The Second Sheffield Colloquium* (ed. John W. Rogerson, Margaret Davies, and M. Daniel Carroll; JSOTSup 207; Sheffield: Sheffield Academic, 1995), 296–314.

rationalistic economic calculation, but God promises to reward those who show such "irrational" kindness to the needy.[8]

A comparison between a parallel legal tradition in Exodus and Deuteronomy illustrates how the prominence of divine blessing as a return for charity functions as a motif in Deuteronomy and also introduces the important question of how reward for beneficence is framed in Greek translations of the Hebrew Scriptures.[9] The Covenant Code in Exod 22:26-27 enjoins that someone who takes a neighbor's coat as a deposit must return it before sundown, or else the mistreated and coatless neighbor, with no proper bedding for the night, will cry out a curse against the oppressor to God, who will hear the cry of the poor and exact vengeance (cf. 22:23-24).[10]

A similar pledge law in Deut 24:13 emphasizes not God's retribution upon a creditor who mistreats a debtor but the "righteousness" credited to one who returns a coat given as a pledge before nightfall:[11]

> You shall certainly return the deposited coat by sundown, so that your neighbor may sleep in the coat and bless you, and to you it shall be as righteousness (צדקה) in the sight of the Lord your God.

Here the action of refusing to keep distrained property overnight in order to ensure that an impoverished debtor has comfortable bedding is part of Israel's responsibility to care for the needy (as is not withholding the wages of poor and needy laborers; cf. Deut 24:14-15). Presumably, if a coat were collected as debt collateral at all, it would have to be returned by the creditor

---

[8]   So Gary A. Anderson, *Charity: The Place of the Poor in the Biblical Tradition* (New Haven: Yale University Press, 2013), 50–51.

[9]   The comparison is suggested in an essay by Michael Satlow, although Satlow does not consider the significance of the LXX's handling of Deut 24:13; see Michael L. Satlow, "'Fruit and the Fruit of Fruit': Charity and Piety among Jews in Late Antique Palestine," *JQR* 100 (2010): 244–77 [262].

[10]   On this passage, see Jonathan Ben-Dov, "The Poor's Curse: Exodus XXII 20-26 and Curse Literature in the Ancient World," *VT* 56 (2006): 431–51; Baker, *Tight Fists or Open Hands?* 2792–2893 (kindle).

[11]   The phrasing in this sentence is not at all meant to imply that a theology of divine retribution is absent from Deuteronomy; it is meant to imply only that the motif of divine retribution is not present in the lending laws of Deut 24:10-13, especially when compared with Exod 22:26-27. On the motif of retribution in Deuteronomy, see Vincent Sénéchal, *Rétribution et intercession dans le Deutéronome* (BZAW 408; Berlin: De Gruyter, 2009); for a thoughtful discussion of the issue of divine retribution from a larger canonical perspective, see Stephen B. Chapman, "Reading the Bible as Witness: Divine Retribution in the Old Testament," *PRSt* 31 (2004): 171–90. Chapman makes the important point that any discussion of retribution should be framed within the larger framework of divine blessing, divine punishment, and divine curse.

each night, an inconvenient situation that might lead to the waiving of the deposit.[12] Such compassion, moreover, is counted as "righteousness" for those who demonstrate it (cf. Deut 6:24-25). One interpretative tradition understands צדקה in Deut 24:13 as a reward from God granted on the basis of one's compassion for the poor, a "merit" accrued through charity.[13] It is also possible that "righteousness" in this verse denotes conduct that conforms to the patterns of the rightly ordered way of life detailed in God's law (cf. Deut 4:8; 16:18-20; 33:21). In this sense, returning a deposited coat to a poor person before nightfall is a concrete embodiment of "righteous," or rightly ordered, social relations within the covenant community.[14]

Regardless of the meaning of Deut 24:13 in the MT, it is notable that the LXX translator of Deuteronomy renders the verse as follows:

> ἀποδόσει ἀποδώσεις τὸ ἐνέχυρον αὐτοῦ περὶ δυσμὰς ἡλίου, καὶ κοιμηθήσεται ἐν τῷ ἱματίῳ αὐτοῦ καὶ εὐλογήσει σε, καὶ ἔσται σοι ἐλεημοσύνη ἐναντίον κυρίου τοῦ θεοῦ σου.

> You shall surely return his pledge at about sunset, and he shall sleep in his garment, and he shall bless you, and it shall be to you ἐλεημοσύνη before the Lord your God.

This text is intriguing, and very important for the present study, because of the LXX translator's rendering of צדקה with ἐλεημοσύνη, for ἐλεημοσύνη is the noun most often rendered "alms" or "almsgiving" in modern translations

---

[12] So Walter Brueggemann, *Deuteronomy* (AOTC; Nashville: Abingdon, 2001), 238.

[13] Jack R. Lundbom, *Deuteronomy: A Commentary* (Grand Rapids: Eerdmans, 2013), 325; cf. Ben-Dov, "Poor's Curse," 439–41, including the Jewish commentators referenced in n. 19. Lundbom cites a fifth-century BCE Aramaic papyri that promises that, if the governor of Judea provides assistance in rebuilding the Jewish temple at Elephantine, "a credit (וצדקה) it will be to you before Ya'u God of Heaven" (*ANET*[3], 492). The view that צדקה in Deut 24:13 means "merit" is supported by the observation that in the immediate literary context (24:10-15) the opposite of "righteousness" is "guilt" (חטא) and by the parallel with both Deut 6:25 and Gen 15:6 (hence the NRSV's translation: "It will be to your credit").

[14] Daniel I. Block, *How I Love Your Torah, O LORD! Studies in the Book of Deuteronomy* (Eugene, Ore.: Cascade, 2011), 16. Deut 24:13 has been a minor flashpoint in debates about justification since the Protestant Reformation. In his *Institutes of Christian Religion*, for example, Calvin concedes that Deut 24:13 (along with Deut 6:25 and Ps 106:30-31) identifies a precept of the law as "righteousness," but he avers that, because perfect obedience to the law is impossible due to weakness of the flesh, this text does not undermine his doctrine of justification by faith (John Calvin, *Institutes of the Christian Religion: The First English Version of the 1541 French Edition* [trans. Elsie Anne McKee; Grand Rapids: Eerdmans, 2009], 365).

of the LXX, the NT, and second-century Christian literature. Within LXX Deuteronomy, צדקה is translated with ἐλεημοσύνη only in 6:25 and 24:13. This same translation is also found in the Greek Psalms (LXX Pss 23:5; 32:5; 34:24 [S and La^G]; and 102:6) and Isaiah (1:27; 28:17; 59:16).[15] As is clear from the Greek versions of Psalms and Isaiah, the LXX translators did regularly employ ἐλεημοσύνη as a translation of צדקה to speak of God's mercy or compassion, and not "almsgiving," per se:[16]

He it is that will receive blessing from the Lord and *mercy* (ἐλεημοσύνη; MT: וצדקה מאלהי ישעו) from his divine savior. (LXX Ps 23:5, NETS)

[The Lord] loves mercy and justice (ἀγαπᾷ ἐλεημοσύνην καὶ κρίσιν; MT: אהב צדקה ומשפט); the earth is full of the mercy (ἔλεος) of the Lord. (LXX Ps 32:5, NETS)

The Lord is one who performs merciful deeds (ποιῶν ἐλεημοσύνας ὁ κύριος) and judgment for all who are wronged. (Ps 102:6)[17]

For [Zion's] captivity shall be saved with judgment and with mercy (μετὰ ἐλεημοσύνης). (Isa 1:27, NETS)[18]

The Lord saw it, and it did not please him that there was no judgment. And he saw, and there was no man, and he took notice, and there was none who helped; so he defended them with his own arm, and with compassion he upheld them (τῇ ἐλεημοσύνῃ ἐστηρίσατο). And he put on righteousness (δικαιοσύνη) like a breastplate and placed a helmet of salvation on his head, and he clothed himself with a garment of vengeance and with his cloak, as one about to render retribution, reproach to his enemies. (Isa 56:15b-18, NETS)

---

[15] In contrast, the LXX translates צדקה or צדק with δικαιοσύνη more than 170 times.

[16] So John A. L. Lee, *A Lexical Study of the Septuagint Version of the Pentateuch* (SBLSCS 14; Chico, Calif.: Scholars Press, 1983), 108. Lee's gloss for ἐλεημοσύνη is "mercy, pity"; cf. Heiligenthal, "Werke," 290–93.

[17] The NETS translates the phrase ποιῶν ἐλεημοσύνας ὁ κύριος as "one who performs acts of pity is the Lord," although the NETS also supplies a footnote that suggests "perhaps *alms*" for ἐλεημοσύνας.

[18] As is well known, the Greek translation of Isaiah provides a deeply contextualized, sometimes innovative, rendering of its source text. The Greek translation of Isa 1:27 offers a rendering that highlights the restoration of Zion's captives by God's mercy, establishing a theme that runs throughout Greek Isaiah. On this particular text, see especially the discussion in J. Ross Wagner, *Reading the Sealed Book: Old Greek Isaiah and the Problem of Septuagint Hermeneutics* (FAT 88; Tübingen: Mohr Siebeck, 2013), 165–95.

In Greek versions of both Psalms and Isaiah, therefore, when צדקה is trans-lated by ἐλεημοσύνη this rendering marks ἐλεημοσύνη as a kind action from, or characteristic of, the compassionate and merciful God. Similarly, ἐλεημοσύνη in the LXX's rendering of the Deuteronomic pledge law in Deut 24:13 denotes compassion or mercy that one will receive from God on the basis of one's fair treatment of a poor debtor.

The notion that ἐλεημοσύνη in Deut 24:13 refers to God's mercy is sup-ported by the other text in LXX Deuteronomy in which צדקה is rendered by ἐλεημοσύνη—namely, Deut 6:25. There, in summarizing the results of obedience to God's commandments, Moses declares:

καὶ ἐλεημοσύνη ἔσται ἡμῖν, ἐὰν φυλασσώμεθα ποιεῖν πάσας τὰς ἐντολὰς ταύτας ἐναντίον κυρίου τοῦ θεοῦ ἡμῶν, καθὰ ἐνετείλατο ἡμῖν κύριος.

And there will be merciful action (ἐλεημοσύνη) for us, if we are careful to keep all these commandments before the Lord our God, as he has commanded us.

The MT states that the Israelites will be considered "righteous" (צדקה) if they adhere to God's commandments. But the LXX frames the outcome of collective obedience to the Law as God's mercy upon Israel. Deuteronomy 6:25 clarifies the rendering of צדקה with ἐλεημοσύνη in 24:13: God will show mercy to those who act mercifully to the poor.[19]

The observation that ἐλεημοσύνη in the LXX often means "mercy" or "compassion" when it translates צדקה is crucial for the ensuing analysis of several other texts in the Septuagint, the New Testament, and the early church fathers that employ the noun ἐλεημοσύνη to refer to merciful action on behalf of the poor. At this point, it is important briefly to clarify the lin-guistic theory that shapes the translation and interpretation of the noun ἐλεημοσύνη in this chapter and elsewhere in this study. Most discussions of this term, and certainly most dictionary entries for ἐλεημοσύνη, proceed on the basis of an assumed lexical polysemy. Thus, in consulting the entries for ἐλεημοσύνη in standard Greek lexicons, all of which are organized according to a principle of lexical polysemy, one is presented with a variety of glosses and asked to disambiguate between multiple senses:

[19] So John William Wevers, *Notes on the Greek Text of Deuteronomy* (SBLSCS 39; Atlanta: Scholars Press, 1995), 126. Wevers writes, "In later Hebrew צדקה comes to mean 'mercy,' and 'deeds of mercy,' and so 'almsgiving,' and this apparently influenced the translator. So what LXX is saying is that 'we will have mercy (i.e., God will be charitably disposed toward us) if we diligently practice πάσας τὰς ἐντολὰς ταύτας before the Lord.'"

LSJM (so also LEH)[20]
1. pity, mercy
2. charity, alms

BDAG
1. exercise of benevolent goodwill, alms, charitable giving w. focus on attitude and action as such
2. that which is benevolently given to meet a need, alms w. focus on material as such

EDNT
1. pity, kindness
2. alms

Louw-Nida
1. to give to those in need as an act of mercy—"acts of charity, alms, giving to the needy" (57.111)
2. that which is given to help the needy—"gift, money given to the needy, charity donation" (57.112).

---

[20] Takamitsu Muraoka's lexicon of the Septuagint offers an interesting contrast in that, like Louw-Nida, Muraoka's general procedure is to offer one or more definitions of a word instead of a series of glosses or translation equivalents, although Muraoka's lexicon is arranged according to words and not semantic domains, unlike Louw-Nida (Muraoka, *A Greek-English Lexicon of the Septuagint* [Louvain: Peeters, 2009]). For a critique of Muraoka's failure consistently to adhere to this principle in practice, see John A. L. Lee, "Review of T. Muraoka, *A Greek-English Lexicon of the Septuagint*," *BIOSCS* 43 (2010): 115–25. To be clear, Muraoka favors definitional polysemy. That is, many words are defined according to multiple senses. Muraoka's entry for λόγος, for example, offers six different definitions. The entry in Muraoka for ἐλεημοσύνη, however, provides only one definition, according to the format described in the introduction, which indicates that definitions are printed in italics: "*kindly, charitable disposition, compassion.*" The definition itself is somewhat confusing since it appears to offer both a definition (i.e., "*kindly, charitable disposition*") and a one-word gloss (i.e., "*compassion*"), a common inconsistency in this lexicon, as pointed out in Lee's review, that could be remedied by printing the gloss ("*compassion*") in plain text. After this "definition" in Muraoka's entry for ἐλεημοσύνη come two descriptions: (1) "a. human attribute and obj. of ποιέω," followed by a citation of Gen 47:29 and Tob 4:7 (G¹), followed by the note "pl. w. ref. to acts of charity" and a reference to Tob 12.9 (G¹), and (2) "b. divine attitude" (followed by a citation of Deut 24:13 and 6:25). The point of highlighting this entry is to suggest that Muraoka's *definition* of the word is actually monosemic, even if the definition identifies as an attitude (i.e., "*disposition*") something that seems to be an action in the LXX (i.e., "merciful action/deeds").

Interestingly, the multiple senses defined for ἐλεημοσύνη in these lexicons do not agree with one another.[21] LSJM and EDNT clearly distinguish between ἐλεημοσύνη as pity/mercy/kindness and ἐλεημοσύνη as charity/alms, although EDNT's glosses do not include the act of "almsgiving." Louw-Nida, on the other hand, does not offer pity/mercy/kindness as a semantic domain for ἐλεημοσύνη, presumably assuming that the term in the New Testament distinguishes only between the act of giving to the needy (for which, curiously, Louw-Nida includes the gloss "alms," a word that would presumably fit better in the second definition) and the thing that is given to help the needy, without indicating that the word can denote a feeling or disposition. BDAG's definition parallels this distinction between the act and the gift, although the first definition in BDAG seems to conflate kindness in a general sense (i.e., "benevolent goodwill") with the act of charitable giving.

The point of this exercise of looking at how various Greek lexicons treat the word ἐλεημοσύνη is not to parse or choose between competing definitions but to suggest that there is an attractive alternative to lexical polysemy. While spelling out this different theoretical perspective in any detail would demand a different project altogether, a convincing case can be made that the most fruitful and methodologically coherent perspective on lexical semantics is to adopt a *monosemic bias* before conceding lexical polysemy. Monosemy is the semantic theory that words have a univocal lexical meaning that is adjusted by pragmatic and contextual factors.[22] While some words in *Koinē* Greek can have distinct lexical senses without being homonyms (although often a distinction between polysemy and homonymy is difficult to establish), a more helpful semantic perspective is to begin with the assumption that each word has a univocal lexical meaning, conceding polysemy only when necessary. With regard to the word ἐλεημοσύνη, the working assumption in a monosemic perspective would be that ἐλεημοσύνη has the univocal lexical meaning of "merciful act," drawing ἐλεημοσύνη into close semantic

---

[21] On one hand, some lack of agreement might be expected since the chronological and textual range of BDAG/EDNT/Louw-Nida is different from that of LSJM/LEH/Muraoka. On the other, given both the infrequency with which the word ἐλεημοσύνη appears outside of Jewish and Christian literature and the likelihood, therefore, that early Christian usage was influenced by the Septuagint, it would be unusual if the "semantic range" (in the polysemous model reflected among these lexicons) were not similar between the LXX and NT.

[22] See the definition in Thorstein Fretheim, "In Defense of Monosemy," in *Pragmatics and the Flexibility of Word Meaning* (ed. Németh T. Enikö and Károly Bibok; Current Research in the Semantics/Pragmatics Interface 8; Amsterdam: Elsevier, 2001): "a lexical item with a univocal meaning which will inevitably be modified in context by a process of inferential enrichment of the encoded lexical meaning" (80).

relationship with its cognate ἔλεος ("mercy"), and that pragmatic adjustments in context, especially the literary co-texts in which the lexeme appears, can enrich this encoded lexical meaning.[23] To be sure, there are numerous instances in which ἐλεημοσύνη is appropriately translated "almsgiving" (or, perhaps better, "the merciful act of almsgiving"), but a monosemic bias contends that only context allows for this ad hoc construction of meaning. In practice, the semantic perspective of monosemy demands greater attention to lexical pragmatics and with it an avoidance of the parceling out of various "senses" of the word ἐλεημοσύνη.[24]

To return to Deut 24:13, it should be reasonably clear that the word ἐλεημοσύνη in the Greek translation of Deuteronomy is best rendered "merciful action" and not "almsgiving." In considering the word ἐλεημοσύνη in other contexts, however, it will be important to note that a bias in favor of lexical monosemy will allow for a rendering of ἐλεημοσύνη as "almsgiving" or "alms" only where there exist particular, contextual markers that indicate that the merciful act is specifically the merciful act of providing material assistance to the needy. Too often translators and interpreters render ἐλεημοσύνη as "almsgiving" without recognizing that the lexeme connotes merciful action and not charitable giving per se.

Care for the Poor and Reward in Proverbs

While the motif of divine blessing for charitable action is particularly prominent in Deuteronomy, it is also found elsewhere in the Old Testament, notably in the book of Proverbs. As a preeminent example of Jewish Wisdom literature, the marked emphasis on honesty and generosity for the poor in Proverbs is not rooted in the remembrance of God's deliverance of the

---

[23] Although ἐλεημοσύνη and ἔλεος can be synonymous, a general distinction would be that the former denotes the practice of mercy while the latter denotes the feeling of mercy. See R. Bultmann, "ἔλεος, κτλ," *TDNT*, 486; Jan Joosten, "חסד 'bienveillance' et *ELEOS* 'pitié': Réflexions sur une équivalence lexicale dans la Septante," in *"Car c'est l'amour qui me plaît, non le sacrifice": Recherches sur Osée 6:6 et son interprétation juive et chrétienne* (ed. J. Bons; JSJSup 88; Leiden: Brill, 2004), 25–42.

[24] For the semantic perspective presented in this section, I am deeply indebted to Benjamin J. Lappenga's excellent dissertation and the literature cited therein: *Paul's Language of Ζῆλος: Monosemy and the Rhetoric of Identity and Practice* (BIS 137; Leiden: Brill, 2015). For other works in the field of biblical studies that discuss lexical monosemy, see Gregory P. Fewster, *Creation Language in Romans 8: A Study in Monosemy* (Linguistic Biblical Studies 8; Leiden: Brill, 2013); Stanley Porter, "Greek Linguistics and Lexicography," in *Understanding the Times: New Testament Studies in the 21st Century; Essays in Honor of D. A. Carson on the Occasion of His 65th Birthday* (ed. Andreas J. Köstenberger and Robert W. Yarbrough; Wheaton, Ill.: Crossway, 2011), 19–61.

Israelites from bondage in Egypt, nor does Proverbs ground its exhortations to charity in specific appeals to the law. Instead, the discourse about wealth and poverty in Proverbs displays traditional scribal wisdom that emerges from reflection on the divinely created cosmic order, an order that governs the physical world and social relations within it.[25] The book of Proverbs has a complicated compositional history, and issues of wealth and poverty, and justice and charity, loom large in various proposals regarding editorial stages of the canonical text.[26] For the purposes of this study, however, it is appropriate to focus on several themes and sayings as they appear in the final form of the Masoretic Text and in early Greek translation of the book.

The first text in Proverbs that identifies a connection between giving and material reward offers a helpful framework with which to begin an analysis of the relationship between benevolence for the needy and recompense in the book of Proverbs. In the discourse of the father to the son in Proverbs 1–9, the father figure promises material reward for generous giving: "Honor the Lord with your wealth and with the first fruits of all your produce. And your barns will be filled with grain, and your vats will burst with new wine" (MT 3:9-10). The text does not explicitly instruct giving to the needy, and the reference to giving from the firstfruits should be interpreted as a command to present this produce to the priest in the temple cult.[27] In the larger context of Proverbs, however, the activity of honoring the Lord with wealth (הוֹן) should be seen as a practice that includes the provision of material support for the needy, not least because of the claim in Proverbs that lending to the poor is lending to God (19:17). Such an interpretation of Prov 3:9 is strengthened by Prov 14:31, which employs the same verb (כבד) in claiming that "those who oppress the poor taunt their Maker, but those who are kind to the needy

---

[25] See, e.g., Leo G. Perdue, "Wisdom Literature," in Joel B. Green et al., *Dictionary of Scripture and Ethics* (Grand Rapids: Baker, 2011).

[26] See, e.g., R. Norman Whybray, *Wealth and Poverty in the Book of Proverbs* (JSOTSup 99; Sheffield: JSOT Press, 1990).

[27] So Michael V. Fox, *Proverbs 1–9: A New Translation with Introduction and Commentary* (AB 18A; New York: Doubleday, 2000), 151–52. That Prov 3:9 is the only instance in the book in which cultic sacrifice is stipulated has sometimes led to the claim that the sacrificial cult is minimized or rejected altogether in Proverbs. While there is doubtless a critique of improperly offered sacrifices in the book (see 7:14; 14:9; 15:8; 20:25; 21:27), by no means does Proverbs (or other Jewish wisdom literature) disavow cultic sacrifice, even if the book is more directly focused on the cultivation of virtuous behavior (21:3). On this point, see Jonathan Klawans, *Purity, Sacrifice, and the Temple: Symbolism and Supersessionism in the Study of Ancient Judaism* (Oxford: Oxford University Press, 2006), 87–89; Leo G. Perdue, *Wisdom and Cult: A Critical Analysis of the Views of Cult in Wisdom Literatures of Israel and the Ancient Near East* (SBLDS 30; Missoula, Mont: Scholars Press, 1977).

honor God" (ומכבדו חנן אביון). Showing kindness to the needy, according to
the logic of Proverbs, is to honor the Lord with wealth.

Interestingly, Prov 3:10 assures material, and specifically agricultural,
prosperity for those who honor God with wealth and give the firstfruits of
their produce: "And your barns will be filled with grain, and your vats will
burst with new wine." The promised blessing in verse 10 serves to inspire
obedience to the command in verse 9.[28] The saying, then, might be read as a
transparent articulation of a theology of mechanistic retribution: if you do
X for the Lord (i.e., give to the poor and observe cultic offerings), you will be
blessed with Y (i.e., agricultural success). There is no way of avoiding, here
and elsewhere, the close connection between act and consequence in Proverbs: giving for a return is part and parcel of the theology of this text, not to
be explained away, even as the link between act and consequence throughout
the book of Proverbs admits a variety of explanations.[29]

At the same time, however, the quixotic description of the return on one's
disposal of goods in Prov 3:10—barns filled with plenty, wine vats bursting
with wine—might invite a nonliteral understanding of this blessing, with the
lavishness of the reward pointing to an idealized exchange, an exaggeration
characteristic of the ways in which the book of Proverbs employs the rhetoric
of wealth and material prosperity to motivate the pursuit of wisdom and a
life of embodied righteousness. In this sense, the promise of material prosperity in 3:10, and elsewhere (cf. Prov 3:13-15; 8:18-21), does not so much
offer an empirically verifiable law of retribution—similar to that sometimes
propounded by proponents of today's so-called prosperity theology—as it
communicates a symbolic vision in which wealth is a symbol designed to
encourage readers in the pursuit of wisdom. This reading of Proverbs is perhaps suggested by the book's prologue itself, which intimates that the goal of
the instruction is "to understand a trope and a figure, the words of the wise
and their riddles" (1:6).[30]

[28] Timothy J. Sandoval, *The Discourse of Wealth and Poverty in the Book of Proverbs*
(BINS 77; Leiden: Brill, 2006), 104.

[29] See the helpful discussion in Tova Forti, "The Concept of 'Reward' in Proverbs:
A Diachronic of Synchronic Approach?" *CBR* 12 (2014): 129–45. As is well known,
some texts in Proverbs envision a pragmatic/utilitarian connection between deed and
consequence in the sense that recompense is the (natural?) result of one's actions, while
other texts in Proverbs depict God as the active agent who rewards or punishes human
beings on the basis of their deeds. Forti's proposal for reconciling these different perspectives is astute: "[T]he dual presence of the human and divine systems is a function of the
seam between the author's didactic-utilitarian purpose and the conventional sapiential
religious-moralistic view" (129).

[30] I am indebted here to Sandoval, *Discourse of Wealth and Poverty*.

Occasionally in Proverbs, charity is commanded without any explicit mention of reward for beneficence or punishment for stinginess or injustice. In Prov 3:27-28, for example, the fictive son to whom the discourse is addressed is given concrete instructions not to refuse the good that belongs to someone else—a statement that in the LXX reads, "Do not hold back from doing good to a needy person" (μὴ ἀπόσχῃ εὖ ποιεῖν ἐνδεῇ)—and not to delay in helping a neighbor when the son has the means to provide assistance immediately. In this command, there is no specific promise of reward or punishment, although the words are embedded in a larger rhetorical context that makes clear that acceptance of this instruction will lead to the fear and knowledge of the Lord (2:5). In general, however, proverbs endorsing charity and care for the poor, even as observations about the workings of the world, tend to be framed in the language of retribution. Positively, "a generous person will be enriched, and one who gives water will get water" (11:25); those who are kind to the poor are happy (14:21); the generous, who share their bread with the poor, are blessed (22:9); God will reward those who give bread and water to hungry and thirsty enemies (25:21-22);[31] and the one who gives to the poor will lack nothing (28:27). Even a king who judges the poor with honesty will see his throne established forever (29:14). Negatively, those who refuse to sell grain, perhaps during times of famine or food shortage, will be cursed (11:24); one who closes an ear to the cry of the poor will cry out and not be heard (21:13; cf. 23:10-11); those who rob, crush, or plunder the poor will be plundered by the Lord (22:23); and cursed will be one who turns a blind eye to the poor (28:27).[32] Oppressing or mocking the poor is akin to insulting their Creator (14:31; 17:5). The saying in Prov 28:27 articulates a fitting summary of this relationship between benevolence for the needy and reward in the book of Proverbs, for the maxim promises not only blessing to the one who gives to the poor but also execration for the one who ignores the disadvantaged: "Whoever gives to the poor will lack nothing, but one who turns a blind eye will get many a curse" (NRSV; cf. 14:31; 17:5).

Interestingly, while the Masoretic Text of Proverbs certainly stresses the need to assist the poor, the theme of charity is even more prominent in the Greek translation of Proverbs. Earlier, for example, a slight difference between the MT and LXX of Prov 3:27 was observed, for the Greek translator includes the word "needy" (ἐνδεής) to specify that those to whom good

---

[31] While the recipients of assistance in Prov 25:21-22 are called "enemies" and not "the poor," they are characterized as hungry and thirsty, and the heaping of coals of fire on their heads consists of the material provision of bread and water. This is almsgiving.

[32] Closely related is the notion that the greedy will suffer punishment (1:19; 15:27); see Sandoval, *Discourse of Wealth and Poverty*, 115–54.

is due are the poor: "Do not hold back from doing good to a needy person (εὖ ποιεῖν ἐνδεῇ)." Elsewhere, entire clauses advocating charity are present in the LXX but absent in the MT version of Proverbs:

MT (13:11): Dishonest money dwindles away, but whoever gathers money little by little makes it grow. (TNIV)

הון מהבל ימעט וקבץ על־יד ירבה

LXX (13:11): Property gained hastily with lawlessness is contracted, but the one who gathers for himself with godliness will be multiplied. The righteous one is compassionate and he lends.

ὕπαρξις ἐπισπουδαζομένη μετὰ ἀνομίας ἐλάσσων γίνεται, ὁ δὲ συνάγων ἑαυτῷ μετ᾽ εὐσεβείας πληθυνθήσεται. δίκαιος οἰκτίρει καὶ κιχρᾷ.

MT (17:5): Those who mock the poor insult their Maker; those who are glad at calamity will not go unpunished. (NRSV)

לעג לרש חרף עשהו שמח לאיד לא ינקה

LXX (17:5): The one who laughs at the poor angers his Maker, and the one who rejoices at a person being destroyed will not go unpunished. But the one who has compassion will be shown mercy.

ὁ καταγελῶν πτωχοῦ παροξύνει τὸν ποιήσαντα αὐτόν, ὁ δὲ ἐπιχαίρων ἀπολλυμένῳ οὐκ ἀθωωθήσεται. ὁ δὲ ἐπισπλαγχνιζόμενος ἐλεηθήσεται.

More examples could be cited, but the Greek translation of Proverbs characteristically emphasizes compassion for the needy more strongly than the MT. These variances are best explained as representing a thematic concern for the translator of the LXX rather than as differences based on the Greek translator's use of an alternate Hebrew *Vorlage*.[33] This point is important because the LXX Proverbs served as a primary source for early Christian reflection on the wisdom and virtue of charity.

Additionally, within Proverbs several specific sayings figure prominently in later Jewish and Christian discourse about the meritorious and atoning value of almsgiving. First, the promise in Prov 10:2 and 11:4 that "righteousness" (צדקה/δικαιοσύνη) rescues from death is alluded to in discussions of

[33] See Ronald L. Giese Jr., "Compassion for the Lowly in Septuagint Proverbs," *JSP* 11 (1993): 109–17. Other texts highlighted by Giese that emphasize the theme of compassion for the lowly in LXX Proverbs include 14:21; 19:7; and 22:9. My use of the phrase "the translator" of LXX Proverbs does not imply that only one individual was responsible for this translation.

charity in both Tobit (4:10; 12:9) and Sirach (29:12), as well as later Jewish (*b. Shab.* 156) and Christian (*2 Clem.* 16.4; Pol. *Phil.* 10.2; Cyprian, *Ep.* 51.22; *Laps.* 35; *Dom. or.* 32–33; *Eleem.* 5–6, 20) literary sources:[34]

MT (10:2): Treasures of wickedness do not profit, but righteousness delivers from death.[35]

לֹא־יוֹעִילוּ אוֹצְרוֹת רֶשַׁע וּצְדָקָה תַּצִּיל מִמָּוֶת

LXX (10:2): Treasures will not profit the lawless, but righteousness will deliver from death.

οὐκ ὠφελήσουσιν θησαυροὶ ἀνόμους, δικαιοσύνη δὲ ῥύσεται ἐκ θανάτου.

It is noteworthy that the LXX renders צדקה not with ἐλεημοσύνη but with δικαιοσύνη, making it highly unlikely that the Greek translator understood the saying as advocating "almsgiving."[36] The notion that the wicked might gain riches is itself an indication of the paradoxical nature of Proverbs, for other sayings indicate that it is the righteous who will prosper, not the wicked (3:8-9, 15-16; 10:22). Although it has been claimed that Prov 10:2 serves as a basis for a theology in which care for the poor delivers one from eternal punishment, such a reading stumbles as an account of the exchange dynamics envisioned in Proverbs, for the book of Proverbs itself reflects no belief in postmortem existence.[37] In context, both the Hebrew and Greek versions of Prov 10:2 contrast ill-gotten material wealth with moral and social rectitude.[38] Given the close correlation, though perhaps not identification, between the wise and the righteous throughout Proverbs (e.g., 1:3; 2:9; 10:31; 11:9), this saying likely observes that the righteous characteristically

---

[34] Often, early Christian allusions are to Tobit, which is shaped by Proverbs, and not to Proverbs itself.

[35] Cf. Prov 11:4 (MT): "Wealth does not profit in a day of anger, but righteousness delivers from death." The phrase וּצְדָקָה תַּצִּיל מִמָּוֶת is identical in Prov 10:2 and 11:4, although Prov 11:4 is absent from the LXX.

[36] Anderson's decision to translate צדקה in Prov 10:2 and 11:4 as "almsgiving" because "this was the norm in the Second Temple period" is linguistically problematic; see Anderson, *Charity*, 197. Furthermore, Anderson's claim that "the concept of a 'treasury in heaven' is born" in Sirach's interpretation (in 29:12) of Prov 10:2 fails to account for the fact that the language of "heaven" is nowhere used in either saying (see the discussion in the following chapter).

[37] English translations that render the phrase בְּיוֹם עֶבְרָה in Prov 11:4 as a definite (e.g., NRSV: *the* day of wrath") instead of "in a day of anger" perhaps feed into an unwarranted "eschatologizing" of Proverbs.

[38] For this understanding of "righteousness" in Proverbs, see Sun Myung Lyu, *Righteousness in the Book of Proverbs* (FAT II/55: Tübingen: Mohr Siebeck, 2012).

act in ways that mitigate (untimely) death.[39] The history of interpretation of this text, however, especially among Christian authors, moves in an eschatological direction (cf. Wis 1:15; cf. Tertullian, *Pat.* 7.13; Herm. *Vis.* 3.9.5–6).

Second, it is worth noting that Prov 10:12, while not ostensibly about charity, became one of the texts to which allusion is often made in early Christian advocacy of atoning almsgiving, a hermeneutical innovation perhaps assisted by an allusion to this saying in 1 Pet 4:8:[40]

MT (10:12): Hatred stirs up controversy, but love covers over all offenses.

שנאה תעורר מדנים ועל כל־פשעים תכסה אהבה

LXX (10:12): Hatred awakens strife, but friendship covers all who do not love strife.

μῖσος ἐγείρει νεῖκος, πάντας δὲ τοὺς μὴ φιλονεικοῦντας καλύπτει φιλία.

Third, a saying located in Prov 16:6 in the MT and 15:27 in the LXX offers an interesting possible connection between human compassion and atonement for sin:

MT (16:6): Through love and faithfulness atonement for sin is made; and through fear of the Lord evil is avoided.

בחסד ואמת יכפר עון וביראת יהוה סור מרע

LXX (15:27): One who receives a bribe destroys himself, but one who hates the receiving of bribes is saved. By merciful acts and faithful deeds[41] sins are cleansed, but by the fear of the Lord everyone turns away from evil.

ἐξόλλυσιν ἑαυτὸν ὁ δωρολήμπτης, ὁ δὲ μισῶν δώρων λήμψεις σῴζεται. ἐλεημοσύναις καὶ πίστεσιν ἀποκαθαίρονται ἁμαρτίαι, τῷ δὲ φόβῳ κυρίου ἐκκλίνει πᾶς ἀπὸ κακοῦ.

---

[39] On the relationship between righteousness and wisdom in Proverbs, see the discussion in Lyu, *Righteousness in the Book of Proverbs*, 54–62.

[40] See chap. 7 for a fuller discussion of this issue.

[41] LXX Prov 15:27 renders the singular אמת with the unusual dative plural πίστεσιν, perhaps "indicating that 'deeds [plural] of faithfulness' cleanse an individual from sins, not simply faith in abstraction" (Christopher M. Hays, "By Almsgiving and Faith Sins Are Purged? The Theological Underpinnings of Early Christian Care for the Poor," in *Engaging Economics: New Testament Scenarios and Early Christian Reception* [ed. Bruce W. Longenecker and Kelly D. Liebengood; Grand Rapids: Eerdmans, 2009], 260–80 [269]). My translation attempts to capture this unusual construction.

The Hebrew version of this saying in Prov 16:6a presents a number of interpretive difficulties. This proverb proposes a means of remedying sin in the form of חסד and אמת and a means of avoiding wickedness in the form of fear of the Lord. But the saying leaves unresolved the question of whether it is human or divine love (חסד) and faithfulness (אמת) that makes possible atonement for sin. Does atonement (כפר) in this context designate God's act of forgiving human sin? Or does atonement involve some sort of appeasement of iniquity or the rending of broken social relations among humans? It is sometimes suggested that the parallelism in this verse between its two main clauses indicates that "love and faithfulness" are human attributes or actions, for "fear of the Lord" in Proverbs is one of wisdom's cardinal virtues, to be cultivated by attentive readers of the discourse.[42] Thus, since the second line describes the human act of fearing the Lord, חסד and אמת in verse 6a must be human acts as well.[43] If it is indeed human love and faithfulness that atone for sin, perhaps this text functions as part of a larger critique of cultic sacrifice in Proverbs, with the saying in 21:3 then emblematic of a dismissal of the temple cult: "To do righteousness and justice is more acceptable to the Lord than sacrifice" (NRSV). Divine forgiveness for sin can be achieved through human love and faithfulness, either rendering the sacrificial cult unnecessary or adding human love and faithfulness as necessary human virtues that complement and render effective sacrificial practice.[44]

The issue is complicated, however, by the fact that the book of Proverbs does advocate cultic sacrifice in 3:9, as was discussed above. Moreover, while a number of sayings in Proverbs do critique the inappropriate offering of sacrifices, especially sacrifices offered by the wicked and the unjust (7:14; 14:9; 15:8; 20:25; 21:27), cultic sacrifice as such is never rejected. Perhaps, then, "love" and "faithfulness" in Prov 16:6a are to be interpreted as divine, and not human, attributes or actions. Interestingly, although it is often very difficult to discern any clear structure among the various sayings in the document, Prov 16:1-9 appears to be a unified section framed by two sayings that

---

[42] See esp. Prov 1:7 (cf. 1:29; 2:5; 8:13; 9:10; 10:27; 14:26-27; 15:16, 33; 19:23; 22:4; 23:17; 24:21); cf. Sandoval, *Discourse of Wealth and Poverty*, 45–49.

[43] So Bruce K. Waltke, *The Book of Proverbs, Chapters 15–31* (NICOT; Grand Rapids, Eerdmans, 2005), 13.

[44] This latter interpretation is offered by Waltke, who does not believe that Proverbs rejects cultic sacrifice: "The epigrammatic proverb points only to the human virtues that complement the sacrificial system to make atonement (Lev. 1:4; 4:4; 16:21; *passim*). Unless a person is characterized by unfailing love, the sacrificial system is of no avail (1 Sam. 15:22). The guilty sinner cannot trust himself to the divine grace mediated through the cultus 'if he is not zealous in his relations to his fellowmen, to practice love and truth' (cf. Matt. 6:12, 14-15; Luke 7:47; Jas. 1:26-27; 2:8, 12-18)." Waltke, *Book of Proverbs*, 13–14.

emphasize the contrast between human planning and the Lord's direction
(vv. 1, 9).[45] The entire unit in Prov 16:1-9 stresses the activity of the Lord,
and the note regarding God's punishment of the arrogant in verse 5 ("All
those who are arrogant are an abomination to the Lord; be assured, they will
not go unpunished" [NRSV]) might be seen as contrasting with God's "love
and faithfulness" in verse 6. In the larger canonical context, חסד and אמת
are regularly paired as divine attributes, notably in the account of the Lord's
appearance to Moses in Exod 34:6-7:

> [6]The Lord passed before him, and proclaimed, "The Lord, the Lord,
> a God merciful and gracious, slow to anger, and abounding in *steadfast
> love and faithfulness* (ורב־חסד ואמת), [7]keeping *steadfast love* (חסד) for
> the thousandth generation, forgiving iniquity and transgression and
> sin, yet by no means clearing the guilty, but visiting the iniquity of the
> parents upon the children and the children's children, to the third and
> the fourth generation." (NRSV)

Indeed, as is well known, some form of this confession is echoed at least eight
additional times in the Old Testament (Num 14:18; Neh 9:17; Pss 103:8;
86:15; 145:8-9; Joel 2:13; Nah 1:3; Jonah 4:2). Although only in Ps 86:15
does the phrase "abounding in חסד and אמת" recur in this confessional statement, חסד and אמת are regularly paired as attributes of the loving and faithful God, especially in the Psalms (e.g., Gen 24:27; 32:10; 2 Sam 2:6; 15:20;
Pss 25:10; 40:10-11; 57:3; 61:8; 85:10; 89:14, 24; 92:2; 98:3; 100:5; 108:4;
115:1; 117:2; 138:2). Even elsewhere in Proverbs the pairing of these two
nouns appears always to refer to God's love and faithfulness: in Prov 3:3 the
son is exhorted not to allow חסד and אמת to forsake him in the sense that
God's gracious character provides a framework for adherence to his father's
teaching; in 14:22 those who plan good find חסד and אמת, presumably from
God; and in 20:28 it is said that God's חסד and אמת preserve the king.[46]

     In light of this context, it seems best to understand חסד and אמת in MT
Prov 16:6 as divine characteristics, and thus the text might be paraphrased:
"Through God's love and faithfulness sin is atoned for [by means of the sac-
rificial cult]." That is, the sacrificial cult is God's gracious provision, and sac-
rifices, when rightly offered, are the means by which the loving and faithful
God atones for the iniquity of his people.[47]

---

[45] Roland E. Murphy, *Proverbs* (WBC 22; Nashville: Thomas Nelson, 1998), 118.

[46] C. John Collins, "Proverbs and the Levitical System," *Presb* 35 (2009): 9–34
[28–29].

[47] As Collins summarizes this reading: "[T]he sacrificial system, which mediates
blessings such as atonement through the sin offering, the guilt offering, and the burnt

The MT of Prov 16:6 is admittedly open to a variety of construals, but the best reading is one that understands חסד and אמת as attributes of God. It is not entirely clear, however, that the Greek translator of Proverbs understood this saying in this way. The recensional history of this section of LXX Proverbs is complex, and it appears that the translator of Proverbs has significantly reworked the material in 15:27–16:9, transposing several verses and omitting others.[48] It seems that the Greek translator's substantial editorial activity serves more emphatically to emphasize the theme of mercy than justice and the fear of the Lord.[49]

With regard to this specific saying in LXX 15:27, for example, the LXX translator has pulled the saying from MT 16:6 together with a saying about bribery (found in MT 15:27): "One who receives a bribe destroys himself, but one who hates the receiving of bribes is saved." In contrast to the MT, the placement of the verse about the cleansing of sin in the LXX does not connect the verse to God's judgment of the arrogant as in MT 16:5, even as the parallel verse in LXX 16:5 claims that the arrogant are impure and adds the claim that the one who "unjustly joins hands [i.e., participates in a false business dealing] will not go unpunished." Instead, the two sayings stitched together in LXX 15:27 appear to indicate that the specific sin cleansed by "merciful acts and [deeds of] faithfulness" (ἐλεημοσύναι and πίστις) is bribery:[50]

---

offering, is a provision stemming from the Lord's steadfast love and faithfulness, by which he graciously made a covenant with his people and preserves that people; and the proper response to that covenant, and to the steadfast love and faithfulness on which it rests, is to fear the Lord, and thus to turn away from doing evil—to begin to realize in one's own experience the covenant ideal of properly functioning humanity—rather than to presume on the sacrifice" ("Proverbs and the Levitical System," 30; for a similar reading of Prov 16:6, see Perdue, *Wisdom and Cult*, 165).

[48] For a brief summary, see Emanuel Tov, *The Greek and Hebrew Bible: Collected Essays on the Septuagint* (VTSup 72; Leiden: Brill, 1999), 426–27.

[49] This is the thesis of the insightful study by Ruth Scoralick, "Salomos griechische Gewänder—Beobachtungen zur Septuagintafassung des Sprichwörterbuches," in *Rettendes Wissen: Studien zum Fortgang weisheitlichen Denkens im Frühjudentum und im frühen Christentum* (ed. Karl Löning and Martin Fassnacht; Alter Orient und Altes Testament 300; Winona Lake, Ind.: Eisenbrauns, 2002), 43–75. On the question of whether differences between the MT and LXX versions of Proverbs are due to the LXX working from a different *Vorlage* or to the LXX translator freely altering a source text that fairly closely resembled the MT, I am persuaded by the arguments of Johann Cook (NETS, "To the Reader of Proverbs"), Scoralick, and others that differences between the MT and LXX of Proverbs are largely due to the translator's creative reshaping of material.

[50] J. Cook, NETS, 622. In this context, the dative plural πίστεσιν refers not to faith in the abstract but to "deeds of faithfulness"; so also Hays, "By Almsgiving and Faith," 269.

One who receives a bribe destroys himself, but one who hates the
receiving of bribes is saved. By merciful acts[51] and faithful deeds sins
are cleansed, but by the fear of the Lord everyone turns away from evil.

Moreover, if this placement of the saying about ἐλεημοσύνη and the alleviation of sin indicates that bribery is cleansed by "merciful acts and faithfulness," then it appears that, in contrast to the interpretation of the MT of
Prov 16:6 above, the Greek translator of Proverbs understood חסד and אמת
to be human actions.

The notion that in LXX Prov 15:27 ἐλεημοσύνη and πίστις are human
deeds is also strengthened by the use of the noun ἐλεημοσύνη elsewhere in
LXX Proverbs. While some instances of the noun ἐλεημοσύνη in LXX Proverbs are ambiguous and could plausibly refer to either God's mercy or human
compassion (e.g., 3:3; 19:22; 20:28), LXX Prov 14:22 differs from the MT in
such a way as to make clear that ἐλεημοσύνη and πίστις are human actions:

MT (14:22): Do not those who plan evil go astray? Those who plan
good find love and faithfulness.

הלוא־יתעו חרשי רע וחסד ואמת חרשי טוב

LXX (14:22): Those who go astray devise evil things, but the good
devise mercy and truth. Mercy and faithfulness the planners of evil
things do not understand. But acts of mercy and faithfulness are with
planners for good things.

πλανώμενοι τεκταίνουσι κακά, ἔλεον δὲ καὶ ἀλήθειαν τεκταίνουσιν
ἀγαθοί. οὐκ ἐπίστανται ἔλεον καὶ πίστιν τέκτονες κακῶν; ἐλεημοσύναι δὲ
καὶ πίστεις παρὰ τέκτοσιν ἀγαθοῖς.

The cognate ἔλεος with πίστις as the object of the verb τεκταίνω in 14:22a
indicates that ἐλεημοσύνη and πίστις in verse 14:22b are "with" planners for
good things in the sense that these people practice merciful deeds and faithfulness. Similarly, Prov 21:21 speaks of "a way of righteousness and merciful

---

[51] My translation reflects the discussion of monosemy above. Hays writes of the
LXX's rendering of חסד with ἐλεημοσύνη in Prov 15:27 that the LXX "seems to be functioning as an interpretative translation" ("By Almsgiving and Faith," 274). Hays continues:
"It is entirely proper to think of almsgiving as an expression of חסד, and in this respect the
translation is appropriate, if a bit narrow" (274). But translating חסד with ἐλεημοσύνη is
"narrow" only if one has determined that ἐλεημοσύνη means "almsgiving," which is, in
fact, how Hays consistently translates the noun throughout his essay. If ἐλεημοσύνη, on
the other hand, means "merciful action," it is not so clear that this does not come close to
the Hebrew חסד; see Joosten, "חסד 'bienveillance' et ELEOS 'pitié.'"

deeds" (ὁδὸς δικαιοσύνης καὶ ἐλεημοσύνης) as an honorable pattern of human life. The praiseworthy woman of Proverbs 31 is also described as practicing ἐλεημοσύνη with the result that her children are built up and become wealthy (31:28). Thus, it seems clear that in 15:27 the phrase ἐλεημοσύναις καὶ πίστεσιν ἀποκαθαίρονται ἁμαρτίαι should be understood as indicating that, in some way, human deeds of mercy and faithfulness cleanse sins, especially, though perhaps not exclusively, the sin of bribery. LXX Prov 15:27, with its promise that sins are cleansed by merciful acts and faithful deeds, became a key text in early Christian support of the atoning value of almsgiving (Clement of Alexandria, *Strom.* 2.15; Cyprian, *Laps.* 35; *Eleem.* 2; *Apos. Con.* 2.35; 3.1.4; 7.12; cf. Ps.Ign. *Hero* 5).

Finally, ~~Prov 19:17~~ provides an influential statement that equates care for the poor with lending to God, an act of beneficence that merits divine recompense:

> MT (19:17): Whoever has compassion on the poor lends to the Lord, and he will recompense him for his deed.

> מלוה יהוה חונן דל וגמלו ישלם־לו

> LXX (19:17): One who acts mercifully to a poor person lends to God, and he will recompense him according to his gift.

> δανίζει θεῷ ὁ ἐλεῶν πτωχόν, κατὰ δὲ τὸ δόμα αὐτοῦ ἀνταποδώσει αὐτῷ.

There is not a substantial difference between the Hebrew and Greek versions, as both imagine a divine economy in which material support given to the needy metaphorically constitutes a loan to God. The extent to which charity can be called an act of lending (לוה/δανείζω) to God is clarified in the second part of the proverb: God, the proxy recipient, will pay back the loan to the generous lender. ~~The notion that care for the poor constitutes a loan to God that the Creator will recompense features as a key component in early Jewish and Christian discourse about the meritorious value of almsgiving,~~ for later authors also imagine a triangular relationship of exchange between the poor recipient, the generous lender, and God.[52]

---

[52] E.g., Irenaeus, *Haer.* 4.18; Clement of Alexandria, *Strom.* 3.6; *Paed.* 2.13; 3.4; Cyprian, *Eleem.* 15–16, 26; *Laps.* 35; *Dom. or.* 33; *Const. ap.* 3.1.4; 7.1.12; Chrysostom, *On Repentance and Almsgiving,* 7.24; Gregory of Nazianzus, *Select Orations* 14; Ambrose, *Tob.* 16.55; Augustine, *Serm.* 38.8; 42.2; 123.5; 357.5; Jerome, *Comm. Eph.* 5.1; *Comm. Eph.* 120.1; cf. Luke 6:28; for the citation of *Midrash Tannaim zum Deuteronomium* on Deut 15:10, see Anderson, *Charity,* 30. Several modern authors contend that Prov 19:17 contains the earliest hint that almsgiving results in the accumulation of heavenly treasure

"Righteousness" and Reward in Daniel 4

One of the most important scriptural texts linking care for the poor with the alleviation of sin is found in ~~Dan 4:27~~, a verse that figures prominently in early Christian discourse about the atoning value of almsgiving. After Daniel recounts and interprets a troubling dream of Babylon's King Nebuchadnezzar early in the book's narrative (2:1-49), a second sequence reports the content of a subsequent dream of Nebuchadnezzar (4:9-18 [4:6-15]) and Daniel's interpretation of the vision (4:19-27 [4:16-24]).[53] In his dream, the king sees a great tree at the center of the earth, a tree that reaches the height of heaven, with foliage and fruit to provide shade and food for animals, birds, and all living beings (4:10-12 [4:7-9]). This idyllic scene is interrupted by the appearance of a heavenly figure who cries out, "Cut down the tree and chop off its branches, strip off its foliage and scatter its fruit" (4:14 [4:11], NRSV). The angel, however, declares that the tree's stump and roots are to be left in the ground and, in a shift from horticultural to anthropological imagery, chained with iron and bronze (4:15a [4:12a]), a picture that corresponds to the description of the human figure's reduction to an animallike existence in the remainder of the dream (4:15b-17 [4:12b-14]).

As was the case earlier in the narrative, Daniel is asked to provide an interpretation (4:8, 18 [4:5, 15]). Seemingly aware of the horrifying implications of this dream for Nebuchadnezzar, Daniel initially hesitates to serve as seer (4:19 [4:16]). When pressed, however, Daniel reveals that the tree is the king and that the declaration of the heavenly figure regarding the beastly

---

(so Nathan Eubank, *Wages of Cross-Bearing and Debt of Sin: The Economy of Heaven in Matthew's Gospel* [BZNW 196; Berlin: De Gruyter, 2013], 27; Bradley C. Gregory, *Like an Everlasting Signet Ring: Generosity in the Book of Sirach* [DCLS 2; Berlin: De Gruyter, 2010], 192–93; Anderson, *Sin*, 140–41). The problem with describing Prov 19:17 as a foundational text for the concept of "heavenly treasure" is that the saying promises no such thing. The reward envisioned in Prov 19:17 may be called "heavenly" only in the sense that the God who established the heavens (Prov 3:19; 8:27) is the one who recompenses, but not in the sense that there is treasure accumulated in heaven in a spatial or metaphorical or eschatological sense.

[53] Citing this passage is complicated because Dan 4:1-3 in the NRSV corresponds to 3:31-33 in the MT. This material in Theodotian's text (Th) is found at the end of chapter 3 and numbered 3:98-100 in the Göttingen critical edition, but the same material, along with additional information, is found at the end of chapter 3 (i.e., 3:34a-c) in the Old Greek (OG) text. For the sake of reference, I have provided the versification of the NRSV with the numbers of the Ziegler/Munich edition of the Göttingen critical edition of the Septuagint in parentheses. Joseph Ziegler, Olivier Munich, and Detlef Fraenkel, eds., *Susanna, Daniel, Bel et Draco* (2nd ed.; Vetus Testamentum Graecum 16/2; Göttingen: Vandenhoeck & Ruprecht, 1999).

state of the human figure in the vision is a decree of God regarding Nebuchadnezzar: he will be driven away from humans and compelled to live with wild animals until he learns "that the Most High has sovereignty over the kingdom of mortals, and gives it to whom he will" (4:25 [4:22]).

At the conclusion of Daniel's interpretation of this dream that portends judgment upon the king until he acknowledges God's sovereignty over human kingdoms, Daniel offers Nebuchadnezzar a charge that might allow the king to avert the impending debacle:

> Therefore, O king, may my counsel be acceptable to you: break from your sins with justice (בצדקה פרק), and your iniquities with mercy to the oppressed (ועויתך במחן ענין), so that your prosperity may be prolonged. (MT 4:27 [4:24])

The meaning of the Aramaic צדקה (ṣidqāh) here is important and debated. It has been suggested that, especially combined with the parallel במחן ענין (bmiḥan ʿānāyin, "mercy to the oppressed") in the second half of the clause (cf. Pss 37:21; 112:4–5), this passage represents "the first Jewish testimony for the use of the word in the meaning of 'alms, charity.' "[54] Certainly, the Hebrew צדקה (ṣĕdāqāh) came to denote "almsgiving" in postbiblical Hebrew, and in rabbinic literature צדקה becomes a kind of technical term for material support of the poor.[55] It is not entirely apparent, however, that Daniel's statement to Nebuchadnezzar should be interpreted in such a limited sense, with the phrase translated, "Redeem your sins by *almsgiving* and your iniquities by generosity to the poor."[56]

In the present context, Daniel is addressing a king whose responsibility is to maintain justice throughout the land. Nebuchadnezzar is not called privately to make charitable contributions to the poor from his personal resources; as king he is exhorted to govern in such a way that his kingdom reflects the values of the sovereign God whose power he has failed

---

[54] Franz Rosenthal, "Sedaka, Charity," *HUCA* 23 (1950–1951): 427–28; cf. Anderson, *Sin*, 139–41; Satlow, "Fruit and the Fruit of Fruit," 262–63.

[55] Gregg E. Gardner, "Charity Wounds," in *The Gift in Antiquity* (ed. Michael L. Satlow; Oxford: Wiley-Blackwell, 2013), 173–88; Yael Wilfand Ben Shalom, "Poverty, Charity and the Image of the Poor in Rabbinic Texts from the Land of Israel" (Ph.D. diss, Duke University, 2011), 64–70.

[56] This is the translation given in Gary A. Anderson, "How Does Almsgiving Purge Sins?" in *Hebrew in the Second Temple Period: The Hebrew of the Dead Sea Scrolls and of Other Contemporary Sources* (ed. Steven E. Fassberg, Moshe Bar-Asher, and Ruth A. Clements; STDJ 108; Leiden: Brill, 2013), 7–8.

to acknowledge.[57] A broader view of the scope of צדקה in Dan 4:27 fits the larger canonical context in which rulers—especially rulers of Israel— are regularly charged with doing "justice and righteousness," a social ideal often associated with the creation and administration of equitable and liberating laws that protect all people, especially the vulnerable.[58] The verb פרק as an imperative demands that Nebuchadnezzar "break off" his sins and iniquities by acting as a righteous and just ruler. To be sure, Daniel's charge indicates that justice and mercy to the oppressed are two sides of the same coin, so in no sense should Daniel's appeal be abstracted from the concrete manifestation of justice evidenced by merciful action on behalf of the marginalized. But to translate the phrase בצדקה פרק as "redeem your sins by almsgiving" runs the risk of missing the larger sociopolitical context in which Nebuchadnezzar would rightly follow Daniel's instruction. Indeed, when Nebuchadnezzar ultimately comes to his senses and blesses the Most High God, he praises the King of heaven, "for all his works are truth, and his ways are justice, and he is able to bring low those who walk in pride" (4:37 [4:34]).

Greek translations of this passage from Daniel 4 offer an interesting window into the early reception of the passage and pave the way for this text to play a significant role in early Christian advocacy of atoning almsgiving. Greek Daniel exists in two versions. The history and relationship of these two versions of Daniel are complex, but in general terms the earlier and less well-preserved Old Greek (OG) version appears to be a freer, more dynamically equivalent translation, whereas the so-called Theodotian (Th) version represents a later translation characterized by more formal equivalence to its Hebrew source. The differences between these two versions of Greek Daniel are especially pronounced in chapters 4–6, where the OG differs markedly from the MT and Th, and this difference stands in contrast to the fact that in the rest of Daniel, both the OG and Th appear to be translated

---

[57] So John E. Goldingay, *Daniel* (WBC 30; Dallas: Word, 1989), 81. Choon Leong Seow (*Daniel* [Westminster Bible Companion; Louisville, Ky.: Westminster John Knox, 2003], 71) writes: "Daniel's counsel, however, is simply a call for Nebuchadnezzar to submit to the will of heaven for earthly governance (see Ps. 72:1-2; Isa. 11:3-4; Jer. 22:15-16). This view of government is in accordance with royal ideology throughout the ancient Near East, where legitimate rule is predicated upon 'justice and righteousness' for the oppressed and lowly."

[58] See Moshe Weinfeld, *Social Justice in Ancient Israel and in the Ancient Near East* (Minneapolis: Fortress, 1995), 44–56; Nardoni, *Rise Up, O Judge*, 95–121. See 2 Sam 8:15; 1 Kgs 10:9; 2 Chron 9:8; Ps 72:1-2.

from Hebrew *Vorlagen* similar to the MT.[59] That both versions of Greek Daniel render צדקה with the Greek ἐλεημοσύνη is sometimes adduced as evidence in favor of the translation "almsgiving" or "charity" even for the MT of Dan 4:27.[60]

---

[59] R. Timothy McLay, *The OG and Th Versions of Daniel* (SBLSCS 43; Atlanta: Scholars Press, 1996); idem, "The Old Greek Translation of Daniel IV–VI and the Formation of the Book of Daniel," *VT* 55 (2005): 304–23.

[60] So Gary A. Anderson, "Redeem Your Sins by the Giving of Alms: Sin, Debt, and the 'Treasury of Merit' in Early Jewish and Christian Tradition," *Letter & Spirit* 3 (2007): 47; Garrison, *Redemptive Almsgiving*, 52–53. In his many writings on Dan 4:27 and the topic of charity in particular, Anderson consistently translates ἐλεημοσύνη as "almsgiving." Interestingly, this consistent translation gives the impression that the word is monosemous and not polysemous, but Anderson wrongly assumes that ἐλεημοσύνη is only monosemous in the sense that it denotes "almsgiving"; see Anderson, *Charity*, 33–34. Rosenthal is far more careful in his treatment of ἐλεημοσύνη. He recognizes that Greek translations of צדקה or צדק / צדקה may not reflect "alms proper" in the sense of "charity," although ἐλεημοσύνη "did eventually become the chosen term for charity, alms to the poor" ("Sedaka, Charity," 428–29). Anderson follows Rosenthal in declaring that "the key to translating this verse properly lies in the parallelism of its structure": "To appreciate the meaning of *ṣidqâ'*, we must look at the second half of the verse, for the development of the verbal noun *miḥan* parallels almost exactly the development of *ṣidqâ'*" (*Charity*, 139). Anderson then, following Avi Hurwitz, cites a number of texts from the Psalms and Proverbs (Pss 37:21; 112:4-5; Prov 14:21, 31; 19:17; 28:8) to support the claim that "in later biblical texts both the roots *ṣdq* and *ḥnn* acquire the extended sense [elsewhere 'special meaning'] of giving charitably to the poor" (139). Anderson's position appears to be guilty of reading back into early biblical texts meanings that words later acquired. For a critique of Anderson's linguistic methodology as it relates to his use of Aramaic, see Edward Cook, "Sin and Salvation, Aramaic Style: Reflections on the Aramaic Vocabulary of Sin in the Light of Gary Anderson's 'Sin: A History'" (presented at the Annual Meeting of the SBL, Atlanta, 2010).

OG Dan 4:24 (4:27)	Th Dan (4:24) 4:27
κύριος ζῇ ἐν οὐρανῷ καὶ ἡ ἐξουσία αὐτοῦ ἐπὶ πάσῃ τῇ γῇ· αὐτοῦ δεήθητι περὶ τῶν ἁμαρτιῶν σου καὶ πάσας τὰς ἀδικίας σου ἐν ἐλεημοσύναις λύτρωσαι, ἵνα ἐπιείκεια δοθῇ σοι καὶ πολυήμερος γένῃ ἐπὶ τοῦ θρόνου τῆς βασιλείας σου, καὶ μὴ καταφθείρῃ σε. τούτους τοὺς λόγους ἀγάπησον· ἀκριβὴς γάρ μου ὁ λόγος καὶ πλήρης ὁ χρόνος σου.	διὰ τοῦτο βασιλεῦ ἡ βουλή μου ἀρεσάτω σοι, καὶ τὰς ἁμαρτίας σου ἐν ἐλεημοσύναις λύτρωσαι καὶ τὰς ἀδικίας σου ἐν οἰκτιρμοῖς πενήτων. ἴσως ἔσται μακρόθυμος τοῖς παραπτώμασίν σου ὁ θεός.
The Lord lives in heaven, and his authority is over all the earth. Pray (to him) concerning your sins, and redeem all your injustices with acts of mercy, so that kindness may be given to you and you might live many days on the throne of your kingdom and not be destroyed. Esteem these words, for my word is accurate and your time is up.	Therefore, O king, may my counsel be acceptable to you, and redeem your sins with acts of mercy and your injustices with compassion for the poor. Perhaps God will be patient with respect to your transgressions.

Given the discussion of lexical monosemy above, however, it is not at all clear that the Greek translation of צדקה with ἐλεημοσύνη in either version of Daniel denotes "almsgiving" in the narrow sense of material support for the needy. While the narratives of Daniel 4 in the OG and Th versions share some basic similarities, these accounts also differ in notable ways.[61] As is to be expected, Th generally agrees with the details of the MT, since Th is a more formally equivalent rendering. Thus, as in the preceding discussion of the Aramaic version, the translation of ἐλεημοσύνη in Th should be informed by a similar attention to the context of Daniel's statement. Daniel is speaking to "an unjust king" (βασιλεὺς ἄδικος [Th Dan 3:32]), given to rage and violence (Th Dan 2:12; 3:19), a ruler who not only practices but also compels worship of an idol (Th Dan 3:1-90). Rendering ἐλεημοσύνη in Daniel's charge as "almsgiving" has the potential to imply that the correct course of action for Nebuchadnezzar is for him personally to make charitable contributions to the poor. Daniel's statement, however, indicates that merciful, just, and compassionate leadership will obviate Nebuchadnezzar's sins and injustices:

[61] See T. J. Meadowcroft, *Aramaic Daniel and Greek Daniel: A Literary Comparison*, (JSOTSup 198; Sheffield: Sheffield Academic, 1995), 31–56. Structurally, the material in vv. 3-6 in the MT is absent from the OG (cf. OG 4:15, where the king's court attendants are also not mentioned), and the epistolary introduction that frames the narrative in MT 4:1 (cf. v. 34) is referenced only at the end of the chapter in the OG (4:34b-c).

"Therefore, O king, may my counsel be acceptable to you, and redeem your sins with acts of mercy and your injustices with compassion for the poor. Perhaps God will be patient with respect to your transgressions." To be clear, this Greek translation does frame Daniel's charge to Nebuchadnezzar as an invitation to atone for transgressions by concrete, merciful action on behalf of the poor, and material assistance or charity would certainly have been an aspect of this ἐλεημοσύνη. Indeed, the Th version does develop a new concept by translating the verb פרק ("break off," "release") with λυτρόω ("redeem," "ransom"), introducing an economic metaphor for the alleviation of sin that, when combined with the language of ἐλεημοσύνη, later came to play an important role in the development of atoning almsgiving in early Christianity, especially as Th became the preferred Greek translation of Daniel in the early church. The image of redeeming "sins" and "injustices"— with τὰς ἁμαρτίας and τὰς ἀδικίας as the dual objects of the verb λυτρόω—is also distinctive, since usually in biblical images of redemption it is sinners and not sins that are redeemed.[62]

If Dan 4:27 in Th should be interpreted in the literary context of the seer's address to an unjust king, an unfavorable characterization of Nebuchadnezzar is even more strongly emphasized in the OG version. For example, whereas in the MT and Th the king's vision of the tree serves as a symbol of God's sovereign power over human rulers—a symbol, to be sure, that Daniel interprets with reference to Nebuchadnezzar—in the OG version the dream appears to function as a frightening allegory that depicts a series of one-to-one correspondences between the tree and the fate of Nebuchadnezzar (e.g., OG Dan 4:2, 12-14).[63] The OG explicitly states that the kingdom of Babylon will be taken from Nebuchadnezzar and given to "another, a person disdained in your house" (OG Dan 4:28). This starkly negative depiction of King Nebuchadnezzar in the OG translation of chapter 4 provides the context for Daniel's exhortation, where the king is told not to redeem his sins with acts of mercy but to pray to God concerning his sins and to redeem all his *injustices* with acts of mercy, so that God will extend kindness to him and the king might enjoy a long reign and not be destroyed (OG Dan 4:24). According to OG Dan 4:24, therefore, it is not Nebuchadnezzar's sins (ἁμαρτίαι) that can be redeemed by ἐλεημοσύνη but all his injustices (ἀδικίαι). That it was the Th version—with its wording τὰς ἁμαρτίας σου ἐν

---

[62] This point is developed in more detail in chapter 8.

[63] Meadowcroft, *Aramaic Daniel and Greek Daniel*, 48–51. Nebuchadnezzar is also said to be one who "desolated the house of the living God" (OG Dan 4:19). As Meadowcraft comments, "The [OG] version's attitude towards the king is more adversarial, perhaps reflecting the setting behind chs. 7–12" (55).

ἐλεημοσύναις λύτρωσαι—that came to be favored in the early church is of no small importance for the emergence of the Christian advocacy of the doctrine of atoning almsgiving (*Did.* 4.5–8; *Barn.* 19.8–11; Cyprian, *Eleem.* 5; *Apos. Con.* 3.1.4).

Conclusion

Care for the poor in much of the Old Testament is framed as merciful action that results in reward for the benevolent. Generosity and justice for the needy and powerless are frequently said to be recompensed by God, while at the same time God's judgment and wrath are promised for those who oppress the poor.[64] In this sense, the Old Testament, particularly Deuteronomy and Proverbs, does not share the modern assumption that giving must be free and disinterested, for the expectation of a return for charity is a key aspect of Old Testament ethics, and this connection between charity and reward would come to be shared by early Christian authors who articulated and contextualized their own theologies of generosity in conversation with these scriptural traditions.

---

[64] The discussion here is not exhaustive, and certainly other OT texts featured (though perhaps less prominently) in early Christian discourse about atoning almsgiving. Cyprian, e.g., cites LXX Job 1:5 to claim that almsgiving can purge even the sins of one's children. Mention here should at least be made of the portrayal of the righteous individual in Ps 112 (= LXX Ps 111), not least because the apostle Paul cites Ps 112:9 in 2 Cor 9:9 in the context of an appeal for the Corinthians to give generously to needy believers in Jerusalem. The individual in Ps 112 is described as "merciful and compassionate and righteous" (ἐλεήμων καὶ οἰκτίρμων καὶ δίκαιος), and among his virtuous practices are a compassionate willingness to lend (v. 5). Ps 112:9 (LXX 111:9) is particularly pertinent not only because of Paul's later citation but also because it appears to link generosity with the reward of righteousness: "He dispersed; he gave to the poor; his righteousness remains forever and ever; his horn will be exalted in glory"; see the discussion in chapter 5.

Chapter 2

MERCIFUL DEEDS DELIVER FROM DEATH
Charity and Reward in the Apocrypha

In the middle of the third century CE, perhaps shortly after his election as bishop of Carthage in 248, Cyprian penned what is probably the most important early Christian treatise on atoning almsgiving, an essay entitled *De opere et eleemosynis*. Throughout the discourse, Cyprian draws deeply upon the language of Scripture in order to develop his claim that almsgiving serves to purge the post-baptismal sins of those who show mercy. Among the scriptural texts that figure most prominently in Cyprian's appeal, two documents from a collection that came to be called "the Apocrypha" are particularly influential—namely, Tobit and Sirach.[1] As is the case for other early Christian advocates of atoning almsgiving who employed the Septuagint (or translations derived from it) as an authoritative version, Cyprian regards both Tobit and Sirach as scriptural sources and cites them to promote the atoning efficacy of material support for the poor. A more detailed engagement with Cyprian's *De opere et eleemosynis* in a later chapter will trace the contours of the bishop's scriptural exegesis. But before moving ahead to the third century of the Common Era, it will be helpful to consider the relationship between

---

[1] Cyprian cites Tob 12:8-9 in *Eleem.* 5; Tob 14:10-11 in *Eleem.* 20; Tob 4:6-12 in *Eleem.* 20; Sir 3:30 in *Eleem.* 2; and Sir 29:12 in *Eleem.* 5.

care for the poor and recompense in these two important texts from the Second Temple period.

Tobit

The book of Tobit is a novel, composed in Aramaic during the Hellenistic period, about Jewish families in exile in Assyria in the eighth and seventh centuries BCE. The narrative purports to be recounted by its titular character, Tobit, a pious Jew who is said to have "walked in the ways of truth and righteousness" all the days of his life (Tob 1:3). Following a brief prologue (1:1-2), the book opens with the parallel travails of Tobit—which include his captivity and deportation to Nineveh, his persecution for burying the bodies of his Jewish compatriots, and his blindness provoked by bird feces in his eyes—and a woman named Sarah (the daughter of one of Tobit's relatives in Media), who has been married seven times but whose seven husbands have been killed by a demon on their respective wedding nights (1:3–3:17).[2] After this opening frame, the narrative focuses on the adventures of Tobit's son, Tobias, as he is sent by his father to recover from the city of Rages in Media money that his father had deposited there some twenty years earlier. Tobias is accompanied on his journey by the angel Raphael, disguised as a Jewish kinsmen named Azariah, and on their journey Tobias meets and marries his relative Sarah in the city of Ecbatana. With Raphael's assistance, Tobias vanquishes the demon that had afflicted Sarah in her previous marriages and procures a balm that is used to heal his father's blindness (4:1–12:22). The story concludes with Tobit offering an extended thanksgiving to God (13:1–14:2) and an epilogue that reports the eventual deaths of Tobit and Tobias after long and blessed lives (14:3-15).

At the very beginning of the narrative, Tobit attests that he has walked in truth and righteousness ($\dot{\alpha}\lambda\dot{\eta}\theta\epsilon\iota\alpha$ and $\delta\iota\kappa\alpha\iota\sigma\acute{\nu}\nu\eta$; cf. Prov 8:20) all the

---

[2]   All translations of Tobit, unless otherwise noted, are my own and are taken from the text of G². The textual history of Tobit is complex, as Tobit exists in several Greek textual traditions, the most important of which are the shorter G¹ (preserved in Vaticanus [B], Alexandrinus [A], Venetus [V], POxy 1592²) and the longer G² (preserved in Sinaiticus and partly in POxy 1076³), as well as the Old Latin and four Aramaic (4Q196–199) fragments and one Hebrew fragment (4Q200) from Qumran. The Old Latin translation and the Qumran fragments generally cohere with the G² tradition. Before the discovery of Sinaiticus, Tobit was known among Western churches in its shorter version (= G¹ from B and A), although today the consensus holds that G² represents an earlier textual tradition, with G¹ as a later and abbreviated version. For an extended discussion, see Robert J. Littman, *Tobit: The Book of Tobit in Codex Sinaiticus* (Septuagint Commentary Series 9; Leiden: Brill, 2008), xix–xxv.

days of his life and that he "performed many merciful acts" (ἐλεημοσύνας πολλὰς ἐποίησα) for his kindred (in Palestine?) and for those of his race in exile in Nineveh (1:3, 16).[3] In the first chapter, Tobit's practice of "merciful deeds" (ἐλεημοσύναι) includes a variety of activities (cf. 2:14). Tobit's contribution of the firstfruits and his payment of an assortment of tithes to priests, Levites, and "orphans, widows, and proselytes" in his own country before his exile are ἐλεημοσύναι (1:6-8). Tobit's practice of providing food and clothing for the hungry and naked among his people in Nineveh is ἐλεημοσύνη (1:16-17a). And Tobit's commitment to burying fellow Jews killed in exile is also a practice of ἐλεημοσύνη (1:17b-18).

Moreover, Tobit is twice memorialized later in the narrative as one who performed "acts of mercy." In 7:7 Tobit's relative Raguel laments that "a righteous man and one who performed merciful deeds" (ἀνὴρ δίκαιος καὶ ποιῶν ἐλεημοσύνας) such as Tobit should suffer blindness. The story concludes with the remembrance that, after regaining his sight, Tobit lived for fifty years "in good circumstances and performed acts of mercy" (ἐλεημοσύνας ἐποίησεν [14:2]).[4] At key points in the narrative, then, Tobit's piety is highlighted by evoking his practice of ἐλεημοσύνη.[5] To render ἐλεημοσύνη as "almsgiving" in these descriptions of Tobit's piety, however, would run the risk of implying that Tobit was remembered only for charitable distributions to the needy, when in fact the word ἐλεημοσύνη contributes a broader understanding of Tobit's compassionate actions, one that doubtless includes his charitable giving (so 1:6-8, 17a) but should not be limited to economic dispossession.[6]

---

[3] The text of the G[2] appears to indicate that Tobit's acts of mercy are directed toward two different groups: his relatives and those who were exiled with Tobit in Nineveh. The Vulgate, however, collapses this into one group in exile: *ita ut omnia quae habere poterat cotidie concaptivis fratribus qui erant ex genere inpertiret* (1:3).

[4] It might be argued that if the phrase ἔζησεν ἐν ἀγαθοῖς in 14:2 is taken strictly as a reference to economic prosperity (e.g., "he lived in prosperity" [NRSV]), then the pairing of ἔζησεν ἐν ἀγαθοῖς with ἐλεημοσύνας ἐποίησεν in G[2] might denote "almsgiving" out of economic abundance. The phrase ἔζησεν ἐν ἀγαθοῖς, however, can more broadly denote living "in goodness," specially the good circumstances Tobit enjoyed in the second half of his life in contrast to the spiritual, physical, emotional, and economic hardship he had endured earlier in the narrative; cf. LXX Pss 24:13; 102:5; Prov 11:10; 16:17; Job 21:13; 22:21; 36:11; Sir 12:8, 9; 18:15; *Pss. Sol.* 5.18.

[5] So Merten Rabenau, *Studien zum Buch Tobit* (BZAW 220; Berlin: De Gruyter, 1994), 127.

[6] Roman Heiligenthal, "Werke der Barmherzigkeit oder Almosen: Zur Bedeutung von ἐλεημοσύνη," *NovT* 25, no. 4 (1983): 289–301. Joseph A. Fitzmyer recognizes this point, although he still translates v. 16: "I gave many alms to my relatives, to those of my people" (*Tobit* [CEJL; Berlin: De Gruyter, 2003], 117). On the various ways in which the language of ἐλεημοσύνη is used in both Tobit and Sirach, see Patrick J. Griffin, "A Study

Yet Tobit is not the only exemplar or advocate of the practice of merciful deeds in the narrative. In Tobit's final words of counsel to his son at the end of the story, Tobit reminds Tobias about the tale of Ahikar (14:10b-11a), a man who is cited as an example of the claim that doing ἐλεημοσύνη rescues from death:

> [10]Behold, my child, what Nadin did to Ahikar, who reared him. Was Ahikar not, while still living, forced underground?[7] And God repaid [Ahikar] the dishonor against his face, and Ahikar came out into the light, and Nadin went into the eternal darkness, because Nadin sought to kill Ahikar. Because Ahikar performed an act of mercy (ἐν τῷ ποιῆσαι ἐλεημοσύνην)[8] he came out from the trap of death that Nadin had set for him. And Nadin fell into the trap of death, and it destroyed him. [11]And now, children, behold what an act of mercy does (ἴδετε τί ποιεῖ ἐλεημοσύνη) and what unrighteousness does: it kills!

In the context of Tobit's speech, it is difficult to know the precise reference for the mention of Ahikar's performance of ἐλεημοσύνη in verse 10. Does this refer to Ahikar's acts of mercy more generally? Or does the statement specifically allude to the account of Ahikar's escape from a death sentence at the hands of the Assyrian king Esarhaddon because of Ahikar's earlier deed of saving the life of the man charged with his execution? In this legend, which is only briefly evoked in Tobit 14, Ahikar, an advisor to the Assyrian king Sennacherib, is framed for treason by his adopted nephew, Nadin. As Ahikar is about to be killed, however, he reminds the man given the task of slaying him that Ahikar had earlier delivered the very same executioner from a death sentence levied by the king. Moved by this reminder, the executioner decapitates another prisoner deserving of death and passes off the body as Ahikar's. In some versions of the tale, when the Assyrian king later wishes that he could dispatch Ahikar to travel to Egypt to design a building that bridges heaven and earth, Ahikar's true fate is revealed to the monarch, who then commissions Ahikar for the task. When he returns to his homeland three years later, Ahikar is offered great sums of money, but he asks only for his nephew Nadin to be punished. Nadin is imprisoned, tortured,

---

of *Eleēmosynē* in the Bible with Emphasis upon Its Meaning and Usage in the Theology of Tobit and Ben Sira" (M.A. thesis, The Catholic University of America, 1982).

[7] Literally: "Was he [i.e., Ahikar] not, while living, brought down to the earth?"

[8] Note the accusative singular ἐλεημοσύνην. With most commentators, I regard the pronoun με in Sinaiticus as an error; see Littman, *Tobit*, 158.

and killed.[9] Given the fact that the author of Tobit assumes knowledge of the Ahikar tale throughout the narrative (cf. 1:21-22; 2:10; 11:18; 14:10), it seems highly likely that the "merciful act" that Ahikar performed, of which Tobit reminds Tobias, is Ahikar's compassionate deed of saving the life of the man who would later be assigned his own executioner. Here Ahikar's ἐλεημοσύνη quite literally rescues from death. Awareness of the allusion to the Ahikar account helps to illuminate the gloss on the legend provided in Tobit's last words in the entire book: "And now, children, behold what an act of mercy does (ἴδετε τί ποιεῖ ἐλεημοσύνη) and what unrighteousness does: it kills!" Ahikar's act of clemency later saves his own life, whereas Nadin's unjust act ultimately leads to his death.

Given a monosemic bias that would see the univocal lexical meaning of ἐλεημοσύνη as "merciful act," it is not surprising to find the term ἐλεημοσύνη used to mark such a broad spectrum of merciful deeds performed by humans in Tobit (i.e., 1:3, 16; 2:14; 14:2, 10-11). Interestingly, God, too, is described in Tobit's plaintive prayer near the beginning of the story as one whose "ways are merciful acts (ἐλεημοσύναι) and truth" (3:2). Moreover, Tobit's final prayer of thanksgiving encourages sinners to turn back and do what is righteous (δικαιοσύνη) before God, for perhaps God will look favorably upon them and "do merciful acts for you" (ποιήσει ἐλεημοσύνην ὑμῖν).[10] The book of Tobit does, however, specifically emphasize material care for the poor, or almsgiving, as an integral component of religious piety, and an explicit connection between charity and reward is established in two important speeches in the story.[11]

In chapter four, hoping that his prayer for death will be answered (3:2-6), Tobit summons Tobias and offers his son both instructions about how to procure money that Tobit had deposited with Gabael in Media and a final testament, replete with wisdom for Tobias on how to lead a righteous life (4:1-21). This speech articulates the typically Deuteronomistic perspective that "those who practice truth will prosper in all their deeds" (4:6). Tobit exhorts Tobias to avoid fornication (4:12), pride (4:13), idleness (4:13), injustice (4:14), and drunkenness (4:15). Yet material care for the poor is also a

---

[9] Littman, *Tobit*, xli–xlii; cf. Ingo Kottsieper, "The Aramaic Tradition: Ahikar," in *Scribes, Sages, and Seers: The Sage in the Eastern Mediterranean World* (ed. Leo G. Perdue; FRLANT 219; Göttingen: Vandenhoeck & Ruprecht, 2008), 109–24.

[10] Or "grant mercy to you" (NETS). The phrase from Tob 13:6 is taken from the text of G[1], since there is a lacuna at this point in Sinaiticus; see Griffin, "Study of *Eleēmosynē*," 7–8.

[11] Francis M. Macatangay, "Acts of Charity as Acts of Remembrance in the Book of Tobit," *JSP* 23 (2013): 69–84.

key theme at the beginning and end of Tobit's discourse (4:6b-11, 16-17).
Tobit's first specific instruction states:

> [6]And to all who practice righteousness[12] [7]practice the merciful act
> of almsgiving from your possessions (ἐκ τῶν ὑπαρχόντων σοι ποίει
> ἐλεημοσύνην), and do not let your eye be envious when you practice
> the merciful act of almsgiving (ἐν τῷ ποιεῖν σε ἐλεημοσύνην). Do not
> turn your face away from any poor person, and the face of God will not
> be turned away from you. [8]When you have possessions, according to
> the abundance practice the merciful act of almsgiving from the posses-
> sions. If you have a little, do not be afraid to practice the merciful act of
> almsgiving according to the little that you have. [9]For you will be storing
> up a good treasure for yourself against a day of necessity. [10]Therefore,
> the merciful act of almsgiving delivers from death and keeps one from
> going into darkness. [11]Indeed, the merciful act of almsgiving is a good
> gift, for all who practice it, in the sight of the Most High.[13]

This teaching is then reiterated and slightly expanded near the end of the
instruction (4:16-17):

> [16]Give some of your bread to the hungry and some of your clothing to
> the naked. Give whatever is an abundance for you as a merciful act of
> almsgiving, and do not let your eye be envious when you practice the
> merciful act of almsgiving. [17]Put your bread on the tombs of the righ-
> teous, but do not give it to sinners.

Several notable features of Tobit's speech merit attention. First, the immediate context of the command "practice the merciful act of almsgiving" (ποίει

---

[12] Given the textual uncertainty of Tob 4, there is some confusion about whether
the phrase καὶ πᾶσι τοῖς ποιοῦσι τὴν δικαιοσύνην belongs with the preceding sentence
(RSV, JB, NAB), the following sentence (NRSV), or with 4:19 (Littman, *Tobit*, 88–89.).
Littman argues that no distinction between the righteous and unrighteous as recipients
of charity is made in 1:3 and 1:8. But in those earlier texts the first-person narrator does
emphasize that he practiced merciful acts for "his kindred" (1:3) and for fellow Israelites and "proselytes who had attached themselves to the children of Israel" (1:8). Thus, it
makes sense to understand οἱ ποιοῦντες τὴν δικαιοσύνην in 4:6 as a directive to give to
fellow Israelites, and therefore the phrase καὶ πᾶσι τοῖς ποιοῦσι τὴν δικαιοσύνην belongs
with the sentence that follows.

[13] The translation here is from the G[1] text of Tobit, since there is a lacuna in Sinaiticus from 4:7-19b. Littman provides a text and translation from MS 319. A good argument
can be made that the text of MS 319 should be preferred here, but I have based my translation on G[1] in large part because the text of G[1] largely corresponds to G[2] at this point.
See the discussion in Francis M. Macatangay, *The Wisdom Instructions in the Book of Tobit*
(DCLS 12; Berlin: De Gruyter, 2011), 50–53.

ἐλεημοσύνην) in verse 7 makes clear that here Tobit is advocating the provision of material assistance to those in need (i.e., "almsgiving") as a manifestation of the merciful act called ἐλεημοσύνη. The prepositional phrase ἐκ τῶν ὑπαρχόντων σοι ("from your possessions"; cf. v. 8) and the concern that one's evil eye might jealously begrudge the charitable action (vv. 7, 16) both imply that ἐλεημοσύνη here denotes the allocation of material goods.[14] That verse 16 commands the supply of bread to the hungry and clothing to the naked may indicate that "almsgiving" in this context is primarily envisioned as gifts in kind rather than in coin.[15]

Second, the explicit object of this beneficence is "any poor person" (πᾶς πτωχός [v. 7]). Yet the opening clause "to all who practice righteousness" in

---

[14] On the notion of the "evil eye" here, see Rivka Ulmer, *The Evil Eye in the Bible and in Rabbinic Literature* (Hoboken, N.J.: KTAV, 1994), 43–44. Ulmer cites *m. 'Abot* 5.13 as an interesting thematic parallel.

[15] It is not as if a monetary economy is foreign to the book of Tobit. The central narrative revolves around Tobias' quest to obtain ten talents of silver (ἀργύριον) that Tobit had deposited with Gabael in Media, and Tobit tithes in money (1:7). Interestingly, when Tobit's wife, Anna, has to provide for the family during Tobit's blindness, she is paid a wage (μισθός) for her weaving, a wage that could have been payment in cash or kind, although her employers supplement that wage with the gift of a goat (2:11-14). Gary A. Anderson contends that δῶρον in Tob 4:11, which Anderson views as a translation of the Hebrew noun קרבן, "calls to mind an offering or sacrifice that one might bring to the temple." Anderson draws from this the claim that "Tobit is suggesting that placing coins in the hand of a beggar is like putting a sacrifice on the altar—for both the hand and the altar provide direct access to God" (*Sin: A History* [New Haven: Yale University Press, 2010], 148). (The same argument is offered in Bradley C. Gregory, *Like an Everlasting Signet Ring: Generosity in the Book of Sirach* [DCLS 2; Berlin: De Gruyter, 2010], 236–37.) Anderson's reasoning is significantly flawed, however. First, in the absence of an early Hebrew text of Tob 4:11, it is impossible to know what Hebrew word δῶρον translated. While δῶρον does sometimes translate קרבן in the LXX, the Greek noun also translates many other Hebrew words, including שחד, מנחה, and שׁי. Rather than assuming (without any evidence) that the Greek δῶρον translates a Hebrew word that is sometimes used, especially in Leviticus and Numbers, to refer to a sacrificial gift, the meaning of δῶρον in Tob 4:11 should be assessed in light of its literary context, and it is clear that the word in Tobit means "gift" and not "sacrifice" (see, e.g., 2:14; 13:11). The gift is not a gift to God but a gift to the poor (pace Gregory, *Like an Everlasting Signet Ring*, 237). Anderson's own point regarding the structure of Tob 1, which emphasizes Tobit's acts of mercy (1:3, 16) in Nineveh in contrast to his temple offerings in Israel (1:5-9), should be read to make the opposite point that Anderson draws from this observation: ἐλεημοσύνη in the Diaspora is not at all a "replacement" of sacrifice. Tobit's merciful action on behalf of the needy among his kindred was characteristic of both his sojourn in Nineveh (1:3, 16-20) *and* his experience in Israel, including his participation in temple worship, since Tobit gives a tithe to "the orphans and widows and to the converts who had attached themselves to Israel" (NRSV).

verse 6 suggests that Tobit has in mind particularly the destitute among the people of Israel.[16] The enigmatic saying in verse 17—"Put [or 'pour out'] your bread on the tombs of the righteous, but do not give it to sinners"—may make a similar point regarding ἐλεημοσύνη as being properly directed to righteous fellow Jews, especially if the action of placing bread on tombs of the righteous is interpreted as an allusion to Tobit's willingness to leave a meal in order to attend to the burial of one of his own people murdered in Nineveh (2:2-6).[17]

Third, almsgiving in this context is not merely envisioned as a practice for the wealthy. Instead, Tobit instructs Tobias to give, even in times of material deprivation, "according to the little that you have" (v. 8). Whether living in abundance or scarcity, almsgiving is to be a part of Tobias' upright life.

Fourth, and significantly, Tobit's speech frames the merciful act of almsgiving as a practice that will be recompensed. One dimension of this reward comes in the form of divine favor. Tobias' refusal to turn his face away from the poor will result in God's refusal to turn his face away from Tobias (v. 7); the converse implication of this statement would appear to be that in blessing the poor Tobias will be blessed by God. Indeed, charitable giving is a gift recognized not merely by those who receive this beneficence but by the Most High God (v. 10).

Yet the reward for almsgiving is not only framed in this speech in terms of divine blessing. According to Tobit, sharing possessions with those in need will allow Tobias to store up a good treasure for himself "against a day of necessity" (v. 9). This statement certainly came to be interpreted as an eschatological promise of divine reward, especially as it featured in early Christian discourse about charity as a means of procuring heavenly treasure (so, e.g., 1 Tim 6:17-19). In its context in the narrative of Tobit, however, it is far more likely that the phrase "storing up a good treasure for yourself against a day of necessity" refers simply to security against future fiscal disaster—not unlike the economic misfortune that Tobit himself experiences in the narrative (1:20; 2:10-14; cf. Sir 29:12-13)—by lending to others in the present.[18] In fact, both Tobit's instruction that Tobias should give alms even if he has few possessions (v. 8) and Tobit's and his family's (4:21) experience of moving from abundance to scarcity testify to the fleeting nature of wealth. The vicissitudes of life may mean that one who was

---

[16] See n. 12 above.

[17] Nathan Macdonald, "'Bread on the Grave of the Righteous' (Tob. 4.17)," in *Studies in the Book of Tobit: A Multidisciplinary Approach* (Library of Second Temple Studies 55; ed. Mark Bredin; LSTS 55; London: T&T Clark, 2006), 99–103.

[18] Fitzmyer, *Tobit*, 170–71; Carey A. Moore, *Tobit: A New Translation with Introduction and Commentary* (AB 40A; New York: Doubleday, 1996), 168.

once a giver of alms will become a recipient, and vice versa.[19] Given that the book of Tobit evinces very little, if any, interest in the afterlife and shows no expectation of bodily resurrection, it would be a mistake to read this saying as an eschatological promise.[20] The same can be said about the following assertion: "Therefore, the merciful act of almsgiving delivers from death and keeps one from going into darkness" (v. 10). On one hand, it is ironic that Tobit, who is (self-)acclaimed in the story for his pious commitment to the practice of ἐλεημοσύνη, should utter this affirmation after he has been afflicted by blindness, not least because Tobit will go on to declare upon meeting the disguised angel Raphael, "I lie in darkness like the dead who no longer see the light!" (5:10). Tobit's equation of blindness and death in this statement stands in tension with his assertion that almsgiving "prevents one from going into darkness."[21] Earlier in the story, Tobit's practice of merciful acts for his compatriots leads to the confiscation of his property (1:16-20). More directly, Tobit's ἐλεημοσύνη in the form of burying a murdered Jew leads him to sleep outside at night, which at least indirectly causes his blindness (2:7-10). Blindness is not the "reward" for ἐλεημοσύνη that one expects on the basis of Tobit's speech in chapter 4.

From a literary perspective, this irony might be attributed to the fact that Tobit himself is something of an unreliable character or that he suffers theological blindness that prevents him from seeing that his straightforward theology of retribution is complicated by a narrative in which the reality of

[19] Tobit's own struggle to come to terms with this reality may explain his insistence that his wife return the goat that was given to her in addition to her wages (2:11-14). As one praised for practicing ἐλεημοσύνη, he is now ashamed to be on the receiving end of such beneficence.

[20] On this issue, see Stephan Beyerle, "'Release Me to Go to My Everlasting Home...' [Tob 3:6]: A Belief in an Afterlife in Late Wisdom Literature?" in *The Book of Tobit: Text, Tradition, Theology; Papers of the First International Conference on the Deuterocanonical Books, Pápa, Hungary, 20–21 May 2004* (ed. Geza G. Xeravits and József Zsengellér; JSJSup 98; Leiden: Brill, 2005), 71–88; Jill Hicks-Keeton, "Already/Not Yet: Eschatological Tension in the Book of Tobit," *JBL* 132 (2013): 97–117. For this reason, characterizations of Tobit's speech as advocating "heavenly treasure" are misleading and not grounded in the text. Tobit speaks of storing up "good treasure," not "heavenly treasure." Pace Nathan Eubank, *Wages of Cross-Bearing and Debt of Sin: The Economy of Heaven in Matthew's Gospel* (BZNW 196; Berlin: De Gruyter, 2013), 28–29; Anderson, *Sin*, 9, 12, 144–46.

[21] On the irony of this statement and the testing of Tobit's faith throughout the narrative, see Gary A. Anderson, *Charity: The Place of the Poor in the Biblical Tradition* (New Haven: Yale University Press, 2013), 83–103.

human suffering cannot simply be attributed to disobedience.[22] On the other hand, Tobit's sight is eventually restored (11:7-15). In light of Tobit's earlier equation of blindness with death, perhaps his practice of ἐλεημοσύνη is to be seen as a factor in his deliverance from death and darkness (although not ultimately, since Tobit does eventually die after a long life). In chapter 14 it appears that Ahikar's merciful act of saving the life of his future executioner literally delivers Ahikar from death. In the context of the narrative, then, the statement that ἐλεημοσύνη "delivers from death and keeps one from going into darkness" should be interpreted not as an eschatological promise but as a wisdom saying about the value of merciful deeds in the present world.[23]

The second key speech related to care for the poor and reward in the book of Tobit comes from the lips of the angel Raphael. The angelic visitor gives this speech after Tobias' successful journey with Raphael to Media, the marriage of Tobias and Sarah, and the restoration of Tobit's sight. Raphael summons Tobit and Tobias and offers them a farewell testimony of his own. In the second half of the speech, Raphael reveals his true identity and his role in responding to the prayers of, and healing, Tobit and Sarah (12:11-15). As is true of Tobit's speech in chapter 4, Raphael's words are marked by a Deuteronomistic theology of retribution: "Do good and evil will not overtake you" (v. 7). Key for the study of almsgiving in Tobit, however, are Raphael's comments about the practice of ἐλεημοσύνη in the first half of the speech (12:6-10):

[22] For a penetrating analysis of the narrative along these lines (though without reflection on the irony of Tob 4:10), see Micah D. Kiel, "Tobit's Theological Blindness," *CBQ* 73 (2011): 281–98; cf. Macatangay, *Wisdom Instructions in the Book of Tobit*, 244–48.

[23] Compare the common topos in Greek and Roman moral discourse that, given the insecurity of wealth, sharing one's resources with those in need can lead to reciprocity in the future of this present life. See Aristotle, *Rhet.* 2.5.1383a; Seneca, *Marc.* 9.1; Ovid, *Tr.* 5.8.4–18; cf. Eccl 11:1-2.

Tobit 12:8-9 (G^1)	*Tobit 12:8-9 (G^2)*
^{8}ἀγαθὸν προσευχὴ μετὰ νηστείας καὶ ἐλεημοσύνης καὶ δικαιοσύνης· ἀγαθὸν τὸ ὀλίγον μετὰ δικαιοσύνης ἢ πολὺ μετὰ ἀδικίας· καλὸν ποιῆσαι ἐλεημοσύνην ἢ θησαυρίσαι χρυσίον. ^{9}ἐλεημοσύνη γὰρ ἐκ θανάτου ῥύεται, καὶ αὐτὴ ἀποκαθαριεῖ πᾶσαν ἁμαρτίαν· οἱ ποιοῦντες ἐλεημοσύνας καὶ δικαιοσύνας πλησθήσονται ζωῆς· ^{10}οἱ δὲ ἁμαρτάνοντες πολέμιοί εἰσιν τῆς ἑαυτῶν ζωῆς.	^{8}ἀγαθὸν προσευχὴ μετὰ ἀληθείας^{24} καὶ^{25} ἐλεημοσύνη μετὰ δικαιοσύνης μᾶλλον ἢ πλοῦτος μετὰ ἀδικίας· καλὸν ποιῆσαι ἐλεημοσύνην μᾶλλον ἢ θησαυρίσαι χρυσίον. ^{9}ἐλεημοσύνη ἐκ θανάτου ῥύεται, καὶ αὐτὴ ἀποκαθαίρει πᾶσαν ἁμαρτίαν· οἱ ποιοῦντες ἐλεημοσύνην ^{10}χορτασθήσονται ζωῆς· οἱ ποιοῦντες ἁμαρτίαν καὶ ἀδικίαν πολέμιοί εἰσιν τῆς ἑαυτῶν ψυχῆς.
^{8}Prayer with fasting and merciful action and righteousness is good. A little with righteousness is better than much with unrighteousness. It is better to practice the merciful act of almsgiving than to store up gold. ^{9}For merciful action delivers from death, and it will cleanse every sin. Those who practice merciful action and righteousness will be filled with life, ^{10}but those who sin are enemies of their own life.	^{8}Prayer with truth is good, and the merciful action of almsgiving with righteousness is better than wealth with unrighteousness. It is better to practice the merciful act of almsgiving than to store up gold. ^{9}Merciful action delivers from death, and it cleanses every sin. Those who practice merciful action will be satisfied with life. ^{10}Those who practice sin and unrighteousness are enemies of their own selves.

Both versions of the Greek text of Tobit are cited here because, ~~although the present analysis of Tobit has concentrated on~~ G^2, the phrasing of G^1 ~~will feature significantly in later Christian citation of~~ Raphael's speech in this passage (e.g., 2 Clem. 16.4; Pol. Phil. 10.2; Cyprian, *Eleem.* 5; cf. *Gos. Thom.* 6.1-5; 14.1-3), a point to be considered later. In its literary context, however, much of Raphael's discourse about ἐλεημοσύνη affirms what has already been stated or implied about the value of merciful deeds elsewhere in the narrative. The language of ἀλήθεια, δικαιοσύνη, and ἐλεημοσύνη is clustered here, as in 1:3 (cf. 4:6). Moreover, the contrast between ἐλεημοσύνη and "wealth with unrighteousness," as well as the reference to the activity of

---

^{24} Other witnesses, including G^1 and MS 106 (= G^3) read νηστείας ("fasting"; cf. the Old Latin's *ieiunio*).

^{25} The NRSV's translation of καί as an adversative and its implication that the text prioritizes "almsgiving" over prayer and fasting ("Prayer with fasting is good, *but better than both* is almsgiving with righteousness") is rather unfortunate and has mislead a number of authors (e.g., Charles L. Quarles, "The New Perspective and Means of Atonement in Jewish Literature of the Second Temple Period," *CTR* 2 [2005]: 39–56).

storing up gold in verse 8, implies that, as in 4:7-8, ἐλεημοσύνη is imaged as a merciful act of sharing material goods (i.e., "almsgiving"). Also, as in Tobit's speech in chapter 4, Raphael indicates the practice of ἐλεημοσύνη results in reward for those who act mercifully: indeed, the phrase ἐλεημοσύνη ἐκ θανάτου ῥύεται is the same in 4:10 (G^1) and 12:9 (G^1 and G^2).[26] Additionally, those who practice ἐλεημοσύνη are promised to enjoy a satisfied life (v. 9).

Raphael's speech, however, does offer one notable thematic addition— namely, the assertion that ἐλεημοσύνη purifies every sin (v. 9: αὐτὴ ἀπο- καθαίρει πᾶσαν ἁμαρτίαν). Anderson's argument that the language of "cleansing" (ἀποκαθαρίζω) in Tob 12:9 should be taken as in an economic sense (" 'to clear' in the sense of 'to cancel [an obligation]'") illustrates Ander- son's tendency to force images for the reckoning of sin through ἐλεημοσύνη into his grand economic metaphor that sin is debt. Anderson writes,

> According to Raphael, almsgiving is better than laying up gold because it funds a heavenly treasury rather than an earthly one. But not only that: as was already stated by Tobit in chapter 4, almsgiving can save one from death (a citation from Prov 11:4) as well as 'purge away all sin' (ἀποκαθαριεῖ πᾶσαν ἁμαρτίαν). For all commentators the interpretation of this metaphor seems to be crystal clear. The writer of Tobit has con- ceived of sin as a 'stain' that must be 'cleansed' from the body. The com- parison of sin to a stain is quite common in the Bible. Yet, if this is what our writer has intended then the metaphor does not do justice to the immediate literary context. For giving alms, as Raphael clearly states, allows one to accumulate a proper treasury in heaven as opposed to simply hoarding gold on earth. And if a treasury is the defining feature of almsgiving, in what way can it be used to wash away the stain of sin? Biblical writers do not normally mix metaphors in this way.[27]

There follows an extended discussion of "the way in which terms for 'cleansing' evolve in the postbiblical period," one that loses sight of the narra- tive of Tobit and focuses on Hebrew and Aramaic usage while only consid- ering the Greek word καθαροποιέω, a word that does not even occur in Tobit or anywhere else in the LXX (10). Not only does Anderson impose upon the text the language of "treasury in heaven" in his reading of Tob 12:9, his claim that the phrase αὐτὴ ἀποκαθαριεῖ πᾶσαν ἁμαρτίαν should be translated "[almsgiving] pays off the debt accumulated through sin" ignores the fact that

---

[26] With the exception, of course, of the addition of the conjunction γάρ in G^1.

[27] Gary A. Anderson, "How Does Almsgiving Purge Sins?" in *Hebrew in the Second Temple Period: The Hebrew of the Dead Sea Scrolls and of Other Contemporary Sources* (ed. Steven E. Fassberg, Moshe Bar-Asher, and Ruth A. Clements; STDJ 108; Leiden: Brill, 2013), 10.

"sin" is imaged as defilement/impurity that in need of cleansing elsewhere in the narrative of Tobit (3:14). Anderson's insistence that ἀποκαθαρίζω in Tob 12:9 refers to the paying off of debt is characteristic of his proclivity to force texts into his economic metaphor for sin and his failure to account for the diversity of metaphors used in early Jewish and Christian literature to describe sin and its solution.

In the history of interpretation, this text, along with LXX Prov 15:27 and Th Dan 4:27, figures prominently in later Christian advocacy of atoning almsgiving in the second and third centuries CE. What Raphael means by this declaration in the context of the story of Tobit is not entirely clear, however, in part because the language of sin (ἁμαρτία) is not a major feature of the narrative. In his prayer of lament in chapter 3, Tobit asks God not to punish his sins or unwitting offenses (ἐκδικήσῃς ταῖς ἁμαρτίαις μου καὶ τοῖς ἀγνοήμασίν μου [3:3]) or the sins that his ancestors committed by disobeying God's commandments (3:3-4). Yet in the same prayer Tobit indicates his belief that his unfortunate circumstances, including his blindness, result from God's dealing with him "according to [his] sins" (3:5). This statement stands in some tension with Raphael's assertion in 12:9, since Tobit's commitment to the practice of ἐλεημοσύνη has presumably not cleansed him from every sin, at least according to the perspective of the titular character.[28] Any degree of conflict between Tobit's theological understanding of the relationship between his sin, his blindness, and his practice of ἐλεημοσύνη in his own assessment of his situation in 3:2-6, on one hand, and Raphael's divinely authorized statement that "ἐλεημοσύνη cleanses every sin," on the other, may be yet another indication of Tobit's inability truly to understand the complex nature of human experience, based on Tobit's flawed commitment to a mechanistic theology of retribution.[29]

Since the narrative of Tobit does not develop anything like a robust theology of atonement, it is perhaps tempting to conclude that Raphael's declaration that "ἐλεημοσύνη cleanses every sin" is merely a proverbial saying that does not substantially oppose theologies of atonement in the Hebrew Bible.[30] Or it might be suggested that the "cleansing" of ἐλεημοσύνη is merely

---

[28] Cf. Sarah's avowal in 3:14 (G¹) that she is "pure from all sin with a man" (καθαρά εἰμι ἀπὸ πάσης ἁμαρτίας ἀνδρὸς). As for the language of sin elsewhere in the narrative, Tobit's speech to Tobias in chapter 4 is bracketed by exhortations to flee from sin (4:5, 21), and Tobit's final speech indicates that those who commit sin and injustice will be vanquished from the earth (14:7).

[29] See Micah D. Kiel, The "Whole Truth": Rethinking Retribution in the Book of Tobit (LSTS 82; London: T&T Clark, 2014).

[30] So Moore, Tobit, 270.

a moral purification and that the verb ἀποκαθαίρω should not be viewed as effecting any real atonement for sin.[31] Such interpretative strategies fail, however, to account for both the contours of the narrative in which this statement appears and the reception history of Raphael's declaration in Tob 12:9. Later Christian readings of Tobit 12, such as Cyprian's, will be considered later. But with regard to the narrative context of this statement, it is difficult to avoid the implication that Raphael means what he says: merciful action delivers from death (in the sense of deliverance from physical death discussed above), and it cleanses every sin (in the sense that human transgressions can be purified through the practice of ἐλεημοσύνη). The following statement in verse 10 then may provide a kind of gloss on this assertion by indicating that care for the needy, together with righteousness, is a way to combat injustice: "Those who practice sin and unrighteousness are enemies of their own selves."

The book of Tobit, therefore, establishes a close connection between almsgiving and reward. In the narrative, ἐλεημοσύνη is said to turn God's face upon the generous (4:7-8), to result in the storing up of treasure that can be "cashed in" by donors during times of economic misfortune (4:9), to deliver from death whereas injustice leads to death (4:10; 12:8-9; 14:10-11), and to be a gift to the needy honored by God (4:11). Moreover, the statement in Tob 12:9 that ἐλεημοσύνη cleanses sin affirms, with LXX Prov 15:27 and Th Dan 4:27, the atoning efficacy of almsgiving. Although the book of Tobit is not cited with great frequency in Christian literature through the third century, when Tobit is quoted or alluded to it tends to be featured in discussions of atoning almsgiving.[32]

---

[31] This possibility is suggested but then rejected in Quarles, "New Perspective and Means," 46.

[32] Aside from 2 Clem. 16.4, Tob 12:8-9 is cited in Cyprian, Eleem. 5; and either Tob 4:10 or 12:9 is cited in Pol. Phil. 10.2. On the use of Tobit in the early church, see Susan Docherty, "The Reception of Tobit in the New Testament and Early Christian Literature, with Special Reference to Luke–Acts," in The Scriptures of Israel in Jewish and Christian Tradition: Essays in Honour of Maarten J. J. Menken (ed. Bart J. Koet, Steve Moyise, and Joseph Verheyden; NovTSup 148; Leiden: Brill, 2013), 81–94. For an argument that Jerome's reading of Tob 12:9 played a crucial role in the development of the idea that postmortem alms could shorten time in purgatory, see Danuta Shanzer, "Jerome, Tobit, Alms, and the Vita Aeterna," in Jerome of Stridon: His Life, Writings and Legacy (ed. Andrew Cain and Josef Lössl; Farnham, UK: Ashgate, 2009), 87–103.

Sirach

With the exception of Tobit, no book among the collection of writings known as the Old Testament Apocrypha employs the noun ἐλεημοσύνη more often than Sirach.[33] This long instructional document has a great deal to say about issues of wealth, poverty, generosity, and justice. Two particular texts from Sirach, however, feature prominently in early Christian discourse about the meritorious and atoning value of almsgiving—namely, Sir 3:30 and 29:11-12. It is worth examining these texts in their context in Sirach, even if citations of or allusions to these texts in early Christian literature tend to function as proof-texts of proverbial sayings.

The first passage comes from Sir 3:30–4:10, the first extended discussion of justice in the book:

> [30] A blazing fire water will extinguish,
>> and merciful acts atone for sins.
> [31] The one who pays back benefits thinks about the future,
>> and in a time of falling he will find support.
> [1] Child, the life of the poor do not defraud,
>> and do not put off needy eyes.
> [2] A hungry soul do not grieve,
>> and do not anger a man in his difficulty.
> [3] An angry heart do not trouble,
>> and do not delay giving to one in need.
> [4] A suppliant in distress do not keep rejecting,
>> and do not turn your face away from the poor.
> [5] From one who begs do not turn away an eye,
>> and do not give him an occasion to curse you.
> [6] For if one curses you in the bitterness of his soul,
>> the one who made him will hear his petition.
> [7] Make yourself beloved to a gathering,
>> and for a nobleman bow your head.

[33] I will refer to the book as "Sirach" and the author purportedly responsible for the book as "Ben Sira." As the prologue to Sirach makes clear, the Wisdom of Jesus Son of Sirach was translated by Ben Sira's grandson from Hebrew into Greek sometime after 132 BCE. While the book was mostly known in its Greek translation in antiquity, the discovery of Hebrew portions of Sirach among the Cairo Genizah fragments (designated A–F) and among texts from Masada and Qumran has allowed for the recovery of about two-thirds of a form of the Hebrew text. Many translations of Sirach, such as the NRSV, rely heavily on the Hebrew manuscript tradition (especially MS B). Given my interest in the reception history of Sirach among Greek and Latin Christian texts in the first through the third centuries, however, I will focus on the Greek version of Sirach, using as my text Ziegler's Göttingen edition.

⁸ Incline your ear to the poor,
        and answer him peaceably with gentleness.
⁹ Deliver the wronged from the hand of the wrongdoer,
        and do not be faint-hearted when you render judgment.
¹⁰ Be like a father to orphans
        and instead of a husband to their mother,
and you will be like a son of the Most High,
        and he will love you more than does your mother.[34]

In this unified pericope, verses 30 to 31 address the rewards of ἐλεημοσύνη; verses 1 to 6 stipulate a series of negative behaviors that one should avoid when dealing with the needy, with verse 6 punctuating these injunctions by warning that God will hear the one who curses the abuser of the poor; and verses 7 to 10 issue positive commands related to care for the poor.[35] This unit, therefore, opens with two statements about the benefits accrued for the one who practices mercy for the poor, and these declarations merit unpacking.

In verse 30 the metaphor of water extinguishing a great conflagration is used to illustrate the atoning value of ἐλεημοσύνη: as water extinguishes a burning fire, so merciful practice expiates (ἐξιλάσεται) sin. To translate ἐλεημοσύνη as "almsgiving" in verse 30 ignores the fact that, from a linguistic bias in favor of monosemy, the word means merciful practice broadly conceived, and only specific contextual markers denoting ἐλεημοσύνη as the merciful practice of providing material support to the needy would warrant the translation "almsgiving" or "charity." In the larger context of Sirach, the noun ἐλεημοσύνη includes merciful deeds shown to one's father (3:14) and God's own mercy (17:29)—instances in which the word should hardly be translated "almsgiving"—along with other occurrences in which "merciful deeds" or "merciful practice" sufficiently capture the semantic force of the noun (cf. 7:10; 12:3; 16:14; 17:22; 29:8, 12; 31:11; 35:4; 40:17, 24).[36] In the immediate context of 3:30–4:10, moreover, if verse 30 represents a general statement about the value of ἐλεημοσύνη, then 4:1-10 spells out what ἐλεημοσύνη looks like in practice: not defrauding or ignoring the poor (v. 1),

---

[34] This translation is from the NETS, although I have rendered ἐλεημοσύνη in 3:30 as "merciful acts" rather than "charity."

[35] Verse 7 might appear to be an exception to this focus on charity, although the phrase προσφιλῆ συναγωγῇ σεαυτὸν ποίει in v. 7a should be interpreted as an injunction for fair judgment for the poor among the συναγωγή, especially in light of vv. 8-9, which imagine the recipient of this instruction as a judge called to listen to and defend the poor (cf. 41:18).

[36] See esp. Sir 17:22, where ἐλεημοσύνη and χάρις stand in synonymous parallelism (cf. 40:17).

not grieving or insulting the hungry (v. 2), not troubling or delaying to give to the needy (v. 3), not rejecting or turning away from the destitute (v. 4), not overlooking beggars or inviting curses from them (v. 5), establishing a good reputation among the people (v. 7), listening to the poor and responding with gentleness (v. 8), rescuing the wronged and rendering kind judgment (v. 9), and acting as a father to orphans (v. 10). All of this is ἐλεημοσύνη. There is no doubt that ἐλεημοσύνη in this context includes charity. Yet translation such as "almsgiving" is too narrow if it implies that ἐλεημοσύνη is seen only in the distribution of material goods, for such an understanding ignores the compassion called for by encouraging the poor to be listened to, seen, treated with dignity, and judged fairly by Ben Sira's audience.

In verse 31 the nature of both ἐλεημοσύνη and the recompense that merciful deeds engender is clarified: "The one who pays back benefits thinks about the future, and in a time of falling he will find support." On its own, this statement might be interpreted as wise counsel regarding the repayment of creditors, anticipating the longer discussion of credit in 29:1-7. The point in 3:31 would then be that the practice of repaying a loan (i.e., χάρις) makes it more likely that an individual will find future support in time of need. Taken together with the reference to the atoning power of ἐλεημοσύνη in verse 30, however, this saying appears to suggest that merciful practice itself is a kind of return payment on benefits received; the one who pays back, through merciful deeds, the blessings that he has received will himself, on account of his generosity, find assistance, should he find himself in a position in which he needs to receive ἐλεημοσύνη. Here there is anticipated a theme that we will see more clearly in 29:11-12, and one that is present also in Tobit—namely, that merciful acts, including charity, rescue from trouble in the sense that those who generously give will generously receive when they need assistance.

But how exactly does merciful practice atone for sins, according to the theological grammar of Sirach? It should be noted initially that Ben Sira displays a very positive estimation of the temple cult and the priesthood that maintains it.[37] Readers of Sirach are enjoined to revere, attend to, and honor priests in ways that parallel the call to fear, love, and glorify God (7:29-31), and attention to priests explicitly includes offering cultic sacrifices (7:31; so also 38:11). The extended praise of Wisdom in Sirach 24, which has been suggested as a structural and thematic center of the book, localizes Wisdom's dwelling upon the earth in the Jerusalem temple (24:7-12; cf. 49:11-12)

---

[37] In this section, I draw on the insightful analysis in Gregory, *Like an Everlasting Signet Ring*, 225–32.

and images Wisdom's own service to God in cultic terms (24:10).[38] At the conclusion of the book, in the section known as the "Hymn in Honor of Our Ancestors," Aaron receives extended praise (45:6-22). The section exalts Aaron's everlasting priesthood (45:7, 15), dwells on the beauty of his priestly garments (45:8-13), describes his oversight of sacrificial practices (45:14-16; cf. 46:16), and emphasizes his receipt of priestly gifts (45:20-22). Moreover, the encomium is punctuated by a tribute to the high priest Simon (50:1-21), whose laudable accomplishments include repairing and fortifying the temple (50:1-4) and attending to the holy altar and leading worship while clothed in glorious splendor (50:5-21). It is difficult, therefore, to describe Ben Sira as anything other than an enthusiastic supporter and defender of the Jerusalem priesthood and the sacrificial system.[39]

Sirach's strong endorsement of the priesthood and the Jerusalem temple only throws into sharp relief the possible incongruity of a text like Sir 3:30, which declares that merciful deeds atone for sin. Yet there are two texts earlier in Sirach 3 that make parallel claims for atonement outside of the temple, using similar cultic language:

> [3] The one who honors his father atones for sins (ἐξιλάσκεται ἁμαρτίας),
> [4] and like one who lays up treasure (ὁ ἀποθησαυρίζων) is one who glorifies his mother.

> [14] For merciful practice (ἐλεημοσύνη) to a father will not be forgotten, and it will be credited to you against sins.
> [15] In a day of your affliction it will be remember of you; like warm weather upon frost, so will your sins be melted away.

---

[38] Sir 24:10 reads: "In a holy tent I ministered (ἐλειτούργησα) before him [i.e., the Creator]," and the verb λειτουργέω is also used of Aaron's priestly ministry in 45:15. On the relationship between Torah, the priesthood, and the figure of Wisdom in Sirach, see Robert Hayward, "Sacrifice and World Order: Some Observations on Ben Sira's Attitude to the Temple Service," in *Sacrifice and Redemption: Durham Essays in Theology* (ed. Stephen W. Sykes; Cambridge: Cambridge University Press, 1991), 22–34. Hayward argues that the priestly sacrifice of Simon in the Jerusalem temple (50:1-21) is in Sirach depicted as an embodiment of Wisdom herself and a manifestation of the rightly structured primeval world order, concluding that "sacrifice, duly offered by the legitimate priests in the sanctuary chosen by God, is thus to some extent an earthly reflection of that divine order which permeates the universe and on which creation stands" (29–30).

[39] See also Benjamin G. Wright III, "'Fear the Lord and Honor the Priest': Ben Sira as Defender of the Jerusalem Priesthood," in *The Book of Ben Sira in Modern Research: Proceedings of the First International Ben Sira Conference, 28–31 July 1996, Soesterberg, Netherlands* (ed. Pancratius C. Beentjes; BZAW 255; Berlin: De Gruyter, 1997), 189–222.

Sir 3:1-16 is an extended section on the responsibilities of children toward their parents. In 3:3-4, honoring one's father has atoning efficacy, and honoring one's mother stores up treasure (cf. Sir 29:11). The parallelism in these two verses is striking:

(A)   ἐλεημοσύνη to a father will not be forgotten;
(B)   ἐλεημοσύνη will be credited against sins;
(A') ἐλεημοσύνη will be remembered in a day of affliction;
(B') ἐλεημοσύνη will melt away sins.[40]

Properly relating to one's parents both erases past transgressions and allows for the accumulation of treasure that can be used in the future.[41] That one's father is the object of ἐλεημοσύνη in 3:14 is another indication that "almsgiving" as a default translation of this noun is problematic; in the context of Sir 3:1-16, ἐλεημοσύνη functions as part of a cluster of practices that children should show to their parents, including honoring (vv. 3, 5, 8), glorying (vv. 4, 6), serving (v. 7), supporting (v, 12), and indulging (v. 13) their elders. The emphasis on *mercy* in the phrase "merciful practice to a father will not be forgotten" (ἐλεημοσύνη γὰρ πατρὸς οὐκ ἐπιλησθήσεται) in Sir 3:14 is also important because this verse immediately follows the charge in verses 12 to 13 to help and be patient to a father whose mind fails in old age. While there is no reason to exclude a material dimension to ἐλεημοσύνη in this context, it is merciful practice more generally that leads to a credit against sins.[42]

Forgiveness of sin is a complex phenomenon in Sirach, and the author does not appear to limit forgiveness to the sphere of the temple cult, although sins are certainly also forgiven through sacrifice (45:15-16, 23-24; cf. 34:23). Regularly in Sirach, with no explicit connection to temple sacrifice, God's

---

[40] As Gregory points out in his comments on the Hebrew textual tradition, the effect of what I have translated "merciful practice" (or ἐλεημοσύνη) in 3:15 "almost reverses the imagery found in 3:30 since now צדקה is pictured as heat which melts sin, whereas in v. 30 it is the heat of sin that is extinguished by water" (*Like an Everlasting Signet Ring*, 234.).

[41] Gregory, *Like an Everlasting Signet Ring*, 235. Gregory notes that, when sin is imaged in metaphorical terms of "debt," this helps to explain the relationship between "forgiveness (offsetting a negative) and merit (accruing the positive)" in Sirach: "[I]f both the amelioration of sin and almsgiving are understood in terms of debits and credits, it is not difficult to see how an author such as Ben Sira could elide the two."

[42] Gregory's claim that "Ben Sira views צדקה as not just atoning for previous sins, but as being stored up to offset future sins as well" (*Like an Everlasting Signet Ring*, 236) is not an accurate description of the Greek version of Sirach, where the phrase ἀντὶ ἁμαρτιῶν προσανοικοδομηθήσεταί σοι gives no indication that kindness to a father eliminates future sins. The verb προσανοικοδομέω is in the future aspect because of the genre of the wisdom discourse.

forgiveness of sin is offered through repentance (2:11; 5:4-8; 16:11-14; 17:25–18:14; 18:20-21; 21:1-2).[43] Ben Sira also forges a connection between divine pardon and human forgiveness, stating: "Forgive your neighbor a wrong, and then, when you petition, your sins will be pardoned" (28:2, NETS).[44] While it might be maintained that the language of forgiveness in Sirach should be understood in the larger context of Ben Sira's positive esteem for the temple cult—with the implication that repentance should precede proper sacrifice—the use of atonement language in Sirach 3 indicates that ἐλεημοσύνη offers a means of atonement outside of, even if not directly in competition with, the temple cult.[45] Similar perspectives on the atoning efficacy of merciful practice, including particularly the allocation of material goods to the needy, are, of course, found in LXX Prov 15:27, Th Dan 4:27; and Tob 12:8-10.[46] Ben Sira stands in a tradition that, while in no way disparaging or rejecting the atoning efficacy of the temple cult, envisions the alleviation of sin as taking place through merciful action. To be clear, it is not merely ἐλεημοσύνη that atones for sin in Sirach but Torah observance more broadly; ἐλεημοσύνη is a manifestation of a life centered on adherence to the law. This point is made directly in Sir 35:1-5, where keeping the law is equated with sacrificial offering and merciful practice is equated with a sacrifice of praise:

> [1]The one who keeps the law multiplies offerings,
>   [2]and the one who keeps the commandments offers a sacrifice for deliverance.
> [3]The one who pays back a benefit offers the finest wheat flour,
>   [4]and the one who practices merciful deeds (ὁ ποιῶν ἐλεημοσύνην) offers a sacrifice of praise.
> [5]It is pleasing to the Lord to refrain from wickedness,

---

[43] See Roland E. Murphy, "Sin, Repentance, and Forgiveness in Sirach," in *Der Einzelne und seine Gemeinschaft bei Ben Sira* (ed. Ingrid Krammer and Renate Egger-Wenzel; BZAW 270; Berlin: De Gruyter, 1998), 261–70.

[44] Gregory, *Like and Everlasting Signet Right*, 269; cf. Matt 6:12-15; Mark 11:25; John 20:23; Col 3:13. The diverse range of ways forgiveness is actualized in Sirach offers interesting parallels to the language of forgiveness in the Synoptic Gospels; see chap. 4.

[45] The Greek version of Sir 3:30 translates the Hebrew תכפר with ἐξιλάσκομαι, a verb used with reference to sacrificial atonement in Sir 28:5; 34:23; and 45:16, 23 (but cf. 5:6; 16:7; 20:28). In the LXX, ἐξιλάσκομαι regularly translates כפר, especially in Leviticus; see Dirk Büchner, "Some Reflections on Writing a Commentary on the Septuagint of Leviticus," in *Translation Is Required* (ed. Robert J. V. Hiebert; SBLSCS 56; Atlanta: SBL, 2010), 107–17.

[46] Gregory (*Like an Everlasting Signet Ring*, 235–36) also points to Ezek 18:22.

and to refrain from injustice is to atone (ἐξιλασμὸς ἀποστῆναι ἀπὸ ἀδικίας).⁴⁷

The second key passage from Sirach related to the development of meritorious and atoning almsgiving is 29:8-13, which is located at the center of a longer discourse (29:1-20) about the person who practices mercy (ὁ ποιῶν ἔλεος [v. 1]).⁴⁸ The opening statement in verse 1—"He who does mercy will lend to his neighbor, and he who prevails with his hand keeps the commandments"—introduces the topic—namely, the person who practices mercy. This opening assertion also provides a framework through which the discussion of three separate merciful practices should be interpreted, those practices being loans (vv. 1b-7), acts of mercy (vv. 8-13), and surety (vv. 14-20).⁴⁹

The first subsection, on loans, encourages both lending to those in need as a fulfillment of the commandments (vv. 1b, 2a) and paying back what

---

⁴⁷ So Murphy, "Sin, Repentance, and Forgiveness in Sirach," 268–69. Anthony Giambrone ("'According to the Commandment' [Did. 1.5]: Lexical Reflections on Almsgiving as 'The Commandment,'" NTS 60 [2014]: 448–465 [460–61]) cites Sir 35:2 as evidence that "both during the Second Temple period and after, charity held status as a kind of surrogate cult." Given the importance of the cult in Sirach, it is not clear that charity is the substitute implied by Giambrone's statement.

⁴⁸ Daniel J. Harrington views all of Sir 29 as a unified discourse about "money and property," dividing the material as follows: "borrowing and lending" (vv. 1-7), "almsgiving" (vv. 8-13), "guaranteeing the debts of others" (vv. 14-20), and "the necessity of preserving financial independence" (vv. 21-28) (Jesus Ben Sira of Jerusalem: A Biblical Guide to Living Wisely [Collegeville, Minn.: Liturgical, 2005], 97). It seems better, however, to divide vv. 1-20, which focus on generous giving, from vv. 21-28, which outline strategies for moderate consumption.

⁴⁹ So Georg Sauer, Jesus Sirach / Ben Sira (ATDA 1; Göttingen: Vandenhoeck & Ruprecht, 2000), 209–10. For more discussion of the structure of this chapter, see Gregory, Like an Everlasting Signet Ring, 133–35. I agree with Gregory that there are three separate practices discussed in vv. 1-20 (although I would distinguish v. 1a from vv. 1b-7), but I do not agree with Gregory's conclusion that "almsgiving" in vv. 8-13 is a particular kind of loan, with vv. 2-7 representing what Gregory calls "normal" loans and vv. 8-13 describing "special" loans—i.e., alms. Gregory's position is followed by Anderson, Charity, 46–52. Instead of ἐλεημοσύνη representing a particular kind of loan in Sir 29, loans (vv. 2-7) are a particular kind of ἔλεος (v. 1). The difference can be seen in Gregory's problematic translation of the Greek text of Sir 29:1. Gregory renders the phrase ὁ ποιῶν ἔλεος δανιεῖ τῷ πλησίον as "He who lends to his neighbor acts mercifully." But this translation confuses, and switches, the nominative subject ὁ ποιῶν ἔλεος with the verb δανιεῖ. The subject of the sentence is not "he who lends" (which would be ὁ δανείζων) but "he who does mercy" (ὁ ποιῶν ἔλεος). The Greek sentence does not say that the one who lends acts mercifully but says that the one who practices mercy lends to his neighbors; the difference is neither subtle nor insignificant.

one has been loaned in a timely manner (vv. 2b-6) in order to avoid shame and insult. The third subsection, on surety, encourages those with means to guarantee loans for their neighbors (vv. 14) and those who receive surety to remember and honor the kindness of their guarantors (vv. 15-17), while also recognizing that the risky nature of guaranteeing loans can lead to financial ruin or lawsuits (vv. 18-19). The concluding statement in this section offers practical advice that balances the encouragement to provide surety with an acknowledgment of the dangers involved in this merciful act: "Help your neighbor according to your ability, and take care that you yourself do not fall" (v. 20).

Sandwiched in between these materials is a unit that enjoins the practice of ἐλεημοσύνη:

> [8] Nevertheless, with a lowly person be patient,
>   and for merciful acts do not keep him waiting.
> [9] On account of the commandment help a poor person,
>   and according to his need do not turn him away empty-handed.
> [10] Lose silver for the sake of a brother and a friend,
>   and do not let it rust under the stone for destruction.
> [11] Lay up your treasure according to the commandments of the Most High,
>   and it will profit you more than gold.
> [12] Store up merciful practice in your storerooms,[50]
>   and it will deliver you from every mistreatment.
> [13] More than a strong shield and more than a weighty spear,
>   it will fight against an enemy on your behalf.

The transitional marker πλήν, "nevertheless," at the beginning of this section contrasts the ensuing exhortation regarding kindness to those in need with the previous warning about the dangerous entanglements posed by loans (vv. 5-7). In spite of the fact that the repayment of a loan might be delayed (v. 5), or not paid in full or at all (v. 6), resulting in lenders being defrauded (v. 7), Ben Sira insists that his readers should still show mercy to the lowly. Once again, ἐλεημοσύνη should be understood to include "alms-giving" but should not be limited to material distributions to the needy.

---

[50] The image in v. 12 is domestic ("storerooms") rather than commercial ("treasuries") because the noun ταμιεῖον refers to a storage room or private chamber where, presumably, items might be kept for safekeeping (cf. LXX Gen 43:30; Exod 7:28; Deut 28:8; 32:25; Judg 3:24; 15:1; 16:9, 12; 2 Sam 13:10; 1 Kgs 1:15; 21:30; 22:25; 2 Kgs 6:12; 9:2; 11:2; 2 Chron 18:24; 22:11; Isa 26:20; 42:22; Tob 7:15; Ps 105:30; Prov 24:4; Eccl 10:20; Song 1:4; 3:4; 8:2). In Deut 28:8; Ps 143:13; and Prov 3:10 (cf. Ezek 28:16), the word does denote a barn.

The focus in the immediate context, however, is on the provision of material assistance, for ἐλεημοσύνη is imaged as filling the hand of a poor person (v. 9) and losing money (ἀργύριον) for the sake of a brother and friend (v. 10). Such beneficence on behalf of the poor is encouraged "on account of the commandment" (χάριν ἐντολῆς) in verse 9. That readers are exhorted in verse 11 to "lay up your treasure according to the *commandments* of the Most High," combined with the reference to keeping "the commandments" (τηρεῖ ἐντολάς) in verse 1, should caution against the attempt to identify a singular commandment behind the injunction in verse 9, although the apostle Paul's rhetoric of charity in 1 Tim 6:17-19 might suggest that "the commandment" in Sir 29:9 and elsewhere came to be understood as the practice of providing for the needs of the poor.[51]

Of particular note is the relationship between merciful practice and reward in Sir 29:8-13. Already Sir 17:22 has declared of the divine reward for ἐλεημοσύνη: "A man's practice of mercy is like a signet with him, and a person's kindness [God] will preserve as the apple of his eye." Negatively, in 29:10 failure to part with silver for the sake of a brother and friend is described as hiding the money under a stone where the coinage will rust, an image that may have informed the discourse on possessions in Matt 6:19-21 (cf. Matt 25:14-30). The statement is engagingly ironic, for the reader is instructed to lose (ἀπόλεσον) his money by giving it away to his kin or friend, while the economically cautious course of action—that is, burying the money in the ground for safekeeping, with a stone marking its placement—will actually result in the true loss of possessions.[52]

The irony of verse 10 is clarified in verses 11 to 13, where Ben Sira unpacks the positive reward associated with the practice of ἐλεημοσύνη. Instead of hiding treasure in the ground, the reader is offered a means of profit outside of the confines of the seemingly "rational" economic behavior reflected in the attempt to conceal one's funds. Reiterating the notion—already advanced in verses 1 and 9—that helping those in need is a demonstration of law observance (cf. Sir 35:1), Ben Sira encourages laying up treasure, presumably by giving to the poor, according to "the commandments of the Most High," with the encouragement that this dispossession "will profit you more than gold" (v. 11). The nature of this return on one's investment is then spelled out more

---

[51] See chap. 5. Generally, Deut 15:7-11 is suggested as providing the legal background for the reference to "the commandment(s)" in Sir 29:1-20; Gregory, *Like an Everlasting Signet Ring*, 186–87; Benjamin G. Wright III, *Praise Israel for Wisdom and Instruction: Essays on Ben Sira and Wisdom, the Letter of Aristeas and the Septuagint* (JSJSup 131; Leiden: Brill, 2008), 77.

[52] Gregory, *Like an Everlasting Signet Ring*, 189.

clearly in the following two verses: "Store up merciful practice in your store-rooms (σύγκλεισον ἐλεημοσύνην ἐν τοῖς ταμιείοις σου), and it will deliver you from every mistreatment. More than a strong shield and more than a weighty spear, it will fight against an enemy on your behalf."

Sirach 29:11-13 is also sometimes interpreted as one of the first texts advocating almsgiving as a means of making a deposit in a heavenly treasury.[53] Certainly the notion that care for the poor is a righteous behavior that results in heavenly reward became a key theme in later Jewish and Christian discourse about almsgiving, and this is a key eschatological motif in the New Testament (Mark 10:17-31; Matt 6:1-21; 19:16-30; Luke 12:33-34; 18:18-30; 1 Tim 6:17-19; cf. Jas 5:1-7).[54] In the context of Sirach, however, the wise instruction of 29:11-13 refers not to heavenly (and certainly not to eschatological) reward but to the more mundane (but no less important) principle that those who are generous to the needy will receive assistance from others, should these benefactors come to find themselves in difficult circumstances. The principle of reciprocity invoked here is at most only loosely theological, for it is never stated (as in Prov 19:17, for example) that God will be the one to recompense those who practice ἐλεημοσύνη, and Sirach exhibits no expectation of recompense in an afterlife.[55] As in Tobit, what is imagined in

[53] Particularly notable is Gary Anderson's treatment of this passage in *Charity*, 46–49. Anderson translates Sir 29:11 in this way: "Lay up your treasure [in heaven . . .] and it will *profit* you more than gold" (emphasis in original). Anderson goes on to write, "Ben Sira introduces an idea that will emerge as a key theme in the preaching of Jesus—the treasury in heaven. Though Ben Sira does not provide any details as to how this works, one must presume that the poor person serves as a sort of conduit through which one can convey goods from earth to heaven. . . . The money expended as charity returns to the donor as a credit to a heavenly bank account" (49). But Ben Sira has not introduced the notion of a treasury in heaven at all; Anderson has introduced this concept, as is clear in Anderson's insertion (on the basis of no textual evidence whatsoever) of the bracketed phrase "in heaven" into his translation.

[54] For other Jewish texts that employ the imagery of storing up heavenly reward on the basis of deeds in the present life, see 2 Macc 12:39-45; *Pss. Sol.* 9:5 (cf. Wis 2:22); *2 Bar.* 14:12-13; 24:1-2; 4 Ezra 7:77; 8:31-36; *m. 'Abot* 3:15-17; *t. Pe'ah* 1:2-3; cf. 2 Tim 4:6-8; Col 1:5; 1 Pet 1:4; Klaus Koch, "Der Schatz im Himmel," in *Leben Angesichts des Todes: Beiträge zum theologischen Problem des Todes; Helmut Thielicke zum 60 Geburtstag* (ed. Berhard Lohse and H. P. Schmidt; Tübingen: Mohr, 1968), 47–60; Eubank, *Wages of Cross-Bearing Sin*, 25–52; Tzvi Novick, "Wages from God: The Dynamics of a Biblical Metaphor," *CBQ* 73 (2011): 708–22. Texts that image the day of judgment as a weighing of one's deeds include *1 En.* 38:1-2; 41:1-2; 45:3; 61:1-5; *2 En.* 44:4-5; *T. Ab.* 12–14.

[55] To the extent that there is reward for good deeds after death in Sirach, this reward is envisioned in terms of the remembrance of one's action and the establishment of an eternal name for the righteous; see Samuel L. Adams, *Wisdom in Transition: Act and Consequence in Second Temple Instructions* (JSJSup 125; Leiden: Brill, 2008), 153–213.

this passage, therefore, are situations in which those who help the poor for the commandments' sake are themselves rescued from disaster when their good deeds are remembered by others. The immediate literary context of Sir 29:8-13 makes this clear, for both the discussion of loans and the treatment of surety endorse a *do et des* principle among humans: readers should lend to neighbors so that they will find whatever they need (v. 3); they should pay back loans in order not to make enemies (v. 6); and the kindness of a guarantor should always be remembered (v. 15). In this context, it is clear that the enemy (ἐχθρός) against whom ἐλεημοσύνη fights is not some spiritual force or punishment in the afterlife but the person who would afflict or oppress a practitioner of merciful deeds when that generous donor needs assistance himself.[56] Just as in Tobit 4, deliverance through ἐλεημοσύνη in Sirach 29 refers to security against future fiscal disaster. For those for whom poverty is an ever-present reality and danger, one aspect of the wisdom of showing mercy to those in need is that charity increases the chance that favor will be returned when givers of alms must become recipients.

Thus, the promotion of merciful practice in the Greek version of Sirach displays close similarities to the discourse regarding ἐλεημοσύνη in Tobit: ἐλεημοσύνη is part and parcel of a virtuous life (Sir 7:10; 12:3); ἐλεημοσύνη will be honored and recompensed by God (16:14; 17:22); ἐλεημοσύνη prepares one to receive assistance when trouble befalls (29:11-13; 40:24); and ἐλεημοσύνη establishes solidarity among those who share and is memorialized by the assembly of God's people (31:11; 35:2; 40:17).[57] Moreover, like LXX Prov 15:27, Th Dan 4:27, and Tob 12:8-10, Sir 3:30 asserts the atoning efficacy of merciful deeds. These passages from Greek versions of Proverbs, Daniel, Tobit, and Sirach represent a cluster of scriptural texts that greatly influenced emerging Christian advocacy of atoning almsgiving.

---

[56] In Sirach, the noun ἐχθρός always refers to persons (and not circumstances) who oppose, mock, or trouble Ben Sira's readers in the present or the people of God in the past (see 6:4, 13; 12:8-10, 16; 18:31; 20:23; 23:3; 25:7, 14-15; 29:6; 30:3, 6; 36:6, 9; 42:11; 45:2; 46:1, 5, 16; 47:7; 49:9; 51:8). Someone who does not repay a loan makes an ἐχθρός in 29:6.

[57] Also as in Tobit, ἐλεημοσύνη is demonstrated by God as well as by humans (17:29).

CHAPTER 3

I DESIRE MERCY, NOT SACRIFICE
Cult Criticism and Atoning Almsgiving?

In a discussion of "acts of loving kindness," the post-Tannaitic rabbinic text entitled *Abot de Rabbi Nathan* (*AdRN*) tells a story about an encounter between Rabban Johanan ben Zakkai and Rabbi Joshua. As Johanan was walking down the road, Joshua ran after him and said, with reference to the destruction of the Jerusalem temple, "Woe to us because the house of our life has been destroyed, the place which used to atone for our sins." Johanan answered, "Do not be afraid. We have another atonement instead of it." Joshua asked, "What is it?" Johanan replied by citing Hos 6:6: "For I desire loving kindness and not sacrifice" (*AdRNB* 8).[1]

The traditions within the *AdRN* are notoriously difficult to date. Arguments for the final form of the *AdRN* itself have ranged from the second to the ninth centuries, although the text is generally considered post-Tannaitic.[2]

---

[1] The rendering here draws on the translation from Anthony J. Saldarini, *The Fathers according to Rabbi Nathan (Abot de Rabbi Nathan) Version B: A Translation and Commentary* (SJLA 11; Leiden: Brill, 1975), 75. This story is found in both versions of *AdRN* (A and B).

[2] See, e.g., Hayim Lapin, "The Origins and Development of the Rabbinic Movement in the Land of Israel," in *The Cambridge History of Judaism*, vol. 4, *The Late Roman-Rabbinic Period* (ed. Steven T. Katz; Cambridge: Cambridge University Press, 2006), 216; Shmuel Safrai, ed., *The Literature of the Sages, Part One: Oral Tora, Halakha, Mishna,*

Yet this conversation between Johanan and Joshua encapsulates the basic contours of an influential proposal regarding the emergence of the Christian doctrine of atoning almsgiving. One prominent account of the origins of atoning almsgiving in Jewish and Christian thought presents this tradition as a development of the so-called "prophetic critique of sacrifice" in the Hebrew Bible. According to this view, critiques of ritual sacrifice from Israel's prophets, not least because these criticisms are frequently coupled with calls for the demonstration of justice for the poor, paved the way for the emergence of the doctrine of atoning almsgiving in both Judaism and Christianity.[3] Rabban Johanan articulates something like this thesis when he responds to Rabbi Joshua's worry about the destruction of the location of ritual atonement for sin by pointing to a scriptural passage that envisions an alternative mechanism of atonement—namely, חסד ("steadfast love" [NRSV]).

Critical statements regarding Israel's sacrificial practices are not limited to the prophets (see 1 Sam 15:22-23; Pss 40:6-8; 50:5-15; 51:16-19). It is especially in the prophetic literature, however, that critiques of sacrifice are sometimes linked with the notion that God cares more about justice for the poor than offerings in the temple. Passages from Isaiah, Micah, and Amos are representative:

> [11]What to me is the multitude of your sacrifices? says the LORD; I have had enough of burnt offerings of rams and the fat of fed beasts; I do not delight in the blood of bulls, or of lambs, or of goats. [12]When you come to appear before me, who asked this from your hand? Trample my courts no more; [13]bringing offerings is futile; incense is an abomination to me. New moon and sabbath and calling of convocation—I cannot endure solemn assemblies with iniquity. [14]Your new moons and your appointed festivals my soul hates; they have become a burden to

---

Tosefta, Talmud, External Tractates (Compendia Rerum Iudaicarum ad Novum Testamentum, 2 [3:1]; Philadelphia: Fortress, 1987), 387; Tal Ilan, Mine and Yours Are Hers: Retrieving Women's History from Rabbinic Literature (AGJU 41; Leiden: Brill, 1997), 79; Hermann Leberecht Strack and Günter Stemberger, Introduction to the Talmud and Midrash (Minneapolis: Fortress, 1992), 225–27.

[3] This thesis is most clearly advanced by Roman Garrison, the author of the only English-language monograph heretofore written on the subject of atoning almsgiving. Garrison writes, "The Prophets lay much of the theological groundwork for the doctrine of redemptive almsgiving. Good works, notably charity, demonstrate the individual's personal righteousness and these determine whether he is 'acceptable' to the Lord. . . . The development of the doctrine was apparently accelerated by the destruction of the Temple. Its earlier stages may well reflect a discontent with the sacrificial system; this tension is already evident in the Prophets" (Redemptive Almsgiving in Early Christianity [JSNTSup 77; Sheffield: JSOT Press, 1993], 48, 59).

me, I am weary of bearing them. [15]When you stretch out your hands, I will hide my eyes from you; even though you make many prayers, I will not listen; your hands are full of blood. [16]*Wash yourselves; make yourselves clean; remove the evil of your doings from before my eyes; cease to do evil,* [17]*learn to do good; seek justice, rescue the oppressed, defend the orphan, plead for the widow.* (Isa 1:11-17, NRSV)

[6]"With what shall I come before the LORD, and bow myself before God on high? Shall I come before him with burnt offerings, with calves a year old? [7]Will the LORD be pleased with thousands of rams, with ten thousands of rivers of oil? Shall I give my firstborn for my transgression, the fruit of my body for the sin of my soul?" [8]*He has told you, O mortal, what is good; and what does the LORD require of you but to do justice, and to love kindness, and to walk humbly with your God?* (Mic 6:6-8, NRSV)

[21]I hate, I despise your festivals, and I take no delight in your solemn assemblies. [22]Even though you offer me your burnt offerings and grain offerings, I will not accept them; and the offerings of well-being of your fatted animals I will not look upon. [23]Take away from me the noise of your songs; I will not listen to the melody of your harps. [24]*But let justice roll down like waters, and righteousness like an ever-flowing stream.* [25]Did you bring to me sacrifices and offerings the forty years in the wilderness, O house of Israel? (Amos 5:21-25, NRSV)[4]

At first glance, it seems reasonable to assume that the notion that atonement for sin might be obtained by caring for the poor emerged from engagement with the so-called "prophetic critique of sacrifice" in Israel's Scriptures, and the thesis has often been accepted and repeated.[5] Indeed, the logic of this theory proceeds with an almost mathematical precision: (a) prophetic criticism of priestly sacrifice—a practice that served, of course, to remove impurity and sin—plus (b) prophetic exhortations for justice instead of sacrifice

---

[4] In addition to the texts cited above, see Hos 6:6; Jer 7:23. For an insightful treatment of this topic in the Hebrew Bible, see Jonathan Klawans, *Purity, Sacrifice, and the Temple: Symbolism and Supersessionism in the Study of Ancient Judaism* (Oxford: Oxford University Press, 2006).

[5] E.g., Garrison, *Redemptive Almsgiving*; Christopher M. Hays, "By Almsgiving and Faith Sins Are Purged? The Theological Underpinnings of Early Christian Care for the Poor," in *Engaging Economics: New Testament Scenarios and Early Christian Reception* (ed. Bruce W. Longenecker and Kelly D. Liebengood; Grand Rapids: Eerdmans, 2009), 272–73; Bronwen Neil, "Models of Gift Giving in the Preaching of Leo the Great," *JECS* 18 (2010): 257; cf. Gary A. Anderson, *Sin: A History* (New Haven: Yale University Press, 2010), 165–67. Hays' discussion is far more nuanced than most.

equals (c) the idea that sins can be atoned by demonstrating justice or caring for the poor.

This thruway from the so-called prophetic criticism of sacrifice to atoning almsgiving is, however, a dead end for early rabbinic literature and a path trodden by perhaps only one Christian text before the fourth century. Since a key thesis of this book is that Christian promotion of atoning almsgiving emerged as a result of scriptural exegesis, however, it is worthwhile to pause the chronological survey of the story of atoning almsgiving in order to explore one way in which Scripture does not seem to have informed the development of the tradition. Prophetic and other cult-critical texts appear to have played no discernible role in the emergence of Jewish advocacy of atoning almsgiving and feature only occasionally in Christian texts that promote the atoning efficacy of care for the poor. Not only is the textual basis for such a claim generally lacking (i.e., scriptural texts reflecting the so-called prophetic critique of sacrifice are rarely cited or integrated in appeals for atoning alms), but the idea that care for the poor *replaces* sacrifice is problematized by the continuing importance of sacrifice (variously interpreted) in postbiblical Jewish and Christian texts. By examining two related questions, it may be seen that the road does not lead straight from prophetic criticism to atoning almsgiving. First, to what extent do specific texts from the corpus of Israel's prophets that explicitly condemn cultic practice feature in Jewish and Christian texts that advocate for atoning almsgiving? That is, do prophetic voices critical of the sacrificial cult offer scriptural warrants for rabbinic and Christian proponents of atoning almsgiving? Second, to what extent, if at all, do proponents of atoning almsgiving offer disapproval of literal sacrifice, and is such disapproval connected to the concept that sin can be alleviated by rendering assistance to the needy instead?

Atoning Almsgiving and the Critique of Sacrifice in Biblical and Second Temple Jewish Literature?

Given that the concept of atoning almsgiving seems to have emerged in Jewish literature of the Hellenistic period, it might justifiably be asked if those Jewish texts from the Second Temple period that first explicitly advocate for the atoning efficacy of merciful deeds for the needy—namely, Th Dan 4:27; LXX Prov 15:27; Tobit 12:8-10; and Sir 3:30—do so with reference to the so-called prophetic critique of sacrifice. The short answer, which has already been seen in the examination of these texts, is, No. In none of these documents are cult-critical statements from or allusions to Israel's prophets or other Scriptures employed in order to advance the notion of atoning almsgiving.[6] Daniel, Proverbs, Tobit, and Sirach all esteem the sacrificial cult and the Jerusalem temple, even if some of these texts do occasionally condemn the inappropriate offering of sacrifices.[7] In none of these documents is there any indication that, in promoting the atoning significance of almsgiving, the authors/translators of these Second Temple texts drew upon prophetic writings that pit priestly sacrifice against justice for the poor. Indeed, LXX Daniel, Tobit, Sirach, and even LXX Proverbs all hold the Jerusalem temple and its cultic practices in high regard, even if priestly traditions and sacrificial activity are not major themes of any of these documents, with the notable exception of Sirach.

Rabbinic Literature

Johanan and Joshua's conversation in *AdRNB* 8 indicates that, in later rabbinic literature, Hos 6:6 did later come to be interpreted as a text that offers atonement through חסד apart from the sacrificial cult. But what of earlier rabbinic literature? Although the concept of meritorious almsgiving is well represented in later Palestinian Amoraic sources (*y. Pe'ah* 1:1, 15b; *y. Shab.* 6:10, 8; *Lev. Rab.* 34:7-8; cf. *Gen. Rab.* 44:12; *b. B. Bat* 9b; 10a; 11a; *b. Suk.* 49b), perhaps only three texts from the Tannaitic literature emphasize the

---

[6] This claim is not intended to deny that LXX Daniel, Tobit, Sirach, and, perhaps to a lesser extent, LXX Proverbs draw richly upon biblical antecedents in diverse ways. See, e.g., Bernd U. Schipper, "Das Proverbienbuch und die Toratradition," *ZTK* 108 (2011): 381–404; Micah D. Kiel, "Tobit and Moses Redux," *JSP* 17 (2008): 83–98; Jeremy Corley and Vincent Skemp, eds., *Intertextual Studies in Ben Sira and Tobit: Essays in Honor of Alexander A Di Lella, O.F.M.* (CBQMS 38; Washington, D.C.: Catholic Biblical Association of America, 2005); Alexander A. Di Lella, "A Study of Tobit 14:10 and Its Intertextual Parallels," *CBQ* 71 (2009): 497–506. Di Lella's study offers a fascinating look at interextuality as it relates to the rhetoric of almsgiving in Tobit, but he does not show that the so-called prophetic critique features in the narrative of Tobit.

[7] Critiques of improperly offered sacrifices are found in Prov 7:14; 14:9; 15:8; 20:25; 21:27; Sir 7:9; 34:21-31; 35:15; cf. 35:1-13. The positive portrayal of the Jerusalem temple in 1:4-6 and 14:5-7 offers a kind of narrative frame for the book of Tobit; see Moore, *Tobit*, 291. On the role of the temple and cultic sacrifice in the story of Daniel, see Winfried Vogel, *The Cultic Motif in the Book of Daniel* (New York: Peter Lang, 2010); Rodney Alan Werline, "Prayer, Politics, and Social Vision in Daniel 9," in *Seeking the Favor of God*, vol. 2, *The Development of Penitential Prayer in Second Temple Judaism* (ed. Mark J. Boda, Daniel K. Falk, and Rodney A. Werline; SBLEJL 22; Atlanta: Society of Biblical Literature, 2007), 17–32; Johan Lust, "Cult and Sacrifice in Daniel: The Tamid and the Abomination of Desolation," in *Book of Daniel: Composition and Reception*, vol. 2 (ed. John J. Collins and Peter Flint; VTSup 83; Leiden: Brill, 2001), 671–88.

meritorious and/or atoning nature of care for the poor.[8] It is not necessary here to entertain the complicated question of whether and to what extent later rabbinic texts may preserve earlier historical traditions.[9] The point to be made by looking at early rabbinic texts is that, while the Tannaitic literature does occasionally endorse the meritorious or atoning nature of almsgiving, never in Tannaitic sources is this position advanced with reference to the so-called prophetic critique of sacrifice.

For example, in the *Mekhilta de-Rabbi Ishmael Nezikin* 10, Rabbi Ishmael declares, "Come and see how merciful He by whose word the world came into being is to flesh and blood. For a man can redeem himself from the Heavenly judgment by paying money."[10] The string of scriptural citations used to support this claim includes Dan 4:24 ("break off your sins by צדקה").[11] Given the evidence to suggest that, in contrast to our discussion of צדקה in the MT of Dan 4:27, צדקה did come to assume in rabbinic literature the additional meaning "giving (alms) to the poor," it is clear that Ishmael understands redemption from heavenly judgment of sins to occur through monetary distributions to the poor.[12] Yet the text does not invoke the so-called prophetic critique of sacrifice to justify this conviction. Instead, Dan 4:24 serves as a key scriptural proof.

Similarly, *Tosefta Pe'ah* 4, which contains the other two passages in the Tannaitic literature that address the topic of charity and heavenly reward,

---

[8] These three passages are also discussed in Alyssa M. Gray, "Redemptive Almsgiving and the Rabbis of Late Antiquity," *JSQ* 18 (2011): 144–84.

[9] It certainly *could* be the case that a later text like *AdRN* preserves accurate historical information about a first-century figure such as Johanan ben Zakkai. But the methodological approach taken here is to date the tradition on the basis of the date of the compilation, rather than sifting through later corpora in an attempt to discern earlier (i.e., pre-70 or first-century) traditions. On the issue of dating rabbinic traditions, see Strack and Stemberger, *Introduction to the Talmud and Midrash*, 57–60. While some would include Tannaitic traditions preserved only in the Babylonian Talmud in "Tannaitic literature" (*baraitot*), the authenticity of traditions attributed to the Tannaim but preserved only in post-Tannaitic compilations is questionable; see Strack and Stemberger, *Introduction to the Talmud and Midrash*, 197–99.

[10] Jacob Z. Lauterbach, *Mekilta de-Rabbi Ishmael*, vol. 1 (Philadelphia: Jewish Publication Society of America, 1976), 86–88. Redemption from judgement here is shorthand for redemption from judgment of one's sins.

[11] The other scriptural texts cited include 2 Kgs 12:5; Exod 30:12; Prov 13:8; and Job 33:23-24.

[12] Ben Shalom, "Poverty, Charity and the Image of the Poor in Rabbinic Texts from the Land of Israel," 64–70. On צדקה in Rabbinic literature, see Marcus Jastrow, *Dictionary of the Targumim, the Talmud Babli and Yerushalmi, and the Midrashic Literature* (2 vols.; New York: Pardes, 1950).

does not employ cult-critical texts from the Hebrew Scriptures in its advocacy of meritorious almsgiving.[13] First, the story of Monobases' dispossession
of his treasures to the poor during a time of famine in *t. Pe'ah* 4:18 includes
a string of scriptural citations that justify the benevolent—but, from the
perspective of his brothers, foolish—action (Pss 85:11; 89:14; Isa 3:10; Prov
11:30; Deut 24:13; and Isa 58:8).

A. M'ŚH B: Monobases the king [of Adiabene] went and gave [to the
poor; *'md wbzbz*] [all of] his treasures during years of famine.

B. His brothers sent [the following message] to him:

C. "Your ancestors stored up treasures and increased the wealth [left
for them by] their ancestors. But you went and gave away all of these
treasures, both your own and those of your ancestors!"

D. He replied to them, "My ancestors stored up treasures for this lower
[world], but I, [through giving charity (*ṣdqh*)], have stored up treasures for [the heavenly world] above, as it is stated [in Scripture],
*Faithfulness will spring up from the ground below, [and righteousness
(ṣdq) will look down from the sky]* (Ps 85:11).

E. "My ancestors stored up treasures [for the material world], where
the [human] hand can reach (*šhyd šwlṭt bw*), but I have stored up
treasures [for the nonmaterial world], where the [human] hand
cannot reach, as it is stated [in Scripture], *Righteousness (ṣdq) and
justice are the foundation of your throne, [steadfast love and faithfulness
go before you]* (Ps 89:14).

F. "My ancestors stored up treasures [of a type] that produce no [real]
benefits (*pyrwt*), but I have stored up treasures [of (*sic*) the sort that
do produce benefits, as it is stated [in Scripture], *Tell the righteous
(ṣdyq) that it shall be well with them, for they shall reap the benefits
(pyrwt) of their deeds* (Isa 3:10).

G. "My ancestors stored up treasures of money, but I have stored up
treasures of souls (*šl npšwt*), as it is stated [in Scripture], *The fruit of
the righteous (ṣdyq) is a tree of life, and a wise man saves the souls [of
poor people]* (*npšwt*) (Prov 11:30).

---

[13] On the economic practices of *t. Pe'ah* 4, see esp. Gregg E. Gardner, "Competi-
tive Giving in the Third Century CE: Early Rabbinic Approaches to Greco-Roman Civic
Benefaction," in *Religious Competition in the Third Century CE: Jews, Christians, and the
Greco-Roman World* (ed. Jordan D. Rosenblum, Lily Vuong, and Nathaniel P. DesRosiers;
JAJSup 15; Göttingen: Vandenhoeck & Ruprecht, 2014), 81–92; cf. Gregg E. Gardner,
The Origins of Organized Charity in Rabbinic Judaism (Cambridge: Cambridge University
Press, 2015).

H. "My ancestors stored up treasures [that eventually, after their deaths, would benefit only] others, but I have stored up treasures [that will benefit] myself [both in life and in death], as it is stated [in Scripture], *It shall be a righteousness (ṣdq) to you before the Lord your God* (Deut 24:13).

I. "My ancestors stored up treasures in this world, but I have stored up treasures for myself in the world-to-come, as it is stated [in Scripture], *Your righteousness (ṣdqyk) shall go before you, and the glory of the Lord shall be your rear-guard* (Isa 58:8)."[14]

While the narrative clearly indicates Monobases' conviction that he will receive heavenly and lasting treasures in return for his generosity, there is no indication that the reward received by Monobases will be the remission of sin, marking this as a text that presents *meritorious* (or recompensed) but not *atoning* almsgiving. In fact, the only scriptural text that employs the language of salvation denotes the salvation not of the donor but of the recipients of charity: "My ancestors stored up treasures of money, but I have stored up treasures of souls [*šl npšwt*], as it is stated [in Scripture], *The fruit of the righteous [ṣdyq] is a tree of life, and a wise man saves the souls [of poor people] [npšwt]* (Prov 11:30)." Thus, *t. Pe'ah* 4:18 should be taken as an example of meritorious, not atoning, almsgiving.

Two of the six scriptural texts used by Monobases to justify his actions do merit attention, however. Initially, it might seem that the citation of Ps 89:14 ("Righteousness and justice are the foundation of your throne; steadfast love and faithfulness go before you" [NRSV]) hints that Monobases' generosity was motivated by a desire for justice (משפט) for the poor. The citation of Isa 58:8 is also evocative, since the larger literary context of this verse in Isaiah 58, while not offering a critique of sacrifice, does supply a prophetic indictment of the practice of fasting, rooted in the prophet's insistence that a true fast is "to loose the bonds of injustice, to undo the thongs of the yoke, to let the oppressed go free, and to break every yoke . . . to share your food with the hungry and to provide the poor wanderer with shelter" (Isa 58:6-7, NRSV). Might these scriptural citations indicate that *t. Pe'ah* 4:18 presents the notion of meritorious almsgiving in close connection with the theme of justice for the poor in Isaiah? A more likely answer is that all six scriptural texts are selected because they feature the link-root צדק.[15] The use of scrip-

---

[14] Translation from ~~Jacob Neusner, The Tosefta, Translated from the Hebrew: First Division; Zera'im~~ (Hoboken, N.J.: KTAV, 1986).

[15] צדק in Pss 85:11; 89:14; and Isa 58:8; צדיק in Isa 3:10 and Prov 11:30; and צדקה in Deut 24:13.

tural proofs is a common hermeneutical technique in the Tosefta. The proofs that justify Monobases' actions are semantically connected through the ability to explain Monobases' "charity" (צדקה).[16] It does not appear, therefore, that Monobases' citation of Isa 58:8 ("your righteousness will go before you, and the glory of the LORD will be your rear guard" [NIV]) is intended to invoke its larger Isaianic context.

The third Tannaitic text that posits a connection between care for the poor and divine reward is found in *t. Pe'ah* 4:21:

A. Said R. Eleazar b. R. Yosé, "From which [verse may we derive the fact] that charity and righteous deeds are great peace-[makers] and intercessors between [the people of] Israel and their Father in heaven?

B. "It is stated [in Scripture], *For so says the Lord: Do not enter their house of mourning, or go to lament or bemoan them. For I have taken away my peace from this people, says the Lord, [namely], my steadfast love (ḥsd) and mercy (rḥmym)* (Jer 16:5).

C. "*Steadfast love (ḥsd)*—this refers to righteous deeds (*gmylwt ḥsdym*).

D. "*Mercy (rḥmym)*—this refers to charity.

E. "[The verse thus] teaches that charity and righteous deeds are great peace-[makers] between [the people] of Israel and their Father in heaven."[17]

Here R. Eleazar inquires about a scriptural basis for the belief that "charity and righteous deeds" reconcile the people of Israel and God. The answer is given in the form of a citation of Jer 16:5, a text that links "steadfast love" (חסד), interpreted in *t. Pe'ah* 4:21 as a reference to righteous deeds, and "mercy" (רחמים), interpreted as a reference to charity. Again, there is no reference to the prophetic critique of sacrifice. Interestingly, in this passage, the peace established is between God and the corporate body of Israel, not between God and an individual benefactor, as is the case in the Monobases narrative cited above.

There is no evidence, therefore, in these early rabbinic texts that support for meritorious or atoning almsgiving is developed with reference to the

[16] On the importance of scriptural proofs in the *Tosefta*, see Bruce Chilton and Jacob Neusner, *Types of Authority in Formative Christianity and Judaism* (London: Routledge, 1999), 134–41; Marc Hirshman, *The Stabilization of Rabbinic Culture, 100 C.E.–350 C.E.: Texts on Education and Their Late Antique Context* (Oxford: Oxford University Press, 2009), 17–30; A. Gray ("Redemptive Almsgiving," 152–53) also discusses the linkage of these verses through the "root *tz-d-k*, which is implicitly interpreted throughout as referring to *tzedakah* in the sense of 'alms.'"

[17] Translation from Neusner, *Tosefta*.

so-called prophetic critique of sacrifice. Indeed, such a conclusion is hardly surprising, given that the Tannaitic literature generally recognizes the continued importance of sacrificial practices.[18] *Tosefta Rosh Hashanah* 2.9 is often cited as illustrative: "When the Temple is rebuilt, speedily in our days, these things will return to their original status."[19] In general, the early rabbinic response to the devastating destruction of the temple in 70 CE was to hope for its restoration.[20]

As the conversation between Rabban Johanan and Rabbi Joshua in *AdRNB* 8 indicates, later Jewish texts do explicitly connect the destruction of the temple—and with it the end of cultic sacrifice—with the concept of atoning almsgiving. Yet there is no evidence in the Tannaitic literature that atonement for sin through care for the poor was seen to replace or supersede atonement through sacrifice.

Patristic Literature

Turning to Christian literature of roughly the same period, there is a slightly more diverse array of perspectives. In this context, it is sufficient simply to note that appeals to the prophetic critique of sacrifice do not function in most early Christian discussions of the atoning power of almsgiving (e.g., 2 *Clem.* 16.4; *Did.* 4.5–8; *Barn.* 19.8–11; Cyprian, *Eleem.*; cf. Herm. *Sim.* 2.1–10; Clement of Alexandria, *Quis div.* 31–32). It is worth glancing at two of these texts, however, since their authors are well aware of, and explicitly appeal to, the prophetic critique of sacrifice. Yet, interestingly, neither author links this cult criticism with his discussion of atoning almsgiving. There is, however, at least one early Christian text that does draw together the idea that merciful deeds can atone for sin with the so-called prophetic critique of sacrifice, for such a connection is forged in the *Sibylline Oracles*.

The Epistle of Barnabas

The *Epistle of Barnabas* (ca. 70–132 CE) reveals a Christian author well acquainted with the so-called prophetic critique of sacrifice. Indeed, *Barnabas* offers an allegorical reading of Scripture that leads to a novel and wholly negative dismissal of animal sacrifice. In short, the author of *Barnabas*

[18] Naftali S. Cohn, *The Memory of the Temple and the Making of the Rabbis* (Divinations: Rereading Late Ancient Religion; Philadelphia: University of Pennsylvania Press, 2012).

[19] Robert Goldenberg, "Early Rabbinic Explanations of the Destruction of Jerusalem," *JJS* 33 (1982): 517–25.

[20] Klawans, *Purity, Sacrifice, and the Temple*, 211; Cohn, *Memory of the Temple*.

maintains that literal sacrifice always represented a misunderstanding, since God has never desired human offerings (2.6) or a human temple (16.1–10). In *Barnabas*, the sacrificial cult is completely rejected as a symptom of Jewish obduracy, and the treatise contains only one brief indication that Jesus' death is an offering (2.6: προσφορά) that replaces Jewish sacrifice.

At the beginning of a discussion of sacrifices and fasts, the author states, "For [the Lord] has made it clear to us through all the prophets (διὰ πάντων τῶν προφητῶν) that he needs neither sacrifices nor whole burnt offerings nor general offerings (οὔτε θυσιῶν οὔτε ὁλοκαυτωμάτων οὔτε προσφορῶν)" (2.4). This assertion is then supported by a citation of LXX Isa 1:11-13:

> What is the multitude of your sacrifices to me? says the Lord. I am full of whole burnt offerings, and I do not want the fat of lambs and the blood of bulls and goats, not even if you come to appear before me. For who demanded these things from your hands? Do not continue to trample my court. If you bring fine flour, it is in vain; incense is detestable to me; your new moons and Sabbaths I cannot stand. (*Barn.* 2.5)[21]

Interestingly, the text does not go on to cite Isa 1:16-18:

> [16]Wash yourselves; make yourselves clean; remove the evil of your doings from before my eyes; cease to do evil, [17]learn to do good; seek justice, rescue the oppressed, defend the orphan, plead for the widow. [18]Come now, let us argue it out, says the LORD: though your sins are like scarlet, they shall be like snow; though they are red like crimson, they shall become like wool. (NRSV)

Instead, there follows a statement regarding the abolishment (καταργέω) of sacrifices through the offering of the Lord Jesus Christ (2.6), and a loose paraphrase of LXX Jer 7:22-23:

> I did not command your fathers, when they were coming out of the land of Egypt, to bring whole burnt offerings and sacrifices, did I? On the contrary, this is what I commanded them: "Let none of you bear a grudge in his heart against his neighbor, and do not love a false oath." (*Barn.* 2.7–8)[22]

---

[21] Unless otherwise noted, translations of the *Epistle of Barnabas* in this chapter are from Michael W. Holmes, *The Apostolic Fathers: Greek Texts and English Translations* (3rd ed.; Grand Rapids: Baker, 2007).

[22] LXX Jer 7:22-23 reads: "For I did not speak to your fathers or command them, on the day when I led them from the land of Egypt, concerning whole burnt offerings and sacrifice. But this word I commanded them, saying: 'Hear my voice, and I will be God to

After emphasizing the importance of recognizing that God's speech is directed "to us" (ἡμῖν λέγει), the author punctuates this short catena of scriptural citations by quoting Ps 51:17 ("A sacrifice to God is a broken heart; an aroma pleasing to the Lord is a heart that glorifies its Maker") and appealing to the audience to pay careful attention to salvation, "lest the evil one should cause some error to slip into our midst and thereby hurl us away from life" (*Barn.* 2.10).

Yet while here and elsewhere *Barnabas* clearly rejects cultic sacrifice (see esp. *Barnabas* 16 on the temple), the author does not employ or integrate this critique in his advocacy of atoning almsgiving later in the document. Near the end of the letter (19.8–11), in the section of the document that reflects the so-called Two Ways Tradition (18.1–20.2) and that closely parallels material in *Didache* 1–5, the author of *Barnabas* encourages remembrance of eschatological judgment as a motivation for seeking the presence of the saints, either through working to save a life through the word or by working "with your hands for a redemption of your sins" (my translation). As verse 11 clarifies, active and cheerful giving is spurred by remembrance that God is the "good recompenser of the reward" (τίς ὁ τοῦ μισθοῦ καλὸς ἀνταποδότης [my translation]). The significant point here is that, while the author of *Barnabas* employs the so-called prophetic critique of sacrifice earlier in the epistle, his dismissal of sacrifice does not feature in the comments on atoning almsgiving in *Barnabas* 19. In the final form of the text of *Barnabas*, the prophetic critique of sacrifice in 2.4–10 is not connected to, and does not serve as a basis for, the appeal for atoning almsgiving in 19.10–11.[23]

---

you, and you will be a people to me. And you should walk in all my ways that I command you, that it may be well with you.'"

[23] This might be explained as additional evidence that *Barnabas* is a composite text, and it has often been suggested that *Barn.* 18–20 represents traditional material that has been awkwardly included by the author or even interpolated into the text by a later editorial hand. But a strong argument can be made that the "Two Ways Tradition" in the final chapters of *Barnabas* is integral to the theological aims of the letter as a whole (see chap. 8; James N. Rhodes, "The Two Ways Tradition in the Epistle of Barnabas: Revisiting an Old Question," *CBQ* 73 [2011]: 797–816). *Did.* 4.5–8 closely parallels *Barn.* 19.9–12. Unlike *Barnabas*, nowhere does the *Didache* offer criticism of Jewish sacrificial practice, although (not unlike Paul in 1 Cor 8–10) *Did.* 6.3 does reject pagan sacrifice, insisting on abstinence from meat sacrificed to idols (εἰδωλόθυτος), which "involves the worship of dead gods." I find unpersuasive Anthony Giambrone's claim that "the sacral language of 13.3–7 advances the *Didache*'s larger operation of replacing the temple cult" ("'According to the Commandment' [*Did.* 1.5]: Lexical Reflections on Almsgiving as 'The Commandment,'" *NTS* 60 [2014]: 460). Among the texts that Giambrone cites (8.1–2; 14.1–3; and 16.3–8), only 14.1–3 has any "cultic" resonance. Giambrone's equation of the prophets and the poor in *Did.* 13.3–4, with the implication that *Did.* 13.4 directs "dedicated offerings to

Cyprian

Cyprian of Carthage's *De opere et eleemosynis* (ca. 248–249) stands as a preeminent contribution to early Christian discourse about the atoning value of almsgiving, not least because it offers the first systematic discussion of the topic. At the end of an opening section in which he praises the benefactions and mercies of God and Christ, including the Lord's healing of the wounds born by Adam, Cyprian declares that divine love has come to assist frail humans a second time, following baptism, "so that whatever uncleanliness we afterwards contract [that is, after baptism] we may wash away with corporal acts of mercy [*eleemosynis*] (*Eleem.* 1.20–21)." In the next section, Cyprian expands this last assertion by introducing the main thesis of the treatise with reference to three scriptural passages that support his claim. First, in citing a version of LXX Prov 15:27 ("By alms and faith sins are purged away"), Cyprian clarifies that this text does not refer to pre-baptismal sins, which are "cleansed by the blood and sanctification of Christ" (*Eleem.* 2.3–4). Second, Cyprian quotes Sir 3:30 ("As water will quench fire, so alms will quench sin") in order to demonstrate and prove (*ostenditur et probatur*) that the flame of post-baptismal sin is extinguished by *eleemosyna* (*Eleem.* 2.4–8). Although remission of sins is granted only once in baptism, the continual observance of *eleemosyna* imitates baptism in bestowing afresh the indulgence (*indulgentiam*) of God (*Eleem.* 2.9–11). The third scriptural text, from Luke 11:40-41 ("He that made that which is within made also that which is without. But give alms, and behold all things are clean unto you"), seems to indicate how exactly almsgiving is related to baptism: since Jesus speaks of giving alms as an activity that makes things clean for the donor (*vobis munda [sunt] omina*), both practices have to do with washing and cleaning (*Eleem.* 2.12–22).

Building upon this opening biblical exposition, Cyprian's treatise goes on to develop a number of exegetical arguments to advance his claim

---

the hands of beggars," is quite an overreach. Moreover, the term θυσία is used positively in 14.1–3 to describe the activities of a Christian communal meal that takes place on "the Lord's day of the Lord" (κατὰ κυριακὴν δὲ κυρίου). The term θυσία in this context appears to serve as a metaphorical extension of sacrificial language to a Christian communal meal. The citation of Mal 1:11, 14 at the conclusion of this brief passage (14.3) roots the presentation of this Christian θυσία in a *positive* assessment of the role of Jewish sacrifice. There is no explicit connection, however, between the sacrificial language of *Did.* 14 and Jesus' death. Indeed, the Christian θυσία does not appear to remove sins, since confession of sins happens first, "so that your sacrifice may be pure" (ὅπως καθαρὰ ἡ θυσία ὑμῶν ᾖ). See Jonathan A. Draper, "Pure Sacrifice in Didache 14 as Jewish Christian Exegesis," *Neot* 42 (2008): 223–52; Benoît Grimonprez-Damm, "Le 'sacrifice' eucharistique dans la Didachè," *RevScRel* 64 (1990): 9–25.

regarding the atoning power of almsgiving. Indeed, Cyprian's engagement with Scripture is quite extensive.[24] Yet nowhere in the work does Cyprian cite or allude to texts from the corpus of the "prophetic critique of sacrifice." This absence is striking not only because of the frequency with which Cyprian cites scriptural texts throughout the document but also because in several places Cyprian indicates the superiority of almsgiving to the practices of prayer and fasting (so also 2 Clem. 16).[25]

That Cyprian does not in *Eleem.* state the superiority of almsgiving to *sacrifice* is all the more notable because Cyprian was well aware of the prophetic critique of sacrifice by the time *De opere et eleemosynis* was written, likely shortly after Cyprian's election as bishop of Carthage in 248 and just before the outbreak of persecution under Decius in the winter of 249–250.[26] In *Test.* 1.16, an earlier collection of scriptural proof-texts, Cyprian provides a section entitled *Quod sacrificium vetus evacuaretur et novum celebraretur* ("That Old Sacrifices Should Be Voided and New Ones Celebrated") in which he quotes Isa 1:11-12; Pss 50:13-14, 23; 4:5; and Mal 1:10-11 in order to demonstrate from Old Testament proofs the end of animal sacrifice.[27] Such a position is reflected in Cyprian's letters as well. In *Ep.* 76.3, for example, Cyprian suggests that priests should not lament the fact that they no longer offer and celebrate divine sacrifices, noting that the sacred Scripture declares "the sacrifice of God is a broken spirit; God does not despise a contrite and humbled heart" (Ps 51:17; cf. *Ep.* 80.2; *Mort.* 11).

Although the language and concept of sacrifice is absent from *Eleem.*, Cyprian regularly refers to the practice of *sacrificium* elsewhere in his extant

---

[24] Based on the text of Edward V. Rebenack, I count forty-two distinct direct quotations (nineteen from the OT/Apocrypha and twenty-three from the NT) in 529 lines of the Latin text. Rebenack, *Thasci Caecili Cypriani: De opere et eleemosynis; A Translation with an Introduction and a Commentary* (Patristic Studies 94; Washington, D.C.: Catholic University of America Press, 1962). The text and translation of *Eleem.* used here and elsewhere is from Rebenack.

[25] "For neither will he be able to merit the mercy of God, who has not himself been merciful, nor will he obtain anything from God's love through prayers, who has not been humane to the prayer of the poor" (*Eleem.* 5.7–9). Also, in citing Tob 12:8-9 ("Prayer is good with fasting and alms, for alms delivereth from death, and the same purgeth away sins"), Cyprian writes, "[Tobit] shows that our prayers and fasts have less efficacy, if they are not aided by corporal works of mercy, that our prayers alone are of little avail for obtaining our petitions, if they are not accompanied by an abundance of deeds and corporal works of mercy" (*Eleem.* 5.22–24).

[26] See chap. 9 for a discussion of the dating of this document.

[27] In *Eleem.* 5, Cyprian cites Ps 40:2, yet without any reference to vv. 5-6 ("Sacrifice and offering you do not desire, but you have given me an open ear. Burnt offering and sin offering you have not required" [NRSV]).

literary corpus, and these references reflect a wide range of usage, including martyrdom as a sacrifice (*Ep.* 8, 80), liturgy as a sacrifice (*Ep.* 15, 33, 36, 53), the Eucharist as a sacrifice (*Ep.* 62, 65, 67, 71, 74, 75; *Dom. or.* 4, 33), and, less commonly than one might think, Christ's death as a sacrifice (*Unit. eccl.* 17). Given the number of Cyprian's writings devoted to the laxist controversy, it is not surprising that the bishop most frequently employs the language of sacrifice to refer to the actions of the *sacrificati* and the *turificati* (i.e., "those who offered incense") during the Decian persecution. Thus, while the language of sacrifice can be used positively (i.e., when applied to martyrdom, the Eucharist, or the death of Christ) or negatively (i.e., when applied to those who made the sacrifice to the imperial cult) in Cyprian's writings, it does not feature in Cyprian's lengthy discourse on atoning almsgiving, and he never connects the tradition of Old Testament criticism of sacrifice (which was familiar to him) with his advocacy of atoning almsgiving.

In the absence of evidence, it is not easy to explain why a connection between the prophetic critique of sacrifice and atoning almsgiving was not made by the author of *Barnabas* and Cyprian. Both writers cite and make use of the prophetic critique of sacrifice when insisting that literal sacrifice has been replaced by the sacrifice/offering of Christ. Yet neither *Barnabas* nor Cyprian appeals to this scriptural tradition in their promotion of the atoning value of concern for the poor.[28] It appears as if establishing a connection would suit the rhetorical and theological aims of *Barnabas* and Cyprian, yet the link is simply not there. The lack of any explicit connection between cult criticism and atoning almsgiving should caution against assuming a simple equation when discussing the reception history of biblical traditions. Even if it seems that (a) prophetic criticism of priestly sacrifice (a practice that served, of course, to remove impurity and sin) plus (b) prophetic exhortations for justice instead of sacrifice *should equal* (c) the idea that sins can be remitted by showing justice to or caring for the poor, (c) without (a) or (b) is the solution to an equation that does not exist.

---

[28] With regard to a text like the *Didache*, one might argue that the tradition of prophetic critique was simply unknown to the author(s). It is possible that this lack of awareness might also explain the lack of connection between atoning almsgiving and the prophetic critique of sacrifice in *2 Clement*, a document to be discussed in chapters 7 and 8. But given that *2 Clement* is ostensibly a homily on Isa 54—with numerous citations of and allusions to the OT throughout the document, including Isaiah, Jeremiah, Ezekiel, and Malachi—it would be hard to imagine that the author was unaware of the tradition of cult criticism (2.1: Isa 54:1; 3.5: Isa 29:13; 6.8: Ezek 14:14-20; 7.6: Isa 66:24; 14.1: Jer 7:11; 14.2: Gen 1:27; 15.3: Isa 58:9; 16.3: Mal 4:1 and Isa 34:4; 17.5: Isa 66:18, 24; cf. 8.2: Jer 18:1-6; 17.4: Isa 66:18).

Sibylline Oracle 2

It should not be inferred, however, that a connection between prophetic criticism of sacrifice and atoning almsgiving is never forged among early Christian proponents of the atoning efficacy of merciful deeds, for just such a link
is found in book two of the *Sibylline Oracles*:

> 78 Give to the poor at once and do not tell them to come tomorrow.
> 79 With perspiring hand give a portion of corn to one who is in need.[29]
> 80 Whoever gives on account of merciful practice (ὃς δ' ἐλεημοσύνην
> παρέχει) knows that he is lending to God.[30]
> 81 Mercy saves from death (ῥύεται ἐκ θανάτου ἔλεος) when judgment
> comes.
> 82 God wants not sacrifice but mercy (ἔλεος) instead of sacrifice.
> 83 Therefore clothe the naked. Give the hungry a share of your bread.[31]
> 84 Receive the homeless into your house and lead the blind.
> 85 Pity the shipwrecked, for the voyage is uncertain.
> 86 Give a hand to one who has fallen. Save a solitary man.
> 87 All have a common lot, the wheel of life, unstable prosperity.
> 88 If you have wealth, stretch out your hand to the poor.[32]
> 89 The things which God gave you, give of them to one in need.[33]

Here the injunction to "give to the poor" is supported by allusions to both
LXX Prov 19:17 and 10:2:

> *Sib. Or.* (2.80): ὃς δ' ἐλεημοσύνην παρέχει, θεῷ οἶδε δανείζειν.

> Whoever gives on account of merciful practice knows that he is lending
> to God.

> LXX Prov (19:17): δανίζει θεῷ ὁ ἐλεῶν πτωχόν, κατὰ δὲ τὸ δόμα αὐτοῦ
> ἀνταποδώσει αὐτῷ.

---

[29] See *Did.* 1.6.

[30] I have translated the idiomatic phrase ὃς δ' ἐλεημοσύνην παρέχει in a way that
acknowledges the prepositional phrase and maintains the semantic connection between
ἐλεημοσύνη and ἔλεος.

[31] Lines 79–83 and 91–95 are often printed in parentheses, indicating that the
material in these verses represents an addition to the material from the *Sentences of
Pseudo-Phocylides* that comprises much of the text of *Sib. Or.* 2.56–148. I have not included
brackets, however.

[32] Cf. *Barn.* 19.9; *Did.* 4.5.

[33] The translation is slightly amended from James H. Charlesworth, ed., *The Old
Testament Pseudepigrapha*, Vol. 1: *Apocalyptic Literature & Testaments* (New York: Dou-
bleday, 1983); cf. J. L. Lightfoot, *The Sibylline Oracles: With Introduction, Translation, and
Commentary on the First and Second Books* (Oxford: Oxford University Press, 2007).

One who acts mercifully to a poor person lends to God, and he will recompense him according to his gift.

Sib. Or. (2.81): ῥύεται ἐκ θανάτου ἔλεος, κρίσις ὁππόταν ἔλθῃ.

Mercy saves from death when judgment comes.

LXX Prov (10:2): οὐκ ὠφελήσουσιν θησαυροὶ ἀνόμους, δικαιοσύνη δὲ ῥύσεται ἐκ θανάτου.

Treasures will not profit the lawless, but righteousness will deliver from death.[34]

What qualifies Sib. Or. 2.80–81 as atoning almsgiving is that the literary context indicates that mercy here entails the provision of material assistance to those in need: the imperative δίδου ("give") in verse 78 stands at the head of this section; the object of the imperative παράσχου in verse 79 is "grain" (στάχυς); and verses 83 to 86 flesh out the nature of ἐλεημοσύνη/ἔλεος in material terms. What qualifies Sib. Or. 2.80–81 as atoning almsgiving is the statement that mercy saves from death when judgment comes (κρίσις ὁππόταν ἔλθῃ). Here the saying from Prov 10:2 (or possibly Tob 4:10) is located in a decidedly eschatological context, with rescue from "death" in the context of Sib. Or. 2 representing salvation at the time of the final judgment (2.6–55, 149–338), rescue that includes deliverance from fiery destruction (2.196–213), resurrection from the dead (2.221–51), and life immortal in a utopian world (2.313–38). Indeed, the moral instruction adapted from Pseudo-Phocylides in 2.56–148 is bracketed by the scene of a heavenly contest for "the immortal prizes of most noble victory" (2.42–43). The introduction of the scene (2.39–55) imagines God granting "rich gifts and eternal hope" to martyrs, virgins, those who perform justice, those who live in piety and acknowledge the one God, and those faithful in marriage; and the conclusion (2.149–53) depicts the righteous passing through the gate of life as they gain entry to immortality:

149 This is the contest, these are the prizes, these the awards.
150 This is the gate of life and entry to immorality
151 which the heavenly God appointed as reward of victory
152 for most righteous men. But they, when they receive
153 the crown, will pass through this in glory.

---

[34] Since that which rescues from death in Sib. Or. 2.81 is ἔλεος and not δικαιοσύνη as in Prov 10:2, it may well be the case that the allusion is actually to Tob 4:10: διότι ἐλεημοσύνη ἐκ θανάτου ῥύεται.

In this sense, the term "salvific almsgiving" might be a more appropriate descriptor of the benefits of merciful care for the poor in *Sib. Or.* 2. The righteous receive rewards, including entry into the gate of life and entry to immortality.

It is in *Sib. Or.* 2.82, moreover, that there is a connection between atoning almsgiving and the prophetic critique of sacrifice, for the Sibyl cites Hos 6:6: "God wants not sacrifice but mercy (ἔλεος) instead of sacrifice."[35] Interestingly, the rejection of sacrifice is made emphatic by the repetition of the noun θυσία (or θυσίη) at the beginning and end of the statement, negated in the first instance by the negative adverb οὐ and in the second by the preposition ἀντί: οὐ θυσίην, ἔλεος δὲ θέλει θεὸς ἀντὶ θυσίης.[36] That the allusion to Hos 6:6 is part of material in this section (in vv. 79–83) that has been added to a longer extract from Pseudo-Phocyclides in 2.56–148 is clearly evidence of redaction of traditional material, although it is impossible to tell if this insertion belongs to the hand responsible for the earliest Hellenistic-Jewish form of book two or if it should be included as part of later Christian editing of the *Sibylline Oracles*, particularly given the importance that Hos 6:6 assumed in patristic interpretation of the Old Testament.[37] This point is precisely why it is very difficult, if not impossible, to assess the role, if any, that *Sib. Or.* 2.78–89 might have played in the emerging doctrine of atoning almsgiving. Partly because *Sib. Or.* 2 is never clearly cited by the church fathers—and only directly referenced for the first time in the late fifth-century or early sixth-century pagan testimonia collection called *Theosophy*—a precise date for the document is unattainable. Various proposals have suggested that perhaps an original Jewish oracle (comprising both *Sib. Or.* 1 and 2) was completed before the destruction of the Jerusalem temple in 70 CE and that this Jewish text was later subjected to Christian redaction, perhaps around the

---

[35] Gianfrancesco Lusini, "La citation d'Osée 6:6 dans les Oracles Sibyllins," in *"Car c'est l'amour qui me plaît, non le sacrifice": Recherches sur Osée 6:6 et son interprétation juive et chrétienne* (ed. E. Bons; JSJSup 88; Leiden: Brill, 2004), 43–55.

[36] Cf. LXX Hos 6:6: διότι ἔλεος θέλω καὶ οὐ θυσίαν καὶ ἐπίγνωσιν θεοῦ ἢ ὁλοκαυτώματα.

[37] See Maria Cristina Pennacchio, "L'interprétation patristique d'Osée 6:6," in *"Car c'est l'amour qui me plaît, non le sacrifice": Recherches sur Osée 6:6 et son interprétation juive et chrétienne* (ed. E. Bons; JSJSup 88; Leiden: Brill, 2004), 147–78. The issue of the relationship between *Sib. Or.* 2.78–89 (as a section of 2.56–148) and Pseudo-Phocyclides is considered extensively in Lusini, "La citation d'Osée 6:6." It is possible that both Tertullian (*Marc.* 4.27) and Clement of Alexandria (*Strom.* 4.6) interpret Hos 6:6 in ways that parallel its use in *Sib. Or.* 2.81.

middle of the second century CE.[38] But it is also possible that books one and two of the *Sibylline Oracles* should be understood as an originally Christian composition, possibly in response to the material in book three, and not as a Christian redaction of a Jewish source text.[39] Either way, a date for the Christian form of books one and two—whether redacted or an original composition—could seemingly be located anywhere from the middle of the second century to the fourth century (or possibly later), making it impossible to know how precisely to locate this text, with its combination of the themes of atoning almsgiving and the prophetic critique of sacrifice, in the development of atoning almsgiving in the Christian tradition.

It cannot be said that the *Sibylline Oracles* exerted any significant influence on the emergence of the early Christian concept of atoning almsgiving. Not only do the *Sibylline Oracles* likely postdate the most significant nascent Christian advocates of the atoning value of almsgiving in the second and third centuries CE, but the *Sibyllines* themselves do not appear to have been widely known, read, or cited. The most influential literary voices that shaped Christian discourse about the relationship between care for the poor and the alleviation of sin were scriptural ones, including Th Dan 4:27, LXX Prov 15:27, Tob 12:8-10, and Sir 3:30. Yet scriptural influence on the emergence of this tradition is not limited to the Greek translation of Hebrew Scriptures and apocryphal texts, for the writings of the New Testament played an important role, too, as the next three chapters will show.

[38] This is the view of J. J. Collins in Charlesworth, *Old Testament Pseudepigrapha*, 322. Collins' position on a mid-second-century date for the document is supplemented, but not radically altered, by Lightfoot, although Lightfoot argues that *Sib. Or.*1–2 originated as a Christian interpretation of *Sib. Or. 3*. Lightfoot, *Sibylline Oracles*.

[39] So Lightfoot, *Sibylline Oracles*.

CHAPTER 4

GIVE ALMS WITH RESPECT TO THE THINGS WITHIN

Charity and Reward in the Synoptic Gospels and Acts

Given the strong connection between caring for the poor and divine recompense in numerous Jewish scriptural and apocryphal texts, it might seem likely that these traditions would have shaped reflection on the relationship between charity and reward in the New Testament. Yet at least one strand of New Testament interpretation would aim to sever any association between material care of the needy and recompense in the earliest forms of the Jesus movement. Rudolf Bultmann, for example, perhaps the premier European New Testament interpreter in the twentieth century, infamously interpreted Jesus' understanding of the demand of God as a protest against Jewish legalism. Bultmann's signal complaint against "Jewish legalism" was that this form of piety, which "endeavors to win God's favor by the toil of minutely fulfilling the Law's obligations," offers a defective motivation for ethical behavior.[1] Any system in which ethical behavior is motivated by the expectation of reward or punishment or compelled by a formal, unquestioning obedience fails to live up to the radical, genuine obedience characteristic of Jesus' proclamation of the kingdom of God. As Bultmann opines:

---

[1] Rudolf Bultmann, *Theology of the New Testament* (2 vols.; trans. Kendrick Grobel; New York: Scribner's, 1951, 1955; repr. 2 vols. in 1; Waco, Tex.: Baylor University Press, 2007), 1:11.

In principle, when a man's duties are conceived of as the committing or omitting of specific acts under legal requirement, he can completely discharge them and have room left over for extra deeds of merit. So there developed in Judaism the notion of "good works" that go beyond the required fulfillment of the Law (such as almsgiving, various acts of charity, voluntary fasting, and the like) establishing literal merits and hence capable of atoning for transgressions of the Law. This indicates that here the idea of obedience is not taken radically.[2]

At the heart of ~~Bultmann~~'s pejorative assessment of "Jewish legalism," including the "good work" of almsgiving, stands his ~~Kantian impulse to reject the idea that rightly oriented ethical behavior can be motivated by the promise of reward or punishment~~. While Bultmann's derogatory and inaccurate assessment of Jewish religion has long been queried and, from the perspective of many, rightly been put to rest, numerous treatments of New Testament ethics still echo the notion that deeds exhorted or performed on the basis of external motivation, such as the procurement of present or heavenly reward, lead down the path toward legalism.[3] But is such a sentiment supported by the writings of the New Testament themselves, particularly regarding the relationship between charity and recompense? An examination of this issue in the Synoptic Gospels and Acts will highlight ample evidence of meritorious almsgiving in these canonical texts: providing material assistance to the needy is a means of accumulating some reward for the donor, recompense usually, but not always, imaged as eschatological or heavenly reward.[4] The

[2] Bultmann, *Theology of the New Testament*, 1:12.

[3] One influential and pointed critique of Bultmann's view of "Jewish legalism" is found in E. P. Sanders, *Paul and Palestinian Judaism: A Comparison of Patterns of Religion* (Philadelphia: Fortress, 1977), 44–47; cf. Anders Gerdmar, *Roots of Theological Anti-Semitism: German Biblical Interpretation and the Jews, from Herder and Semler to Kittel and Bultmann* (SJHC 20; Leiden: Brill, 2009), 385–90. For an early response to Bultmann's rejection of reward as a motivation for ethics, see Paul S. Minear, *And Great Shall Be Your Reward: The Origins of Christian Views of Salvation* (YSR 12; New Haven: Yale University Press, 1941).

[4] This chapter will focus on the Synoptic Gospels and Acts. The Gospel of John certainly anticipates the blessing of resurrection on the last day for those who believe in the Son of God (5:25, 28-29; 6:39-40, 44, 54; 11:24-26; 14:19), and John 5:28-29 promises "the resurrection of life" to those who have done good things and "the resurrection of judgment" to those who have done evil things; see Marianne Meye Thompson, *The God of the Gospel of John* (Grand Rapids: Eerdmans, 2001), 80–87; Tim O'Donnell, "Complementary Eschatologies in John 5:19-30," *CBQ* 70 (2008): 750–65. But nowhere in the Fourth Gospel is divine or eschatological recompense specifically connected to practices of charity. Given how little John's Gospel dwells on issues of wealth and poverty in comparison with the Synoptics, the absence of any thematic connection in the Gospel of John between

New Testament writings, moreover, appear also to have planted seeds that would, in the second and third centuries, flower into the early Christian concept of atoning almsgiving.

The Gospel of Mark

In comparison with Matthew and Luke, its synoptic successors, the Gospel of Mark has relatively less material related to the relationship between charity and reward. Two texts in Mark's Gospel do, however, connect the provision of material assistance with recompense, and both passages shape the development of this motif in Matthew and Luke.

Mark 9:41-50

Following the first two passion predictions in the Gospel of Mark (8:31-33 and 9:30-32), Mark 9:41-50 offers a short discourse on eschatological reward and loss at the final judgment.[5] This pericope is set within the framework of a larger section (8:22–10:52) in which Jesus teaches the twelve disciples and

---

merciful practice on behalf of the needy and eschatological reward is unsurprising. On the other hand, 1 John 3:14 insists that those who have passed from death to life can be confident of this reality because of their mutual love: "We know that we have passed from death to life because (ὅτι) we love the brothers and sisters. Whoever does not love abides in death" (1 John 3:14). In the context of this letter, "love" is defined, at least in part, by the person who has material possessions who sees and helps a brother or sister in need (1 John 3:17-18; cf. 3 John 5–8).

[5] Many interpreters link 9:41 with the preceding vignette in 9:38-40, an account that relates the observation by one of Jesus' disciples, John, son of Zebedee, that someone unaffiliated with Jesus' close circle of followers was observed casting out demons in Jesus' name. John states, "We forbade him, because he was not following us" (9:38b). This report prompts Jesus to reply that such a person should not be stopped, "for no one who does a deed of power in my name will be able soon afterward to speak evil of me. Whoever is not against us is for us" (9:39b-40, NRSV). Although v. 41 shares with vv. 38-39 the concept of performing an action in Jesus' name, I follow Joel Marcus in viewing v. 41 as the first statement in the ensuing discourse about eschatological reward and loss in 9:41-50 (Marcus, *Mark 8–16: A New Translation with Introduction and Commentary* [AB 27A; New Haven: Yale University Press, 2009], 688.). As Marcus observes, the saying about giving a cup of water to someone who bears the name of Christ in v. 41 is thematically unrelated to vv. 38-40, a point that has led to much speculation about the redactional history of v. 41 (see, e.g., the discussion in Adela Yarbro Collins, *Mark: A Commentary* [Hermeneia; Minneapolis: Fortress, 2007], 449). Conversely, if μισθός in v. 41 is understood as eschatological reward, then this statement makes good sense as an introduction to the material that follows, particularly as the phrase Ὃς γὰρ ἂν in v. 41 is followed by ὃς ἂν in v. 42 and καὶ ἐὰν in vv. 43, 45, and 47.

others about the true nature and cost of discipleship.[6] The unit in 9:41-50
begins with a statement that promises a reward (μισθός) to the person who
provides water to followers of Jesus: "For whoever gives you a cup of water
to drink because you bear the name of Christ, truly I say to you that such a
person will certainly not lose his or her reward" (9:41).

The precise nature of this reward is unclear, although the subsequent
warnings about eternal punishment in verses 42 to 48 strongly suggest that
the reward in verse 41 is eschatological recompense at the final judgment,
which is also how the term μισθός frequently features elsewhere in the New
Testament (Matt 5:12//Luke 6:23; Luke 6:35; 1 Cor 3:8-15; 9:17-18; Rev
11:18; 22:12; cf. 2 Pet 2:13-15).[7] For this reason, and especially if verse 41
is understood as the opening declaration of a new unit about eschatological
reward and loss, those who receive an eschatological reward for provisioning
Jesus' followers are to be understood as fellow disciples and not outsiders
unaffiliated with the Christ-believing community. The saying about offering
a drink of water may have originated in a missionary setting in which Jesus'
earliest disciples required material assistance on their journeys to proclaim
repentance and the kingdom of God (so Mark 6:6b-13; Matt 10:1-15; Luke
9:1-6; 10:1-16). Yet, in the context of Mark's Gospel, the identity of those
who "bear the name of Christ" (v. 41) includes a wider circle than the Twelve,
as is clear in Jesus' statement, "Whoever welcomes one such child in my name
welcomes me" (9:37).[8] Thus, Jesus promises eschatological reward to those
who meet the material needs of fellow followers of Jesus by providing water
to thirsty disciples (9:41). This passage reflects the concerns of a community
marked by the provision of mutual assistance.

Mark 10:17-31

If the saying in Mark 9:41 establishes an explicit yet imprecise link between
charity and reward, then the story of Jesus' conversation with a wealthy
inquisitor (Mark 10:17-22), followed by Jesus' discussion of this episode with
the disciples and Peter (10:23-31), offers a richer account of the relationship
between almsgiving and its return in this world and the next. Coming like

---

[6] Richard A. Horsley, *Hearing the Whole Story: The Politics of Plot in Mark's Gospel*
(Louisville, Ky.: Westminster John Knox, 2001), 79–97. Horsely's perceptive analysis of
the motif of the failure of the disciples in this section and elsewhere in Mark's Gospel does
not mitigate the point that the theme of much of Jesus' teaching in Mark 8:27–10:52 is
discipleship.

[7] Marcus, *Mark 8–16*, 688.

[8] So also Mark 13:13: "You will be hated by all people on account of my name" (διὰ
τὸ ὄνομά μου; cf. 16:17).

the preceding discourse in 9:41-50 in the context of the larger unit on discipleship in Mark 8:22–10:52, the story of Jesus' encounter with the rich man narrates the difficulty of accepting Jesus' teachings for one with many possessions.

In this well-known passage, a man approaches Jesus, kneels before him (perhaps adopting a posture of reverent inquiry), and asks, "Good Teacher, what must I do to inherit eternal life?" (v. 17). Jesus immediately eschews the label "good," insisting that "no one is good but God alone" (v. 18). Jesus then reminds his interlocutor of the man's knowledge of the second table of the Ten Commandments, which covers stipulations that govern social relations within the covenant community: "You know the commandments: 'You shall not murder. You shall not commit adultery. You shall not steal. You shall not bear false witness. You shall not defraud. Honor your father and mother'" (v. 19). Jesus' conversation partner answers by expressing his faithfulness in keeping these commandments since his youth (v. 20), a response that prompts Jesus, while looking at him, to love him and say, "You lack one thing: go, sell whatever you have, and give to the poor, and you will have a treasure in heaven; and then come, follow me" (v. 21). The encounter concludes with the narrator's observation that, upon hearing Jesus' statement, the man became sullen (ὁ στυγνάσας) and departed while grieving (λυπούμενος), "for he had many possessions" (v. 22).

At the conclusion of this encounter, the rich man's own narrative is open rather than closed, for the text does not specify whether he obeyed or disregarded Jesus' directives. The ambiguity of the text is often glossed over by a modern interpretative history of this passage that simply assumes the man's failure to become a follower of Jesus.[9] There is obviously some connection between the man's departure and his material prosperity: he leaves shocked and grieving because he has many possessions.[10] Yet the man's dour and grieved parting from Jesus need not indicate a refusal to heed Jesus' charge, although that certainly could be the case. The man's downcast reaction could just as well signal his awareness of the difficult cost of following Jesus, a price to be paid in the hard choice that he will make to sell his possessions, give to the poor, and become a disciple of Jesus. Or the man's sadness could reflect grief over the fact that he had previously devoted his life to the increase of his possessions, perhaps without understanding until his meeting with

---

[9] See the excellent discussion in Andrew D. Clarke, "'Do Not Judge Who Is Worthy and Unworthy': Clement's Warning Not to Speculate about the Rich Young Man's Response (Mark 10.17-31)," *JSNT* 31 (2009): 447–68. The same point is true of this pericope's synoptic parallels in Matt 19:16-22 and Luke 18:18-25.

[10] The γάρ in v. 22b is causal.

Jesus the cost to others of his accumulation, or perhaps without recognizing that he could have been acquiring heavenly treasure through almsgiving instead of earthly goods. The point is that none of this is stated in the text of Mark's Gospel (or in its synoptic parallels). Interpreters, therefore, should be careful not to assume or impose upon the text any specific closure to this man's narrative.

If Mark's Gospel is silent regarding the man's ultimate response to Jesus' command (v. 21), neither is there any clear indication of what the man was lacking, according to Jesus' diagnosis. Have the man's possessions blinded him to the fact that, in spite of his confident assertion of obedience, he has not actually fulfilled the commandments of the second table of the Decalogue? Perhaps his accumulation of possessions has come as the result of social injustice, due either to the man's own nefarious practices or to larger socioeconomic structures that produced unjust wealth disparity.[11] Or has the man dutifully observed the second table of the Ten Commandments but neglected the first by loving his possessions more than God?[12] Again, the text does not say what precisely the man lacked, a fact that also merits interpretive caution. Whatever the reason for the man's lack, Jesus' command offers an antidote that articulates a close relationship between almsgiving and heavenly reward. Jesus tells the man to do three things: go (ὕπαγε),[13] sell

---

[11] Interestingly, in Origen's commentary on the Gospel of Matthew, there is added (perhaps by the Latin translator of the work) a citation of the so-called *Gospel of the Nazarenes* that identifies the man's mistreatment of the destitute as evidence that invalidates his claim to have fulfilled the law and the prophets: "And the Lord said to him: How canst thou say, I have fulfilled the law and the prophets? For it stands written in the law: Love thy neighbor as thyself; and behold, many of thy brethren, sons of Abraham, are begrimed with dirt and die of hunger—and thy house is full of many good things and nothing at all comes forth from it to them! And he turned and said to Simon, his disciple, who was sitting by him: Simon, son of Jona, it is easier for a camel to go through the eye of a needle than for a rich man to enter the kingdom of heaven" (Origen, *Comm. Matt.* XV 14 on 19:16ff.; translation from Wilhelm Schneemelcher, ed., *New Testament Apocrypha*, vol. 1, *Gospels and Related Writings* [rev. ed.; trans. and ed. by R. McL. Wilson; Louisville, Ky.: Westminster John Knox, 1991], 161); see Albertus Frederik Johannes Klijn, "Question of the Rich Young Man in a Jewish-Christian Gospel," *NovT* 8 (1966): 149–55. For an illuminating discussion of the ways in which the social contexts of readers shape answers to the question of the man's lack in the Matthean version of the story, see Gerald O. West, *The Academy of the Poor: Towards a Dialogical Reading of the Bible* (Pietermaritzburg: Cluster, 2003), 1–13.

[12] Robert H. Stein, *Mark* (BECNT; Grand Rapids: Baker, 2008), 470.

[13] As Clarke observes, the man's departure in v. 22 (ἀπῆλθεν) could well be interpreted as a fulfillment of this very command to "go": "Not to have departed would have amounted to disobedience. Indeed, it is only by *going away* that the rich man would be able

whatever he has (ὅσα ἔχεις πώλησον), and give to the poor (δὸς τοῖς πτωχοῖς).[14] Jesus' instruction for the man to divest all his goods is an indication that Jesus is asking him for a radical commitment to discipleship.[15] But Jesus also invites his interlocutor into an exchange relationship in which the man is promised a return on his charitable investment.

The reward that Jesus promises the man for obedience to these imperatives is the possession of "treasure in heaven" (v. 21). This is the first instance of the language of heavenly treasure in the synoptic tradition; aside from specific parallels to this story (Matt 19:21//Luke 18:22), the image is employed elsewhere in both Matthew (6:19-21) and Luke (12:33-34). It is often suggested that in the Synoptic Gospels the concept of charity as a means of accumulating heavenly treasure reflects the influence of Second Temple Jewish texts such as Tobit (4:9) and Sirach (29:11) in which merciful acts are imaged as storing up treasure.[16] A detailed consideration of this point must await an examination of the language of heavenly treasure elsewhere in the synoptic tradition, but here it should be observed that in Mark 10:21 Jesus promises the man not merely future reward (perhaps from other humans) for his dispossession of goods but heavenly reward. The phrase "you will have treasure in heaven" (ἕξεις θησαυρὸν ἐν οὐρανῷ) should be interpreted both spatially and temporally. In Mark's narrative, "heaven" or "the heavens" is not a designation for the ultimate eschatological resting place of followers of Jesus but rather describes the present abode of God (6:41; 7:34; 8:11; 11:25, 30-31; 14:62) and other cosmic figures (12:25; 13:25, 32).[17] Thus, the tearing apart of the heavens in Mark 1:9-11 (cf. 15:38-39) signals God's invasive action of eliminating the barrier between God and creation, and Jesus can affirm in Mark 13:31 that "heaven and earth will pass away, but my words will not

---

to sell and give, and eventually reach the point of *following*" ("Do Not Judge," 462 [emphasis in original]).

[14] The definite article τοῖς is omitted in many early textual witnesses (A, B, W, Ψ, Clement of Alexandria).

[15] On the relationship of this passage to the larger theme of discipleship in Mark's Gospel, see Sondra Ely Wheeler, *Wealth as Peril and Obligation: The New Testament on Possessions* (Grand Rapids: Eerdmans, 1995), 39–56. The final command does not necessarily state that all the proceeds from the man's divestment of all his possessions should be given to the poor, for in that case the text would read something like δὸς ὅσα ἔχεις τοῖς πτωχοῖς. Does this mean that only a certain percentage of the funds from the man's sale of his possessions was to be directed to the destitute? Unfortunately, the text is unclear.

[16] As observed in chapter 3, however, neither Tobit nor Sirach views the storing up of treasure as "heavenly" or eschatological.

[17] The noun οὐρανός in the Second Gospel also denotes "the portion or portions of the universe gener. distinguished from planet earth" (BDAG 5437)—i.e., the sky (4:32; 13:27).

pass away."[18] For Jesus to avow, then, that upon selling his goods and giving to the poor the man will have "treasure in heaven" is to suggest that the man will have a reward with the God who is in heaven. At the same time, although the issue is not developed in detail, it would seem that temporally this divine reward will be obtained at the final judgment, even if it is secured after the man's divestiture in the present, a point suggested both by the previous discourse about eschatological reward and loss in 9:41-50 and by the fact that Jesus' conversation with his interlocutor begins with the man's question about inheriting eternal life (10:17).

After the rich man's departure, Jesus looks to his disciples and opines, "How hard it will be for those who have wealth to enter the kingdom of God!" (10:23). In response to the disciples' perplexity at this statement, Jesus reiterates his observation with the evocative comparison that "it is easier for a camel to go through the eye of a needle than for a rich person to enter the kingdom of God" (10:25), an image that has long been interpreted as an indication that wealth itself disqualifies one from eternal salvation.[19]

This leads the astonished disciples to ask, "Who then can be saved?" To this question, Jesus responds with the axiom, "With human beings it is impossible, but not with God; for all things are possible with God" (10:26-27). At this point, Peter interjects, "Look, we have left everything and have followed you" (10:28). Peter's observation shifts the focus from Jesus' command to the rich man to sell everything and give to the poor to the issue of renunciation, for Peter does not specify that his and others' dispossession resulted in any particular beneficence to the needy.

Nevertheless, Jesus offers a response to Peter's remark that connects abandonment of possessions and family with both this-worldly return and eschatological reward:

[18] On Mark 1:9-11, see Donald H. Juel, *The Gospel of Mark* (Interpreting Biblical Texts; Nashville: Abingdon, 1999), 60–63.

[19] Such an interpretation is ostensibly the one countered in Clement of Alexandria's *Quis div.* 2: "For some, after merely listening in an off-hand way to the Lord's saying, that a camel shall more easily creep through a needle's eye than a rich man into the kingdom of heaven, despair of themselves, feeling that they are not destined to obtain life. So, complying with the world in everything, and clinging to this present life as the only one left to them, they depart further from the heavenward way, taking no more trouble to ask who are the rich men that the Master and Teacher is addressing nor how that which is impossible becomes possible" (trans. Butterworth, LCL). For insightful analysis on the later history of engagement with this passage, see Peter Brown, *Through the Eye of a Needle: Wealth, the Fall of Rome, and the Making of Christianity in the West, 350–550 AD* (Princeton: Princeton University Press, 2012).

[29]Truly I say to you, there is no one who has left house or brothers or sisters or mother or father or children or fields for my sake and for the sake of the gospel, [30]who will not receive a hundredfold now in this age—houses and brothers and sisters and mothers and children and fields, with persecutions—and in the age to come eternal life. [31]But many who are first will be last, and the last will be first. (10:29b-31)

Since this is the only passage in the Gospels (along with its Lukan, but not Matthean, parallel) that ostensibly connects the abandonment of possessions with material blessing in this life, it is a favored text among preachers of the so-called prosperity gospel. Although there are many forms of prosperity teaching, in its most mechanistic expressions Mark 10:29b-31 is interpreted as a promise that giving—usually not to the poor but to the preacher or religious institution requesting the funds—will be rewarded with a massive return on one's "investment" in the form of material blessing in the present life. One prosperity preacher famously and bluntly articulates this interpretive principle in a commentary on 10:29-30, declaiming, "You give $1 for the Gospel's sake and $100 belongs to you; give $10 and receive $1000; give $1000 and receive $100,000. . . . Give one airplane and receive one hundred times the value of the airplane. Give one car and the return would furnish you a lifetime of cars. In short, Mark 10:30 is a very good deal."[20]

Such an interpretation does rightly intuit that the consequence of, and perhaps even the implicit motivation for, the dispossession of goods for Jesus' sake and for the sake of the gospel in Mark 10:29-30 is some form of material reward in this present life (v. 30: νῦν ἐν τῷ καιρῷ τούτῳ), as well as the ultimate reward of eternal life in the age to come. What the mechanistic prosperity theology reading of 10:29-30 is missing, however, is a contextually sensitive understanding of the *nature* of the "material" rewards promised by Jesus in the present life. The interpretation of the abandoned things gained in a hundredfold return in the present age by followers of Jesus—houses, brothers, sisters, mothers, children, and fields—should be defined by the literary context of Mark's Gospel. Following Jesus may result in the difficult, even painful, loss of material possessions and family relationships (1:18-20; 13:12-13). That which is gained, however, is not individual financial prosperity and security but rather an abundance of new family members, and even

---

[20] Gloria Copeland, *God's Will Is Prosperity* (Tulsa, Okla.: Harrison House, 1978), 54; cited in Kate Bowler, *Blessed: A History of the American Prosperity Gospel* (New York: Oxford University Press, 2013), 99. For a nuanced assessment of the phenomenon and global impact of all varieties of theologies of prosperity, see Katherine Attanasi and Amos Yong, eds., *Pentecostalism and Prosperity: The Socio-economics of the Global Charismatic Movement* (New York: Palgrave Macmillan, 2012).

"houses" (οἰκίαι, perhaps "households") and fields, through participation in a new family, oriented around Jesus, comprised of those who do the will of God. Thus, earlier in the narrative, when he is sought by his mother, brothers, and sisters while in Nazareth, Jesus brushes aside their inquiry by asking the crowd, "Who are my mother and my brothers?" (3:33). Then, looking at the crowd gathered around him, Jesus says, "Look, here are my mother and my brothers. Whoever does the will of God is my brother and sister and mother" (3:34-35). The new family promised in Mark 10 is precisely the family comprised of followers of Jesus who do the will of God. Moreover, it is important not to ignore the fact that the things first abandoned and then returned a hundredfold now in this age come "with persecutions" (μετὰ διωγμῶν), a note that reminds readers that even this-worldly blessings available to those who share in the new family gathered around Jesus do not come without hostility and suffering, a key aspect of the motif of discipleship in Mark's Gospel (cf. 4:17; 8:34-38; 10:37-40; 13:9-13). The notion that persecution will accompany those things gained in this age for those who abandon possessions for Jesus' sake and for the sake of the gospel is regularly ignored by many proponents of prosperity theology.

In two of the three passages in the Gospel of Mark in which Jesus explicitly commends or commands material provision for the needy (9:41-50 and 10:17-22), he does so by offering the promise of eschatological reward for those who exercise such care.[21] Exhortations to charity in the Gospel of Mark, therefore, are not disinterested. Instead, appeals to almsgiving in Mark are rooted in the conviction that those who offer material support to those in want will be recompensed for their charitable actions, even as participation in this exchange is framed as an aspect of discipleship. Mark's Gospel, then, can be counted as an advocate of meritorious almsgiving, although there is no sense that charity is broadly atoning in the Second Gospel.

---

[21] The other passage in which Jesus commends charity is Mark 14:3-9. In response to the protests of some who witness a woman anointing Jesus' head with expensive ointment at the house of Simon the leper in Bethany and who insist that proceeds from the sale of the ointment could have been given to the poor, Jesus states, "Let her alone; why do you trouble her? She has performed a great service for me. For you always have the poor with you, and you can show kindness to them whenever you wish; but you will not always have me" (14:6-7, NRSV). Given that in his response Jesus alludes to Deut 15:11—a verse that uses the observation that there will never cease to be need on the earth in order to issue the command, "Open your hand to the poor and needy neighbor in your land" (NRSV)—Jesus "is not, then, devaluing service to the poor but assuming that it will remain a continuing duty in the coming period" (Marcus, *Mark 8–16*, 941). Possibly, Jesus' critique of the practice of "Corban" in Mark 7:9-13 should also be included as a passage in the Second Gospel in which Jesus commends charity.

The Gospel of Matthew

Compared to its Markan source, the Gospel of Matthew contains substantially more material related to the connection between charity and recompense. This should not be surprising, since the First Gospel generally devotes far more attention to the theme of punishment and reward at the final judgment than the other Gospels.[22] The relationship between charity and recompense in the Gospel of Matthew is one aspect—though a crucially important one—of a larger thread that runs throughout the narrative, and in this sense "recompense" is the right word for the motif in Matthew's Gospel because charitable actions result in reward while abuse of and disregard for the poor result in punishment.[23]

Matthew 6:1-21

At the center of the Sermon on the Mount stands Matt 6:1-21, a carefully structured unit contrasting heavenly and earthly rewards.[24] The passage opens with a statement that introduces the theme of the ensuing discourse: "Beware not to practice your righteousness before other people to be seen by them, for then you have no reward with your Father in heaven" (v. 1). In the teaching that follows, Jesus then provides instruction regarding how righteousness (δικαιοσύνη)[25] is to be practiced—namely, through deeds of mercy (vv. 2-4), through prayer (vv. 5-15),[26] and through fasting (vv. 16-18). In each

---

[22] Daniel Marguerat, *Le jugement dans l'Évangile de Matthieu* (2nd ed.; Geneva: Labor et Fides, 1995); Blaine Charette, *The Theme of Recompense in Matthew's Gospel* (Journal for the Study of the New Testament; JSNTSup 79; Sheffield: JSOT Press, 1992).

[23] See the helpful introductory comments in Charette, *Theme of Recompense in Matthew's Gospel*, 11–20.

[24] My understanding of the structure of this passage is influenced by Jonathan T. Pennington, *Heaven and Earth in the Gospel of Matthew* (NovTSup 126; Leiden: Brill, 2007), 242–49; cf. Birger Gerhardsson, "Geistiger Opferdienst ach Matth. 6,1-6, 16-21," in *Neues Testament und Geschichte: Historisches Geschehen und Deutung im Neuen Testament* (ed. Heinrich Baltensweiler and Bo Reiche; Zurich: Theologischer Verlag, 1972), 69–77. Most commentators divide the material differently, usually with 6:1-18 seen as a self-contained unit and 6:19 beginning a new section that includes 6:19-34 (so Dale C. Allison Jr., "The Structure of the Sermon on the Mount," *JBL* 106 [1987]: 423–45).

[25] The NRSV's rendering of δικαιοσύνη in Matt 6:1 as "piety" is rather unfortunate, since the term "piety" in English can imply personal, perhaps even individualistic and private, behavior. This rendering fails to capture the extent to which δικαιοσύνη, according to Matthew's Gospel, is to be shown also in deeds of embodied justice (cf. 5:6, 10, 20; 6:33; 21:32).

[26] The teaching on prayer in vv. 7-15 is an excursus.

section, a practice is discussed by means of a contrast between a negative
assessment of one manifestation of that practice—a manifestation that leads
to earthly reward, particularly in terms of honor precedence for those who
practice such things—followed by instruction commending a positive manifestation of the practice that will merit reward by the heavenly Father:

	Practice	Negative Manifestation	Negative Reward	Positive Manifestation	Positive Reward
6:2-4	Doing a deed of mercy	Practicing mercy while sounding a trumpet like the hypocrites do in the syna-gogues and the streets	Receiving the praise of others	Practicing mercy secretly, so that your left hand does not know what your right hand is doing	"Your Father who sees in secret will reward you."
6:5-6	Prayer	Practicing prayer like the hypocrites, who stand and pray in the synagogues and at the street corners	Being seen by others	Praying to the Father who is in secret in a private room, with the door shut	"Your Father who sees in secret will reward you."
6:16-18	Fasting	Practicing fast-ing while look-ing dismal, like the hypocrites, who disfigure their faces to show others that they are fasting	Being recognized as fasting by others	Fasting with oiled heads and washed faces so that the practice of fasting is observed not by others but by the Father	"Your Father who sees in secret will reward you."

The unit concludes in verses 19 to 21 with a summary of the teaching. This
final précis articulates a positive offer of heavenly reward that balances the
negative warning in verse 1, while also reasserting a warning against the pursuit of earthly treasure:

> [19]Do not store up for yourselves treasures on earth, where moth and
> rust destroy and where thieves break in and steal. [20]But store up for
> yourselves treasures in heaven, where neither moth nor rust destroys

and where thieves do not break in and do not steal. [21]For where your treasure is, there your heart also will be.[27]

The righteous practices to be performed discreetly in this context are "doing a deed of mercy" (ἐλεημοσύνη), prayer (προσεύχομαι), and fasting (νηστεύω), a triad of religious praxis featured elsewhere in earlier Jewish and later Christian literature, notably Tob 12:8-9.[28] Unlike Raphael's exhortation to Tobit and Tobias in Tobit 12, however, in which contextual cues suggest that the verb ποιέω with ἐλεημοσύνη as its object is appropriately rendered "to practice the merciful act of almsgiving" (at least in Tob 12:8b), in Matt 6:2-4 ἐλεημοσύνη should be translated "merciful deed."[29] In this context, ἐλεημοσύνη may well include giving alms to the poor, particularly since the necessity of Jesus' disciples providing material support of the needy is clearly a Matthean emphasis (25:31-46). But translations should be wary not to restrict ἐλεημοσύνη to "the *giving* of alms," not least because, while the term ἐλεημοσύνη is not used in the narrative outside of 6:2-4, the long discussion of charity and reward in Matt 25:31-46 includes feeding the hungry, provisioning the thirsty with water, welcoming the stranger, clothing the naked, caring for the sick, and visiting those in prison. The list of actions in Matt 25:31-46 is probably the best definition of ἐλεημοσύνη in the Gospel of Matthew, even though the noun ἐλεημοσύνη is not used there. To understand the action described in Matt 6:2-4 as "giving alms" is potentially to restrict these merciful deeds to monetary distributions.

The conclusion of this unit in verses 19 to 21 clarifies the spatial location of God's rewards for discreet practices of righteousness—namely, heaven. Almost all modern English translations of Matt 6:1 depict practicing righteousness before others in order to be seen by them as resulting in those who do conspicuous righteous acts having "no reward *from* your Father in

---

[27] For a tradition-historical study of the treasure-in-heaven saying in Matt 6:19-20 and Luke 12:33 (as well as parallels in Mark 10:21; *Gos. Thom.* 76.3; John 6:27; Jas 5:2-3; and Col 3:1-2), see Steven R. Johnson, *Seeking the Imperishable Treasure: Wealth, Wisdom, and a Jesus Saying* (Eugene, Ore.: Wipf & Stock, 2008).

[28] Tob 12:8-9; 2 Clem. 16.1–4; Herm. Sim. 5.3.7–8; cf. *Gos. Thom.* 6, 14.

[29] One of the arguments for rendering the construction ποιῆσαι ἐλεημοσύνην in Tob 12:8 as "to practice the merciful act of almsgiving" is that in Tob 12:8 this action is contrasted with "wealth with unrighteousness" and the activity of storing up gold. It is true that Matt 6:19-20 contrasts storing up treasures on earth with storing up heavenly treasure, but, in the context of Jesus's discourse in Matt 6:1-21, it is not merely ἐλεημοσύνη that results in heavenly reward but also prayer and fasting. The NRSV's translation of the phrase Ὅταν οὖν ποιῇς ἐλεημοσύνην as "So whenever you give alms" would make more sense if δίδωμι was used instead of ποιέω.

heaven."[30] Yet the opening statement in this unit actually promises that there will be no reward "*with* your Father in heaven" (παρὰ τῷ πατρὶ ὑμῶν τῷ ἐν τοῖς οὐρανοῖς) for those who practice public righteousness. The difference between receiving reward "from" and receiving reward "with" the heavenly Father is not insignificant, for verses 19 to 20 contrast treasures located on earth with treasures located in heaven. This contrast between earthly and heavenly treasures is followed by the closing statement that the spatial location of one's treasure is also the location of one's heart (v. 21). The opposite of having "no reward *with* you Father in heaven" in verse 1 is thus captured in verses 19 to 21: the accumulation of heavenly treasure through acts of mercy, prayer, and fasting is stored up *with* God in heaven. Since heaven (or more commonly "the heavens") in Matthew's Gospel is the invisible divine realm where God's will is done (6:10), a realm that stands in contrast to the earth (6:9-10, 19-21; 16:18; 28:16-20), those who practice mercy, pray, and fast in secret, without regard for the accumulation of earthly honor, will be rewarded with treasure in heaven by the God who is in heaven and who grants such reward.[31] Although the heavenly treasure is awarded on the basis of righteous practices for followers of Jesus on the earth—in agreement with Matthew's eschatology the recompense comes in the future (6:4, 6, 18)—this heavenly reward will be realized when God settles accounts on the day of final judgment.[32]

Matthew 10:1-42

The next text in Matthew's Gospel that connects charity and reward comes in the missionary discourse in Matthew 10. In 10:1-42, Jesus summons his

---

[30] Translations that render παρὰ τῷ πατρὶ ὑμῶν as "from your Father" include CEB, ESV, NIV, NJB, NRSV (cf. NAB: "no recompense from your Father"). Interestingly, the NASB translates the phrase "you have no reward *with* your Father who is in heaven."

[31] As Jonathan Pennington concludes in his study of the language of οὐρανός/οὐρανοί in the First Gospel, "Thus, by stepping back and analyzing Matthew's rich and varied use of heaven language we can see that behind it all is an intentional focus on the theme of heaven and earth, specially highlighting the current contrast or tensive relationship between the two realms, between God and humanity. Yet Matthew does not only emphasize the contrast, but also the fact that this contrast or tension will be resolved at eschaton when heaven and earth are reunited through Jesus (6:9-10; 28:18). In fact, only by recognizing the intensity of the tension that currently exists between heaven and earth can we fully appreciate the significance of the eschaton in which the kingdom of heaven will come to earth" (*Heaven and Earth*, 342–43).

[32] Nathan Eubank, "Storing Up Treasure with God in the Heavens: Celestial Investments in Matthew 6:1-21," *CBQ* 76 (2014): 77–92 [91]. My reading of Matt 6:19-21 is shaped by the argument in Eubank's insightful essay.

twelve disciples, gives them authority to cast out unclean spirits and to heal sicknesses, and sends them out with instructions regarding their mission to proclaim the nearness of the kingdom of heaven to the lost sheep of the house of Israel. Jesus' words of commission to the disciples in verses 5 to 42 feature themes of payment and repayment at the beginning and end of the discourse.

After first outlining the scope of their mission (vv. 5-6), the content of their proclamation of the good news (v. 7), and the nature of their healing activity (v. 8a), Jesus exhorts the Twelve, "Freely you received; freely give" (v. 8b). Presumably, this charge to give implies that, just as the disciples have freely experienced the blessings of God's coming kingdom without any payment, they should share, through their proclamation of the good news and works of healing, the blessings of the kingdom with others without any expectation of payment. This instruction is clarified by the next statement, in which Jesus instructs the disciples to take on their mission "no gold, or silver, or copper in your belts, no bag for your journey, or two tunics, or sandals, or a staff; for laborers deserve their food" (vv. 9-10, NRSV). The final clause in verse 10 is slightly puzzling, since the explicit command to give away the blessings of the kingdom of God without payment (v. 8) and the instruction regarding a mission without possessions (vv. 9-10a) appear to be qualified by an allowance that those who labor on behalf of the good news deserve to be supported with food (τροφή).[33] Yet any tension between these statements is minimized if the idea is that the disciples should offer the blessings of the kingdom without expectation of payment and the disciples are not to profit from their proclamation of the gospel, but they may receive basic nourishment in the context of their mission.[34]

---

[33] This is certainly how the saying, as it is known from oral tradition, is interpreted in the Pauline Letters, where it is cited in discussions of support for church leaders in both 1 Cor 9:14 and 1 Tim 5:17. See David G. Horrell, "'The Lord Commanded . . . but I Have Not Used . . .': Exegetical and Hermeneutical Reflections on 1 Cor 9.14-15," *NTS* 43 (1997): 587–603; Wolfgang Harnisch, "Der Paulinische Lohn: (I Kor 9,1-23)," *ZTK* 104 (2007): 25–43.

[34] So Donald A. Hagner, *Matthew 1–13* (WBC 33A; Dallas: Word, 1993), 272. It may not be insignificant, in fact, that Luke's version of the saying reads ὁ ἄξιος γὰρ ὁ ἐργάτης τοῦ μισθοῦ αὐτοῦ ("the laborer is worthy of his wage"), whereas Matthew's version reads ἄξιος γὰρ ὁ ἐργάτης τῆς τροφῆς αὐτοῦ ("the laborer is worthy of his food"). In Matthew's Gospel, the saying advocates not payment but nourishment, perhaps clarifying any tension with the saying in 10:8b; cf. John S. Kloppenborg, "Poverty and Piety in Matthew, James and the Didache," in *Matthew, James, and Didache: Three Related Documents in Their Jewish and Christian Settings* (ed. Huub van de Sandt and Jürgen K. Zangenberg; SBLSymS 45; Atlanta: Society of Biblical Literature, 2008), 224.

If Jesus' commission discourages the Twelve from pursuing or receiving reward in the context of their missionary work aside from having their basic needs met, the conclusion of the discourse promises reward (μισθός) for those who show hospitality to the disciples:

[40]The one who welcomes you welcomes me, and the one who welcomes me welcomes the one who sent me. [41]The one who welcomes a prophet in the name of a prophet will receive a prophet's reward, and the one who welcomes a righteous person in the name of a righteous person will receive a righteous person's reward; [42]and whoever gives even a cup of cold water to one of these little ones in the name of a disciple—truly I tell you, none of these will lose their reward. (10:40-42)

The nature of the rewards discussed in verses 41 to 42 for those who welcome prophets and righteous persons and for those who provide water to the disciples (i.e., "these little ones"; cf. 18:6, 10, 14; 25:40, 45) is not entirely clear on the basis of these sayings alone.[35] In the larger context of Matthew's Gospel, however, the reward in 10:41-42 is best seen as heavenly reward, similar to the discussion in Matt 6:1-21 (cf. Mark 9:41). The section on rewards in verses 40 to 42 follows immediately the saying about losing one's life for Jesus' sake as a means of finding (true) life (v. 39). Moreover, the close parallel between providing "one of these little ones" (ἕνα τῶν μικρῶν τούτων) a drink of water in 10:42 and caring for the Lord himself by, among other things, alleviating the thirst of one whom he calls "one of the least of these brothers and sisters of mine" (ἐποιήσατε ἑνὶ τούτων τῶν ἀδελφῶν μου τῶν ἐλαχίστων) in the discourse about future judgment in 25:40 implies that the reward gained for showing hospitality to Jesus' followers in Jesus' name is recompensed at the final judgment.[36] As in 6:2-4, then, in 10:41-42 a future, heavenly reward is granted on the basis of merciful action in this present life.

Matthew 19:16-30

In many ways, the structure of the story of Jesus' encounter with a wealthy man and the ensuing conversation between Jesus and his disciples in Matt 19:16-30 parallels its Markan source: Jesus is approached by a man who asks about obtaining eternal life (v. 17); Jesus responds by identifying obedience to the commandments as a means of entering into life (vv. 17-19), a reply that

---

[35] Following the twice-repeated "in the name of" formula of v. 41, the statement about giving "in the name of a disciple" (εἰς ὄνομα μαθητοῦ) in v. 42 refers to the "little one" who receives the drink, not the giver (cf. Mark 9:41); so R. T. France, *The Gospel of Matthew* (NICNT; Grand Rapids: Eerdmans, 2007), 415.

[36] France, *Gospel of Matthew*, 413.

leads the man to claim that he has, in fact, kept the commandments and to ask what he still lacks (v. 20); Jesus then says, "If you wish to be perfect, go, sell your possessions, and give to the poor, and you will have treasure in the heavens, and come, follow me" (v. 21); the man leaves grieving because he has many possessions (v. 22); this encounter prompts Jesus to inform his disciples about the difficulty of a rich person entering the kingdom of heaven (vv. 23-24), an assessment that astounds the disciples and causes them to ask, "Who then can be saved?" (v. 25); this question leads Jesus to say, "For human beings it is impossible, but for God all things are possible" (v. 26). As in Mark's account, Jesus promises his conversation partner that obeying the commands to sell possessions and give to the poor will result in the accumulation of heavenly treasure. Also as in its Markan source, the conclusion of the man's story is open-ended because his ultimate response is not narrated.

Matthew's account differs significantly from Mark's, however, in the second part of the discussion between Jesus and his disciples (Matt 19:27-30), where the Markan note that those who abandon material possessions will receive reward "*in this age* . . . and in the age to come eternal life" (Mark 10:30) is omitted. In the Matthean version of this story, Jesus responds to Peter's assertion and question ("Look, we have left everything and followed you. What then will there be for us?" [v. 27]) by saying:

> [28] Truly I tell you who have followed me that, at the renewal of the world (ἐν τῇ παλιγγενεσίᾳ), when the Son of Man sits on his glorious throne, you also will sit on twelve thrones, judging the twelve tribes of Israel. [29] And everyone who has left houses or brothers or sisters or father or mother or children or fields for the sake of my name will receive a hundredfold and will inherit eternal life. [30] But many who are first will be last, and the last first. (19:28b-30)

There is no indication in Jesus' answer in Matthew 19 that those who follow him will be rewarded in the present age for the abandonment of family and possessions. The temporal phrase "at the renewal of the world" (ἐν τῇ παλιγγενεσίᾳ) in verse 28 modifies the following clause that describes the Son of Man sitting on his glorious throne, indicating that the judgment exercised by the twelve disciples over the twelve tribes of Israel happens at the dawn of the new eschatological age.[37] Having abandoned everything in order to follow Jesus in the present age, the disciples are promised authority to

---

[37] So Donald A. Hagner, *Matthew 14–28* (WBC 33B; Dallas: Word, 1995), 564; David C. Sim, "The Meaning of Palingenesia in Matthew 19.28," *JSNT* 50 (1993): 3–12. For other passages that image followers of Jesus participating in eschatological rule, see Rev 3:21; 20:6; 1 Cor 6:2-3; cf. Dan 7:22-27.

judge Israel in the age to come, a reversal reiterated in the contrast between the first and the last at the conclusion of the pericope (v. 30). Moreover, not only the disciples but "everyone" (πᾶς) who abandons possessions and family for the sake of Jesus' name will receive a hundredfold return and will inherit eternal life. Matthew's omission of the clause "now in this age" (νῦν ἐν τῷ καιρῷ τούτῳ) in Mark 10:30 indicates that the reward for this dispossession is eschatological and not this-worldly, although Matthew does preserve a distinction between the hundredfold return and eternal life, perhaps in the sense that the hundredfold return is envisioned as heavenly reward at the final judgment for those who have also been granted eternal life, the very object of the rich man's desire (v. 16).[38]

That Matthew would remove reference to present rewards for the abandonment of family and possessions in his account of Jesus' encounter with the rich man is entirely consistent with the eschatological perspective found throughout the First Gospel. The eschatology of Matthew's Gospel is complex, but one of the most characteristic aspects of Matthean eschatology is its marked emphasis on recompense according to deeds at the final judgment.[39] Expectation of the final judgment is a central theme in Matthew, and the function of this motif within the narrative is primarily to inspire moral behavior in light of the coming judgment. The ethical motivation of Matthew's judgment motif can be seen especially in Jesus' speeches, where Jesus regularly teaches his disciples to live in the present in light of the reality of hell and the final day of judgment, when the righteous will be separated from the unrighteous (Matt 5:12, 21-30; 6:1-21; 7:13-14, 21-27; 10:40-42; 13:24-30, 36-43, 47-50; 16:27; 18:8-9, 23-35; 19:27-30). Throughout the narrative of Matthew, the practice of righteousness, including sharing resources with the needy, is grounded in the expectation that everyone will be rewarded

---

[38] On the distinction between the hundredfold return and eternal life, see Hagner, *Matthew 14–28*, 564.

[39] Andries G. Van Aarde, "'On Earth as It Is in Heaven': Matthew's Eschatology as the Kingdom of the Heavens That Has Come," in *Eschatology of the New Testament and Some Related Documents* (ed. Jan G. van der Watt; WUNT II/315; Tübingen: Mohr Siebeck, 2011), 35–63; David J. Neville, "Toward a Teleology of Peace: Contesting Matthew's Violent Eschatology," *JSNT* 30 (2007): 131–61; Klaus Wengst, "Aspects of the Last Judgment in the Gospel according to Matthew," in *Eschatology in the Bible and in Jewish and Christian Tradition* (ed. Henning Graf Reventlow; JSOTSup 243; Sheffield: Sheffield Academic, 1997), 233–45; Vicky Balabanski, *Eschatology in the Making: Mark, Matthew and the Didache* (SNTSMS 97; Cambridge: Cambridge University Press, 1997); David C. Sim, *Apocalyptic Eschatology in the Gospel of Matthew* (SNTSMS 88; Cambridge: Cambridge University Press, 2005).

and/or punished at the final judgment on the basis of how they have lived in the present life.[40]

Matthew 25:31-46

Nowhere is the relationship between eschatological judgment and ethics more evident in the First Gospel than in chapters 24 to 25, the fifth and final discourse in the narrative. Jesus' teaching in these chapters begins with Matthew's adaptation in 24:1-36 of the apocalyptic discourse in Mark 13, material that concludes in verse 36 with the note that no one—neither the angels of heaven nor the Son—knows the day or the hour of end of the age but the Father. To the material from Mark 13 that serves as the basis for Matt 24:1-36, the author of the First Gospel then appends three passages that emphasize the necessity of being ready for the coming of the Son of Man at an unexpected hour (24:37-44, 45-51; 25:1-13).[41] The parable of the Talents (25:14-30) stresses the importance of servants acting responsibly while the "Lord" of the household is away; the servant who is not faithful with the talent entrusted to him has his talent taken away and is thrown into "the outer darkness, where there will be weeping and gnashing of teeth" (v. 30, NRSV). Finally, the apocalyptic discourse in Matthew 24–25 concludes in 25:31-46 with Jesus' depiction of the scene of final judgment, when all the nations are gathered before the Son of Man as he is seated on his glorious throne and the Son of Man "will separate them from one another, just as a shepherd separates the sheep from the goats" (v. 32).[42]

Significantly for the topic of charity and reward in Matthew's Gospel, the Son of Man's sifting between the sheep and the goats is determined on the basis of whether those gathered from the nations have cared for the needy. The righteous sheep are blessed by the Father, given the inheritance of the kingdom prepared from the foundation of the world, and received

---

[40] Cf. Richard B. Hays, *The Moral Vision of the New Testament: Community, Cross, New Creation; A Contemporary Introduction to New Testament Ethics* (San Francisco: HarperCollins, 1996), 106–7.

[41] Matt 24:42 does adapt Mark 13:35.

[42] On the history of interpretation of this difficult passage, including particularly the identity of πάντα τὰ ἔθνη in v. 32 and "the least of these brothers and sisters of mine" in v. 40, see Sherman W. Gray, *The Least of My Brothers: Matthew 25:31-46; A History of Interpretation* (SBLDS 114; Atlanta: Scholars Press, 1989). For a provocative analysis of the ways in which this text features in contemporary evangelical Christian preaching, see Jeannine K. Brown, "Matthew's 'Least of These' Theology and the Subversion of 'Us/Other' Categories," in *Matthew: Texts @ Contexts* (ed. Nichole Wilkinson Duran and James P. Grimshaw; Minneapolis: Fortress, 2013), 287–301.

into eternal life (vv. 35, 40). The sheep are identified and rewarded because they have provided for the king himself by feeding the hungry, provisioning the thirsty with water, welcoming the stranger, clothing the naked, caring for the sick, and visiting those in prison (vv. 34-40). When the righteous express their ignorance regarding their performance of these merciful deeds, inquiring about when they have done the things for which they are rewarded (vv. 37-39), the king responds, "Truly I tell you, just as you did it to one of the least of these brothers and sisters of mine, you did it to me" (v. 40).[43] So closely linked are Jesus and his followers that showing material kindness to Jesus' disciples is to do the same for Jesus himself. In a very real way, then, by caring for fellow disciples, the sheep embody the secret performance of merciful deeds advocated in Matt 6:2-4, for the righteous are not even aware of the extent to which their ἐλεημοσύνη has ministered to Christ.[44] Conversely, the goats are sent away "into the eternal fire prepared for the devil and his angels" (v. 41), cursed and banished to eternal punishment (v. 46) because of their failure to perform merciful deeds for followers of Jesus who are hungry, thirsty, strangers, naked, sick, and imprisoned. Nothing is stated or implied about the motivations of those sheep who have acted mercifully on behalf of the destitute, although the motif of divine judgment on the basis of how individuals have cared for the marginalized strongly suggests that, here as elsewhere in Matthew's Gospel, ethics are motivated by eschatology.[45]

[43] On the motif of the sheep's ignorance, see Sigurd Grindheim, "Ignorance Is Bliss: Attitudinal Aspects of the Judgment according to Works in Matthew 25:31-46," *NovT* 50 (2008): 313–31. Grindheim's study helpfully illuminates the interrelationship between attitude and action as it bears on the Matthean theme of judgement, even if Grindheim is guilty of introducing Pauline terminology and theological concepts into the discussion (so rightly Nathan Eubank, *Wages of Cross-Bearing Sin: The Economy of Heaven in Matthew's Gospel* [BZNW 196; Berlin: De Gruyter, 2013], 3). Moreover, Grindheim wrongly identifies the reason for the surprise of the righteous blessed by the king for their care for the poor: they are not surprised *that* they are rewarded for their charity; rather, the righteous are surprised because they do not seem to have anticipated that the Son of Man has been the true object of merciful deeds shown to fellow Christians.

[44] Grindheim, "Ignorance Is Bliss," 323. To be sure, the term ἐλεημοσύνη is not used in Matt 25:31-46, but the noun is an apt summary of the scope of merciful deeds of the righteous in this passage. That the "least of these brothers and sisters of mine" in vv. 40 and 45 are followers of Jesus is debated, but the restriction of this phrase to followers of Jesus is demanded by the use of the term ἀδελφός elsewhere in Matthew (cf. 5:22-24, 47; 7:3-5; 12:48-50; 18:15, 21, 35; 23:8; 28:10). For the view that the "least of these brothers and sisters of mine" are Christian missionaries, see Joong Suk Suh, "Das Weltgericht und die Matthäische Gemeinde," *NovT* 48 (2006): 217–33.

[45] Sim, *Apocalyptic Eschatology*, 222–42.

The scene of the Son of Man's judgment of the righteous and unrighteous in Matt 25:31-46 offers a fitting and evocative climax of the motif of divine reward for merciful deeds or punishment for their absence in the Gospel of Matthew. Matthew's Gospel envisions a universal judgment of all people—including followers of Jesus—on the basis of deeds performed in this life, and an important measure of one's righteousness is care for needy disciples of Jesus.[46] In this sense, merciful action toward needy disciples in Matthew's Gospel is primarily meritorious in the sense that practices of merciful care for the poor result in heavenly reward at the final assize, when the works of all people will be judged.

At the same time, however, it could be argued that, because care for the poor in the Gospel of Matthew represents a significant element of Jesus' proclamation, charity is broadly atoning in the sense that adherence to Jesus' teaching of a better righteousness is one of several ways in which the alleviation of sin is narrated in the First Gospel. Certainly, Jesus' identity as one who saves from sin is foundational in Matthew's story. At a key moment in the narrative, after the record of the genealogy of "Jesus the Messiah, son of David, son of Abraham" (1:1-17), Jesus' birth is foretold to Joseph by an angel of the Lord, and the angel's prediction is punctuated by the declaration that Mary "will bear a son, and you are to name him Jesus, for he will save his people from their sins" (1:21). This statement in Matt 1:21, in which the main character of the story is named and his commission is identified, can be viewed as programmatic for the mission of Jesus in the Gospel of Matthew.[47] But what does it mean, within the literary framework of Matthew's Gospel, for Jesus to "save his people from their sins"?

One common answer to this question connects the prediction that Jesus will save his people from their sins in Matt 1:21 with references elsewhere in the Gospel to the death of Jesus as an event that accomplishes forgiveness. The Last Supper tradition in the Gospel of Matthew, for example, records Jesus' statement, with reference to the cup, "Drink from it, all of you; for this is my blood of the covenant, which is poured out for many for the forgiveness of sins" (26:27b-28, NRSV). There is no doubt that Matt 26:28

---

[46] I thus prefer to interpret πάντα τὰ ἔθνη in v. 32 in a universal sense, including "the gentile nations, Israel, and also the *corpus mixtum* of the Christian church" (Hagner, *Matthew 14–28*, 742).

[47] Warren Carter, *Matthew and Empire: Initial Explorations* (Harrisburg, Pa.: Trinity International, 2001); Boris Repschinski, "'For He Will Save His People from Their Sins' (Matthew 1:21): A Christology for Christian Jews," *CBQ* 68 (2006): 248–67. For much of the argument in this section, I am influenced by Thomas R. Blanton IV, "Saved by Obedience: Matthew 1:21 in Light of Jesus' Teaching on the Torah," *JBL* 132 (2013): 393–413.

frames Jesus' death as a liberating, vicarious sacrifice that accomplishes the forgiveness of sins.[48] Yet forgiveness of sin in the narrative of Matthew's Gospel (as in Mark's) is also made available before the crucifixion of Jesus takes place and often occurs or is promoted apart from, or at least without any direct connection to, the cross: John's practice of baptism of repentance is accompanied by the confession of sins (3:1-12); Jesus instructs his disciples to pray for forgiveness of their debts (ὀφειλήματα) and notes that if they forgive others their trespasses (τὰ παραπτώματα αὐτῶν), then the heavenly Father of the disciples will forgive them, but if the disciples do not forgive others, neither will they be forgiven by the Father (6:12, 14-15; cf. 12:31-32); Jesus himself offers forgiveness of sins to a paralytic man whom he heals, a proclamation of clemency that provokes the ire of scribes who observe the episode (9:2-8); and in response to a question from Peter, Jesus opines that a member of "the church" who sins against Peter should be forgiven seventy-seven times (18:21-22), a principle that is illustrated in the ensuing parable of the unforgiving servant (18:23-35). While the cross is the ultimate means of atonement in Matthew's Gospel, it is not the only means by which forgiveness of sin is narrated.

To raise questions about the dynamics of forgiveness in Matthew's Gospel is also to raise questions about the reasons that forgiveness is needed. Matthew's Gospel reflects an understanding, common among Jews of the Second Temple period, of "sin" (ἁμαρτία) and "lawlessness" (ἀνομία) as failure to obey the teachings of Torah. In Matthew, moreover, Jesus is characterized as the authoritative teacher of Torah whose instruction intensifies (but does not mitigate or transcend) the law by summoning his followers, as participants in the kingdom of heaven, to a more faithful obedience to Torah and a surpassing righteousness than that of the scribes and Pharisees (5:17-20). In this sense, it might be argued that Jesus' *teaching* "saves his people from their sins." That is, those who follow Jesus and obey Torah as it is interpreted and, notably, summarized (22:34-39) by him are saved from their sins in the sense that adherents to Jesus' teaching do not violate God's will as it is revealed in Torah. In Matthew's Gospel, Jesus' mission of saving his people from their sins is both preventative, in that those who follow Jesus' instruction are saved

---

[48] So Donald Senior, *The Passion of Jesus in the Gospel of Matthew* (Collegeville, Minn.: Liturgical, 1985), 64–71; John Nolland, *The Gospel of Matthew: A Commentary on the Greek Text* (NIGTC; Grand Rapids: Eerdmans, 2005), 1078–84. The assumption that the cross is an atoning sacrifice may also be implicit in the so-called "ransom saying" in 20:28, although this is disputed; see J. Christopher Edwards, *The Ransom Logion in Mark and Matthew: Its Reception and Its Significance for the Study of the Gospels* (WUNT II/327; Tübingen: Mohr Siebeck, 2012).

from committing future sins, and restorative, in that Jesus' death on the cross is a sacrificial offering that brings forgiveness for transgressions of Torah that have been or will be committed.

The Gospel of Luke and the Acts of the Apostles

It has long been observed that, among early chroniclers of the life and teaching of Jesus, the author of the Gospel of Luke has a special interest in issues related to riches, poverty, and possessions, a concern reflected also in the second volume of this author's account, the Acts of the Apostles. The wealth of material in Luke–Acts related to economics and eschatology is paralleled in the earliest Christian literature only by the Gospel of Matthew, a narrative with which Luke–Acts shares much in common but with which Luke–Acts also differs in some important respects. If a general survey of the theme of wealth and poverty in Luke–Acts would threaten to overwhelm with its scope, the relationship in Luke between charity and reward is slightly more manageable.[49] Where in Luke–Acts is care for the needy or the divestiture of goods connected with some notion of reward, so that those who give (away) receive something in return?

Luke 11:37-41

Among early Christian proponents of atoning almsgiving, Luke 11:41, along with 1 Pet 4:8, is one of the most oft-cited texts among the writings that came to be called the "New Testament" in support of the notion that the practice of ἐλεημοσύνη can cleanse sin. In Jesus' conversation with an unnamed Pharisee at a meal hosted by that Pharisee, Jesus responds to his host's astonishment that he does not wash before the meal by saying:

> Now you Pharisees clean the outside of the cup and of the dish, but the inside of you is full of greed and wickedness. Foolish people! Did not the one who made the outside make the inside also? So give alms with respect to the things within, and see, everything is clean for you (πλὴν τὰ ἐνόντα δότε ἐλεημοσύνην, καὶ ἰδοὺ πάντα καθαρὰ ὑμῖν ἐστιν). (11:39-41)

Both the narrative setting of Jesus' exchange with his host, a Pharisee, and the woes against the Pharisees and the scribes that follow in verses 42 to

---

[49] For the most thorough and relevant treatment of issues of wealth, poverty, and possessions in Luke–Acts, see Christopher M. Hays, *Luke's Wealth Ethics: A Study in Their Coherence and Character* (WUNT II/275; Tübingen: Mohr Siebeck, 2010).

52 (cf. the collusion of "the scribes and the Pharisees" in v. 53) indicate that audience of the statements in verses 39 to 41 (and therefore the recipients of the command to give ἐλεημοσύνη in v. 41) consists of Pharisees.[50]

English translations of Luke 11:41, perhaps reflecting a concern lest the text be read to suggest that almsgiving itself purifies, have often struggled over the phrase τὰ ἐνόντα δότε ἐλεημοσύνην, generally preferring to view the construction as a double accusative of object-complement so that Jesus enjoins giving as alms the things inside (e.g., ESV: "But give as alms those things that are within") or giving alms in expression of what is truly within those commissioned to give (e.g., CEB: "Therefore, give to those in need *from the core of who you are* and you will be clean all over").[51] Yet careful attention to the narrative context suggests that translations like the ESV ("give *as alms* those things that are within") make little sense, since Jesus has just said in verse 39 that the inside of the Pharisees is full of greed and wickedness (τὸ δὲ ἔσωθεν ὑμῶν γέμει ἁρπαγῆς καὶ πονηρίας). How can greed and wickedness be given as alms?

A far better understanding of the construction τὰ ἐνόντα δότε ἐλεημοσύνην views τὰ ἐνόντα as an accusative of respect, resulting in the rendering "give alms *with respect to the things within*."[52] In this sense, the practice of ἐλεημοσύνη alleviates the problem that is "within" the Pharisees—namely, greed and wickedness. The phrase that punctuates this conversation then reiterates the cleansing effect of merciful action on behalf of the needy: "Give alms with respect to the things within, *and see, everything is clean for you.*" That is, both the outside of the cup and the dish (since the Pharisees will

---

[50] In light of the discussion of the semantics of ἐλεημοσύνη in chapter 2, the phrase δότε ἐλεημοσύνην in Luke 11:41 and 12:33 appears to represent a pragmatic adjustment of the univocal lexical meaning "merciful act." When ἐλεημοσύνη is the object of the verb δίδωμι, as it is in Luke 11:41 and 12:33 (cf. Acts 3:2, 3, 10), what is given is not a merciful act but an object—namely, "alms." This contextual semantic adjustment is clarified by the two paired commands in Luke 12:33: Πωλήσατε τὰ ὑπάρχοντα ὑμῶν καὶ δότε ἐλεημοσύνην ("Sell your possessions and give alms").

[51] On the grammatical category of double accusative of object-complement, see Daniel B. Wallace, *Greek Grammar beyond the Basics: An Exegetical Syntax of the New Testament with Scripture, Subject, and Greek Word Indexes* (Grand Rapids: Zondervan, 1997), 181–89. The NIV (1984) tries to solve the problem by adding a phrase that is nowhere implied in the Greek text: "But give what is inside <the dish> to the poor, and everything will be clean for you." This expansive rendering, which also puzzlingly translates δότε ἐλεημοσύνην as "give to the poor," is modified in the NIV (2011): "But now as for what is inside you—be generous to the poor, and everything will be clean for you." John Nolland argues that τὰ ἐνόντα should be taken as an accusative of respect, but then renders this "as an expression of what is inside" (*Luke 9:21–18:34* (WBC 35B; Dallas: Word, 1993).

[52] I follow the reading of C. Hays, *Luke's Wealth Ethics*, 120–23.

continue to dine with clean vessels) and the inside of the Pharisees will then be cleansed through the practice of ἐλεημοσύνη.[53] The inside-outside dichotomy in Luke 11:39-41 does not contrast internal drives with the external manifestation of the Pharisees' actions, as if the Pharisees do the right things for the wrong motivations, for Jesus' ensuing speech in verses 42 to 44 makes clear that the Pharisees do not do the right things. Jesus' contrast between the inside and outside of the Pharisees instead plays on the imagery of dining utensils and on a distinction between moral and ritual purity.[54] ~~The Pharisees are ritually pure but morally impure, and Jesus offers almsgiving as a means of purifying the greed and wickedness within them so they will be morally pure~~ (which they are not) ~~as well as ritually pure~~ (which they are). The "reward" offered to the Pharisees here through the practice of almsgiving is internal moral purity from greed and wickedness, their sin here being imaged as an impurity that needs cleansing. In this sense, Luke 11:41 is perhaps the one text in the New Testament that most clearly advocates the concept of atoning almsgiving, if "atoning almsgiving" is meant to describe merciful action on behalf of the needy that cleanses human sin.

[53] On this point, I would differ from Hays, who, in a discussion of how Jesus' advocacy of the purifying effects of almsgiving corresponds to Jewish scriptural traditions, asserts, "The part of Jesus' claim that does not cohere with Jewish assumptions is the contention that proper attention to almsgiving (and deeds of that sort) excuses a person from rigorous observance of purity law" (C. Hays, *Luke's Wealth Ethics*, 121). I see no evidence, either in this passage or in the rest of Luke's Gospel, that Jesus assumes that Pharisees will not continue to keep purity laws. Peter's vision regarding clean and unclean food in Acts 10, as well as the role of Cornelius in Peter's changing perspective (see below), is not a narrative development anticipated in Luke 11. Indeed, as Hays himself acknowledges, ~~the portrayal of Paul in Acts—a portrait that shows Paul embracing circumcision for Timothy (16:3), undergoing purification rituals (21:22-26), and remaining ceremonially clean in the temple (24:18)—shows the author of Luke–Acts does not envision or advocate a wholesale rejection of purity laws.~~

[54] Here I follow the distinction between ritual and moral impurity made by Jonathan Klawans, who writes, "(1) While ritual purity is generally not sinful, moral impurity is a direct consequence of grave sin. (2) A characteristic feature of moral impurity is its deleterious effect on the land of Israel. Ritual impurity, in contrast, poses no threat to the land. (3) While ritual impurity often results in a contagious defilement, there is no personal-contact contagion associated with moral impurity. . . . (4) While ritual impurity results in an impermanent defilement, moral impurity leads to a long-lasting, if not permanent, degradation of the sinner, and, eventually, of the land of Israel. (5) While ritual impurity can be ameliorated by rites of purification, that is not the case for moral impurity. Moral purity is achieved by punishment, atonement, or, best of all, by refraining from committing morally impure acts in the first place" (*Purity, Sacrifice, and the Temple: Symbolism and Supersessionism in the Study of Ancient Judaism* [Oxford: Oxford University Press, 2006], 55).

Not insignificantly, Jesus immediately goes on to chastise his Pharisaic interlocutors for ignoring the justice (κρίσις) and the love of God (ἡ ἀγάπη τοῦ θεοῦ):[55] "Woe to you Pharisees, because you give a tenth of your mint, rue, and all other kinds of garden herbs, but you neglect the justice and the love of God! These you ought to have done, without neglecting the others" (11:42; cf. Matt 23:23). Jesus assumes that the Pharisees will continue to observe the tithe laws stipulated in the Scriptures, but they have not practiced justice and the love of God. In this context, it is appropriate to envision ἡ ἀγάπη τοῦ θεοῦ as a practice that the Pharisees ought to have embraced (as opposed to viewing τοῦ θεοῦ as a subjective genitive that denotes God's love for humans), not least because the nearest co-textual parallel is found in Jesus' conversation with a legal expert in Luke 10:25-37.[56] In that earlier conversation, in response to a lawyer's question about how to inherit eternal life, Jesus asks what is written in Torah, to which the lawyer responds, "You shall love the Lord your God with all your heart, and with all your soul, and with all your strength, and with all your mind; and your neighbor as yourself" (10:27, NRSV). The exchange implies that loving God is inseparable from loving one's neighbor, a point driven home by the only other Lukan passage that speaks of human beings loving God—namely, Luke 16:13, where Jesus says, "No slave can serve two masters; for a slave will either hate the one and love the other, or be devoted to the one and despise the other. You cannot serve God and wealth." In the context of Luke 16, loving God entails the proper use of wealth.

The pairing of the justice (κρίσις) and the love of God (ἡ ἀγάπη τοῦ θεοῦ) in Luke 11:42, therefore, implies that the Pharisees, though they may appear to have acted justly and loved God through their practices of purity and tithing, have, in fact, failed properly to love God and to embody God's justice because they have failed to love their neighbors. They have greedily held to possessions rather than loving their neighbors through the merciful practice of almsgiving. This passage also suggests that, from a Lukan perspective, "giving alms," or ἐλεημοσύνη, and "justice" are not contrasting or even different practices.[57] In the world of Luke–Acts, ἐλεημοσύνη denotes "charity" not as a one-sided transaction but rather as a "merciful act" that involves

---

[55] The genitive τοῦ θεοῦ governs both articular nouns.

[56] C. Hays, *Luke's Wealth Ethics*, 122–23.

[57] While the noun κρίσις is used of the eschatological day of judgment elsewhere in the Gospel of Luke, including earlier in chapter 11 (cf. 10:14; 11:31-32), in Luke 11:43 the notion that κρίσις is a human practice (e.g., ταῦτα δὲ ἔδει ποιῆσαι) indicates that the term denotes "administration of what is right and fair, right in the sense of justice/righteousness" (BDAG).

relationships of reciprocity and solidarity, for the one who performs ἐλεημοσύνη one day may need to receive ἐλεημοσύνη the next.

~~Luke 12:32-34~~

The next passage in which merciful deeds are connected with reward comes immediately after the parable of the Rich Fool (12:13-21) in a discourse directed to the disciples (v. 22):[58]

> [32]Do not be afraid, little flock, for it is your Father's good pleasure to give you the kingdom. [33]Sell your possessions, and give alms (δότε ἐλεημοσύνην). Make purses for yourselves that do not wear out, an unfailing treasure in heaven, where no thief comes near and no moth destroys. [34]For where your treasure is, there your heart will be also. (12:32-34)

The string of aorist imperatives in verse 33 (πωλήσατε τὰ ὑπάρχοντα ὑμῶν καὶ δότε ἐλεημοσύνην· ποιήσατε ἑαυτοῖς βαλλάντια μὴ παλαιούμενα) suggests that these injunctions are closely related: selling possessions and giving alms enable the making of purses that do not wear out, a treasury that will not be exhausted. In this sense, almsgiving is the antidote to the punishment experienced by those who store up treasures for themselves but are not rich toward God, as exemplified in the parable of the Rich Fool in 12:16-21. The reward for almsgiving in Luke 12:33-34, then, is the accumulation of heavenly treasure. As in Mark and Matthew, the image of "heavenly treasure" represents an early Christian development of the notion, found in various Second Temple texts such as Tobit and Sirach, that merciful action on behalf of the needy results in reward. Luke's Gospel, along with its synoptic companions, envisions heavenly reward as eschatological merit on the basis of the performance of ἐλεημοσύνη in the present life.

Luke 14:7-14

In chapter 14, at another Lukan meal scene that takes place at the home of a leader of the Pharisees, Jesus instructs his host about the need to care for the poor, the crippled, the lame, and the blind by sharing food and hospitality with the excluded.[59] Jesus informs the one who had invited him that,

---

[58] That the disciples are the recipients of this teaching is additionally emphasized by the phrase τὸ μικρὸν ποίμνιον in 12:32.

[59] John T. Carroll, "Luke's Portrayal of the Pharisees," *CBQ* 50 (1988): 604–21. On the dynamics of reciprocity in this text, see Martin Ebner, "Symposion und Wassersucht, Reziprozitätsdenken und Umkehr: Sozialgeschichte und Theologie in Lk 14,1-24," in

by extending table fellowship to the destitute and to those whose disabled bodies open them to economic vulnerability, the Pharisee will be blessed. Although the poor, the crippled, the lame, and the blind cannot repay him (presumably with a return invitation; cf. v. 13), the Pharisee will be repaid "at the resurrection of the righteous" (v. 14; ἀνταποδοθήσεται γάρ σοι ἐν τῇ ἀναστάσει τῶν δικαίων). Given that Jesus speaks of repayment in terms of a return invitation to a lunch or dinner by one's friends, kin, or wealthy neighbors (v. 12), it may be implied that the repayment for provisioning the needy at the resurrection of the righteous is here envisioned as an invitation, on the basis of one's care for the marginalized, to an eschatological (messianic?) banquet.[60] Yet while the precise nature of the recompense at the resurrection is not spelled out, the notion that the Pharisee will receive future, eschatological reward on the basis of welcoming the marginalized to his table is clearly stated.

Luke 16:1-9

The next key, though admittedly vexing, text that connects charity and reward is found in Luke 16:1-9, a parable of a dishonest manager that Jesus tells to his disciples. When the household manager of a certain rich man is accused of wasting the rich man's possessions, the manager is asked to give an account of his management and notified of the termination of his employment (vv. 1-2). Recognizing his bleak chances of future employment, particularly given his unsuitability for manual labor and his unwillingness to beg, the household manager hatches a plan so that, once his job is taken away, people will still welcome him into their homes (vv. 3-4). The household manager summons his master's debtors and, one by one, dramatically reduces their exorbitant debts (vv. 5-7). The punch line of the parable is as puzzling as it is provocative:

> [8]And his master commended the dishonest manager because he had acted shrewdly; for the children of this age are more shrewd in dealing with their own generation than are the children of light. [9]And I tell you, make friends for yourselves by means of dishonest wealth so that when it is gone, they may welcome you into the eternal homes. (16:8-9, NRSV)

Paulus und die antike Welt: Beiträge zur zeit- und religionsgeschichtlichen Erforschung des paulinischen Christentums (ed. David C. Bienert, Joachim Jeska, and Thomas Witulski; FRLANT 22; Göttingen: Vandenhoeck & Ruprecht, 2008), 115–35.

[60] See Dennis E. Smith, *From Symposium to Eucharist: The Banquet in the Early Christian World* (Minneapolis: Augsburg Fortress, 2003).

In light of the connection between charity and recompense elsewhere in the Gospel of Luke, the parable of the dishonest manager can be read as a story about meritorious almsgiving.[61] In this reading, the dishonest manager is held out as a model of imitation for the disciples of Jesus because the manager employs his master's resources to procure future security. The reasoning is a fortiori: if such a dishonest man (ἀδικία [v. 8]) is commended because he acts shrewdly in safeguarding his future by giving away things that are not his own, how much more will this apply to the disciples as they make use of God's possessions? The parable is punctuated in verse 9 by an exhortation to make friends with the poor or those in need by means of unrighteous wealth so that, when the money is gone, those friends will welcome the disciples into the eternal homes.[62] In this sense, already the contrast between the rich man and Lazarus is anticipated (16:19-31): whereas the rich man, who did not welcome Lazarus into his home before death, is not welcomed by Lazarus to Abraham's bosom, the disciples, through almsgiving, will make friends in this life with those who need assistance and who cannot reciprocate, and those friends will, in turn, welcome the disciples into heavenly abodes. The story of the rich man and Lazarus, in fact, underscores the negative recompense that awaits those, especially the wealthy, who fail to show mercy to the destitute.[63]

Luke 18:18-30

Jesus' encounter with the rich ruler in Luke 18 offers another opportunity to reflect on the relationship between almsgiving and reward in the Gospel of Luke. In spite of several minor differences, the story is similar to its Markan antecedent, making a detailed analysis of the passage unnecessary, since the same themes emerge: the commission to sell everything and give to the poor, an act of dispossession that will result in heavenly treasure (v. 22); a call to follow Jesus (v. 22); the man's sadness when faced with Jesus' charge, yet with an open ending that does not report his ultimate response (v. 23); the conversation between Jesus and his audience (including Peter) about the impossibility of the rich entering the kingdom of God (vv. 23-28); and Jesus'

[61] See Francis E. Williams, "Is Almsgiving the Point of the 'Unjust Steward'?" *JBL* 83 (1964): 293–97; so also Outi Lehtipuu, "The Rich, the Poor, and the Promise of an Eschatological Reward in the Gospel of Luke," in *Other Worlds and Their Relation to This World* (ed. Tobias Nicklas et al.; JSJSup 143; Leiden: Brill, 2010), 229–46.
[62] I would differ from Williams, who understands the friends of v. 9 as "a personification of the almsdeeds which are performed with the 'mammon of unrighteousness'" ("Is Almsgiving the Point," 295).
[63] See esp. Lehtipuu, "Rich, the Poor, and the Promise," 235–37.

offer of both present and future reward for those who leave homes and families for the sake of the kingdom of God (v. 29). As in Mark's Gospel, Jesus'
promise of "many times more" this-worldly reward (i.e., "in this age"), in the
context of the Lukan narrative, signifies participation in the new family, oriented around Jesus, comprised of those who "hear the word of God and do
it" (8:21).[64] And in addition to reaping the benefit of sharing in kinship net-
works reconfigured around Jesus in this age, those who abandon homes and
relatives are also promised life in the age to come.

Luke 19:1-10

Perhaps the most distinctively Lukan feature of the story of the rich ruler in
Luke 18:18-30 is its juxtaposition with the narrative of Zacchaeus the tax
collector in 19:1-10. For while the response of the rich ruler in Luke 18 is not
explicitly narrated, Zacchaeus stands as a model of repentance and rightly
ordered economic practice. As an exemplar of the Lukan motif of reversal,
this wealthy chief tax collector is one whom readers might initially expect
to be an outsider with regard to the kingdom of God (cf. 6:24; 12:16-21;
16:19-31), yet the story concludes with Jesus' declaration, "Today, salvation
has come to this house, because he, too, is a son of Abraham" (v. 9).

The question of what provokes this response from Jesus has occasioned
no small debate. Should Zacchaeus' statement in verse 8 be read as a defense
of habitual practices in which he is already engaged or as a statement of
repentance and resolution, marking acts of economic justice and restitution
that he will demonstrate in the future?

> ἰδοὺ τὰ ἡμίσιά μου τῶν ὑπαρχόντων, κύριε, τοῖς πτωχοῖς δίδωμι, καὶ εἴ
> τινός τι ἐσυκοφάντησα ἀποδίδωμι τετραπλοῦν.

> Look, half of my possessions, Lord, I am going to give [or "I give"] to
> the poor, and if I extorted anyone of anything I am going to pay back
> [or "I pay pack"] four times as much.

While good arguments can be made for both options, the context, particularly the emphatic "today" (σήμερον) at the beginning of Jesus' response,
suggests that the present verbs δίδωμι and ἀποδίδωμι should be understood
to denote Zacchaeus' future resolve, in light of his meeting with Jesus, to
commit himself to new practices of economic justice.[65]

---

[64] So Joel B. Green, *The Gospel of Luke* (NICNT; Grand Rapids: Eerdmans, 1997),
658–59; in addition to 8:19-21, see also 9:5-62; 12:51-53; 14:25-26.

[65] So Dennis Hamm, "Zacchaeus Revisited Once More: A Story of Vindication or
Conversion?" *Bib* 72 (1991): 248–52.

If this is the case, then what is the relationship between Zacchaeus' embrace of almsgiving and reparations, on one hand, and Jesus' declaration of salvation, on the other? Is Zacchaeus "saved" by his repentance, symbolized by his changed economic practices? If salvation in the Gospel of Luke principally means status reversal, participation in the kingdom of God, and membership in the community gathered around Jesus, then it is easy to see how Zacchaeus' statement of repentance in verse 8 both symbolizes and effects the salvation of his household, even as Zacchaeus' response would also be impossible without Jesus' intentional (v. 5) and boundary-crossing (v. 7; cf. 5:30; 15:2) initiative personally to engage Zacchaeus.[66]

Acts of the Apostles

When the author of Luke–Acts narrates the early church's mission in the second volume of his work, the Acts of the Apostles, there is not necessarily a clear connection between giving and reward, particularly since notes of eschatological reward for generous sharing are muted in Acts in comparison with the Gospel of Luke. That is not to say that the story of Acts is unconcerned with the economic practices of the earliest followers of Jesus after the resurrection. Initially, for instance, Luke emphasizes the believers' willing divestiture of goods in order to meet the material needs of members of the Christ-believing community in Jerusalem (Acts 2:45; 4:34-35).[67] The summary statement in 2:42-47 at least implicitly connects the generosity of those who would sell their possessions and goods to give to those in need—along with the other practices described in this section, to be sure—with the numerical increase of "those who were being saved" (v. 47). Here the benefit of generosity is corporate, both in the sense that sharing resources establishes and solidifies the κοινωνία (v. 42) of the believers and in the sense that the church's care for the needy—assistance that would certainly have included the provision of food (cf. vv. 42, 46)—was part of the Christ-believing community's attractive public witness in Jerusalem.[68]

---

[66] See Joel B. Green, *The Theology of the Gospel of Luke* (New Testament Theology; Cambridge: Cambridge University Press, 1995), 76–101.

[67] On these statements in the larger context of Luke's wealth ethics, and for an informative analysis of some literary, historical, and economic questions raised by these passages, see C. Hays, *Luke's Wealth Ethics*, 190–210.

[68] The story of the healing of the paralytic man in Acts 3:1-10 does not directly bear on the relationship between care for the needy and reward, but it does feature a concentration of the term ἐλεημοσύνη. The noun is used three times (3:2, 3, 10) to refer to the object of the man's request at the "Beautiful Gate." Translations that render the noun ἐλεημοσύνη as "money" (CEB) or "to beg" (NAB, NASB, NIV, NJB) both unnecessarily

Acts 9:36-42 and 10:1-48

The stories of Tabitha (9:36-42) and Cornelius (10:1-48) are sometimes discussed with reference to atoning and/or meritorious almsgiving, the former because Tabitha's resuscitation from the dead is preceded by the observation that she was "full of good works and merciful deeds, which she continually performed" (9:36: αὕτη ἦν πλήρης ἔργων ἀγαθῶν καὶ ἐλεημοσυνῶν ὧν ἐποίει), the latter because the Gentile centurion is noted for his practice of ἐλεημοσύνη, even to the extent that an angel of the Lord declares that Cornelius' "merciful actions have ascended as a remembrance before God" (10:4: αἱ ἐλεημοσύναι σου ἀνέβησαν εἰς μνημόσυνον ἔμπροσθεν τοῦ θεοῦ).[69] Tabitha's story should not be seen as an example of meritorious or atoning almsgiving, however. While Tabitha's body is raised to life by Peter, her healing is only, at best, indirectly related to her characterization as a disciple "full of good works and merciful deeds" (v. 36). Tabitha's pious and beneficent life may be the reason that the disciples in Joppa send an urgent request for Peter immediately to come from Lydda (v. 38), as well as the cause of the grief experienced by Joppan widows at Tabitha's death (v. 39). But there is no suggestion in the narrative that Tabitha is resuscitated because of her merciful deeds.

The story of Cornelius' encounter with Peter is more complex and suggestive. This account concludes with the baptism of Cornelius, a Gentile

---

limit the request to a financial transaction (as if the man were ringing a Christmas bell for the Salvation Army outside of a department store) and fail to highlight the fact that "a merciful act" (ἐλεημοσύνη) is exactly what Peter provides the paralytic man. Peter makes clear, of course, that his ἐλεημοσύνη does not consist of "gold or silver" (3:6), but nevertheless Peter does not reject the request. Instead, Peter responds, "What I have I give to you: in the name of Jesus Christ [stand up and] walk!" (3:6). In context, Peter does perform ἐλεημοσύνη. The only other instance of the use of the word ἐλεημοσύνη in Acts occurs in 24:17, when Paul, while standing trial before Felix, says of his final trip to Jerusalem: "Now after some years I came to bring alms (ἐλεημοσύνας ποιήσων) to my nation and to offer sacrifices" (NRSV). As in Luke 11:41 and 12:33, the context seems to suggest a pragmatic adjustment to the meaning "merciful act." It may well be the case that ἐλεημοσύνη in this context refers to donations to the temple. For an argument that ἐλεημοσύνη does not refer to the collection for Jerusalem mentioned in 1 Cor 16:1-4; 2 Cor 8:1-9:15; and Rom 15:25-33, see David J. Downs, "Paul's Collection and the Book of Acts Revisited," *NTS* 52 (2006): 50–70; pace Klaus Berger, "Almosen für Israel," *NTS* 23 (1977): 180–204.

[69] See the discussion in Roman Garrison, *Redemptive Almsgiving in Early Christianity* (JSNTSup 77; Sheffield: JSOT Press, 1993), 66–68. Cyprian invokes Tabitha's story in support of atoning almsgiving (*Eleem.* 6).

officer in the Roman army, and his household, an episode that occupies a central place in the unfolding narrative in Acts of the inclusion of Gentiles among the community of God's people.[70] Cornelius' performance of prayers (αἱ προσευχαί) and merciful deeds (αἱ ἐλεημοσύναι) are certainly import- ant to his depiction as a devout, God-fearing Gentile (v. 2).[71] Not only is the introduction to Cornelius framed with reference to his merciful deeds and prayers (v. 2), but the angel of God who visits Cornelius reports that these practices have ascended as a remembrance (μνημόσυνον) before God (v. 4), a statement reiterated later in the narrative when Cornelius recapitu- lates before Peter and others his conversation with the heavenly messenger (v. 31). In Acts 10:4, therefore, Cornelius' prayers and merciful deeds arise as a remembrance before God, and in Acts 10:31 Cornelius summarizes the angel as saying that the centurion's prayer and merciful deeds have been remembered before God.

What is the relationship between Cornelius' piety, including his perfor- mance of ἐλεημοσύναι, and God's remembrance of him? Without suggesting any particular literary relationship, the characterization of Cornelius' piety parallels that of Tobit in interesting ways.[72] Tobit's own exemplary piety is introduced at the beginning of the narrative with reference to Tobit's per- formance of merciful deeds (ἐλεημοσύναι [1:3]), his pilgrimages to Jerusa- lem to offer tithes and firstfruits and to participate in festivals (1:4-8), his endogamous marriage (1:9), his abstention from unclean food (1:10-11), and an expanded list of Tobit's ἐλεημοσύναι, a list that includes giving food and clothing to the needy and burying the dead among his people (1:16-18). Later in the story, when the angel Raphael reveals his true identity to Tobit and

---

[70] For canonical and narrative analyses of this episode, see Robert W. Wall, "Peter, 'Son' of Jonah: The Conversion of Cornelius in the Context of Canon," *JSNT* 29 (1987): 79–90; van Thanh Nguyen, *Peter and Cornelius: A Story of Conversion and Mission* (ASMMS 15; Eugene, Ore.: Wipf & Stock, 2012). My reading of the Cornelius story owes much to C. Hays (*Luke's Wealth Ethics*, 234–37), whose interpretation I have fol- lowed closely at points.

[71] Much of the discussion about the character of Cornelius has centered on the ques- tion whether the term "god-fearer" (φοβούμενος τὸν θεὸν [10:2]) is a technical term that refers to Gentile sympathizers to Judaism; for a helpful overviews of the debate, see Craig S. Keener, *Acts: An Exegetical Commentary*, vol. 2, 3:1–14:28, (Har/Com ed.; Grand Rap- ids: Baker, 2013), 1750–53; Dietrich-Alex Koch, "The God-Fearers between Facts and Fiction: Two Theosebeis-Inscriptions from Aphrodisias and Their Bearing for the New Testament," *Stud. Theol.* 60, no. 1 (2006): 62–90.

[72] Susan Docherty, "The Reception of Tobit in the New Testament and Early Chris- tian Literature, with Special Reference to Luke–Acts," in *The Scriptures of Israel in Jewish and Christian Tradition: Essays in Honour of Maarten J. J. Menken* (ed. Bart J. Koet, Steve Moyise, and Joseph Verheyden; NovTSup 148; Leiden: Brill, 2013), 85.

Tobias (in Tobit 12), for instance, Raphael's declaration of "the whole truth" affirms that Tobit's and Sarah's prayers (3:1-15) were presented by Raphael as a remembrance before God: "And now when you and your daughter-in-law, Sarah, prayed, it was I who brought the remembrance (μνημόσυνον) of your prayer before the Holy One, and when you would bury the dead, similarly I was present with you."[73] The noun μνημόσυνον in Leviticus and Numbers occasionally refers to the memorial portion of a sacrificial offering (e.g., LXX Lev 2:2, 9, 16; 5:12; 6:8; Num 5:15, 26; cf. Sir 35:5-6; 38:11; 45:16), but in Tobit prayer is a "remembrance" (μνημόσυνον) before God.[74]

Like Tobit, then, Cornelius offers prayers and merciful deeds that rise to God for divine remembrance (10:4, 31). Both of these pious men—one a faithful Jew, one a Gentile centurion—receive God's consideration and favor in part because of their practice of ἐλεημοσύνη. Within the narrative world of Luke–Acts, Cornelius' performance of merciful deeds can be fruitfully considered in light of Jesus' statement to the Pharisees in Luke 11:41 regarding the purifying power of ἐλεημοσύνη: "So give alms with respect to the things within, and see, everything is clean for you (πάντα καθαρὰ ὑμῖν ἐστιν)." In Jesus' encounter with the Pharisees in Luke 11, the Pharisees are concerned about external purity (vv. 38-39a), but Jesus accuses them of being internally unclean, full of greed and wickedness on the inside (v. 39b), and offers the practice of almsgiving as a means of becoming entirely clean.

Similarly, the story of Peter's encounter with Cornelius turns on the issue of clean and unclean. When Peter receives a vision of a large sheet containing all kinds of four-footed animals, reptiles, and birds being let down from the open heaven, followed by a voice instructing Peter, "Get up, Peter; kill and eat" (10:10-13), Peter initially rejects this command, reasoning that he has never eaten anything "profane and unclean" (οὐδέποτε ἔφαγον πᾶν κοινὸν

---

[73] Technically, Raphael says that Tobit's and Sarah's prayers were a μνημόσυνον ("remembrance") before God and that Raphael was with Tobit when he buried the dead (καὶ ὅτε ἔθαπτες τοὺς νεκροὺς ὡσαύτως συμπαρήμην σοι). Yet in context it is likely that Raphael's presence *with* Tobit precedes his bringing this act as a remembrance before God, and earlier in the chapter Tobit's practice of burying his fellow Israelites is defined as ἐλεημοσύνη (cf. Tob 1:16-18). On the theme of remembrance in Tobit, see Francis M. Macatangay, "Acts of Charity as Acts of Remembrance in the Book of Tobit," *JSP* 23 (2013): 69–84.

[74] I am not inclined to see either the author of Tobit or the author of Acts as adopting a "stock appropriation of sacrificial language for describing non-cultic acts of piety" (C. Hays, *Luke's Wealth Ethics*, 236) because the language of "remembrance" (μνημόσυνον) is not specifically "cultic," although it is used in Leviticus and Numbers to refer to an aspect of a cultic presentation. Hays assumes that μνημόσυνον is a technical term for cultic offering when it is not.

καὶ ἀκάθαρτον [10:14]).[75] In response, the voice charges Peter, "What God has made clean, you must not consider profane" (10:15). Given that Peter's vision contains a sheet full of animals that Peter is instructed to eat, it might naturally be assumed that the implication of this revelation concerns the legitimate consumption of unclean *food*. Interestingly, however, Peter offers a different interpretation of the vision when he meets with Cornelius and Cornelius' household in Caesarea: "You yourselves know that it is unlawful for a Jewish man to associate or visit with a foreigner. But God has shown me that I should not call *any person* profane or unclean" (10:29). ~~According-ing to Peter's interpretation in Acts 10:28-29, the vision shown to him by God related to the designation of profane or unclean *people*, not animals or food, a point reiterated in Peter's retelling of the episode in 11:4-17.~~ Peter's re-narration moves directly from the voice's instruction not to call profane the things God has made clean (v. 9) to a description of the Holy Spirit's descent upon Cornelius and the centurion's household, with the implication that those baptized by the Holy Spirit are not unclean (vv. 11-17).[76]

The point of the story is not that Peter can enter into fellowship with Cornelius only because the centurion's prayers and deeds of mercy purify him, for missionary encounters with Gentiles earlier (8:26-40) and later in Acts do not assume that Gentile recipients of the gospel message must exhibit the same piety as Cornelius.[77] Moreover, Cornelius' prayers and merciful deeds (προσευχαί καὶ ἐλεημοσύναι) are said to have come before God as a "remembrance," not as an atoning sacrifice for sins. Nevertheless, it is difficult to ignore the connection between Cornelius' piety—exhibited partly through his practice of ἐλεημοσύνη—and the command to Peter, "What God has made clean, you must not consider profane" (10:15). God is the one who makes Cornelius (and other things and people) clean.[78] But the logical

---

[75] On the importance of rendering the conjunction καί as "and" instead of "or," see Mikeal C. Parsons, "'Nothing Defiled AND Unclean': The Conjunction's Function in Acts 10:14," *PRSt* 27 (2000): 263–74.

[76] The difference between the account of Peter's vision and Peter's interpretation of it has sometimes been used to speculate about different traditions or redactional elements in the narrative; see, e.g., François Bovon, "Tradition et rédaction en Actes 10:1-11,18," *TZ* 26 (1970): 22–45.

[77] So C. Hays, *Luke's Wealth Ethics*, 236; pace Berger, "Almosen für Israel," 180–204.

[78] God is the subject of the verb καθαρίζω both times it occurs in the Cornelius narrative (10:15; 11:9). In an unpublished paper graciously shared with me, Timothy Reardon has argued that Acts 15:9 also refers to the cleansing of Cornelius and that the phrase τῇ πίστει τὸ καθαρίσας should be linked with the preceding clause and taken as a dative of respect: "making no distinction between our faith and theirs, on account of

outworking of Jesus' earlier statement in Luke 11:41 would seem to imply that God's cleansing of Cornelius happens in concert with Cornelius' performance of merciful deeds. In the context of the narrative of Luke–Acts, Cornelius embodies the instruction of Jesus regarding ἐλεημοσύνη in the Gospel of Luke: his prayers and ἐλεημοσύνη are closely connected to his purity. It can be said, therefore, that Cornelius' practice of merciful deeds is, at the very least, a sign, if not the cause, of his status as a Gentile neither profane nor unclean (10:28).[79]

Acts 20:35

The final passage in Acts in which giving and reward are connected comes at the conclusion of Paul's speech to the Ephesian elders at Miletus in Acts 20. This discourse—which comes in the larger context of a protracted depiction of the internal, communal practices of the church (20:1–21:17)—is somewhat unique in Acts in that it is the only speech of Paul's directed at disciples of Jesus.[80] Paul's address concludes with a commendation of the Ephesian elders to God and to the message of God's grace (v. 32) and a call for the listeners to imitate Paul's example by caring for the weak, an appeal rooted in the words of Jesus:

> [32]And now I commend you to God and to the message of his grace, a message that is able to build you up and to give you the inheritance among all who are sanctified. [33]I coveted no one's silver or gold or clothing. [34]You know for yourselves that I worked with my own hands to support myself and my companions. [35]In all this I have given you an example that by such work we must support the weak, remembering the words of the Lord Jesus, for he himself said, "It is more blessed to give than to receive." (20:32-35, NRSV)

Much commentary on Paul's citation of Jesus' teaching in verse 35 has focused on the relationship of this quotation to the teaching of the historical Jesus

---

having cleansed their hearts." According to Reardon, the cleansing of "their hearts," which happens apart from or before faith, represents the cleaned life of Cornelius through the act of almsgiving.

[79] As Christopher Hays summarizes, "By doing alms Cornelius exemplifies that his Gentile ethnicity *has not* rendered him unclean. The very thing that Jesus tells the Pharisees will cleanse their impurity becomes evidence of Cornelius's own purity" (*Luke's Wealth Ethics*, 236 [emphasis in original]).

[80] For perceptive analysis of this speech in its literary context, see Beverly Roberts Gaventa, "Theology and Ecclesiology in the Miletus Speech: Reflections on Content and Context," *NTS* 50 (2004): 36–52.

and parallels to this phrase in Greco-Roman literature.[81] What is often not observed, however, is that the saying "It is more blessed to give than to receive" echoes the same notion of self-interested giving seen in the Synoptic Gospels, including the Gospel of Luke. In the context of Paul's exhortation, practices of "giving" and "receiving" refer to material provision of the needy (20:34-35). Paul does not prohibit the reception of assistance, even as he encourages the elders of the Ephesian church to imitate his example of working to support himself, his companions, and "the weak" (οἱ ἀσθενοῦντές)—that is, the poor and marginalized.[82] Instead, Paul indicates that the act of giving is more blessed (μακάριος) than the act of receiving. According to the logic of verse 35, then, to give to the needy and vulnerable brings blessing upon those who provide this material support. Such a perspective on the "interested" nature of giving not only fits the literary context of Luke–Acts but also coheres with key elements of rhetoric of almsgiving in the Pauline Epistles.

Conclusion

There can be little doubt that the Synoptic Gospels and Acts regularly, and sometimes emphatically, emphasize the connection between caring for the poor and divine recompense. Almsgiving in these canonical writings is broadly meritorious in the sense that those who practice merciful deeds are often promised reward for their material care of the needy. Occasionally, the precise nature of this reward is not clearly defined. Yet the Synoptic Gospels and Acts frequently (though not exclusively) extend the reward for charity into the eschatological future, a development not seen in texts like Deuteronomy, Proverbs, Tobit, and Sirach. It is particularly in these three scriptural narratives of Jesus' life that divine recompense for merciful deeds comes to be understood as extending beyond this life into the next. And this emphasis on the eschatological reward for almsgiving would come to shape the development of Christian theology in the second and third centuries.

Moreover, if there is one text among the Synoptic Gospels and Acts that most decisively shaped the emergence of the notion of atoning almsgiving, it is Luke 11:41: "So give alms with respect to the things within, and see, everything is clean for you." Cyprian's treatise *De opere et eleemosynis*, for example, opens with the citation of three scriptural texts that frame his entire discussion of almsgiving as an antidote to post-baptismal sin: Prov 16:6 (LXX

---

[81] Craig S. Keener, *Acts: An Exegetical Commentary*, vol. 3, 15:1–23:35 (Grand Rapids: Baker, 2014), 3062–67.

[82] So Bruce W. Longenecker, *Remember the Poor: Paul, Poverty, and the Greco-Roman World* (Grand Rapids: Eerdmans, 2010), 151–52.

15:27); Sir 3:30; and Luke 11:40-41.[83] In his gloss on these verses, Cyprian comments that in this text Jesus is

> teaching, obviously, and showing that not the hands ought to be washed but the heart, and that uncleanliness ought to be removed on the inside rather than on the outside; moreover, that he who has cleansed that which is within has also cleansed that which is without and, when, his mind has been cleansed, has begun to be clean in his skin also and his body. Next, instructing and showing by what means we are able to be clean and purified, He added that corporal works of mercy [i.e., alms] must be done. In His mercy, He admonishes that mercy be done, and, since He seeks to save those whom He has redeemed with great price, He teaches that they, who after the grace of baptism have been defiled, can be cleansed again. (*Eleem.* 2)[84]

Cyprian's interpretation of Luke 11:41 is far from idiosyncratic. In a sermon on Leviticus that identifies six "remissions of sin in the Gospel" in addition to baptism, Origen lists almsgiving third, after baptism and martyrdom, and he glosses the point with a citation of Luke 11:41: "For the Savior says, 'but nevertheless, give what you have and, behold, all things are clean for you'" (*Hom. Lev.* 2.4.5).[85] Similarly, near the end of a sermon on John 17, John Chrysostom pauses to consider how, in the same way that children often enjoy toy chariots and dolls more than the real thing, sinful people find pleasure in earthly wealth and glory instead of lasting heavenly treasure (*Hom. Jo.* 81). Chrysostom then cites Dan 4:27 and Luke 11:41 in an appeal for his hearers to nourish the soul and provide a remedy for the wounds the soul receives through lust, anger, sloth, reviling, revenge, and envy by almsgiving, "which can be placed on every wound." Chrysostom argues that the practice of almsgiving effects transformation among those who give and leads them to eternal reward:

> He that practices showing mercy to him that needs, will soon cease from *covetousness*; he who continues in giving to the *poor*, will soon cease from *anger*, and will never even be high-minded. For as the physician continually tending wounded *persons* is easily sobered,

---

[83] On Cyprian's use of Scripture in this treatise, see David J. Downs, "Prosopological Exegesis in Cyprian's *De opere et eleemosynis*," *JTI* 6 (2012): 279–94.

[84] The translation is from Edward V. Rebenack, *Thasci Caecili Cypriani: De opere et eleemosynis; A Translation with Introduction and a Commentary* (Patristic Studies 94; Washington, D.C.: Catholic University of America Press, 1962). For other appeals to Luke 11:41 in discussions of atoning almsgiving, see *Orig. Hom. Lev.* 2.4.5.

[85] For a longer discussion of this passage in Origen's *Hom. Lev.*, see chap. 7.

beholding *human nature* in the calamities of others, so we, if we enter upon the work of aiding the *poor*, shall easily become *truly* wise, and shall not admire riches, nor deem present things any great matter, but despise them all, and soaring aloft to heaven, shall easily obtain the *eternal* blessings, through the *grace* and loving kindness of *our Lord Jesus Christ*; to whom, with the Father and the *Holy Ghost*, be *glory* for ever and ever. (*Hom. Jo.* 81)[86]

Even a cursory glance at the early reception history of Luke 11:41 suggests that the verse can be taken as a statement that almsgiving has the power to cleanse human sin, particularly greed and wickedness.[87] To the question asked in the opening line of Robert Lowry's hymn, "Nothing but the Blood" ("What can wash away my sin?"), the author of Luke–Acts seems to answer, and a number of his earliest interpreters certainly do answer, "ἐλεημοσύνη."

---

[86] In his *Enchiridion on Faith, Hope, and Love*, Augustine discusses the relationship of almsgiving to repentance. Augustine defines "suitable repentance" as marked by almsgiving, yet he is also wary not to allow that "gross sins, such as are committed by those who shall not inherit the kingdom of God, may be daily perpetrated, and daily atoned for by almsgiving" (*Enchir.* 70). As Augustine goes on to comment, "The life must be changed for the better; and almsgiving must be used to propitiate God for past sins, not to purchase impunity for the commission of such sins in the future" (70). Later Augustine cites Luke 11:41, claiming that this passage applies to "every useful act that a man does in mercy," including caring for anyone who is hungry, thirsty, naked, stranger, fugitive, sick, imprisoned, captive, weak, blind, sorrowful, sick, wanderer, perplexed, or sinner. Augustine's citation of 11:41 is complicated by the fact that his Latin text may read quite differently than the Greek; cf. the Vulgate: *Verumtamen quod superest, date eleemosynam: Et ecce omnia munda sunt vobis.*

[87] On the possibility that Tertullian interpreted Luke 11:41 in support of atoning almsgiving, see J. Ramsey Michaels, "Almsgiving and the Kingdom Within: Tertullian on Luke 17:21," *CBQ* 60 (1998): 475–83.

CHAPTER 5

STORING UP TREASURE
FOR A GOOD FOUNDATION
Almsgiving and Reward in the Pauline Epistles

Sometime around 49 or 50 CE, the apostle Paul, as a delegate of the church in Antioch, traveled to Jerusalem to meet with leaders of the early Jesus movement located there. Paul was accompanied by two associates from Antioch: Barnabas and Titus (a Gentile). According to Paul's recollection of this visit in Gal 2:1-10, the meeting ostensibly addressed and affirmed Paul's circumcision-free mission to the Gentiles, while also asseverating Peter as apostle to the circumcised (v. 8). Paul's account in Galatians 2 concludes with the memory of James, Peter, and John recognizing the grace of God given to Paul, extending to Paul and Barnabas the "right hand of fellowship," and agreeing to a binary mission that would send Paul and Barnabas to bring the good news to Gentiles and the Jerusalem leaders to the Jews (v. 9). After narrating the agreement regarding the validity of his mission to the Gentiles, Paul appends the request from the Jerusalem leaders that Paul and his companions "remember the poor," an entreaty, Paul indicates, that he was enthusiastic to oblige: "They asked only one thing, that we continue to remember the poor, which was the very thing I was eager to do" (v. 10).

In modern biblical scholarship, the request made by the Jerusalem apostles that Paul and the Antioch delegates "remember the poor" has regularly been interpreted in a local sense—namely, that "the poor" in Gal 2:10 are poor believers in Jerusalem for whom the apostles ask material assistance. The appeal to "remember the poor" in 2:10 is then often understood as a reference to—indeed, the origin of—the relief fund that Paul later organized among the largely Gentile churches of his mission for "the poor among the saints" in Jerusalem (Rom 15:26). Paul calls this project "the collection for the saints" (1 Cor 16:1), and he refers to it in several of his letters (i.e., 1 Cor 16:1-4; 2 Cor 8:1-9:15; Rom 15:14-32).

There are, however, numerous problems with linking the request to "remember the poor" in Gal 2:10 with the later Pauline collection for Jerusalem. Perhaps most significantly, there is no clear reason that the request to "remember the poor" should be localized to Jesus-believers in Jerusalem.[1] Instead, the Jerusalem leaders who ask the Antioch delegates to "remember the poor" are concerned that Paul and Barnabas, in the context of their mission to non-Jews, continue to remind pagan converts that caring for the poor is an integral part of the gospel witness. While Jewish communities in the Greco-Roman world, formed as they were by scriptural traditions in which care for the needy was a religious requirement, regularly developed practices of providing assistance for the destitute, concern for the poor, though not entirely absent, was not a prominent social value for most pagans.[2] In commissioning the Antioch delegates to bring the gospel of Jesus Christ to the Gentile world, therefore, the Jerusalem leaders wanted to ensure that the good news proclaimed by Paul and Barnabas to pagans would not ignore an essential Jewish conviction and practice, deeply embedded in Old Testament scriptural texts and in the Jesus tradition: the people of God should care for the poor. Thus, at the heart of Paul's own presentation of his mission as apostle to the Gentiles stands a commitment, agreed to by him and the Jerusalem apostles, to "remember the poor."

[1] For a discussion of the chronology of the collection, see David J. Downs, *The Offering of the Gentiles: Paul's Collection for Jerusalem in Its Chronological, Cultural, and Cultic Contexts* (WUNT II/248; Tübingen: Mohr Siebeck, 2008). In that earlier work, I argued that the reference to remembering the poor in Gal 2:10 should be connected to the collection from Antioch with which Paul was involved (Acts 11:27-30) and not associated with the later Pauline collection for Jerusalem. While I would still contend that Gal 2:10 should be separated from the later Pauline collection for Jerusalem referenced in 1 Cor 16:1-4; 2 Cor 8:1-9:15; and Rom 15:14-32, I am now no longer convinced that the request to "remember the poor" in Gal 2:10 refers only to the Antioch collection. I have been persuaded by the trenchant argument of Bruce W. Longenecker that "the poor" in Gal 2:10 should not be localized in Jerusalem; Longenecker, *Remember the Poor: Paul, Poverty, and the Greco-Roman World* (Grand Rapids: Eerdmans, 2010), 157–206.

[2] Longenecker, *Remember the Poor*, 60–107.

Paul's agreement with the leaders of the Jerusalem church that charity be essential to his mission as apostle to the Gentiles is then fleshed out in numerous allusions and appeals to practices of almsgiving in the letters ascribed to Paul.[3] Not only did Paul spend a number of years organizing a relief fund for "the poor among the saints in Jerusalem" (Rom 15:26) among the largely Gentile churches of his mission, but his letters both encourage readers to share material resources with the needy (Rom 12:13, 16; Eph 4:28; 1 Thess 5:14; Titus 3:14; cf. Gal 6:9-10) and refer to specific practices of caring for the poor, including communal meals (1 Cor 11:17-34; cf. 2 Thess 3:6-13) and provision for widows (1 Tim 5:3-16). Indeed, when discussing the Jerusalem collection in a letter to the Corinthians, Paul reminds his readers in Corinth that participation in the collection is a means of glorifying God "by your obedience to the confession of the gospel of Christ and by the generosity of your partnership-forming contribution (κοινωνία) for them and for *all*" (2 Cor 9:13). Here Paul intimates that Corinthian κοινωνία for believers in Jerusalem, as demonstrated through material support for the collection, would be one particular manifestation of practices of generosity and almsgiving to which the Corinthians would be committed for *all*.[4] Moreover, Paul himself, according to his testimony, often lived in or near a state of material deprivation (1 Cor 4:11-12; 2 Cor 11:23-27; Phil 4:11-12) and regularly worked to support himself through manual labor (1 Thess 2:9; 2 Thess 3:7-9; 1 Cor 4:12; 9:3-12; 2 Cor 11:27; cf. Acts 18:3; 20:34-35).[5] As such, Paul appears occasionally to have received charitable assistance from some

---

[3] From a historical-critical perspective, many New Testament interpreters would want to distinguish between the seven Pauline Letters whose authorship by the historical Paul is not generally contested, on one hand, and the six so-called Disputed Paulines (i.e., Ephesians, Colossians, 2 Thessalonians, 1–2 Timothy, and Titus), on the other. I myself, in fact, have occasionally written about the economic practices described in the Pauline Epistles with the assumption that it is possible to distinguish between authentic and pseudonymous Pauline Letters (e.g., Downs, "Paul's Collection and the Book of Acts," 50). In this chapter, however, I shall make no such distinction among the thirteen letters attributed to the apostle Paul in the canon of the New Testament, for I no longer find historical and literary arguments for the pseudonymous nature of the Disputed Paulines convincing. The claim that all thirteen canonical letters attributed to Paul are authentic obviously shapes my interpretation of the evidence in significant ways. Defending this position on the authenticity of the thirteen canonical letters in any kind of detail is not possible here, but for an insightful recent article questioning the "consensus" view with regard to one particular "disputed" epistle, see Paul Foster, "Who Wrote 2 Thessalonians? A Fresh Look at an Old Problem," *JSNT* 35 (2012): 150–75.

[4] Longenecker, *Remember the Poor*, 140, 187–88.

[5] Todd D. Still, "Did Paul Loathe Manual Labor? Revisiting the Work of Ronald F. Hock on the Apostle's Tentmaking and Social Class," *JBL* 125 (2006): 781–95; Steven

of the churches or individuals associated with his mission (2 Cor 11:7-12; Phil 4:10-20; Rom 16:1-2, 23; cf. Phlm 22), even while he also sometimes vigorously refused to request or receive compensation for his work (1 Thess 2:9-12; 1 Cor 9:3-18; 2 Cor 2:17; 11:7-11). Given the numerous references or allusions to practices of care for the poor in Paul's letters, and given the Jewish theological context in which these practices emerged, it is not surprising that the Pauline Epistles regularly frame care for the needy as a practice that receives recompense, both divine and human.[6]

1 Timothy 6:6-19

This exploration of the relationship between charity and reward in the Pauline Epistles will begin with an oft-neglected but illuminating passage: 1 Tim 6:6-19.[7] Material from 1 Timothy has regularly been ignored in the study

---

J. Friesen, "Poverty in Pauline Studies: Beyond the So-Called New Consensus," *JSNT* 26 (2004): 323–61; Longenecker, *Remember the Poor*, 298–316.

[6] Negatively, failure to care mercifully for the poor subjects the Corinthians to Paul's censure (1 Cor 11:17) and divine judgment (1 Cor 11:27-32). In his critical assessment of the Corinthians' failure to practice the Lord's Supper, Paul indicts the Corinthians for showing contempt to the "have-nots," presumably because some of the "have-nots" are not sufficiently provisioned by this substantive meal while others drink (and eat) to excess (1 Cor 11:21-22). In contrast, Paul encourages the Corinthians to recognize that—unless the community embodies a concern for others, particularly the poor, modeled on the self-giving love of Jesus Christ—it cannot rightly proclaim the Lord's death (11:20, 23-26). Paul exhorts the Corinthians not to eat of the bread or drink of the cup of the Lord's Supper without discerning the corporate body of Christ—i.e., at the very least feeding all members of Christ's body—or else they will invoke divine judgment against themselves (11:28-29). In fact, Paul implies that failure rightly to discern the body of Christ during this corporate meal has already resulted in weakness, illness, and death among some members of the community (11:30). This claim may imply that both those who overconsume and those whose hunger is neglected suffer harmful physical consequences as a result of the distorted practice of the Lord's Supper at Corinth. An interesting text in light of Paul's claim in 1 Cor 11:30 is Herm. *Vis.* 3.9.2–5a: "Now listen to me and be at peace among yourselves, and be concerned with one another and assist one another; and do not partake of God's creation in abundance by yourselves, but also share with those in need. *For by overeating some people bring on themselves fleshly weaknesses and injure their flesh, while the flesh of those who do not have anything to eat is injured because they do not have enough food, and their bodies are wasting away.* This lack of community spirit is harmful to those of you who have, yet do not share with those in need. Look to the coming judgment" (translation from Michael W. Holmes, *The Apostolic Fathers: Greek Texts and English Translations* [3rd ed.; Grand Rapids: Baker, 2007], 487–89).

[7] The organization of the Pauline material in this chapter is broadly thematic and not chronological, not least because I am hesitant to place too much confidence in any particular chronological arrangement of the Pauline Letters. For a recent attempt, see

of gift-giving practices among the Pauline churches because of the common scholarly assumption that the letter is a pseudonymous composition, one that illustrates only the subsequent thoughts of a second-rate imitator of the apostle Paul. Yet 6:6-19 offers a revealing perspective on the relationship between almsgiving and recompense, particularly if the passage is treated as an important aspect of the canonical portrait of Paul. In fact, 6:17-19 can provide a helpful lens through which to view other Pauline texts in which some kind of reward is imagined or offered for those who practice merciful deeds.[8]

Among the interpretative challenges offered by the final chapter of 1 Timothy, one literary and one theological question are especially resistant to easy answers. First, how does the personal charge to Timothy in 6:11-16 relate to its present literary context, particularly since the directives given to Timothy in verses 11 to 14, which are punctuated by a brief doxology in verses 15 to 16, appear at first glance to interrupt the focused teachings on wealth found in verses 6 to 10 and verses 17 to 19? Second, does the instruction to the rich in verses 17 to 19, with its suggestion that the wealthy are able through generous deeds to store up a treasury of credit from which funds can be used to purchase reward in the next life, contradict or stand in tension with the Pauline doctrine of justification by faith and not works?

The Literary Unity of 6:6-19

The literary structure of 1 Timothy 6 has frequently puzzled interpreters. The instructions to slaves in 6:1-2a conclude and naturally belong together with the household code from the previous chapter.[9] It is more difficult to discern the organization and thematic relationship of the material that

---

Douglas A. Campbell, *Framing Paul: An Epistolary Account* (Grand Rapids: Eerdmans, 2014).

[8] A longer version of this section appears in David J. Downs, "The God Who Gives Life That Is Truly Life: Meritorious Almsgiving and the Divine Economy in 1 Timothy 6," in *The Unrelenting God: Essays on God's Action in Scripture in Honor of Beverly Roberts Gaventa* (ed. David J. Downs and Matthew L. Skinner; Grand Rapids: Eerdmans, 2013), 242–60.

[9] The material in the household code also addresses the treatment of older and younger men and women (5:1-2), support of widows (5:3-16), and the payment, discipline, and appointment of elders (5:17-25); see David G. Horrell, "Disciplining Performance and 'Placing' the Church: Widows, Elders, and Slaves in the Household of God (1 Tim 5,1–6,2)," in *1 Timothy Reconsidered* (ed. Karl P. Donfried; Colloquium Oecumenicum Paulinum 18; Leuven: Peeters, 2008), 109–34. The directive that Timothy stop drinking only water in 5:23 does appear to be something of a digression, although it is probably linked to the preceding and following material through the concept of purity (so Jürgen Roloff, *Der Erste Brief an Timotheus* [EKKNT 15; Zürich: Benziger & Neukirchener, 1988], 315).

follows, not least because two sections that deal directly with the topic of wealth, verses 6 to 10 and 17 to 19, are ostensibly separated by a personal charge to Timothy in verses 11 to 16.[10] Paul's charge to Timothy in verses 11 to 16 has been characterized as an "intrusion,"[11] an interpolation,[12] an awkwardly placed baptismal or ordination tradition,[13] or an example of a pseudo-Paulinist's tendency to combine material in a rough and disjointed manner.[14]

Yet it is possible that the charge to Timothy in 1 Tim 6:11-16 actually continues, rather than interrupts, Paul's discourse about wealth in verses 3 to 10 and verses 17 to 19. This proposal centers on the nature of the unspecified "commandment" that Timothy is exhorted to keep in verse 14.[15] In verses 13 to 14, Paul issues a solemn charge for Timothy to keep "the commandment" (τηρῆσαί σε τὴν ἐντολήν), yet there is no immediate indication of what specific action(s) keeping this commandment is intended to entail:

> [13]I charge you in the presence of God, who gives life to all things, and of Christ Jesus, who testified before Pontius Pilate with respect to the good confession, [14]*to keep the commandment unblemished and above reproach until the manifestation of our Lord Jesus Christ,* [15]which he will

---

[10] The discussion of wealth in 6:6-10 is linked to the previous material on false teaching in 6:3-5 by the repetition and alteration in v. 6 (Ἔστιν δὲ πορισμὸς μέγας ἡ εὐσέβεια μετὰ αὐταρκείας) of the phrase πορισμὸν εἶναι τὴν εὐσέβειαν in v. 5 that is used to describe the mistaken belief of false teachers that godliness is a means of profit; see Peter Dschulnigg, "Warnung vor Reichtum und Ermahnung der Reichen: 1 Tim 6,6–10.17-19 im Rahmen des Schlußteils 6,3-21," *BZ* 37 (1993): 60–77.

[11] Martin Dibelius and Hans Conzelmann, *The Pastoral Epistles: A Commentary on the Pastoral Epistles* (trans. Philip Buttolph and Adela Yarbro; Hermeneia; Philadelphia: Fortress, 1972), 87.

[12] James David Miller, *The Pastoral Letters as Composite Documents* (SNTSMS 93; Cambridge: Cambridge University Press, 1997), 88–95.

[13] Roloff, *Timotheus*, 340–45; Ernst Käsemann, "Das Formular einer neutestamentlichen Ordinationsparänese," in *Neutestamentliche Studien für Rudolf Bultmann: Zu seinem siebzigsten Geburtstag* (ed. Walther Eltester; BZNW 21; Berlin: De Gruyter, 1954), 261–68.

[14] Samuel Bénétreau, "La richesse selon 1 Timothée 6,6-10 et 6,17-19," *ETR* 83 (2008): 49–60.

[15] My understanding of this passage owes much to Nathan Eubank, "Almsgiving Is 'the Commandment': A Note on 1 Timothy 6.6-19," *NTS* 58 (2012): 144–50. Other proposals for the meaning of "the commandment" include (1) the specific instruction in vv. 11-12, (2) Timothy's baptismal or ordination commission, (3) the entire epistle, (4) the life of faith as it is summarized in vv. 11-12, (5) Timothy's ministry or commitment to Christ, (6) the "deposit of faith" in 1 Tim 6:20, (7) the gospel as a "rule of life," or (8) a reference to Jesus tradition; see the listing and discussion in I. Howard Marshall, *A Critical and Exegetical Commentary on the Pastoral Epistles* (ICC; London: T&T Clark, 1999), 663–65.

make known at the proper time—he who is the blessed and only Sovereign, the King of kings and the Lord of lords, [16] who alone has immortality, who dwells in unapproachable light, whom no human has seen or is able to see; to him be honor and might forever. Amen. (6:13-16)

If "the commandment" in verse 14 refers to the practice of caring for the poor, then 1 Tim 6:11-16 is not an interruption of a discourse on the proper use of wealth but rather an important exhortation within that discourse, one that concludes in verses 18 to 19 with a call for rich believers to share their resources generously.[16] In order to support the claim that "the commandment" in verse 14 refers to almsgiving, evidence from the Second Temple period, from the Jesus-movement in the first and second centuries, and from rabbinic Judaism may be cited to suggest that almsgiving, or merciful practice, was understood as "the commandment" in a widely attested idiom.[17]

---

[16] Eubank, "Almsgiving," 145.

[17] Eubank points out that numerous rabbinic texts employ the term מצוה ("commandment") to refer to the activity of providing material assistance to the needy (i.e., "almsgiving"), with the Aramaic phrase בר מצוותא denoting a "man of almsgiving" ("Almsgiving," 144–47); cf. Saul Lieberman, "Two Lexicographical Notes," *JBL* 65 (1946): 67–72. Gary A. Anderson glosses בר מצוותא as "'a generous person,' that is, one who is in the habit of giving alms" (*Sin: A History* [New Haven: Yale University Press, 2010], 174). Although this usage of the term מצוה to mean "almsgiving" probably only became common in the fourth century of the Common Era, Eubank suggests that an earlier parallel, outside of rabbinic literature, might be found in the *Testament of Asher* 2.8, a text that has been dated to around 200 CE, although it also likely incorporates earlier traditions (see Joel Marcus, "The *Testaments of the Twelve Patriarchs* and the *Didascalia Apostolorum*: A Common Jewish Christian Milieu?" *JTS* 61 [2010]: 596–626). Eubank also identifies Sir 29:1 ("The merciful lend to their neighbors; by holding out a helping hand they keep the commandments" [NRSV]); Sir. 29:8-13; Matt 19:16-22 (and pars.); and *Did.* 1.5 as texts that might suggest a link between almsgiving and obedience to the commandment(s). Sir 29:9 reads, "On account of *the commandment* help a poor person, and according to his need do not turn him away empty-handed." Even the prominence ascribed to merciful practice in the moral instruction of Tobit might be relevant to the possibility of the idiom (e.g., 4:5-11; 12:8-10; 14:8-11; cf. Anderson, *Sin*, 174). More recently, Anthony Giambrone has questioned the usefulness of some of this lexical evidence. But rather than rejecting Eubank's thesis Giambrone qualifies it by suggesting that there is a "genetic relation" between Sir 29:9 and later Greek usage of ἡ ἐντολή as a reference to almsgiving. Giambrone also posits that the phrase κατὰ τὴν ἐντολήν in *Did.* 1.5, 13.5, and 13.7 is a "reference to the command to give to the poor," a reference "one syntactic step away from the full semantic shift" ("'According to the Commandment' [*Did.* 1.5]: Lexical Reflections on Almsgiving as 'The Commandment,'" *NTS* 60 [2014]:457, 464–65). I would propose two additional pieces of evidence. First, Polycarp cites 1 Tim 6 (vv. 7, 10), followed by the exhortation that readers should "follow the commandment of the Lord" (Pol. *Phil.* 4.1). This text is important evidence from the reception history of

With regard to the structure and argument of 1 Timothy 6, then, viewing "the commandment" in verse 14 as a reference to almsgiving both continues the discussion of wealth in verses 6 to 10 and anticipates the advice
for the rich to share their wealth in verses 17 to 19. Indeed, verses 17 to 19
neatly recapitulate the basic elements of the personal charge to Timothy in
verses 11 to 16:

Charge[18] to Timothy (vv. 11-16)	Instructions to the Rich (vv. 17-19)
Flee these things (i.e., the love of money in v. 10)	Do not be haughty, nor hope in the uncertainty of wealth (v. 17)
Instead of the love of money, pursue righteousness, godliness, faith, love, endurance, gentleness (v. 12)	Instead of hoping in wealth, hope in God (v. 17)
Take hold (ἐπιλαβοῦ) of the eternal life and keep the commandment (i.e., to give alms [vv. 12-14])	Generously share resources, thus storing up a good foundation for the future, so that they may take hold (ἵνα ἐπιλάβωνται) of the life that is truly life (vv. 18-19)[19]

---

1 Tim 6 that "the commandment (of the Lord)" was understood as almsgiving (David J.
Downs and Wil Rogan, "'Let Us Teach Ourselves First to Follow the Commandment of
the Lord' [Pol. Phil. 4.1]: An Additional Note on Almsgiving as 'The Commandment,'"
article in preparation). Second, with a clear allusion to Tob 12:8-9 and a quotation of
1 Pet 4:8, 2 Clem. 16.4 states, "Therefore, merciful practice is good as repentance for sin.
Fasting is better than prayer, but merciful practice is better than both, and 'love covers a
multitude of sins.' Prayer from a good conscience delivers from death. Blessed is everyone who is found full of these things, for merciful practice lightens the burden of sin."
The author of 2 Clement then immediately follows this call to repentance in the act of
ἐλεημοσύνη in 16.4 with another exhortation to repent and a reminder that repentance
involves the practice of "the commandments" in 17.1: "For if we have commandments (εἰ
γὰρ ἐντολὰς ἔχομεν) that we should practice this [i.e., repentance, which is demonstrated
through ἐλεημοσύνη, according to 2 ~~Clem.~~ 16.4], to draw people away from idols and to
instruct them, how much more wrong is it that a person who already knows God should
perish?" J. Ramsey Michaels also argues that Tertullian (Against Marcion 4.35.12–13 and
4.36.4–5; cf. 4.27.6–9) understood "the commandment" (praeceptum) as Jesus' command
to give alms in Luke 11:41 ("Almsgiving and the Kingdom Within: Tertullian on Luke
17:21," CBQ 60 (1998): 475–83).

[18] Paul employs the verb παραγγέλλω in v. 13 to issue the formal charge to Timothy,
and then in v. 17 Timothy is instructed to "charge" (παράγγελλε) the rich in the present age
"not to be haughty, nor to hope in the uncertainty of wealth, but to hope in God, who richly
grants to us all things for enjoyment" (cf. the use of παραγγέλλω in 1 Tim 1:3; 4:11; 5:7).

The entirety of 1 Tim 6:6-19, then, encourages an appropriate theological perspective on, and the proper employment of, wealth.[20]

Indeed, the two adjectives used to describe *how* "the commandment" in verse 14 is to be kept—ἄσπιλος and ἀνεπίλημπτος, "unblemished" and "above reproach"—make sense especially in the context of Timothy's oversight of material distributions to the needy, a role surely intended in Paul's instructions regarding material support for widows in 1 Tim 5:3-16.[21] If the intended recipients of the directives in 5:7 ("Give these instructions, so that *they* may be above reproach") are family members who provide for widows (as opposed to the widows themselves),[22] then the adjective ἀνεπίλημπτος has already been used in the letter to describe the "irreproachable" character of those charged with the responsibility of caring for the needy. To be sure, this summons to impeccable moral conduct in 5:7 should not be limited to matters of financial integrity, for, in the act of providing responsible care for godly widows, family members demonstrate their general character and reputation (cf. 1 Tim 3:1-13).

In the context of directives about how to care for the socially and economically marginalized, however, the issue of integrity when managing and distributing material resources is almost certainly at the forefront in the purpose-clause ἵνα ἀνεπίλημπτοι ὦσιν in 1 Tim 5:7. Moreover, the contentious history of Paul's efforts to organize a relief fund for impoverished believers in Jerusalem—an endeavor that led to charges of fiscal mismanagement and impropriety against the apostle in Corinth (cf. 2 Cor 11:7-9; 12:14-21)—demonstrates the importance of caring for the poor in a manner that is "unblemished and above reproach" (1 Tim 6:14). Although not offering an exact linguistic correspondence, Paul's statements in 2 Cor 8:16-24

---

[19] Cf. the reference to "God, who gives life to all things," in v. 13.

[20] As Eubank summarizes his argument, "If 'the commandment' [in 1 Tim 6:14] refers to almsgiving then the author would simply be telling Timothy the same thing that Timothy is to tell the rich: instead of pursuing money, pursue eternal life and give alms" ("Almsgiving," 149).

[21] If this reading is accepted, a related question concerns the particular role that Timothy himself is intended to play in the distribution of alms in Ephesus. This question broaches larger issues concerning the structure and development of church leadership in 1 Timothy, the Pastoral Epistles, and second-century Christianity. My own view is that, in keeping "the commandment" of almsgiving, Timothy is intended to manage and oversee material contributions to the poor in a way similar to Paul's organization of the Jerusalem collection, even if Timothy's leadership is mediated by local ἐπίσκοποι (3:1-7) and διάκονοι (3:8-13).

[22] So William D. Mounce, *Pastoral Epistles* (WBC 46; Nashville: Thomas Nelson, 2000), 283.

about his plans to collect offerings in Corinth for the saints in Jerusalem with at least two appointed delegates from the Macedonian churches represent a thematic parallel to the instruction given to Timothy in 6:14:

> [20]We are taking this preparation lest anyone blame us concerning this lavish gift that is being administered by us. [21]For we pay attention to what is honorable, not only "in the sight of the Lord" but also "in the sight of human beings." (2 Cor 8:20-21)[23]

In the same way, Paul charges Timothy to keep "the commandment" of providing for the needy in a manner that is unblemished and above reproach, lest Timothy encounter in Ephesus similar opposition to that experienced by Paul in Corinth during the apostle's efforts to arrange a contribution for needy believers in Jerusalem.

Meritorious Almsgiving in 1 Timothy 6:17-19

A solution to the literary unity of 1 Tim 6:6-19 that sees the entire passage as a discourse about the proper use of wealth sheds important light on the exhortation in 6:17-19, a text that has often beguiled interpreters because of the implication of verse 19 that wealthy believers can accrue for themselves future treasure in exchange for generously sharing their resources:

> [17]To the rich in the present age, charge them not to be haughty, nor to hope in the uncertainty of wealth, but to hope in God, who richly grants to us all things for enjoyment— [18]that is, to do good, to be rich in good works, to be generous, [to be] willing to share, [19]storing up for themselves a good foundation for the future, so that they may take hold of the life that is truly life.

It has been suggested that verses 18 to 19 reflect the "completely un-Pauline" notion that good works provide a foundation for the future.[24] Among those not inclined to posit so sharp a discontinuity between the soteriology of 1 Timothy (or the so-called Pastoral Epistles in general), on one hand, and the undisputed Pauline Epistles, on the other, a common strategy for explaining the relationship between charity and reward in verse 19 is to draw a distinction between *demonstrating* one's godliness and *earning* one's salvation.[25]

---

[23] For a more detailed description of the troubles faced by Paul in his efforts to raise funds for Jerusalem, see Downs, *Offering of the Gentiles*, 40–60, 138–39.

[24] Helmut Merkel, *Die Pastoralbriefe* (NTD 9/1; Göttingen: Vandenhoeck & Ruprecht, 1991), 52 (my translation).

[25] E.g., Phillip H. Towner says of the ἵνα-clause at the end of v. 19, "[I]t requires not an earning of salvation or eternal life, but rather a demonstration of genuine godliness in

This-Worldly or Eschatological Reward?

Before considering an alternative perspective on the relationship between generosity and reward, it is worth asking if 1 Tim 6:17-19 refers to eschatological realities and divine recompense at all. In the economic world of Greco-Roman antiquity, episodic or conjunctural poverty was an ever-present threat for all but a very small number of the economic elite. Might 1 Tim 6:17-19 then simply advocate the wisdom of generously sharing one's resources with others in the hope that the recipients of such beneficence would reciprocate, should the original donor run into financial hardship at some point in the future? Even those in verse 17 characterized as "the rich in the present age" (οἱ πλούσιοι ἐν τῷ νῦν αἰῶνι) need not be exempt from economic trouble, especially if this term denotes those members of the early Christian movement who possess moderate to significant surplus resources but are not representatives of the imperial or regional elite. Thus, it is worth pondering whether those whose generosity allows them to store up for themselves a good foundation for the future might simply be securing potential assistance in this life through the reciprocal exchange of goods and services.

The hope of such this-worldly reciprocation has already been shown to be used as motivation for merciful practice in the teachings of Tobit and Sirach. In fact, Tob 4:6-11, which is often highlighted as a passage with intriguing thematic and linguistic parallels to 1 Tim 6:17-19, envisions this very scenario. In a speech commissioning his son, Tobias, into the world, Tobit says:

> [6]And to all who practice righteousness [7]practice the merciful act of almsgiving from your possessions, and do not let your eye be envious when you practice the merciful act of almsgiving. Do not turn your face away from any poor person, and the face of God will not be turned away from you. [8]When you have possessions, according to the abundance

---

the present age" (*The Letters to Timothy and Titus* [NICNT; Grand Rapids: Eerdmans, 2006], 428). Similarly, William Mounce comments, "There is no suggestion that the rich can earn their way to heaven by doing these things; Paul is spelling out the results of certain actions. Salvation in the [Pastoral Epistles] is by God's grace and mercy alone (cf. 1 Tim 1:12-17)" (*Pastoral Epistles*, 368). I. Howard Marshall's interpretation is slightly more nuanced in that he perceives v. 19 to be focused on "reward" instead of salvation, but Marshall nevertheless emphasizes the same distinction between earning and demonstration. "The purpose clause might almost be thought to suggest that people can lay up a treasury of credit for their generous deeds which will win reward in the next life (for the motif see Tobit 4:9); but 2 Tim 1.9 forbids this idea. Rather, we have the normal NT teaching that lack of the expression of faith in good works is an indication of the lack of faith itself, and conversely" (*Critical and Exegetical Commentary*, 673–74).

practice the merciful act of almsgiving from the possessions. If you have a little, do not be afraid to practice the merciful act of almsgiving according to the little that you have. [9] *For you will be storing up a good treasure for yourself against a day of necessity.* [10] Therefore, the merciful act of almsgiving delivers from death and keeps one from going into darkness. [11] Indeed, the merciful act of almsgiving is a good gift, for all who practice it, in the sight of the Most High.

Tobit's claim that sharing possessions with those in need will allow Tobias to store up a good treasure for himself "against a day of necessity" (v. 9) should not, in the narrative context of Tobit, be read as an eschatological promise of divine reward.[26] Instead, Tobit's statement about "storing up a good treasure for yourself against a day of necessity" refers simply to security against future fiscal disaster by lending to others in the present. Even the following assertion, that "almsgiving delivers from death and keeps you from going into the darkness," need not refer to the afterlife, since it might be implied that the practice of ἐλεημοσύνη literally saves from physical death, as merciful practice is said to have done for Ahikar in Tob 14:10. The idea that generosity can rescue from economic misfortune is also reflected in Sir 29:12-13: "Store up merciful practice in your storerooms, and it will deliver you from every mistreatment. More than a strong shield and more than a weighty spear, it will fight against an enemy on your behalf." In a world where sudden material peril is an ever-present reality, sharing generously with others can secure against future fiscal disaster.

Moreover, although pagan authors in Greco-Roman antiquity do not promote the practice of almsgiving with the same frequency as Jewish and Christian writers, a common topos in Greek and Roman moral discourse is the notion that, given the insecurity of wealth, sharing one's resources with those in need can lead to reciprocity in the future of this life.[27] In the same way, Paul advises the Corinthians that they ought to contribute to a relief fund for believers in Jerusalem because, although the Corinthians are presently experiencing an abundance when compared with the need of Jerusalem, at some point in the future the situations might be reversed, with the abundance of the saints in Jerusalem supplying the needs of the Corinthians

---

[26] See the discussion of this text in chap. 3.

[27] See Aristotle, *Rhet.* 2.5.1383a; Seneca, *Marc.* 9.1; Ovid, *Tr.* 5.8.4–18; Abraham Malherbe, "Godliness, Self-Sufficiency, Greed, and the Enjoyment of Wealth: 1 Timothy 6:3-19 Part II," *NovT* 53 (2011): 73–96, esp. 78–88.

(2 Cor 8:13-14).[28] Thus, a reference to "storing up a good foundation for the future" does not necessarily denote an eschatological reward from God.

Yet it seems unlikely that 1 Tim 6:17-19 refers to a this-worldly return on one's generous sharing with the needy. The instruction is specifically directed to "the rich in the present age" (τοῖς πλουσίοις ἐν τῷ νῦν αἰῶνι) in verse 17, a phrase that frames the injunction in the context of an eschatological dualism (cf. Gal 1:4; 2 Tim 4:10; Titus 2:12). Also, given the overlap between the language of "storing up a good foundation for the future" in verse 19 and gospel traditions that employ similar terminology with reference to the storing up of heavenly treasure (Matt 6:19-20; 19:21; Luke 12:21, 33-34), it is likely that the phrase εἰς τὸ μέλλον in verse 19 refers to the eschatological future. Finally, although the phrase "life that is truly life" (τῆς ὄντως ζωῆς) in verse 19 is not the equivalent of "eternal life" (cf. 1 Tim 6:12), the expression does appear to designate an eschatological reward of some sort (see below). On balance, then, the traditional eschatological reading of 1 Tim 6:17-19 is still to be preferred, and therefore the dynamic between human action and divine recompense merits consideration.

What Kind of Eschatological Reward?

If Paul's promise in 1 Tim 6:19 about rich believers "taking hold of life that is truly life" through almsgiving offers some kind of eschatological reward, does the generosity of the rich simply demonstrate their godliness or does it earn them salvation?[29] The suggestion that the text is about not "earning" but "demonstrating" one's salvation fails adequately to account for both the economic language of verse 19a and the purpose clause of verse 19b (ἵνα ἐπιλάβωνται τῆς ὄντως ζωῆς). On the other hand, the view that the phrase "the life that is truly life" (τῆς ὄντως ζωῆς) in verse 19b denotes the attaining of "eternal life," with the implication that eternal life (or salvation) is that which is purchased through generosity, also misses the mark. An attractive alternative is that Paul claims that those who are rich in the present age are able to accumulate heavenly treasure through the generous sharing of material resources in this life (v. 19a), and this heavenly treasure allows them to take hold of reward, not salvation, in the next life (v. 19b).[30]

[28] On the need to interpret 2 Cor 8:13-14 as a reference to an exchange of material resources (instead of the spiritual and material reciprocity discussed in Rom 15:26-27), see Downs, *Offering of the Gentiles*, 137–39.

[29] For some scholars who draw this distinction, see n. 26 above.

[30] Christopher M. Hays criticizes the strategy of "simplistically" drawing a distinction between "earning heaven" and "'demonstrating' godliness." Hays' primary reason for this claim is his conviction that the purpose clause of v. 19b (ἵνα ἐπιλάβωνται τῆς ὄντως

The section opens with an indication of the intended recipients of the instruction: "to the rich in the present age" (v. 17). It is difficult to know how exactly these believers should be plotted on a scale of economic stratification. Likely, these members of the audience are not imperial or even civic elites but rather Christians of (relatively) moderate surplus resources whose lives are not marked by subsistence-level existence, but whose economic level does not reach the highest 1 to 3 percent of the population.[31] The content of the mandate that Timothy is told to communicate to believers of means is spelled out in two negative infinitive clauses in verse 17: the first, with a verb that Paul seems to have coined on his own, μὴ ὑψηλοφρονεῖν, instructs believers not to be haughty; the second, μηδὲ ἠλπικέναι, charges them to hope not in the uncertainty of wealth but in God, "who richly grants to us all things for enjoyment."

That earthly possessions should be employed "for [the purpose of] enjoyment" (εἰς ἀπόλαυσιν) is often linked to Paul's anti-ascetic affirmation earlier in the letter that "everything created by God is good, and nothing is to be rejected, if it is received with thanksgiving, for it is made holy by God's word and prayer" (1 Tim 4:4-5), a statement motivated by the rejection of marriage and the demand for abstinence from certain foods by false teachers (4:3).[32] In this sense, "enjoyment" (ἀπόλαυσις) is realized not in self-indulgence or in greedy consumption but in the humble acknowledgment that God is the one who richly grants all things for the purpose of enjoyment.[33]

ζωῆς) "indicates a more robust relationship between the generosity and the attainment of eternal life." According to Hays, "This passage clearly indicates that munificence will somehow be directly beneficial for attaining eternal life" ("By Almsgiving and Faith Sins Are Purged? The Theological Underpinnings of Early Christian Care for the Poor," in *Engaging Economics: New Testament Scenarios and Early Christian Reception* [ed. Bruce W. Longenecker and Kelly D. Liebengood; Grand Rapids: Eerdmans, 2009], 275). Hays also writes, "To imply that the only alternative to 'demonstrating' is 'earning' evinces a lack of theological reflection on the manner in which works could be involved in attaining eternal life" (275).

[31] I am drawing on Friesen, "Poverty in Pauline Studies," 323–61. Friesen excludes the Pastoral Epistles from consideration in his discussion of economic stratification and the Pauline churches, however (but cf. 348n79).

[32] So, e.g., I. Marshall, *Critical and Exegetical Commentary*, 672; Towner, *Letters*, 426; Luke Timothy Johnson, *The First and Second Letters to Timothy: A New Translation with Introduction and Commentary* (AB 35A; New York: Doubleday, 2001), 310.

[33] Abraham Malherbe offers an exegetical perspective that clarifies the means by which the rich in this world realize their enjoyment of the wealth that God has richly supplied them. Malherbe suggests that, while the prepositional phrase εἰς ἀπόλαυσιν might be absolute because it is not followed by a genitive or accusative noun specifying the object of enjoyment, "it is possible to read ἀγαθοεργεῖν as in apposition to and epexegetic of εἰς ἀπόλαυσιν, πλουτεῖν as epexegetic of ἀγαθοεργεῖν, and εἶναι as epexegetic of ἀγαθοεργεῖν" ("Godliness," 89). That is, a string of epexegetical infinitives describes *how* wealth is to be

True enjoyment of wealth is found in the employment of material resources to perform good works, most specifically through the generous and charitable disposal of wealth. This "hedonistic" liberality, moreover, allows those who practice benevolent sharing to "[store] up for themselves a good foundation for the future, so that they may take hold of the life that is truly life" (v. 19). It seems entirely appropriate to speak of "meritorious almsgiving" in 1 Tim 6:19 in the sense that acts of mercy and distributions of material assistance have the potential to secure merit for donors. The metaphor is mixed, combining the economic and/or agricultural imagery of "storing up" or "treasuring up" goods (ἀποθησαυρίζω) with the architectural image of laying the foundation (θεμέλιος) of an edifice.[34] To borrow language from the anthropological literature on gift-exchange, this is "interested" giving, in the sense that givers are encouraged to anticipate some return, even if the reciprocity comes from God in the form of heavenly reward and not from the human recipients of the assistance.[35]

As noted above, however, it is the purpose clause ἵνα ἐπιλάβωνται τῆς ὄντως ζωῆς at the end of verse 19 that has caused the most difficulties. In what sense are the rich in the present age encouraged to engage in almsgiving so that, as a result, they may take hold of the life that is truly life? On one hand, the common distinction between earning and demonstrating salvation disregards the syntax of the text, for it is clear that saving up heavenly treasure is advocated *for the purpose of* taking hold of true life. On the other hand, "life that is truly life" in verse 19 should not be conflated with the earlier charge to Timothy in verse 12: "Take hold of the eternal life to which you were called and about which you confessed the good confession before many

---

enjoyed by listing three actions through which enjoyment of wealth is manifested: by doing good, by being rich in good works, and by being generous and sharing. As Malherbe comments on the significance of this reading: "What is striking is that the purpose for the gift of wealth is not the proper use of it, which is attended by enjoyment; rather, the purpose is enjoyment, which is explicated by the three infinitives that follow. Whatever the local circumstances, if there were any that were responsible for this inversion, the author wishes the benevolent use of one's wealth to be an expression or means of enjoyment rather than, say, something done out of duty or compulsion. The enjoyment in view is not centered on the self but is other-directed. . . . The reason for enjoyment is that this is what God intends in providing richly. What is required is not reflection but action" (91–92).

[34] Jerome D. Quinn and William C. Wacker present an interesting argument that the term θεμέλιος "has a double meaning of the base for a building and a deposit of money that produces interest" (*The First and Second Letters to Timothy: A New Translation with Notes and Commentary* [Eerdmans Critical Commentary; Grand Rapids: Eerdmans, 2000], 555–56).

[35] See, e.g., Jacques T. Godbout and Alain Caillé, *The World of the Gift* (trans. Donald Winkler; Montreal: McGill-Queen's University Press, 1998).

witnesses."[36] The instructions are similar—not least because both feature the verb ἐπιλαμβάνομαι—but they are not *identical*. For one thing, the wording is different, and it is significant that Paul did not write ἵνα ἐπιλάβωνται τῆς αἰωνίου ζωῆς in verse 19. Moreover, "eternal life" in verse 12 is a reality that Timothy is instructed to grasp in the present, "a goal to be achieved here and now in this world and not just at the end of the contest."[37] In verse 19, however, both the notion that the rich store up for themselves a heavenly foundation *for the (eschatological) future* (εἰς τὸ μέλλον) and the aorist subjunctive ἐπιλάβωνται indicate that, whatever it is, "life that is truly life" is not possessed by the rich in the present. Everything about verse 19 suggests that the object of the verb ἐπιλαμβάνομαι is a prize to be seized in the future, and this differs markedly from the charge to Timothy in verse 12.

Life That Is Truly Life and Divine Judgment

Much rests, then, on the precise meaning of the phrase τῆς ὄντως ζωῆς, a term that does not find a precise parallel in biblical literature. A statement in Philo of Alexandria's *De congressu eruditionis gratia* may offer some assistance, however. In this treatise, Philo offers an extended allegorical meditation on Gen 16:1-6 in order to bolster the belief (held by Stoics but rejected by Cynics and Epicureans) that an encyclical education (i.e., a liberal arts curriculum) was a necessary precursor to the study of philosophy.[38] In discussing an individual's sojourns into the lands of Egypt, which is the symbol of the passions and associated with childhood, and Canaan, which is the symbol of wickedness and associated with youth, Philo cites Lev 18:1-5, a passage in which God tells the Israelites not to follow the statutes of the Egyptians or the Canaanites but to obey instead the Lord's commandments, for "the one who does them shall live in them" (*Congr.* 86).[39] Philo then provides commentary on the text:

> So then true life (ἡ πρὸς ἀλήθειαν ζωή) is walking in the judgments and commandments of God, so that the practices of the godless must

[36] See, e.g., Merkel, *Pastoralbriefe*, 52; Quinn and Wacker, *Timothy*, 556; Towner, *Letters*, 428.

[37] I. Marshall, *Critical and Exegetical Commentary*, 660.

[38] See Alan Mendelson, *Secular Education in Philo of Alexandria* (Cincinnati: Hebrew Union College Press, 1982). In Philo's allegorical interpretation, heaven-born men like Abraham must "enter into" Hagar, who represents encyclical education, before passing on to Sarah, who stands for virtue.

[39] Translations of *De congressu* are modified from Philo, *On Mating with Preliminary Studies*, in *Philo*, vol. 4 (trans. F. H. Colson and G. H. Whitaker; LCL; Cambridge, Mass.: Harvard University Press, 1932).

be death. And what the practices of the godless are we have been told. They are the practices of passions and evils, from which spring the many multitudes of the impious and the workers of unholiness. (*Congr.* 87)

Philo's interpretation of Lev 18:1-5 here has generated much discussion, not least because of the role that Leviticus 18 plays in the soteriology of several Old Testament and Second Temple Jewish texts, including the Pauline Epistles.[40] The key point is Philo's presentation of his concept of "true life," which he defines here rather precisely by means of a predicate participle: "True life is walking in the judgments and commandments of God" (περιπατοῦντός ἐστιν ἐν ταῖς τοῦ θεοῦ κρίσεσι καὶ προστάξεσιν).

Philo employs the concept of "true life" in a variety of ways in his many writings. Sometimes the phrase "true life" is used in a Platonic sense to denote a person's rational soul (i.e., the incorporeal and animating aspect of a person that results from God's life-giving breath; *Leg.* 1.32, 35), sometimes it describes authentic spiritual life in contrast to destruction and death (*Leg.* 3.52; *Migr.* 21; *QG* 1.70; cf. *Her.* 201; *Leg.* 3.35), and sometimes it serves as a general reference to wise or virtuous existence (*Leg.* 2.93; *Mut.* 213; *Her.* 53; cf. *Virt.* 17; *Somn.* 2.64).[41] In *Congr.* 87 and elsewhere in Philo's corpus, however, the phrase "true life" designates the *reward* that one receives from God for virtuous behavior. For example, in *QG* 4.238, "true life" is the "prize" (ἆθλον) for Jacob's discipline, in contrast to the death that results for the wicked and evil person. In *QG* 4.46, "true life" is a reward denied to those who seek "low and base and earthly things," for they die with respect to "true life." Similarly, in *Post.* 45, "true life" (τὴν ἀληθῆ ζωὴν) is the promised outcome for a good person, as opposed to the individual who follows the example of Cain and dies with respect to virtue. Together, "[t]hese three passages show that 'true life' is a *reward* for the virtuous soul while death is the *recompense* for the wicked soul."[42] This reward can take the form of eternal life (*Spec.* 1.345), but it can also simply reflect God's favorable judgment—either in the present or in the future—of one's virtue, often in contrast to divine punishment of impious behavior (*Post.* 12, 45; *QG* 1.16; cf. *Mut.* 216; *Gig.* 14).[43] In *Congr.* 87,

---

[40] See esp. Preston M. Sprinkle, *Law and Life: The Interpretation of Leviticus 18:5 in Early Judaism and in Paul* (WUNT II/241; Tübingen: Mohr Siebeck, 2008), 101–14.

[41] On this diversity, see Dieter Zeller, "The Life and Death of the Soul in Philo of Alexandria: The Use and Origin of a Metaphor," *SPhilo* 7 (1995): 19–55.

[42] Sprinkle, *Law*, 112 (emphasis added).

[43] On the complex and sometimes inconsistent dynamic of reward and punishment in Philo's writings, see Alan Mendelson, "Philo's Dialectic of Reward and Punishment," *SPhilo* 9 (1997): 104–25.

for instance, "true life" entails both obedience to God's commandments and, significantly, walking in the "judgments" of God. Interestingly, in his gloss on the text of LXX Lev 18:1-5, Philo substitutes the word κρίσεις for κρίμα (i.e., LXX Lev 18:4: κρίματά μου ποιήσετε), perhaps suggesting more strongly than his source text the theme of God's active judgment of human virtue or wickedness.[44] True life, according to Philo, involves not only obedience to God's statutes but also the positive judgment of one's behavior by God.[45]

Without positing any sort of literary relationship, I would suggest Paul in 1 Tim 6:19 utilizes the phrase "life that is truly life" (τῆς ὄντως ζωῆς) in a manner that parallels Philo's notion of "true life" as a reward for honorable action in *Congr.* 87, although certainly Paul does not locate this concept in an allegorical narrative of the virtuous soul's journey to God. In short, to "take hold of the life that is truly life" in 6:19 is to live in light of the judgments and commandments of God in the sense that, through their generosity, the rich store up for themselves a heavenly treasure for the future *so that*, at the eschatological judgment, they can take hold of the heavenly reward that will be given to those who have lived in light of God's future judgment and in obedience to God's commands. One advantage of this proposal is that it coheres with the suggestion that "the commandment" in 6:14 refers to care for the needy. Enjoyment of wealth—which is demonstrated in doing good, performing good works, and generously sharing one's possessions—leads to the accumulation of heavenly treasure, and from these funds believers are able to "purchase" not salvation but "true life"—that is, the reward given to those who have obeyed God's commands, especially, in this context, the command to give alms.

A second advantage is that this reading of the phrase τῆς ὄντως ζωῆς is entirely compatible with the Pauline notion that, while the salvation of those in Christ is determined solely by divine grace and not on the basis of human merit or action, believers should anticipate a future eschatological

---

[44] For another example of Philo's interpretation of a scriptural text that more strongly emphasizes divine judgment than its biblical antecedent, compare Num 25:1-18 and 31:1-18 with *Virt.* 45 (cf. *Virt.* 174). This interpretative strategy is not exactly common in Philo, however. Elsewhere Philo appears to distance God from active punishment of the wicked; see Mendelson, "Dialectic," 106–23.

[45] In spite of the fact that Sprinkle's analysis of the concept of "true life" in Philo is very helpful, the theme of divine judgment is muted in his interpretation of *Congr.* 87. While Sprinkle initially follows Colson in translating the phrase ἐν ταῖς τοῦ θεοῦ κρίσεσι καὶ προστάξεσιν as "in the judgments and commandments of God," his summary statement and later translations omit reference to divine judgment: e.g., "Philo considers the key feature in Lev 18:5 to be the 'true life' that consists in *walking in the commandments* of God" (*Law*, 106 [emphasis added]); "true life is walking in the *statutes* and *ordinances* of God (110n48 [emphasis added]).

judgment according to deeds (Rom 2:6-10; 1 Cor 3:12-15; 4:4-5; 2 Cor 5:10; 1 Tim 5:24-25; 2 Tim 4:6-8, 14).[46] It is not "eternal life" that one obtains with the heavenly treasure accrued on the basis of obedience to God's commands but rather the prize of God's affirmative judgment at the final assize. In the conclusion to his commentary on 1 Tim 6:19, Calvin offers the following summary:

> So far are we from rendering full payment, that, if God should call us to strict account, there is not one of us who would not be a bankrupt. But, after having reconciled us to himself by free grace, he accepts our services, such as they are, and bestows on them a reward which is not due. This recompense, therefore, does not depend on considerations of merit, but on God's gracious acceptance, and is so far from being inconsistent with the righteousness of faith, that it may be viewed as an appendage to it.[47]

Because Calvin recognizes that 1 Tim 6:19b promises a reward for good works, he does not force upon the text an artificial distinction between "earning" and "demonstrating" one's salvation. Yet Calvin also perceptively, if briefly, captures the complex dynamic of divine and human action at work in the economic exchange described in 1 Timothy 6.[48] If 1 Timothy 6 does promote meritorious almsgiving in the sense that the rich in the present age are able to obtain future heavenly treasure through the generous sharing of material resources in the present (vv. 17-19), this exchange of possessions for heavenly reward must be located in a larger literary and theological context in which Paul insists that all things come from God.[49] As Calvin rightly intu-

---

[46] See Kent L. Yinger, *Paul, Judaism, and Judgment according to Deeds* (SNTSMS 105; Cambridge: Cambridge University Press, 1999); Michael F. Bird, *The Saving Righteousness of God: Studies on Paul, Justification, and the New Perspective* (Paternoster Biblical Monographs; Milton Keynes: Paternoster, 2007), 155–78; Kyoung-Shik Kim, *God Will Judge Each One according to Works: Judgment according to Works and Psalm 62 in Early Judaism and the New Testament* (BZNW 178; Berlin: De Gruyter, 2010).

[47] John Calvin, *Commentaries on the Epistles to Timothy, Titus, and Philemon* (trans. William Pringle; Grand Rapids: Eerdmans, 1948), 172–73.

[48] Calvin's aversion to the term "merit" is evident, and this aversion should be located in the larger theological and historical context of Calvin's work; see Charles Raith, "Calvin's Critique of Merit, and Why Aquinas (Mostly) Agrees," *ProEccl* 20 (2011): 135–66. Here and elsewhere Calvin allows that God rewards human action, but for Calvin the reward is not merited because God is the cause of human action because human beings act while being acted upon by God (*Antidotes* 3.111; *BLW* 3.318).

[49] For further development of this point with reference to 1 Timothy, see Downs, "God Who Gives Life," 259–60. The charge to Timothy in 6:11-14 emphasizes Timothy's service to God (v. 11), Timothy's calling by God (v. 12), and God's dynamic identity as

ited, the motif of God's creating, redeeming, and sustaining action in 1 Tim
6:6-19 must be appreciated in order to obtain a properly theological perspective on the topic of human beneficence. With respect to the issue of meritorious almsgiving in 6:17-19 in particular, those who secure the treasure of a
good foundation in order to take hold of life that truly is life do so with funds
they have already received from God, for all that they are and all that they
have to share comes from God. Thus, even the human action of meritorious
almsgiving is located in a larger divine economy in which God is proclaimed
to be the source and provider of all things.

Philippians 4:10-20

If 1 Tim 6:17-19 promises eschatological reward for (relatively) wealthy
donors who generously share their material resources, the conclusion of
Paul's Letter to the Philippians frames recompense for giving in communal eschatological terms. At the end of the epistle, Paul acknowledges that
the Philippians have provided him with material support during his present
imprisonment (4:10-20).[50] In the context of that recognition, Paul highlights
the Philippians' partnership in his suffering and mission, while framing that
partnership as an economic and spiritual exchange:[51]

---

the one "who gives life to all things" (v. 13). The last of these three statements stresses
God's role "as the creator of life and sustainer of the universe," a cosmological affirmation
that anticipates the doxology in vv. 15b-16 (so Towner, *Letters*, 413). Moreover, the dox-
ological material that punctuates the charge to Timothy in 6:15b-16 clearly echoes the
exalted description of God earlier in the letter (1:17). These emphatic confessions of God's
uniqueness, sovereignty, immortality, and glory at the beginning and end of 1 Timothy
provide a properly theological frame for the entire epistle. So Greg A. Couser, "God and
Christian Existence in the Pastoral Epistles: Toward Theological Method and Meaning,"
NovT 42 (2000): 262–83; Vasile Mihoc, "The Final Admonition to Timothy (1 Tim 6,3-
21)," in *1 Timothy Reconsidered* (ed. Karl P. Donfried; Colloquium Oecumenicum Paulinum 18; Leuven: Peeters, 2008), 135–52.

[50] It is often observed that Paul acknowledges the Philippians' contribution but
does not thank them for it. For an insightful study of the omission of the language of
"thanksgiving" in Phil 4:10-20 in the context of the three-way relationship that Paul
envisions between God, himself, and the Philippians, see David E. Briones, *Paul's Financial Policy: A Socio-theological Approach* (LNTS 494; London: Bloomsbury, 2013). Briones argues that "Paul's 'thanks' is intentionally 'thankless' because the Philippians are
mediators of God's commodity, not the source" (126); cf. Thomas R. Blanton IV, "The
Benefactor's Account-Book: The Rhetoric of Gift Reciprocation according to Seneca and
Paul," *NTS* 59 (2013): 396–414.

[51] On the economic context of this partnership, see Julien M. Ogereau, "Paul's
κοινωνία with the Philippians: *Societas* as a Missionary Funding Strategy," *NTS* 60
(2014): 360–78.

¹⁴Nevertheless, you did well in sharing with me as partners (συγ-
κοινωνήσαντές μου) in my affliction. ¹⁵Moreover, you Philippians know
that at the beginning of the gospel, when I departed from Macedonia,
no other church partnered with me in an account of giving and receiving (οὐδεμία μοι ἐκκλησία ἐκοινώνησεν εἰς λόγον εἰς λόγον δόσεως καὶ
λήμψεως) except you alone; ¹⁶for even when I was in Thessalonica, you
sent for my need more than once. ¹⁷It is not that I am seeking the gift
(τὸ δόμα), but I am seeking the profit that increases to your account (τὸν
καρπὸν τὸν πλεονάζοντα εἰς λόγον ὑμῶν). ¹⁸I have been paid in full, and
I have an abundance. I have been fully supplied now that I have received
from Epaphroditus the gifts you sent, a fragrant offering, a sacrifice
pleasing and acceptable to God. ¹⁹And my God will fully supply you
every need of yours, according to his riches in glory in Christ Jesus.
(4:14-19)

Paul's use of the language of "partnership" (συγκοινωνέω, κοινωνέω)
here—particularly as the partnership is described as "an account of giving
and receiving" (εἰς λόγον δόσεως καὶ λήμψεως)—is elsewhere paralleled in
texts of Greco-Roman antiquity to describe economic or business partner-
ships.[52] There is undoubtedly an economic aspect to Paul's partnership with
the Philippians—namely, that the Philippians have provided material support to Paul on several occasions (vv. 10, 14, 16-18). Yet when the apostle
indicates that the return on the Philippians' investment in Paul's need is a
"profit" that increases to their common account (τὸν καρπὸν τὸν πλεονάζοντα
εἰς λόγον ὑμῶν [v. 17]), Paul appears to be thinking of an exchange of material blessings for spiritual ones. In fact, Paul assumes in verses 14 to 19 a
material-spiritual exchange similar to that which he discusses explicitly in
Rom 15:26-27. In Romans 15, Paul writes with reference to the support of
the collection for impoverished believers in Jerusalem by the churches of
Macedonia and Achaia:

²⁶For Macedonia and Achaia were pleased to make a certain
partnership-forming contribution (κοινωνίαν τινὰ ποιήσασθαι)[53] for
the poor among the saints in Jerusalem. ²⁷For they were pleased to do
this and, indeed, they are their debtors. For if in spiritual things the

---

[52] Ogereau, "Paul's κοινωνία," 363–70. The verb πληρόω, which Paul employs in
vv. 18 and 19, was often used to record full payment of economic transactions in inscrip-
tions and papyri.

[53] For the translation of κοινωνία as "partnership-forming contribution," which
aims to highlight both social and material aspects of the word, see Downs, *Offering of
the Gentiles*, 16–17; cf. Robert Jewett, *Romans: A Commentary* (Hermeneia; Minneapolis:
Fortress, 2007), 928–29.

Gentiles have received a contribution from them, the Gentiles ought
also to be of service to them in material things.

In Rom 15:27 the "spiritual blessings" that flow from Jerusalem to the Gentile churches in Macedonia and Achaia probably refer to the gospel itself,
including the gospel's power and soteriological benefits.[54] The dynamic of
partnership in Phil 4:10-20, and throughout the letter, involves, according to
Paul, a similar exchange of material and spiritual blessings, although these
are mediated by the God who is the source of all blessing.[55] In both Romans
15 and Philippians 4, moreover, Paul frames the material-spiritual exchange
in terms of reciprocity and solidarity.

Paul does not unpack the precise nature of the return on the Philippians' investment in Phil 4:17. In the larger context of the letter, however, it is
likely that the phrase "profit that increases to your account" in 4:17 evokes
the eschatological "fruit of righteousness" mentioned in Phil 1:10, the first
instance in Philippians in which Paul employs the noun καρπός. Paul's prayer
in Phil 1:9-11 expresses the hope:

> [9] that your love may overflow more and more with knowledge and full
> insight [10] to help you to determine what is best, so that in the day of
> Christ you may be pure and blameless, [11] having produced the har-
> vest of righteousness (πεπληρωμένοι καρπὸν δικαιοσύνης) that comes
> through Jesus Christ for the glory and praise of God. (NRSV)

When the actions of the Philippians are assessed on the day of judgment,
their generous support of Paul's material needs will serve as part of the "fruit
of righteousness" that increases to their heavenly account.[56] This is meri-

---

[54] Jewett, *Romans*, 931.

[55] So Briones, *Paul's Financial Policy*, 58–130. As Chrysostom comments on this
exchange: "How did they enter into partnership? By reason of giving material things and
receiving spiritual things. You see, just as sellers and buyers enter into partnership with
each other, giving and taking from each other (that's a partnership), so too is it in this
case. I mean, there's nothing, there's really nothing more profitable than this buying and
selling. After all, while it happens on earth, it's perfected in heaven: the buyers have been
stationed on earth, but they buy and strike bargain over heavenly things, depositing the
price on earth. No, don't despair—the heavenly things can't be bought with money, money
can't buy them, but it's the intention of the one who pays the money, their philosophy; no,
it's being above the things of life, their love of humanity, their almsgiving" (*Hom. Phil.*
162–63; trans. Pauline Allen, *John Chrysostom, Homilies on Paul's Letter to the Philippians*
[SBLWGRW 16; Atlanta: Society of Biblical Literature, 2013], 304).

[56] So G. Walter Hansen, *The Letter to the Philippians* (Pillar New Testament Commentary; Grand Rapids: Eerdmans, 2009), 321–22. Given 2 Cor 8:13-14, it should
not automatically be assumed that the reference to God's provision of the needs of the

torious almsgiving, but since no individual donors or any particular group within the Philippian congregation is singled out, it is meritorious almsgiving framed in a communal context.

Galatians 4:12-15

In Gal 4:12-15, when recounting his initial visit to and announcement of the gospel among the Galatians, Paul reminds the Galatians of the care that they provided to him despite, or because of, the apostle's suffering some sort of physical affliction:

> [12]You did me no wrong [i.e., when I came to you]. [13]You know that it was because of a physical infirmity that I first announced the good news to you; [14]though my condition put you to the test, you did not scorn me or spit at me; instead, you readily received me as if I were an angel of God, as Christ Jesus. [15]What has become of your blessedness before God (ποῦ οὖν ὁ μακαρισμὸς ὑμῶν)? For I testify that, had it been possible, you would have torn out your eyes and given them to me.[57]

Instead of despising Paul or spitting upon him—common reactions to the sick and diseased in the ancient world, often inspired by the belief that such hostility was a means of warding off the evil forces held to be responsible for illness (cf. Pliny, *Nat.* 28.36, 39; Theocritus, *Id.* 6)—the Galatians, Paul recounts, welcomed the infirm apostle as they would have welcomed an angel of God or even Christ. Moreover, Paul testifies that the Galatians would

---

Philippians in v. 19 excludes *material* blessing. As Hansen writes, "The increase in fruit to the Philippians' account is the answer to Paul's prayer that *love may abound more and more* (1:9). Sacrificial gifts produce spiritual growth in the givers as well as support for the recipients. But while the fruit accruing to their account refers to spiritual growth in the Philippians, it also refers to God's provisions to supply all their needs. God met Paul's needs while he was suffering in many ways, including the gifts sent by the Philippians. Paul assures the Philippians that the fruit of their gifts will be that God will meet all their needs in many ways as well" (322 [emphasis in original]).

[57] This translation is from Longenecker, *Remember the Poor*, 174. In an earlier essay, Longenecker argues persuasively that the phrase ὁ μακαρισμὸς ὑμῶν be understood as "an objective genitive with God as its implied object" (103). The noun μακαρισμός in Gal 4:15 should be viewed as a reference to divine favor in part because this is how the noun is employed in Rom 4:6-9, the only other place where the noun occurs in Paul's letters. In Rom 4:6-9, μακαρισμός (vv. 6, 9) and μακάριος (vv. 7, 8) "refer to the pouring out of divine favor, specifically defined as God's forgiveness of the lawless acts (ἀνομίαι) of covenant outsiders and the covering of sins" (Bruce W. Longenecker, "'Until Christ Is Formed in You': Suprahuman Forces and Moral Character in Galatians," *CBQ* 61 [1999]: 92–108 [103]).

have sacrificially removed their own eyes and given them to Paul, were such an ocular transplant possible. Paul thus narrates his first encounter with the Galatians so as to highlight their cruciform love for the weak: "Rather than observing practices of prudent self-preservation that were dictated by their culture, the Galatians had already exhibited practices of culturally imprudent self-giving to one in need (and dangerously so)—practices that could only have been enlivened by the Spirit of the Son, in Paul's view."[58]

This narrative then illuminates the question that Paul asks the Galatians in 4:15: "What has become of your blessedness before God (ποῦ οὖν ὁ μακαρισμὸς ὑμῶν)?" Paul poses this query because, from his perspective at the time he is writing the letter, the Galatians have allowed themselves to be turned against Paul by influential teachers of a false gospel (1:6-9; 3:1-5; 4:8-11; 5:2-12).Yet the question implies that the Galatians had earlier received divine blessing because of their generous care for Paul, a blessing now called into question due to the false teachers' success in compelling the Galatians to abandon the gospel and its cruciform pattern of existence (cf. 5:11; 6:12-14). The precise nature of the "blessedness" the Galatians received before God because of their hospitality for the infirm apostle is not spelled out, but this divine favor does seem to have been a reality in the present and not eschatological reward.[59]

---

[58] Longenecker, *Remember the Poor*, 213; on Paul's appeal to cruciform love in Gal 4, see also Benjamin J. Lappenga, "Misdirected Emulation and Paradoxical Zeal: Paul's Redefinition of 'The Good' as Object of ζῆλος in Galatians 4:12-20," *JBL* 131 (2012): 775–96.

[59] Some would argue that Gal 6:9-10 should also be included among the Pauline passages that promise reward for almsgiving: "Let us not become tired of doing good, for we will reap at the right time if we do not give up. So then, whenever we have opportunity, let us work for the good for all, and especially for those who belong to the household of faith." Longenecker, e.g., has followed Bruce W. Winter in arguing that "the phrase 'to do the good' (ἐργαζώμεθα τὸ ἀγαθὸν) that appears in 6:10 is (virtually) technical terminology in the ancient world for bestowing material benefits on others" (*Remember the Poor*, 142.; cf. Winter, *Seek the Welfare of the City: Christians as Benefactors and Citizens* [Grand Rapids: Eerdmans, 1994], 11–40). It is not clear that the language "doing good" in Gal 6:9 or elsewhere represents a *terminus technicus* for benefaction, however. Paul employs the phrase τῷ ἐργαζομένῳ τὸ ἀγαθόν in Rom 2:10 in a context in which τὸ ἀγαθόν as the object of ἐργάζομαι, yet there Paul clearly refers to good deeds in general and not almsgiving in particular. There is little doubt that charitable concern for the needy is included in the charge "let us not become tired of doing good," but it would be a stretch to read this general exhortation to doing good and the promise of reaping for persistence in this action as a statement of "meritorious almsgiving." (Nor do I find convincing Larry W. Hurtado's claim that "the whole of Gal 6:6-10, then, is a single, cohesive appeal urging the Galatians

2 Corinthians 8–9

One economic endeavor of signal importance for the apostle Paul was the relief fund that he organized among the largely Gentile churches of his mission in Macedonia, Achaia, and Galatia for believers in Jerusalem, a project that Paul calls "the collection for the saints" (1 Cor 16:1). It would be difficult to overstate the significance of this collection for Paul's mission as apostle to the Gentiles. That the organization and implementation of the relief fund demanded a considerable amount of Paul's time and energy over the course of a number of years is revealed in his comments about the project in 1 Cor 16:1-4; 2 Cor 8:1–9:15; and Rom 15:14-32. So portentous was the collection for Paul that he reports in Rom 15:30-31 his willingness to risk both his life and the possible rejection of his efforts by the church there in order to deliver the funds personally to Jerusalem.

Paul's most extended statements about the collection for Jerusalem are found in 2 Corinthians 8–9, a section in which Paul delicately exhorts his readers in Corinth to resume contributions to the offering after some members of the church had experienced conflict with the apostle, presumably over financial matters, and abandoned the project as a consequence.[60] In 2 Corinthians 8–9, then, Paul cautiously encourages the Corinthians to adopt a reoriented theological conception of the collection and so resume their participation in the offering. In these chapters, Paul adopts a variety of rhetorical appeals to accomplish this aim: (1) he emphasizes the example of the Macedonians, who have generously contributed to the fund, in spite of their deep poverty (8:1-6); (2) he highlights the paradigmatic grace (χάρις) of the Lord Jesus Christ, "who became poor for your sakes, although he was rich, so that by his poverty you might become rich" (8:9); (3) he draws upon the principle of ἰσότης, or equality (not merely a philosophical concept for Paul but a notion deeply rooted in the narrative of God's gracious provision of manna to the Israelites in the wilderness [8:13-15]); (4) he suggests that both he and the Corinthians will be shamed if believers come from Macedonia to Corinth and find the contribution for Jerusalem unfinished (9:1-5); (5) he paints an agricultural metaphor to suggest that giving to the collection is like sowing seed, a metaphor that emphasizes the generative activity of God in the act of human beneficence (9:6-10); and, finally, (6) he punctuates this

---

to share their material goods with others." See Hurtado, "The Jerusalem Collection and the Book of Galatians," *JSNT* 5 [1979]: 46–62 [53].)

[60] On the history of the collection, see Downs, *Offering of the Gentiles*, 30–72.

appeal by indicating that true generosity results in thanksgiving and praise to God, the one from whom all benefactions ultimately originate (9:11-15).[61]

The promise of future recompense for donors figures twice in Paul's appeal for the Jerusalem collection in 2 Corinthians 8–9.[62] The first instance in which support of the collection is linked with reward offers the possibility that recipients of the Corinthians' generosity in Jerusalem will reciprocate with material support for the Corinthians in the future, should the Corinthians face financial hardship. In 2 Cor 8:13-14, Paul writes, "It is not that others should have relief and you affliction, but it is a matter of equality. At the present time your abundance is for their need, so that their abundance may be for your need, so that there may be equality." The reciprocal relationship described in 2 Cor 8:13-14 is not the same type of material-spiritual exchange discussed in Phil 4:10-20 and Rom 15:26-27. Instead, Paul paints a scenario in which the Corinthians themselves may experience future economic distress and require material assistance from believers in Jerusalem. Here the Corinthian saints are not depicted as "poor," especially in comparison with the present need among believers in Jerusalem, but their financial situation is tenuous enough that Paul presents them as possible recipients of offerings from the saints in Jerusalem at some point in the future. In an economic context of mass episodic or conjunctural poverty, such a scenario is quite plausible. Paul's principle of "equality" is then fleshed out with a citation of

---

[61] Elsewhere I have argued that a number of linguistic expressions in Paul's rhetoric depict the collection in cultic terms (1 Cor 16:1-2; 2 Cor 8:6, 11-12; 9:12; Rom 15:16, 27-28). In metaphorically framing the activity of collecting money for the poor among the saints as an act of cultic worship, Paul underscores the point that the fulfillment of mutual obligations within the Christian community results in praise, not to human donors, as the dominant ideology of patronage or euergetism would have suggested, but to God, the one from whom all benefactions come. Even the very human action of raising money for those in material need originates in ἡ χάρις τοῦ θεοῦ ("the grace of God") and will eventuate in χάρις τῷ θεῷ ("thanks to God"; cf. 2 Cor 9:14-15). Downs, *Offering of the Gentiles*, 120–60.

[62] In light of the eschatological usage of the verb ἀποθησαυρίζω in 1 Tim 6:19, one wonders if perhaps Paul's employment of the cognate θησαυρίζω in 1 Cor 16:2 (cf. Rom 2:5; 2 Cor 12:14), when providing the Corinthians instructions for gathering funds for the Jerusalem collection, might allude to a storing up of heavenly treasure. The phrase κατὰ μίαν σαββάτου ἕκαστος ὑμῶν παρ᾽ ἑαυτῷ τιθέτω θησαυρίζων ὅ τι ἐὰν εὐοδῶται can be translated, "On the first day of every week [or 'Every Sunday'], each of you individually should set aside, *storing up whatever one gains*." Does "setting aside" refer to the gathering of the funds and "storing up" refer to the storing up of heavenly treasure through that which is contributed? The following ἵνα clause makes this possibility unlikely, for the "storing up" is an actual saving up of funds for the Jerusalem collection "so that there need not be collections when I come."

Exod 16:18: "As it is written, 'The one who had much did not have too much, and the one who had little did not have too little.'" The mutual sharing of material resources between believers in Corinth and Jerusalem (and Macedonia; cf. 8:1-6) results not in absolute economic parity but in a leveling of capital so that no one has too much and no one has too little. Interpreted in light of the distribution of resources in Greco-Roman antiquity (see chap. 1), this scenario envisions those of moderate to low means—those facing the threatening realities of "shallow," conjunctural poverty—providing financial support to a community presently marked by a greater lack of resources, even destitution. The model of "almsgiving" in 2 Cor 8:13-14, therefore, does not involve the transfer of funds along a vertical axis from those with an abundance of assets to those with minimal resources (i.e., from the "rich" to the "poor"). Instead, Paul imagines a "mutualism" that entails a more or less horizontal exchange of resources among those of lesser means.

The notion that those on the lower rungs of the economic ladder might be exhorted to demonstrate material assistance for others is supported earlier in this same chapter. As Paul reports in 2 Cor 8:1-6, the Macedonians demonstrated a wealth of generosity by contributing to the relief fund for Jerusalem in spite of their own material deprivation:

> [1]We make known to you, brothers and sisters, the benefaction of God that has been given to the churches of Macedonia, [2]for during a great ordeal of affliction, the abundance of their joy and their *deep poverty* have abounded in the wealth of their sincere concern. [3]For in accordance with their means, I testify, and beyond their means, they gave of their own volition, [4]petitioning us earnestly for the benefit of partnering in the ministry for the saints. [5]And not simply as we expected, but they gave themselves first to the Lord and then to us through the will of God, [6]so that we urged Titus that, as he had previously started, so he should also complete this benefaction among you as well.

Doubtless, Paul's brief narrative sketch of the actions of the Macedonians is characterized by some degree of rhetorical flourish. In attempting to encourage the Corinthians to resume their support of the collection for Jerusalem, Paul highlights the Macedonians' willing beneficence in spite of their own lack of resources. Yet Paul's rhetorical strategy must be taken as essentially an accurate description of the impoverished reality of the Macedonians' financial position, or else his account of their situation would be proved false when representatives of the Macedonian churches arrived in Corinth, as Paul states in 2 Cor 8:16-24 that they will do. Moreover, such a false presentation of the situation of the Macedonians would imperil Paul's already fragile

attempt to convince the Corinthians to resume their support for the Jerusalem collection. This passage from the Corinthian correspondence, therefore,
provides an example of financial assistance for the destitute coming from
those who are themselves relatively impoverished.[63]

The second promise of future recompense for support of the Jerusalem
collection in 2 Corinthians 8–9 is found in 9:6-12. Paul begins this section by summarizing the point to which his comments in verses 1 to 5 have
been leading:

> [6]The point is this: The one who sows sparingly, will also reap sparingly,
> and the one who sows blessedly will also reap blessedly. [7]Each person
> [should give] as much as he has decided in his heart, not reluctantly or
> under compulsion, for God loves a cheerful giver. [8]And God has the
> power to provide for you every benefit in abundance, so that, always
> possessing all sufficiency in every respect, you may abound in every
> good work.

Paul's agricultural maxim in verse 6 (literally, "the one who sows sparingly,
sparingly that one will reap") provides proponents of the so-called prosperity
gospel with the metaphor of "sowing seeds," an image that is regularly used
to encourage "tithing" and other financial investments in Christian ministries as a means of prospering those who give.[64] It is impossible to avoid the
sense that Paul encourages the Corinthians to give to the Jerusalem collection because their generosity will benefit *both* the recipients of their gift and
the Corinthians themselves. The motivation for giving in this context is not
merely self-interest, since both the poor believers in Jerusalem and the Corinthians benefit from this exchange, but some measure of reward is implied.[65]
This is hardly an appeal to dis-interested giving.

---

[63] There may also be parallels among both Jewish communities and Greco-Roman
voluntary associations for care for the needy being given by individuals who themselves
might require material assistance (cf. Pliny, *Ep.* 10.93; Acts 6:1-7; 11:27-30; *m. Demai* 3.1;
see the discussion in Downs, *Offering of the Gentiles*, 102–12).

[64] For a thoughtful analysis of the rhetoric of "sowing" in the preaching of certain
Word of Faith evangelists, see Jonathan L. Walton, "Stop Worrying and Start Sowing!
A Phenomenological Account of the Ethics of 'Divine Investment,'" in *Pentecostalism and
Prosperity: The Socio-economics of the Global Charismatic Movement* (ed. Katherine Atta-
nasi and Amos Yong; New York: Palgrave-Macmillan, 2012), 107–29.

[65] Pace Ralph P. Martin: "The appeal is to a motive which is not one of reward so
much as a disinterested concern to reach out to the Jerusalem saints in their need, and the
issue is not the amount of the gift so much as the involvement it reflects (8:12)" (*2 Corinthians* [WBC 40; Dallas: Word, 2002], 289).

The nature of this reward is clarified in 9:9-12, however, for Paul appeals to LXX Ps 111:9 and returns to the agricultural metaphor of sowing and its implications for Corinthian participation in the collection:

> [9]As it is written: "He scatters abroad, he gives to the poor; his righteousness endures forever." [10]And he who supplies the seed to the sower and bread for food will supply and multiply your seed and will increase the harvest of your righteousness, [11]while you are enriched in every respect for all generosity, which will produce thanksgiving to God through us. [12]For this ministry of service not only supplies the needs of the saints but also abounds with many thanksgivings to God.

A key issue related to the nature of the blessedness promised to the one who sows blessedly in verse 6 involves the identity of the subject of Paul's citation of LXX Ps 111:9 in verse 9, for whether the "he" who scatters abroad, who gives to the poor, and whose righteousness endures forever, is God or a generous human is ambiguous. On one hand, God might be taken as the subject of the Psalm in Paul's citation of it because God is the subject of the preceding and following verses (i.e., "God has the power to provide" [v. 8]; "he who supplies the seed to the sower . . ." [v. 10]) and because the enduring righteousness of God is affirmed in LXX Ps 110:3. On the other, the subject of LXX Ps 111:9 itself is not God but the blessed individual who fears the Lord (μακάριος ἀνὴρ ὁ φοβούμενος τὸν κύριον), and the enduring righteousness of the generous Israelite is twice affirmed in the Psalm (111:3, 9). Even if a close reading might suggest that Paul cites LXX Ps 111:9 as a description of the practices of the generous almsgiver ("he scatters abroad, he gives to the poor") and the future for such a generous person ("his righteousness endures forever"), the initial ambiguity regarding the subject of the scriptural citation may evocatively provoke reflection on "the relationship between divine and human grace and righteousness." That what is said of God's enduring righteousness in LXX Psalm 110 is affirmed of the one who fears God in LXX Psalm 111 encourages readers "to reframe their understandings of benefaction and righteousness within the larger vision offered by those two psalms, viewed from the vantage point of their fulfilment in Christ."[66] In this sense, perhaps the most fitting commentary on Paul's reading of LXX Ps 111:9—"He scatters abroad, he gives to the poor; his righteousness endures forever"—is found earlier in the letter, where Paul indicates that God made the sinless Christ "to be sin, so that in him we might become the righteousness

---

[66] David I. Starling, "Meditations on a Slippery Citation: Paul's Use of Psalm 112:9 in 2 Corinthians 9:9," *JTI* 6 (2012): 241–56 [254].

of God" (2 Cor 5:21). Through union with Christ, believers do not merely participate in but become the righteousness of God.

Yet assuming that the phrase "his righteousness endures forever" (ἡ δικαιοσύνη αὐτοῦ μένει εἰς τὸν αἰῶνα) in Paul's citation of LXX Ps 111:9 refers, at least in part, to those who give generously to the collection for Jerusalem (and, presumably, by extension to all those in Christ who give to the poor), Paul in 2 Cor 9:9 appears to suggest that "righteousness" is the blessed outcome for the one who sows blessedly. Indeed, this is precisely the point Paul clarifies in his ensuring statements, where he insists that the God who provides seed to the one who sows and provides bread for food "will supply and multiply your seed and will *increase the harvest of your righteousness,* while you are enriched in every respect for all generosity, which will produce thanksgiving to God through us" (9:10b-11). Members of the body of Christ who give generously to the collection for Jerusalem (or to the poor more generally; cf. 2 Cor 9:13) will not only be supplied by God with the means to meet the needs of those who lack but also be rewarded by God with an increased harvest of righteousness.

It would be difficult to overstate the extent to which Paul in these two chapters frames contributions to the collection for Jerusalem as acts authenticated and empowered by God's gracious action.[67] Yet even as the God of abundance supplies the Corinthians with the very material resources that they are called liberally to share with believers in Jerusalem, God also increases "the material and spiritual benefits that would accrue to them and to the poor in Jerusalem as a result of their generous benevolence."[68] The Corinthians are enriched in every way for their great generosity, generosity that produces thanksgiving not to the Corinthians but to the God who stands behind and empowers their munificence. It should be clear that Paul's call for the Corinthians to care for impoverished believers is hardly "dis-interested" giving. On the other hand, the reward for this divinely graced charity is not more financial prosperity for the Corinthians but rather the harvest of being in right-relationship with God and others.

---

[67] See Downs, *Offering of the Gentiles,* 131–46.

[68] Murray J. Harris, *The Second Epistle to the Corinthians* (NIGTC; Grand Rapids: Eerdmans, 2005), 644.

Conclusion

Nowhere in Paul's letters does the apostle intimate that sins can be cleansed, covered, lifted, or redeemed by almsgiving.[69] Paul tends to frame sin and its solution primarily as transgressions that have been atoned for by the sacrificial death of Jesus or as an enslaving cosmic power that has been defeated by Jesus' death and resurrection.[70] Yet Paul does advocate meritorious almsgiving in the sense that care for the poor will be recognized and rewarded by God, both in the present and in the future (1 Tim 6:17-19; Phil 4:14-19; Gal 4:12-15; 2 Cor 9:6-12). To be sure, the hope of recompense is far from the only ethical warrant for charity in the Pauline Epistles. Other grounds for almsgiving in Paul's letters include the warning that failure to care for the needy will result in divine judgment (1 Cor 11:17-34), the possibility that those presently in a position to give financial assistance may soon need to receive aid from others (2 Cor 8:13-15), the notion that communal solidarity is forged through the exchange of material and spiritual blessings (2 Cor 8–9; Rom 15:26-27; Phil 4:15-16), the conviction that sharing with the needy is an imitation of the self-giving love of Christ (2 Cor 8:9), and the idea that care for the poor is central to gospel witness in missionary activities (Gal 2:10). Yet the practice and promotion of almsgiving in the Pauline Letters is far from dis-interested, for, as Paul says to Timothy, those who have wealth in the present age should enjoy their possessions by doing good, by being generous, by being rich in good works, by sharing, thus "storing up for themselves a good foundation for the future, so that they may take hold of the life that is truly life" (1 Tim 6:18-19).

[69] Paul is not, as Garrison suggests, "a vital link in the chain of development of the doctrine of redemptive almsgiving" (*Redemptive Almsgiving*, 70).

[70] The literature on sin and atonement in the Pauline Letters is immense; for a representative sampling of recent English-language scholarship, see James D. G. Dunn, *The Theology of Paul the Apostle* (Grand Rapids: Eerdmans, 1998), 79–162, 207–33, 317–412; David A. Brondos, *Paul on the Cross: Reconstructing the Story of Redemption* (Minneapolis: Fortress, 2006); Udo Schnelle, *Theology of the New Testament* (trans. M. Eugene Boring; Grand Rapids: Baker, 2009), 248–53, 275–82; Frank J. Matera, *God's Saving Grace: A Pauline Theology* (Grand Rapids: Eerdmans, 2012), 84–124; Michael J. Gorman, *The Death of the Messiah and the Birth of the New Covenant: A (Not So) New Model of the Atonement* (Eugene, Ore.: Cascade, 2014); Simon Gathercole, *Defending Substitution: An Essay on Atonement in Paul* (ASBT; Grand Rapids: Baker, 2015).

CHAPTER 6

LOVE COVERS A MULTITUDE OF SINS
Atoning Almsgiving in 1 Peter 4:8 and Its Early Christian Reception

Outside of the Synoptic Gospels, Acts, and the Pauline Epistles, several New Testament texts urge or allude to practices of caring for the needy (Heb 13:1-5, 15-16; cf. 10:34; Jas 1:27; 2:1-13, 14-17; 5:1-6; 1 John 3:16-17; cf. 1 Pet 2:11-17; 3:13-17).[1] Yet if there is one saying from New Testament that figured as significantly in the emerging Christian concept of atoning almsgiving

---

[1] The book of James, in particular, warns of God's judgment against those who do not act impartially or mercifully toward the poor (2:9-13). James (5:1-3) also issues a stinging prophetic indictment against the rich who have defrauded laborers and harvesters: "[1]Come now, rich people, weep and cry out over the miseries that are coming upon you. [2]Your riches have become rotten, and your clothes have become moth-eaten. [3]Your gold and silver have become rusty, and their rust will be a witness against you, and it will eat your flesh like fire. You have stored up treasure in the last days."

It is possible that Jas 5:2-3 draws upon a Jesus saying from Q tradition (cf. Matt 6:19-20; Luke 12:33; so Steven R. Johnson, *Seeking the Imperishable Treasure: Wealth, Wisdom, and a Jesus Saying* (Eugene, Ore.: Wipf & Stock, 2008), 97–100). If so, James' version of the saying differs significantly from Matthew's and Luke's, however. In Jas 5:3, e.g., θησαυρίζω refers not to storing up heavenly treasure but to storing up treasure for themselves *in* the last days (but cf. Luke 12:21). The phrase ἐν ἐσχάταις ἡμέραις indicates not that the rich are storing up treasure *for* the last days (pace NRSV; Johnson, *Seeking the Imperishable Treasure*, 99–100) but that, in the last days, which James believes have already come, the rich have set aside resources for themselves while simultaneously defrauding the needy,

175

as Luke 11:41, it is a dictum found in 1 Pet 4:8: "Love covers a multitude of sins." When the author of 1 Peter makes this declaration, however, the affirmation does not clearly name the actor(s) and/or the recipient(s) of such love, nor does the statement indicate whether it is the subject(s) or object(s) of love whose sins are covered. The assertion comes in the context of paraenetic instruction rooted in the conviction that God's eschatological judgment is close at hand:

> [7]The end of all things is near. Therefore, be sensible and self-controlled for prayers. [8]Above all, have constant love for one another, because *love covers a multitude of sins.* [9]Be hospitable to one another without grumbling. [10]Each of you should employ whatever gift he or she has received to serve one another as faithful administrators of the many forms of God's grace. [11]If anyone speaks, that person should speak as one speaking words from God. If anyone serves, that person should serve with the strength God supplies, so that in all things God might be glorified through Jesus Christ, to whom belong glory and dominion forever and ever. Amen. (1 Pet 4:7-11)

An answer to this question "Whose love covers the sins of whom in 1 Pet 4:8?" is not readily discerned by the syntax of the text. Four primary explanations have been suggested by modern interpreters:[2] (1) God's love covers human sins;[3] (2) human love for others covers the sins (through forgiveness)

---

making the rich subject to God's judgment (so Patrick J. Hartin, *James* [SP; Collegeville, Minn.: Liturgical, 2009], 228).

[2] See the helpful listing in Leonhard Goppelt, *Der erste Petrusbrief* (KEK 12/1; Göttingen: Vandenhoeck & Ruprecht, 1978), 283–85. The following interpretations are not necessarily mutually exclusive, however. Lewis R. Donelson (*I & II Peter and Jude: A Commentary* [NTL; Louisville, Ky.: Westminster John Knox, 2010], 128–29), for example, opines that the saying in 1 Pet 4:8b is not clear, suggesting that "the syntax of the verse produces both" the idea that the sins of those who love are forgiven and the idea that the sins of the ones loved are forgiven. This is also the view of Donald P. Senior (with Daniel J. Harrington), *1 Peter, Jude and 2 Peter* (Sacra Pagina 15; Collegeville, Minn.: Liturgical, 2008), 124: "Although the precise meaning is elusive, the general sense is that in loving others one carries out the primary command of the gospel, with the result that forgiveness and reconciliation abound (both among members of the community and in the eye of God), and therefore God's judgment about other lesser failings is abated."

[3] Daniel Keating, *First and Second Peter, Jude* (CCSS; Grand Rapids: Baker, 2011), 103. This also appears to be the interpretation offered by Duane F. Watson and Terrance D. Callan (*First and Second Peter* [Paideia; Grand Rapids: Baker, 2012], 102–3), although Watson depicts human love as a kind of trigger that activates God's love. After discounting interpretations 2, 3, and 4 above, Watson writes, "Rather, Christ's sacrifice takes away sin (1:18-19; 2:24; 3:18), and that sacrifice becomes effective in covering sin when love is exercised. In 1 Clement the exercise of love brings God's forgiveness and the

of the objects of such love;[4] (3) human love for others suppresses sins in the sense that loving action prevents the occurrence of future transgressions among the people of God;[5] and (4) human love for others atones for the sins of those who demonstrates such love, with atonement for sin coming either in the present or at the time of future, eschatological judgment.[6]

Among these interpretative options, the fourth is favored by several early Christian advocates of atoning almsgiving, who understand 1 Pet 4:8 as indicating that providing material assistance to the needy atones for the sins of the donor. Yet the notion that this verse might promote the atoning power of almsgiving is seen as problematic by many modern interpreters, perhaps especially among interpreters representing Protestant traditions suspicious of the notion that atonement for sin can be obtained on the basis of a human deed like caring for the poor.[7] One commentator, for example,

covering (*epikalyptō*) of sins (50.5–6; cf. 49.5). Loving others brings God's love into play. Whether mutual love forgives the sins of the one loving and/or the sins of the one loved is unclear (cf. *1 Clem.* 50.5), but the emphasis on mutuality in community indicates that love covers the sins of both"; cf. Ben Witherington III, *Letters and Homilies for Hellenized Christians*, vol. 2, *A Socio-rhetorical Commentary on 1–2 Peter* (Downers Grove, Ill.: InterVarsity, 2007), 204.

[4] Thomas R. Schreiner, *1, 2 Peter, Jude* (NAC 37; Nashville: B & H, 2003), 212–13: "When believers lavish love on others, the sins and offenses of others are overlooked"; Douglas Harink, *1 & 2 Peter* (BTCB; Grand Rapids: Baker, 2009), 113; John H. Elliott, *1 Peter: A New Translation with Introduction and Commentary* (AB 37B; New York: Doubleday, 2000), 751; Peter H. Davids, *The First Epistle of Peter* (NICNT; Grand Rapids: Eerdmans, 1990), 158–59; Wayne Grudem, *1 Peter* (TNTC; Grand Rapids: Eerdmans, 1988), 173; Goppelt, *Petrusbrief*, 284; C. E. B. Cranfield, *I & II Peter and Jude: Introduction and Commentary* (TBC; London: SCM Press, 1960), 114; W. C. van Unnik, "Teaching of Good Works in 1 Peter," *NTS* 1 (1954): 92–110. This interpretation is also earlier advanced by Martin Luther, *Commentary on Peter and Jude* (trans. John Nichols Lenker; Grand Rapids: Kregel Classics, 1990), 179–82.

[5] Karen H. Jobes, *1 Peter* (BECNT; Grand Rapids: Baker, 2005), 278–79; cf. the comments by J. Ramsey Michaels (*1 Peter* [WBC 49; Waco, Tex.: Word, 1988], 247) that "sin" in 1 Peter is fundamentally social in nature and that "sin as a social phenomenon can indeed be blotted out by the love that Christ commanded and demonstrated." Michaels also argues that "the meaning of 'cover' in its context in 1 Peter is neither to conceal sin illegitimately (as in Ps 31[32]:5 LXX), nor precisely to atone for it, but rather to obliterate it or make it disappear" (247).

[6] Norbert Brox, *Der erste Petrusbrief* (4th ed.; EKK 21; Zürich: Benziger, 1993), 205; Karl H. Schelkle, *Die Petrusbriefe, der Judasbrief* (5th ed.; HTKNT 13/2; Freiburg: Herder, 1980), 118; J. N. D. Kelly, *The Epistles of Jude and Peter* (BNTC; London: Harper, 1969), 178; Ceslas Spicq, *Les Épîtres de Saint Pierre* (SB; Paris: Gabalda, 1966), 150; Leslie Kline, "Ethics for the End Time: An Exegesis of 1 Peter 4:7-11," *ResQ* 7 (1963): 113–23.

[7] See, e.g., the comments by J. N. D. Kelly: "It is much more likely that the writer's point is that at the coming judgment his readers will receive mercy for their own sins (of

finds this understanding of 1 Pet 4:8 to be unpersuasive on theological and literary grounds:

> Such an interpretation finds in a person's love for others a kind of "secondary atonement," an interpretation rendered questionable by the assertion of [the author of 1 Peter] that sins against God have been taken away by Christ (1.18-19; 2.24; 3.18).[8]

This perspective is surely correct to emphasize the soteriological priority ascribed to the death of Christ throughout 1 Peter. In this letter, Christ is the paschal lamb whose blood ransomed believers from the empty life of the past (1:18-19); Christ, the one whose wounds bring healing, "bore our sins in his body on the cross, so that, having died to sins, we might live for righteousness" (2:24); and Christ is the righteous one who "suffered for sins once for all" in order to bring the readers to God (3:18). At the same time that the cross is the climactic point in the narrative of God's work to establish a

---

which he has been constantly reminding them: i. 14; ii. 1; 11 f.; iv. 1-4) provided in the meantime their mutual love does not falter. Forgiveness is God's free gift, and there is no suggestion of its being merited; but the gospel teaches (Lk. vii. 47) that he who loves much has many sins forgiven him and that at the final assize (Mt. xxv. 31-46) what will be decisive will be the love, or lack of love, we have displayed in our actions. . . . For the growth of the (potentially dangerous) notion that works of charity help to secure forgiveness, cf., e.g., 1 Clem. l. 5; Did. iv. 6; Barn. xix. 10; Polycarp, Phil. x. 2" (Epistles of Jude and Peter, 178). Schreiner insists that it "flies in the face of the rest of the New Testament and even 1 Peter (1:18-19; 2:24-25; 3:18) to see the love of believers as somehow atoning for their own sins" (1, 2 Peter, Jude, 212).

   [8]   Paul J. Achtemeier, 1 Peter: A Commentary on 1 Peter (Hermeneia; Minneapolis: Fortress, 1996), 296. Achtemeier's assessment is muted in comparison with John Calvin's polemical response to his Roman Catholic opponents: "Peter confirms his exhortation with the view that nothing is more necessary than to cherish mutual love. . . . This is the plain meaning of the words. It appears from this how absurd the Papists are, in seeking to deduce from this passage their own satisfactions, as though almsgiving and other duties of charity were a kind of compensation to God for blotting out their sins. It is enough to point out in passing their gross ignorance, for in a matter so clear it would be superfluous to add many words" (The Epistle of Paul the Apostle to the Hebrews and the First and Second Epistles of St. Peter [Calvin's Commentaries 12; trans. William B. Johnston; ed. David W. Torrance and Thomas F. Torrance; Grand Rapids: Eerdmans, 1963], 304); cf. Reinhard Feldmeier (The First Letter of Peter [Waco, Tex.: Baylor University Press, 2008], 218–19), who notes that the "fuzziness" and "ambivalence" of 1 Pet 4:8 contradicts "other statements of the letter about Christ's reconciling work." Space does not permit extended reflection on the influence of Calvin's reading of 1 Pet 4:8 upon subsequent Protestant exegesis, but I suspect Calvin's polemical assessment of Roman Catholic interpretations sets the stage for later and continued Protestant reticence to view ἀγάπη in 4:8 as a human action with atoning efficacy.

community of hope (2:5-10), however, so also the exiled community to which the epistle of 1 Peter is written is called to imitate the self-giving love demonstrated in the example (ὑπογραμμός) of Christ, in whose footsteps God's elect are called to walk (2:21-25).[9] Indeed, 1 Pet 4:1-2 picks up on the affirmation of Christ's vicarious suffering in 3:18 ("For Christ also suffered for sins once for all") by exhorting readers, on the basis of Christ's bodily suffering, to face suffering with the same resolve as Christ, positing some connection between suffering in the flesh and the elimination of sin: "Since therefore Christ suffered in the flesh, arm yourselves also with the same intention (for whoever has suffered in the flesh has finished with sin), so as to live for the rest of your earthly life no longer by human desires but by the will of God" (NRSV). Might there not be, then, in 1 Peter an organic relationship between the self-giving and atoning love of Jesus Christ, on the one hand, and a cruciform love shown by believers that has the power to alleviate the sins of those who demonstrate such love, on the other?

An exploration of 1 Pet 4:8 in light of its early Christian reception sheds interesting light on this question. How do early Christian authors, particularly early Christian advocates of atoning almsgiving, understand the identity of the actor who displays love and the relationship between the removal of sins through the death of Christ and the alleviation of sins through human love in 4:8? Does the claim that the sins of those who act charitably can be covered by their love for others within the community of faith necessarily compromise the conviction that atonement for sins results from the sacrificial death of Christ? An examination of the use of this verse among second- and third-century advocates of atoning almsgiving shows that several early Christian interpreters employ this text in documents that emphasize *both* the unique, atoning significance of the cross *and* the possibility of atonement for sin through the practice of almsgiving. This exercise in *Wirkungsgeschichte*, therefore, has the potential to reshape interpretative traditions that would sever any connection between human love and atonement in the reading of 1 Pet 4:8.

---

[9]   On the theme of *imitatio Christi* in 1 Peter, see Clifford A. Barbarick, "The Pattern and the Power: The Example of Christ in 1 Peter" (Ph.D. diss., Baylor University, 2011); J. de Waal Dryden, *Theology and Ethics in 1 Peter* (WUNT II/209; Tübingen: Mohr Siebeck, 2006), 163–91.

When Is the Saying "Love Covers a Multitude of Sins" a Citation of 1 Peter 4:8?

Before proceeding to a survey of the reception of 1 Pet 4:8 in the first three centuries of the Common Era, it is necessary briefly to address the question of how it is possible to know that early Christian writers who state that "love covers a multitude of sins" are, in fact, citing 4:8. As is well known, there is a close, though not exact, similarity between the phrase ἀγάπη καλύπτει πλῆθος ἁμαρτιῶν ("love covers a multitude of sins") in this verse and both the MT of Prov 10:12b (כל־פשעים תכסה אהבה) and a parallel construction in Jas 5:20.[10] Given that the phrase in 1 Pet 4:8 does not match LXX Prov 10:12b (πάντας δὲ τοὺς μὴ φιλονεικοῦντας καλύπτει φιλία, "friendship covers all who are not fond of strife"), and that the author of 1 Peter regularly cites the LXX instead of the MT when evoking the Jewish Scriptures (including citations of or allusions to Proverbs in 1 Pet 2:17c; 3:6; 4:18; 5:5), many have suspected that the author of 1 Peter is not quoting Prov 10:12b directly but instead citing an early Jewish or Christian maxim based on the Hebrew *Vorlage*.[11] If this is the case, how can it be known that an assertion that "love covers a multitude of sins" among the church fathers represents a citation of 1 Pet 4:8 and not an independent evocation of the same free-floating proverb, loosely based on the MT of Prov 10:12, also cited by the author of 1 Peter?

The patristic writers who do cite the phrase "love covers a multitude of sins" tend to treat the saying as a proverbial maxim (or proof-text) anyway, typically failing explicitly to connect the expression to its literary context in 1 Peter, sometimes even conflating it with Pauline material. On the other hand, in all but two of the examples under consideration, the case for 1 Pet 4:8 functioning as the source text is strengthened by an exact correspondence of the Greek wording (i.e., in 1 Clem. 49.5; 2 Clem. 16.4; Clement of

---

[10] Jas 5:20 reads: γινωσκέτω ὅτι ὁ ἐπιστρέψας ἁμαρτωλὸν ἐκ πλάνης ὁδοῦ αὐτοῦ σώσει ψυχὴν αὐτοῦ ἐκ θανάτου καὶ καλύψει πλῆθος ἁμαρτιῶν ("You should know that whoever brings a sinner back from wandering will save the sinner's soul from death and will cover a multitude of sins" [NRSV]). The primary differences between 1 Pet 4:8 and Jas 5:20 are (1) the future form of the verb καλύπτω in James and (2) the fact that the subject of the verb in Jas 5:20 is not ἀγάπη but ὁ ἐπιστρέψας ἁμαρτωλὸν ἐκ πλάνης ὁδοῦ αὐτοῦ. Some manuscripts of 1 Peter read καλύψει in 4:8, but this is likely due to the influence of Jas 5:20 (so Goppelt, *Petrusbrief*, 284).

[11] So Achtemeier, *1 Peter*, 295–96; Jobes, *1 Peter*, 278; Elliott, *1 Peter*, 750–51; on the use of the LXX in 1 Peter, see esp. Karen H. Jobes, "The Septuagint Textual Tradition in 1 Peter," *Septuagint Research: Issues and Challenges in the Study of the Greek Jewish Scriptures* (ed. Wolfgang Kraus and R. Glenn Wooden; Atlanta: Society of Biblical Literature, 2006), 311–33.

Alexandria, ~~*Quis div. 37; Strom.* 4.18; *Paed.* 3.91.3). Since the Greek phrase ἀγάπη καλύπτει πλῆθος ἁμαρτιῶν is unique to 1 Pet 4:8 in the scriptural tradition, when the idiom is found with the very same wording in the writings of second- and third-century Christian authors, 1 Pet 4:8 is highly likely to have been the source text.~~ Because Origen's *Homiliae in Leviticum* exists only in Rufinus' Latin translation, it is impossible to consult the Greek text of Origen's work. Origen's locution *Quoniam charitas cooperit multitudinem peccatoram*, however, is preceded by an indication that these words are spoken by an apostle (*Et apostolus dicit*), making it almost certain that Origen is citing a text he considers to have been written by the apostle Peter (*Hom. Lev.* 2.4.5 [PG 12:418B]). The only potential ambiguity exists in the *Did. apost.* 2.3.2, which credits the saying to the "Lord," and in Tertullian's *Scorp.* 6.10–11. Yet even if it could be shown that a particular writer is not citing 1 Pet 4:8 but instead quoting a traditional aphorism, this would only push the question of reception history back beyond 1 Peter, so that the citation of the saying in the canonical epistle of 1 Peter would be yet an earlier instance of the reception of the early Jewish (or perhaps Jewish-Christian) proverb. ~~Since the precise form of the proverbial saying ἀγάπη καλύπτει πλῆθος ἁμαρτιῶν is not found in any extant literary source earlier than 1 Peter, 4:8 is usually the best option as the source text when the phrase appears in the writings of the church fathers.~~

The Reception of 1 Peter 4:8 in the Second and Third Centuries

1 Clement

~~The earliest citation of 1 Pet 4:8 is found in *1 Clem.* 49.5,~~ a document probably composed anywhere from the latter part of the first century CE until the middle part of the second.[12] In a letter aimed at producing "peace and harmony" (εἰρήνη καὶ ὁμόνοια [*1 Clem.* 63.2]) within the fractious Christ-believing community in Corinth, the author of *1 Clement*, writing on behalf of the church in Rome, calls directly for the practice of love among the Corinthians in *1 Clem.* 49.1–55.6. With allusions to 1 Pet 4:8 and 1 Cor 13:4-7, the author begins this appeal with an "Encomium to Love" (49.2–6):

[12] For discussions of the date of *1 Clement*, see Horatio E. Lona, *Der erste Clemensbrief: Übersetzt und erklärt* (KAV 2; Göttingen: Vandenhoeck & Ruprecht, 1998), 75–78. The range of 80–150 CE is suggested by Laurence L. Welborn, "On the Date of First Clement," *Biblical Research* 29 (1984): 35–54. A pre-70 CE date for *1 Clement* is argued by Rev. Thomas J. Herron, *Clement and the Early Church of Rome: On the Dating of Clement's First Epistle to the Corinthians* (Steubenville, Ohio: Emmaus Road, 2010).

²Who is able to describe the bond of God's love? ³Who is in a position to declare the greatness of its beauty? ⁴The height to which love leads is indescribable. ⁵Love binds us to God. *Love covers a multitude of sins.* Love bears all things. Love is patient in all things. There is nothing vulgar in love, nothing proud. Love has no schism; love does not cause division; love does all things in harmony. Everyone chosen by God has been made perfect in love; without love nothing is pleasing to God. ⁶In love has the Master received us. On account of the love he had for us, our Lord Jesus Christ gave his blood for us by God's will—his flesh for our flesh and his life for our life.[13]

~~In this context, 1 Pet 4:8 is cited not in connection with the practice of alms-giving but rather as part of a general appeal for love as a way of embodying the commandments of Christ (49.1) and modeling the example of Christ (49.6). Given that material assistance to the needy is not an issue in the present context of 1 Clement, this earliest quotation of 1 Pet 4:8 does not function as an appeal to atoning almsgiving.~~[14]

The citation of the saying "love covers a multitude of sins" in *1 Clem.* 49.5 reflects an interesting ambiguity, one inherent in the phrase ἀγάπη καλύπτει πλῆθος ἁμαρτιῶν itself and then employed in the context of the rhetorical appeal to love in this section of *1 Clement*. The accent of the praise of love in *1 Clement* 49 falls on divine love *for* humans: the encomium opens with the question, "Who is able to describe the bond of God's love?" (τὸν δεσμὸν τῆς ἀγάπης τοῦ θεοῦ [v. 2]); the statement that "love binds us to God" implies that this union is accomplished by God (especially given the parallel with the rhetorical question in v. 2); and the section concludes with the acknowledgment that "in love has the Master received us" and the confession that "on account of the love he had for us, our Lord Jesus Christ gave his blood for us by God's will" (v. 6). In context, then, the assertion "love covers a multitude of sins" in *1 Clem* 49.5 might appear to suggest that it is God's love that covers human sins.[15]

---

[13] The identification of this section as an "encomium to love" is found in ~~Odd Magne Bakke's~~ excellent study, *"Concord and Peace": A Rhetorical Analysis of the First Letter of Clement with an Emphasis on the Language of Unity and Sedition* (WUNT II/141; Tübingen: Mohr Siebeck, 2001), 191.

[14] That is not to suggest that the author of *1 Clement* is entirely uninterested in the relationship between faith and finance, although issues of wealth, poverty, and possessions are not major themes in the letter. The author does allude to the practice of Christians selling themselves into slavery in order to "ransom others" (ἑτέρους λυτρώσονται) in *1 Clem.* 55.2; see Jennifer A. Glancy, *Slavery in Early Christianity* (Oxford: Oxford University Press, 2002), 82–83.

[15] So Bakke, *Concord and Peace*, 338–39.

On the other hand, the language of ἀγάπη throughout *1 Clem.* 49.1–55.6, and elsewhere in the letter, undeniably aims at the promotion of embodied "love" among the divided believers in Corinth. If the emphasis at the beginning and end of the encomium to love in *1 Clem.* 49.1–5a and 49.6 is on God's love for humans, the same cannot be said of 49.5b, where "love has no schism" (σχίσμα), an allusion to Corinthian factionalism (cf. 2.6; 46.9; 54.2), where "love does not cause division" (οὐ στασιάζει), precisely the opposite of the seditious action against the Corinthian presbyters (47.6; cf. 4.12; 43.2; 46.7; 51.3; 55.1), and where "love does all things in harmony" (ποιεῖ ἐν ὁμονοίᾳ), a virtue that the author consistently hopes to inculcate among his Corinthian readers (9.4; 11.2; 20.3, 10–11; 21.1; 30.3; 34.7; 50.5; 60.4; 61.1; 63.2; 65.1).[16]

The dynamic interplay between divine and human love is nicely captured at the beginning of the following section, where the author asks, presumably with reference to God's love, "Who is worthy to be found in ἀγάπη, except those whom God considers worthy?" Yet this question is then followed by the exhortation, "Let us ask and petition, therefore, from God's mercy, in order that we may be found blameless in love, standing apart from human partisanship" (50.2). Blamelessness in love, a human virtue, is the opposite of human strife. Moreover, after expressing the hope that those perfected in love by God's grace will be revealed at the visitation of Christ's kingdom in verse 3 and providing scriptural support for that hope by citing Isa 26:20 in verse 4, the author of *1 Clement* then states, "We are blessed, beloved, if we keep the commandments of God in the harmony of love, so that through love our sins may be forgiven" (50.5). But through whose love are sins forgiven? The language of keeping "the commandments of God in the harmony of love" suggests that ἀγάπη here is a human action manifested when the Corinthians reject schism, whereas the citation of LXX Ps 31:1-2 in the following sentence ("For it is written, 'Blessed are those whose lawless behavior was forgiven and whose sins were covered over [ἐπεκαλύφθησαν]. Blessed is the person to whom the Lord will not reckon sin, and in whose mouth there is no deceit'") would seem to indicate that sins are forgiven or covered through God's love. Thus, according to the theological logic of *1 Clem.* 49.1–50.6, the forgiveness and/or covering of sin involves both divine and human ἀγάπη.

---

[16] On the concept of ὁμόνοια in *1 Clement*, see Cilliers Breytenbach, "Civic Concord and Cosmic Harmony: Sources of Metaphoric Mapping in *1 Clement* 20:3," in *Encounters with Hellenism: Studies on the First Letter of Clement* (ed. Cilliers Breytenbach and Laurence L. Welborn; AGJU 53; Leiden: Brill, 2004), 182–96; David J. Downs, "Justification, Good Works, and Creation in Clement of Rome's Appropriation of Romans 5–6," *NTS* 59 (2013): 415–32.

Clement of Alexandria

A connection between 1 Corinthians 13 and 1 Peter 4 is also found in the writings of Clement of Alexandria. The association of these Pauline and Petrine texts is not surprising, since the Alexandrian presbyter explicitly cites *1 Clement* when quoting 1 Corinthians 13 and 1 Peter 4 together in *Stromata* 4.18 [111.3]. In that context, Clement of Alexandria quotes the encomium to love found in *1 Clem.* 49.5, a citation followed immediately by quotes from *1 Clem.* 50.1–2 and 1 Cor 13:1, 3 [111.4–5].[17] Given the explicit dependence of Clement of Alexandria upon the text of *1 Clement* 49, it is useful to consider the witness of Clement of Alexandria out of chronological order. What is particularly noteworthy about Clement of Alexandria's use of 1 Pet 4:8, however, is that once he employs the text in order to support the meritorious value of almsgiving and once, ostensibly, to reject it.

The earlier of the two citations is found in Clement's homiletic treatise *Quis dives salvetur.*[18] The date of this document is uncertain, but it was most likely penned before the *Stromata.*[19] In *Quis dives salvetur*, Clement uses Jesus' conversation with a rich man in Mark 10:17-31 to reflect on the dangers of wealth for believers who posses it, an increasingly important pastoral issue in the context of emerging Christian affluence in late second-century Alexandria. As a means of dealing with the potential problem of riches among his readers, Clement identifies the *desire for wealth* as an evil to be avoided (*Quis div.* 12) and calls prosperous believers to live modestly and simply as the exterior result of their inner detachment from goods (*Quis div.* 26; cf. *Paed.* 3.10–11). While rich believers are not instructed to abandon their possessions, they are challenged to share their resources generously with their materially impoverished brothers and sisters, for the poor can serve as advocates with God on behalf of the rich. Clement famously describes this exchange of alms for prayer with a commercial metaphor:

[17] On Clement of Alexandria's sources, see Annewies van den Hoek, "How Alexandrian Was Clement of Alexandria? Reflections on Clement and His Alexandrian Background," *HeyJ* 31 (1990): 179–94. For a study of Clement that emphasizes the primacy of Scripture in the writings of the presbyter, see Eric Osborn, *Clement of Alexandria* (Cambridge: Cambridge University Press, 2005).

[18] For a detailed and insightful treatment of the relationship between almsgiving and soteriology in Clement's *Quis dives salvetur*, see Helen Rhee, *Loving the Poor, Saving the Rich: Wealth, Poverty, and Early Christian Formation* (Grand Rapids: Baker, 2012), 77–88.

[19] See the discussion in Henny Fiskå Hägg, *Clement of Alexandria and the Beginnings of Christian Apophaticism* (Oxford: Oxford University Press, 2006), 61–70.

What beautiful business! What a divine market! You purchase with money something incorruptible, and you give the perishing things of this world in exchange for heavenly things. Set sail, O Rich Man, for this festal assembly, if you are wise. And if it is necessary, go around the whole earth without considering dangers or toils, that here you might purchase a heavenly kingdom. (*Quis div.* 32)

In *Quis div.* 37, Clement turns to the topic of God's love, which is demonstrated most profoundly in the sacrificial love of God's Son, who gave himself up as a ransom (λύτρον ἑαθτὸν ἐπιδιδοὺς). The sacrifice of Christ provides a model for Christians, since believers cannot hoard temporal things of the world while claiming to love their brothers and sisters. Clement then offers a praise of love modeled on 1 Corinthians 13 and *1 Clement* 49, with allusions to 1 Pet 4:8 and 1 John 4:18:

> But you learn "the more excellent way," which Paul shows, for salvation (ἐπὶ σωτηρίαν). "Love does not seek its own" (1 Cor 13:5), but is poured out upon the brother. For this brother, love flutters with passion; for this brother, it is sensibly mad. "Love covers a multitude of sins" (ἀγάπη καλύπτει πλῆθος ἁμαρτιῶν [1 Pet 4:8]). Perfect love casts out fear (1 John 4:18). Love does not boast, is not puffed up, does not rejoice in injustice, but it rejoices in the truth. Love bears all things, believes all things, hopes all things, endures all things. Love never fails. Prophecies fail; tongues cease; healings are left behind on the earth. But these three things remain: faith, hope, love. And the greatest of these is love (cf. 1 Cor 13:4-13). (*Quis div.* 37)

The citation opens with an indication that fraternal love is "for salvation." Moreover, the gloss that Clement provides for this chain of scriptural citations in the following sentence demonstrates his interpretation of 1 Pet 4:8 as a statement about human love that results in atonement for sin for the one demonstrating that love: "And if someone implants love in his soul, even if he was born in sin, and even if he has done many forbidden deeds, that person is able to counteract his mistakes by increasing love and by accepting pure repentance" (*Quis div.* 38). For sinners who fall into transgression after receiving the baptismal seal and redemption (τὴν σφραγῖδα καὶ τὴν λύτρωσιν), God will forgive the penitent, and true repentance is demonstrated by the wealthy when they assist needy believers (*Quis div.* 39). As Clement summarizes his point in this section: "With regard to transgressions previously committed, God gives release. But with regard to those transgressions that will come, each individual [obtains remission] for himself" (*Quis div.* 40). Thus, in context, Clement of Alexandria employs 1 Pet 4:8 in the rhetorical construction of an argument regarding the atoning value of demonstrating material love for the poor. For this reason, ~~Clement of Alexandria is frequently highlighted as a leading proponent of atoning almsgiving, an interpretation that certainly adheres to the main themes of *Quis dives salvetur.*~~[20]

The complexity of Clement's thought, however, and the variety of ways in which Clement can appeal to a single biblical text has often been underestimated, as can be seen in a second later citation of the saying from 1 Pet 4:8. In a section of the *Stromata* devoted to the topic of martyrdom, Clement of Alexandria again draws upon the apostle Paul, 1 Peter, and *1 Clement*, this time in order to describe the attitude toward death held by "the gnostic" (ὁ γνωστικός). It is important to realize that "the gnostic" for Clement of Alexandria in the *Stromata* is almost a technical term that reflects Clement's Platonic epistemology. Clement makes a distinction between three types of knowledge: (1) sensual knowledge, which is false; (2) spiritual knowledge; and (3) logical knowledge, the latter two of which are true.[21] The Christian gnostic is the individual who, through faith and love, possesses true knowledge, able to undertake a journey of detachment from the world and union with God (*Strom.* 7.12.74–80). It is this philosophical and epistemological context that frames Clement of Alexandria's apparent denial, or at least diminishment, of the meritorious nature of almsgiving in his commentary on 1 Corinthians 13 and 1 Peter 4 in *Stromata* 4.18.[22] There Clement writes:

> Therefore, the noble and holy manner of our philanthropy, according to Clement [i.e., the author of *1 Clement*], seeks the common good, either by martyrdom or by teaching in deed and word, the latter of which is twofold, unwritten and written. This is love: to love God and to love neighbor. This leads to indescribable heights (cf. *1 Clem.* 49.4). *Love covers a multitude of sins* (1 Pet 4:8). Love bears all things. Love is patient in all things. Love joins us to God. Love does all things in harmony. Everyone chosen by God has been made perfect in love. Without love nothing is pleasing to God. There is no explanation of the perfection of love, it is said. Who is worthy to be found in it, except the one whom God considers worthy (*1 Clem.* 50.1–2)? Take, for example, the apostle Paul. "If I give my body," he says, "but do not have love, I am

[20] So Roman Garrison, *Redemptive Almsgiving in Early Christianity* (JSNTSup 77; Sheffield: JSOT Press, 1993), 129–30; see the nuanced analysis in Rhee, *Loving the Poor,* 82–83.

[21] *Strom.* 6.2.4–6.3.1; 4.54.1; 7.1.1; cf. Hägg, *Clement of Alexandria,* 208–12.

[22] On Clement's concept of ὁ γνωστικός, see Andrew C. Itter, *Esoteric Teaching in the Stromateis of Clement of Alexandria* (VCSup 97; Leiden: Brill, 2009), 175–96; and Judith Kovacs, "Divine Pedagogy and the Gnostic Teacher according to Clement of Alexandria," *JECS* 9 (2001): 3–25.

a noisy gong or a clanging symbol." If it is not from an elective disposition, by gnostic love, that I testify, Paul says, but by fear; and if, then, by
anticipated reward I rattle my lips to testify to the Lord that I confess
the Lord, then I am an ordinary man, ringing out the Lord's name,
but not knowing him. For there is indeed a people that loves with the
lips, and there is another that hands over the body to be burned (cf. Isa
29:13). "And if I give away all my possessions," he says, not according to
the principle of affectionate fellowship, but according to the principle
of recompense, either from the person who received the benefaction or
from the Lord who has promised, "and if I have all faith so as to move
mountains," and repel shadowy passions, and if I am not faithful to the
Lord on account of love, "I am nothing," as one reckoned with and no
different from the multitude, especially in comparison with the one
who testifies as a gnostic. (*Strom.* 4.18.111–12)

Clement begins this section by defining love broadly as love of God
and love of neighbor. This introduction is followed by an encomium to love
expressly patterned after *1 Clement* 49. Clement of Alexandria then offers
the apostle Paul as an example of love and its limitations, conflating 1 Cor
13:1 ("If I speak in the tongues of mortals and of angels, but do not have love,
I am a noisy gong or a clanging cymbal") and 13:3 ("if I give my body"). Clement's gloss on this Pauline material reflects his conviction that "gnostic love"
(δι᾿ ἀγάπης γνωστικῆς) cannot be motivated by fear, for fear, as the opposite
of faith, demonstrates a lack of knowledge (*Strom.* 6.9.75–76; 6.12.98). Nor
can the anticipation of reward motivate authentic love: the Christian gnostic
must demonstrate love because of the good itself, not because of the hope
of honor (cf. *Strom.* 4.6.29.4). With regard to the dispossession of material
resources, Clement interprets the first condition in 1 Cor 13:3—κἂν ψωμίσω
πάντα τὰ ὑπάρχοντά μου—to mean a dispossession of goods not based on a
principle of affectionate fellowship (οὐ κατὰ τῆς κοινωνίας τῆς ἀγαπητικῆς
λόγον) but on the basis of an expectation of recompense for the charitable
action (ἀλλὰ κατὰ τὸν τῆς ἀνταποδόσεως), recompense either from the one
who receives the benefaction or from the Lord. The one who engages in
almsgiving with the hope of human or divine requital is nothing, particularly
when compared with the Christian gnostic. There is, therefore, a very different presentation of the motivation for benevolence than one finds in *Quis
dives salvetur*: whereas 1 Pet 4:8 is cited in *Quis div.* 37 as part of an extended
appeal for almsgiving that is concerned with the benefits that accrue for the
donor—including atonement for sin—in *Stromata* 4, Clement insists that

the Christian gnostic will be motivated to show love by knowledge and faith, not by any self-interest on the part of the giver of alms.[23]

The difference between the varying motivations for the practice of merciful deeds in *Quis dives salvetur* and *Stromata* should not be attributed to an inconsistency or a profound chronological development in Clement's thought. Instead, the differences reflect Clement's progressive and teleological view of salvation and ethics. In short, *Quis dives salvetur* is addressed primarily to baptized Christians of some means who have not progressed very far along the path to perfection.[24] The *Stromata*, on the other hand, is concerned with the spiritually advanced Christian gnostic who strives for the ethical goal of ἀπάθεια, the elimination of irrational passions from the soul and likeness to God.[25]

2 Clement

A citation of 1 Pet 4:8 that strongly emphasizes the atoning value of merciful action (ἐλεημοσύνη) is found in the anonymous second-century homily called 2 Clement.[26] In the section of the document from 15.1 to 18.2, there is

[23] In addition to these two passages, Clement of Alexandria also cites 1 Pet 4:8 in *Paed.* 3.91.3, although there the reference is more generally to an attitude and practice of love toward one's neighbor. In that context, Clement has been discussing biblical exhortations to righteous Christian living, referring in 3.85.1 to 1 Pet 1:17-19 in order to remind readers that because they have been ransomed by the blood of Christ (ἀλλὰ τιμίῳ αἵματι ὡς ἀμνοῦ ἀμώμου καὶ ἀσπίλου Χριστοῦ) they are fenced in from the corrupting power of sin by the cross. The way of salvation, according to Clement, is the way of repentance, and this repentance is seen most clearly in (1) true prayer, which includes clothing the naked (citing Isa 58:7-9); (2) true fasting, which includes the end of oppression and injustice (citing Isa 58:4-7); and (3) true sacrifice, which includes a broken heart (citing Isa 1:11-14). After citing material from Luke 17:3-4 on the necessity of showing forgiveness to penitent sinners and from Luke 3:13-14; Deut 1:17; 16:19; Isa 1:17 on the requirement to demonstrate no partiality in judgment, Clement quotes 1 Pet 4:8: "Ἀγάπη," φησί, "καλύπτει πλῆθος ἁμαρτιῶν." The edition cited is M. Marcovich, ed., *Clemntis Alexandri Paedagogus* (VCSup 61; Leiden: Brill, 2002).

[24] For this reason, readers of *Quis dives salvetur* are encouraged to seek out friendship with righteous men who will tutor them in the ways of God (*Quis div.* 31).

[25] See the excellent account of Clement's theology and ethics in David P. O'Brien, "Rich Clients and Poor Patrons: Functions of Friendship in Clement of Alexandria's *Quis dives salvetur*" (Ph.D. diss., University of Oxford, 2004).; cf. Christopher M. Hays, "Resumptions of Radicalism: Christian Wealth Ethics in the Second and Third Centuries," *ZNW* 102 (2011): 261–82 [262–67].

[26] For thorough discussions of the context of 2 Clement, see especially Andreas Lindeman, *Die Clemensbriefe* (HNT 17; Tübingen: J. C. B. Mohr, 1992), 189–96; and Wilhelm Pratscher, *Der zweite Clemensbrief* (KAV 3; Göttingen: Vandenhoeck & Ruprecht, 2007), 9–64. Garrison's arguments that 2 Clement should be associated with the church

a notable emphasis on the theme of eschatological judgment at the day of the Lord's appearing (17.4). Beginning with a call to repentance and to renounce the pursuit of pleasure, the key text for the purpose of this investigation is found in 16.1–4:

> [1] Therefore, brothers and sisters, since we have received no small opportunity to repent, while we have time, let us turn to the God who has called us—that is, while we still have one who receives us. [2] For if we renounce these pleasures and conquer our soul by refusing to do its evil desires, we will share in the mercy of Jesus. [3] But you know that "the day" of judgment is already coming like a "blazing oven," and "some of the heavens will be melted," and the whole earth will be like lead being melted in a fire, and then both the hidden and public works of people will become visible. [4] Therefore, merciful practice (ἐλεημοσύνη) is good as repentance for sin. Fasting is better than prayer, but merciful practice (ἐλεημοσύνη) is better than both, and "love covers a multitude of sins." Prayer from a good conscience delivers from death. Blessed is everyone who is found full of these things, for merciful practice (ἐλεημοσύνη) lightens the burden of sin.

The passage is replete with scriptural resonance. First, two citations of the OT—from LXX Mal 4:1 and LXX Isa 34:4—locate the call to repentance in the context of eschatological urgency. For this reason, translations of the opening clause καλὸν οὖν ἐλεημοσύνη ὡς μετάνοια ἁμαρτίας that imply that "almsgiving *is as good as* repentance for sins" miss the mark, although such a rendering is grammatically possible.[27] From the perspective of the author, ἐλεημοσύνη is good because it is a means of, or perhaps a sign of,

---

in Rome are unconvincing and have not persuaded many supporters (*Redemptive Almsgiving*, 99–107). In his recent commentary on *2 Clement*, Christopher M. Tuckett argues against a literary relationship between 1 Peter and *2 Clement*, positing instead that "the common allusion to the verse from Proverbs in 1 Peter, *1 Clement*, and *2 Clement*, with common wording which agrees strikingly against the LXX version, suggests a common tradition circulating in some early Christian circles, including the provenances of these writings; but it is probably impossible to say more" (*2 Clement: Introduction, Text, and Commentary* [Oxford Apostolic Fathers; Oxford: Oxford University Press, 2012], 267).

[27] Michael W. Holmes (*The Apostolic Fathers: Greek Texts and English Translations* [3rd ed.; Grand Rapids: Baker, 2007], 123) renders the phrase: "almsgiving is good, therefore, as is repentance from sin"; cf. the alternate rendering in Ehrman, *Apostolic Fathers*, 1:19: "giving to charity, therefore is good, so too is repentance from sin." Both Lindemann ("Gut also ist Almosen, wie Buße für Sünde," *Clemensbriefe*, 247) and Pratscher ("Gut also ist Almosen, wie Abkher von der Sünde," *Der zweite Clemensbrief*, 196) translate the phrase along the lines I am suggesting.

repentance for sin. ~~Merciful practice is not merely as good as repentance; it is repentance.~~[28]

2 Clement 16.4 contains the citation of 1 Pet 4:8 (along with Tob 12:8-9): "Fasting is better than prayer, but merciful practice is better than both, and love covers a multitude of sins; prayer from a good conscience delivers from death." Drawing on Tob 12:8 (G^1: "Prayer with fasting and merciful action and righteousness is good"), ~~the author of 2 Clement asserts the superiority of merciful practice over prayer, but he goes beyond Tobit by declaring that ἐλεημοσύνη is better than both~~ fasting and prayer.[29] Without denying the essential goodness of any of these practices (cf. 2 Clem. 2.2, where readers are encouraged "to offer up prayers to God sincerely"), the author constructs a hierarchy of praxis:

"merciful practice"/ἐλεημοσύνη (as repentance for sin)

fasting

prayer

If merciful practice is depicted as a means or sign of repentance in 16.4a, it may also be ranked above fasting and prayer simply because caring for the needy most clearly demonstrates the one thing that the preacher desires most from his audience—namely, repentance (8.1–3; 9.8; 13.1; 16.1; 17.1; 19.1).[30]

---

[28] Here the narrative of Jesus' interaction with Zacchaeus in Luke 19:1-9 presents itself for comparison, although I am not suggesting that there is a literary relationship between Luke and 2 Clement. Zacchaeus' repentance is embodied in his declaration that he will give half of his possessions to the poor and pay back fourfold those whom he has defrauded (19:8; reading δίδωμι and ἀποδίδωμι as futuristic presents; see chap. 5). Luke 19:1-9, therefore, offers a reminder that repentance in early Christianity often has deeply social implications. Zacchaeus receives salvation—which in this context means restoration to the people of God from his status as a marginalized outsider—and as a demonstration of his repentance he commits himself to a life of almsgiving and justice (see Guy D. Nave Jr., *The Role and Function of Repentance in Luke–Acts* [Academia Biblica 4; Atlanta: Society of Biblical Literature, 2002]; on salvation as status reversal in the Gospel of Luke, see Joel B. Green, *The Theology of the Gospel of Luke* [New Testament Theology; Cambridge: Cambridge University Press, 1995], 22–49).

[29] On the relationship between 2 Clement and Tobit, see the detailed analysis in Christopher M. Tuckett, "Tobit 12,8 and 2 Clement 16,4," *ETL* 88, no. 1 (2012): 129–44.

[30] ~~In this sense, I find the introduction of the language of ἐλεημοσύνη in 2 Clem. 16.4 far less "strained" than Tuckett (2 Clement, 272). Moreover, it is probably no accident~~

The reference to 1 Pet 4:8 is also significant for the theological claim advanced by the author.[31] With an emphasis on the eschatological context of ethics similar to that found in 1 Peter 4, the author of *2 Clement* interprets this saying from 1 Pet 4:8 as an indication that the human love demonstrated through the practice of ἐλεημοσύνη signifies one's repentance and covers a multitude of sins for the one who shows mercy to the needy. All those who hear this sermon are commissioned as agents in this mutual assistance, for all are called to repentance.

Didascalia Apostolorum

A link between 1 Pet 4:8, the forgiveness of sins, and the provision of material assistance to the needy is also forged in the *Didascalia Apostolorum*. The material contained in this pseudonymous church order, probably of Syrian provenance, is extremely difficult to date, not least because it is a composite text, the result of a complex and lengthy editing process, a development finally completed in the third or early fourth century.[32] The relevant passage, *Didasc.* 2.3–4, articulates some of the necessary qualifications for the Christian bishop:

> [2.3] And he [i.e., the bishop] should be examined to determine whether he is without blemish in the affairs or the world, and also in his body, for it is written: "Observe that there be no blemish in him who stands up to be priest (Lev 21:17)." 2. He should also not be prone to anger, for the Lord says: "anger even destroys the wise" (Prov 15:1). And he should be merciful, compassionate and full of love, for the Lord

---

that a sermon based on Isa 54 should privilege demonstrations of social justice within the community of faith over the ritual observance of fasting and prayer. Here a text like Isa 58, along with other prophetic witnesses that call for justice instead of cultic practice (cf. Hos 6:6), may stand in the background of the author's thought, although such a connection is impossible to substantiate.

[31] In their essay on the use of the NT in *2 Clement*, Andrew F. Gregory and Christopher M. Tuckett do not discuss the relationship between *2 Clem.* 16.4 and 1 Pet 4:8, attributing the linguistic parallels to "common language" (see "*2 Clement* and the Writings That Later Formed the New Testament," in *The Reception of the New Testament in the Apostolic Fathers* [ed. Andrew F. Gregory and Christopher M. Tuckett; Oxford: Oxford University Press, 2005], 251–92). In his commentary, Tuckett identifies the saying "love covers a multitude of sins" as "traditional within early Christian circles" (*2 Clement*, 275).

[32] See Alistar Stewart-Sykes, *The Didascalia Apostolorum: An English Version with Introduction and Annotation* (STTEEMT 1; Turnhout: Brepols, 2009). More recently, Joel Marcus has argued for a date in the second or third century; see "The *Testaments of the Twelve Patriarchs* and the *Didascalia Apostolorum*: A Common Jewish Christian Milieu?" *JTS* 61 (2010): 596–626.

says: "love covers a multitude of sins" (cf. 1 Pet 4:8). [2.4] And his hand
should be stretched out to give, and he should be compassionate to the
orphans together with the widows, and compassionate to the poor and
to the stranger. He should be illustrious in his ministry and faithful
in the ministry. He should have contrition in his soul, and not shame.
And he should know who deserves to receive, 2. for if there is a widow
who has possessions, or has the means by which she might provide for
the nourishment of her body, and another who, though not a widow,
is in need, whether through sickness, or through raising children, or
through bodily infirmity, it is to her that he should stretch forth his
hand. 3. But if there should be someone who is dissolute, or drunken,
or idle, and is in need of bodily nourishment, he is not worthy of charity, and not from the church. (2.3.1–2.4.3)[33]

The virtues expected of a bishop include mercy, compassion, and love,
the last of which evokes a citation of the phrase "love covers a multitude of
sins." Given that the statement is attributed to "the Lord," it is possible that
the *Didascalia Apostolorum* is citing a Christian proverb, understood here as
a dominical tradition, instead of 1 Pet 4:8. Nevertheless, the saying is related
to the practice of merciful deeds for the needy, even if the notion that compassion for the poor redeems sin is not explicitly developed in this text: "And
his hand should be stretched out to give, and he should be compassionate to
the orphans together with the widows, and compassionate to the poor and
to the stranger." While it is not expressly stated that giving to the powerless
and poor atones for sin, the fact that this assertion immediately follows at
citation of the saying "love covers a multitude of sins" makes the connection
possible. At the very least, the bishop's material care for the marginalized
demonstrates that "he is without blemish in the affairs of the world."

Tertullian

Tertullian cites 1 Pet 4:8 in *Scorpiace*, a treatise on the necessity and goodness of martyrdom (cf. 1.12–2.2) likely composed ca. 212 CE.[34] In challeng-
ing certain opponents who suggested that martyrdom was evil, Tertullian
insists that martyrdom—frequently the fate of those who refuse to commit
idolatry—is the will of God, and that, since God is good, what God wills is
good, even if what God wills is painful (5.1–6.11). As part of this argument,
Tertullian develops two analogies. First, just as medical treatments such as

---

[33] The translation is from Stewart-Sykes.

[34] On this date, see Geoffrey D. Dunn, *Tertullian* (The Early Church Fathers; London: Routledge, 2004), 105.

the scalpel, the hot iron, and the pungent juices of mustard are often agonizing when administered, so also martyrdom, though violently painful, leads to salvation (5.5–13). Second, martyrdom is like an athletic competition, although in this contest God battles with the devil through the virtue of the faithful believer, with the martyr receiving a heavenly reward for victory in the match (6.1–7). In this context, Tertullian notes that God's knowledge of human weakness and the sin that results from it led God to establish "second atonements and the final defences, the contest of martyrdoms and the ritual washing with blood flowing after that" (6.9). The martyrs hand over their lives in a ritual washing of their post-baptismal sin with their own blood:

> For in a proper sense nothing now is able to be reconsidered with the martyrs with whom, in the ritual washing, life itself is handed over. Thus "love covers a multitude of sins," which certainly, while loving God from [its] whole strength, with which it fights in martyrdom, [and] from [its] whole soul, which is handed over for God, moulds a person [into] a martyr. (*Scorp.* 6.10–11)[35]

According to Tertullian's reading of 1 Pet 4:8, the love displayed by martyrs for God results in the sacrificial handing over of life to God and turns the devoted follower who rejects idolatry into a martyr. "Love covers a multitude of sins" in the sense that faithful, loving commitment to God leads one to experience the washing of post-baptismal sin through martyrdom.

Origen

Finally, Origen cites 1 Pet 4:8 in a homily on Leviticus delivered in Caesarea sometime between 238 and 244 (*Hom. Lev.* 2.4.5). In his reflection on the sacrificial laws in Leviticus, Origen observes the variety of sacrificial rituals for the alleviation of sin in Jewish law, ranging from the offering of a spotless bull by the high priest (Lev 4:2-12) to the sacrifice of a goat by the individual Israelite who has committed an unintentional sin (4:27-31). Concerned that some believers may be distressed by the absence of sacrificial practice among Christians, Origen offers a typological interpretation of these diverse sacrifices in Leviticus: Christ's death represents the offering of the fattened bull, a sacrifice that results in the pardon of sins at baptism. For post-baptismal sins, however, there are other ways to alleviate sin, and Origen adds to the atoning sacrifice of Christ six "remissions of sin in the gospel," giving him a list of seven things that produce forgiveness: (1) baptism; (2) martyrdom;

---

[35] The translation is from Dunn, *Tertullian*, 105–34 [118].

(3) almsgiving; (4) forgiving others; (5) converting a sinner; (6) abundant love; and (7) penance:[36]

Now hear how many are the remissions of sins in the gospel. First is the one by which we are baptized "for the remission of sins" (Mark 1:4). A second remission is in the suffering of martyrdom. Third, is that which is given through alms. For the Savior says, "but nevertheless, give what you have and, behold, all things are clean for you" (Luke 11:41). A fourth remission of sins is given for us through the fact that we also forgive the sins of our brothers. For thus the Lord and Savior himself says, "If you will forgive from the heart your brothers' sins, your Father will also forgive you your sins. But if you will not forgive your brothers from the heart, neither will your Father forgive you" (Matt 6:14-15). And thus he taught us to say in prayer, "forgive us our debts as we forgive our debtors" (Matt 6:12). A fifth forgiveness is when "someone will convert a sinner from the error of his way" (Jas 5.20). For thus divine Scripture says, "Whoever will make a sinner turn from the error of his way will save a soul from death and cover a multitude of sins" (Jas 5:20). There is also a sixth forgiveness through the abundance of love as the Lord himself says, "Truly I say to you, her many sins are forgiven because she loved much" (Luke 7:47). And the Apostle says, "Because love will cover a multitude of sins" (1 Pet 4:8). And there is still a seventh remission of sins through penance, although admittedly it is difficult and toilsome, when the sinner washes "his couch in tears" (cf. Ps 6:7) and his "tears" become his "bread day and night" (cf. Ps 41:4), when he is not ashamed to make known his sin to the priest of the Lord and to seek a cure according to the one who says, "I said, 'I will proclaim to the Lord my injustice against myself,' and you forgave the impiety of my heart" (Ps 31:5). What the Apostle James said is fulfilled in this: "But if anyone is sick, let that person call the presbyters of the Church, and they will place their hands on him, anointing him with oil in the name of the Lord. And the prayer of faith will save the sick person, and if he is in sins, they will be forgiven him" (Jas 5:14-15). (Origen, *Hom. Lev.* 2.4.4–5)[37]

---

[36] On the notion of sacrifice in this text, see Robert J. Daly, "Sacrificial Soteriology in Origen's Homilies on Leviticus," *StPatr* 17, no. 2 (1982): 872–78; on the relationship between the cross and atonement in Origen's many writings, see Joseph S. O'Leary, "Atonement," in *The Westminster Handbook to Origen* (ed. John Anthony McGuckin; Louisville, Ky.: Westminster John Knox, 2004), 66–68; cf. Jean Laporte, "Forgiveness of Sins in Origen," *Worship* 60 (1986): 520–27.

[37] This translation is from *The Fathers of the Church*, vol. 83, *Origen; Translation of Homiliae in Leviticum* (trans. Gary Wayne Barkley; Washington, D.C.: The Catholic University of America Press, 1990). Rhee observes that the list seems to be organized in order

Origen writes of the power of alms to atone for sins *and* cites 1 Pet 4:8, but not directly in connection with one another. Almsgiving (or "merciful practice") is the third means of remitting sins (*tertia est, quae per eleemosynam datur*), but in support of this claim Origen quotes Luke 11:41, the other New Testament text most frequently cited by proponents of atoning almsgiving.[38] On the other hand, when 1 Pet 4:8 is evoked by Origen, along with Luke 7:47, it is used to support the contention that "there is also a sixth forgiveness through the abundance of love." Origen's citation of Luke 7:47 indicates that he understands the many sins of the unnamed woman who anoints Jesus' feet with tears, kisses, and perfume in Luke 7:36-50 to have been forgiven *because* she has shown great love.[39] Origen's reading of 1 Pet 4:8, then, should be taken to illustrate that same principle: through profound demonstrations of love (*per abundantiam caritatis*) many sins of those who love abundantly can be covered. Almsgiving would not be excluded from this understanding of abundant love, but it is certainly not the focus of Origen's appropriation of 1 Pet 4:8.[40]

---

of decreasing importance, making almsgiving the most important of the repeatable acts, since baptism and martyrdom are unrepeatable (*Loving the Poor*, 84–85).

[38] See, e.g., Cyprian, *Eleem.*, 2.12–22.

[39] The tendency of many modern translations and commentaries to take the phrase ὅτι ἠγάπησεν πολύ in Luke 7:47 not as causal (indicating the basis of the woman's forgiveness) but as logical (pointing to the woman's loving action *as evidence* that her sins had been forgiven) perhaps suggests the importance of one's larger theological framework for reading the verse. I. Howard Marshall's comment is illuminating: "In favor of [the view that the ὅτι clause should be taken as providing a reason for the woman's forgiveness] one may cite 1 Pet. 4:8 (cf. Prov. 10:12; Jas. 5:20; 1 Clem. 49.5; Matt. 6:14f.; Sir. 17:22; Dan. 4:27), but it is doubtful whether the NT supports the view that love covers, i.e., atones for sin" (*The Gospel of Luke* [NIGTC; Grand Rapids: Eerdmans], 1978, 313). Certainly many of the church fathers did not find this concept as doubtful as Marshall.

[40] For the sake of completeness, mention should also be made of the enigmatic citation of 1 Pet 4:8 in *Gos. Phil.* (II, 3) 78.7–12. In the context of a discussion of knowledge, sin, and freedom, the parable of the Good Samaritan (Luke 10:25-37) is evoked as evidence of the claim that "spiritual love is wine and fragrance" (77.35–36), with the treatment of the injured man's wounds in the parable connected with "spiritual love." The allusion to the Lukan parable is punctuated with this statement: "It [i.e., oil/ointment] healed the wounds, for 'love covers a multitude of sins.'" Here the saying from 1 Pet 4:8 appears to be interpreted as a reference to the loving action of the Samaritan in working to heal the wounds, caused by sin, of the man beaten by robbers. The citation of 1 Pet 4:8 in the *Gospel of Philip* may, in fact, serve to balance the document's general tendency to privilege knowledge over love (but cf. *Gos. Phil.* 45); see Hugo Lundhaug, *Images of Rebirth: Cognitive Poetics and Transformational Soteriology in the Gospel of Philip and the Exegesis of the Soul* (NHMS 73; Leiden: Brill, 2010), 294–96.

Conclusion

What might this exercise in the reception history of one short saying suggest about the "meaning" of 1 Pet 4:8? It is helpful to offer a few comments on the hermeneutical approach known variously as *Wirkungsgeschichte* or "reception history" before considering the implications of this strategy for the interpretation of this verse.

Wirkungsgeschichte and "reception history" have often been equated. Yet they are not merely synonymous, particularly if "reception history" represents a listing of various (and sometimes competing) later interpretations of an earlier text. Merely cataloguing the influence of a text in its post-history is insufficient, for *Wirkungsgeschichte*, at least as Gadamer envisioned the concept, involves not simply a scientific listing of diverse interpretations but a dialogical encounter between a text, the influence of that text, and the interpreter.[41] Consideration of the post-history of a text encourages the identification of one's own, or a tradition's, "interpretative self-consciousness" by showing how others, working within different hermeneutical constructs, have been shaped by engagement with the same text.[42] Attention to the post-history of a text helps to foreground "one's own fore-meanings and prejudices," not in order to reify these presuppositions but to have them challenged and tested.[43] *Wirkungsgeschichte*, thus, involves far more than listing and evaluating the readings of others. If it is true, as Gadamer suggests, that the "meaning" of a text cannot be separated from its history of influence, then

---

[41] As Jonathan Roberts and Christopher Rowland helpfully summarize: "To embrace [*Wirkungsgeschichte*] as a new model of empirical study that intrinsically validates new archival research is to fail to understand what reception history is. Reception history is not about extending our current taxonomy of knowledge simply in order to create further areas of specialism and to resource the continuation of our current proprietorial modes of scholarship. Nor is the ideal of a comprehensive diachronicity an appeal to return to the authoritative received wisdom of the Christian or Jewish tradition as maintained by its orthodox exponents. Rather, it is that the hermeneutical self-consciousness engendered by reception history makes the proprietorial academic and ecclesiastical claims over the biblical texts inadequate and the bracketing out of the particular context of the interpreting subject, whether religious or not, unsatisfactory. The goal of reception history is to develop an open-ended dialogic form of hermeneutics that is not alienated from human experience, and which enables exegesis to regain its interpretative self-consciousness" ("Introduction," *JSNT* 33 [2010]: 131–36 [133]). On the distinction between reception history, reception theory, and *Wirkungsgeschichte*, see Mark Knight's insightful essay in the same issue of *JSNT*: "*Wirkungsgeschichte*, Reception History, and Reception Theory," *JSNT* 33 (2010): 137–46.

[42] Hans-Georg Gadamer, *Truth and Method* (2nd rev. ed.; trans. Joel Weinsheimer and Donald G. Marshall; London: Continuum, 2004), 271.

[43] Gadamer, *Truth and Method*, 269.

the task of engaging the "effective history" of a text is not merely descriptive but also demands "application," not as a second-order determination of how a universal relates to a specific situation but as the central aspect of understanding, for interpretation is always application, according to Gadamer's philosophical hermeneutics.[44] Moreover, many current practitioners of the so-called "theological interpretation of Scripture" would want to emphasize the potential for *Wirkungsgeschichte* to generate an ecclesially rooted engagement with Scripture and tradition that benefits from the wisdom and practices of patristic biblical interpretation.[45] Therefore, far more interesting than a description of how 1 Pet 4:8 was received among some of its earliest Christian interpreters is the claim that this engagement with the effective history of the text stimulates an actualizing (or what Roman Ingarden calls "concretization") of 4:8 for a different context. Particularly for an evangelical Protestantism that has largely balked at the idea that patristic proponents of atoning almsgiving might reflect a faithful hermeneutical embodiment of the early church's inherited Scriptures, two concluding points are significant.[46]

First, among the early appropriations of 1 Pet 4:8 considered above, only the author of *1 Clement* represents the phrase "love covers a multitude of sins" as a reference to God's love for sinners. Yet the author of *1 Clement* also cites the saying "love covers a multitude of sins" in the context of an extended appeal for the Corinthians to love one another in action (*1 Clem.* 49.1–55.6), suggesting that the forgiveness and/or covering of sin involves both divine and human ἀγάπη. In contrast to the evocative ambiguity of the citation of 1 Pet 4:8 in *1 Clem.* 49.5, the other patristic authors who cite 1 Pet 4:8 more directly frame the saying as a statement about human love that covers the sins of those who demonstrate such love. The nature of those affective

---

[44] The phrase "effective history" represents Weinsheimer and Marshall's translation of Gadamer's *Wirkungsgeschichte*. On interpretation and application, see Gadamer, *Truth and Method*, 306–21; see also Jean Grondin, *Introduction à Hans-Georg Gadamer* (Paris: Le Cerf, 1999), 150–66. On meaning, Gadamer writes, "The real meaning of a text, as it speaks to the interpreter, does not depend on the contingencies of the author and his original audience. It certainly is not identical with them, for it is always co-determined also by the historical situation of the interpreter and hence by the totality of the objective course of history" (*Truth and Method*, 296).

[45] Stephen Fowl, however, has recently argued that, while attention to premodern interpretation and the reception of scriptural texts in the early church, on one hand, and *Wirkungsgeschichte*, on the other, "are or can be closely related to each other, they are not necessarily connected" ("Effective History and the Cultivation of Wise Interpreters," *JTI* 7 [2013]: 153–61).

[46] On Roman Ingarden's concept of concretization, see *The Cognition of the Literary Work of Art* (trans. Ruth Ann Crowley and Kenneth R. Olson; Evanston, Ill.: Northwestern University Press, 1973).

demonstrations is certainly not uniform: for Clement of Alexandria in *Quis dives salvetur*, *2 Clement*, and the *Didascalia Apostolorum*, the human love of 1 Pet 4:8 is demonstrated through the provision of material assistance to the needy; for Tertullian, the human love of 1 Pet 4:8 is seen in the martyr's willingness to hand over his or her life to God; for Origen, the human love of 1 Pet 4:8 is shown through abundant charity (cf. *Gos. Phil.* 78). Thus, the different ways in which the saying "love covers a multitude of sins" is appropriated reflect the various pastoral, rhetorical, theological, and historical contexts in which the saying is cited. But in all cases, including *1 Clement*, the ἀγάπη that covers sin is (at least in part) human ἀγάπη.

At the same time, these early interpreters who understand the phrase "love covers a multitude of sins" as a reference to human love for other humans seem to go with the grain of the text of 1 Peter, even though none of these authors evoke or discuss the larger context of 1 Peter 4. Immediately before the statement about love covering a multitude of sins, the author of 1 Peter issues an injunction for mutual love within the community of believers: "Above all, have constant love for one another, because love covers a multitude of sins" (cf. 1 Pet 1:22). In fact, the phrase ὅτι ἀγάπη καλύπτει πλῆθος ἁμαρτιῶν in 1 Pet 4:8b serves as a warrant for the command to mutual love in 4:8a. Moreover, the very next statement in verse 9 expounds on the nature of love within believing community: "Be hospitable to one another without grumbling" (φιλόξενοι εἰς ἀλλήλους ἄνευ γογγυσμοῦ). The call to hospitality in 4:9 makes it clear that the love envisioned is not merely a sentiment, but it involves sacrificial and welcoming action on behalf of the other, perhaps especially the other in material want.[47] Certainly, 4:10-11 emphasizes "the uncalculated grace of God, whose gracious initiative empowers and inspires gracious human response."[48] Yet God's gracious action, as well as an anticipation of God's future judgment, prompts and authorizes human demonstrations of love, including, it would seem, the human love that covers a multitude of sins.

In this sense, perhaps the view that ἀγάπη in 1 Pet 4:8 is human love for others that atones for the sins of those who demonstrate such love reflects a similar theological dynamic to that found at the beginning of 1 Peter 4. Among the realities about Christ's death affirmed in 1 Peter are that (1) the suffering of Christ is a uniquely efficacious atoning act (1:2, 18-19; 2:21-25; 3:18) and (2) the cross is a paradigmatic act to be imitated by those who share in the suffering of Christ (2:21-25; 4:13-16). These two affirmations are

---

[47] See Joel B. Green, *1 Peter* (THNTC; Grand Rapids: Eerdmans, 2007), 144.
[48] Green, *1 Peter*, 144–45.

articulated succinctly in 1 Pet 4:1-2: "Since therefore Christ suffered in the flesh, arm yourselves also with the same intention (for whoever has suffered in the flesh has finished with sin), so as to live for the rest of your earthly life no longer by human desires but by the will of God" (NRSV). Although much ink has been spilled over whether the participial phrase ὁ παθὼν σαρκὶ ("the one who has suffered in the flesh") is a general statement or specifically christological, it seems that the statement can apply both to Christ and to Christians (cf. 4:16): "Christ's once-for-all suffering does away with sin (3:18) so that, in their suffering, his followers might be finished with sin."[49] It is precisely because the suffering of Christ has atoned for sins that followers of Christ can be "through with sin," and this is why, too, the practice of ἀγάπη among God's people can cover a multitude of sins. Thus, *1 Clement, 2 Clement*, Clement of Alexandria, the *Didascalia Apostolorum*, and Origen all seem to stand with 1 Pet 4:8 in using the phrase "love covers a multitude of sins" to promote the social, ecclesiological, and material embodiment of ἀγάπη among the people of God.

Finally, the notion of atoning almsgiving clearly figures in the reading of 1 Pet 4:8 found in *2 Clement* and Clement of Alexandria's *Quis dives salvetur*, and atoning almsgiving is at least marginally connected to the citations of 1 Pet 4:8 in the *Didascalia Apostolorum* and Origen's *Homiliae in Leviticum*. Many modern interpreters reject the view that the phrase "love covers a multitude of sins" in 1 Pet 4:8 can be read as an indication that human love for others atones for the sins of the one who demonstrates love. It is said that such an interpretation compromises or stands in tension with the saving significance of Christ's death, a point so strongly emphasized throughout 1 Peter.

Yet it might be noted that *2 Clement*, for example, opens with a direct exhortation to remember the salvation made available through Christ's suffering:

> [2]And those who listen as though these were little things sin, and we do not realize where we have been called from, by whom, and to what place we were called, and how much suffering Jesus Christ endured for our sake. [3]What repayment then shall we give to him in exchange? Or what fruit can we produce compared to what he has given us? How many holy deeds do we owe him? [4]For he has given us the light. Like a father, he called us children. He saved us when we were perishing. [5]What praise, then, shall we give, or what repayment in return for what we received? (1.2–5)

---

[49] Green, *1 Peter*, 135.

On one hand, the rhetorical questions here emphasize the gracious initiative of Christ's saving death. The theme of the unmerited salvation made possible through Jesus Christ is then continued in the remainder of the prologue to 2 *Clement*, a section that is punctuated with a declaration of salvation on the basis of God's mercy and compassion and an affirmation of calling ex nihilo:

> [6]Our minds were blinded, and we worshiped stones and wood and gold and silver and brass, things made by humans; indeed, our whole life was nothing but death. So while we were thus wrapped in darkness and our vision was filled with this thick mist we recovered our sight, by his will laying the cloud wrapped around us. [7]For he had mercy upon us and in his compassion he saved us when we had no hope of salvation except that which comes from him, even though he had seen in us much deception and destruction. [8]For he called us when we did not exist, and out of nothing he willed us into being. (1.6–8)[50]

Elsewhere, the preacher affirms Christ's actions to save what was perishing (2.3–4) and the saying in "Scripture" (γραφή) that Christ came "not to call the righteous, but sinners" (2.4; cf. Mark 2:17; Matt 9:13). Metaphors for salvation include the removal of a cloud of darkness that blocks sight (1.6; cf. 9.2) and healing from sickness (9.7). The author of 2 *Clement* maintains, like 1 Peter, that salvation has uniquely, decisively, and undeservedly come through the action of Christ. At the same time, the rhetorical questions in 2 *Clem.* 1.3–5 do not necessarily invoke a negative response, for the author of 2 *Clement* is convinced that believers do owe Christ and God much in return, including repentance (9.7–8) and faith and love (15.2).[51]

---

[50] This translation of 2 *Clem.* 1.6–8 is from Holmes, *Apostolic Fathers*, 139.

[51] I take to heart here the critique of my earlier reading of 2 *Clem.* 1.3–5 offered by James A. Kelhoffer, who disagreed with my claim that "the rhetorical questions here emphasize the impossibility of repaying Christ for his suffering 'for our sake'" (Downs, "Redemptive Almsgiving," 516). See Kelhoffer, "Reciprocity as Salvation: Christ as Salvific Patron and the Corresponding 'Payback' Expected of Christ's Earthly Clients according to the Second Letter of Clement," *NTS* 59 (2013): 433–56 [454]. Tuckett, too, writes of 2 *Clem.* 1.3–5, "[T]he answer to these rhetorical questions is perhaps ambiguous. In one way, it might be that the implied answer is 'nothing at all': we can give nothing in return for the wonderful gift of salvation already received. As already noted, the writer's own answer will be rather different: a response *is* required and is regarded as essential. Nevertheless, if there is any truth in the possibility that the section here may reflect the views (and perhaps the formulation) of the community being addressed, the question form may leave the issue open: all would agree that the question follows from the claims made in v. 4. But whereas some might give one answer to the question (claiming that we can give nothing by way of recompense), the author leaves the issue open, at least for the time

Moreover, in *Quis div.* 37, Clement of Alexandria highlights the sacrificial love of God's Son, who gave himself up as a ransom (λύτρον ἑαθτὸν ἐπιδιδοὺς), providing a model of self-giving love for Christians to imitate. Elsewhere in the document, Clement, speaking rhetorically in the voice of the "savior" (ἄκουε τοῦ σωτῆρος), says, "For your sake I wrestled with death and paid your penalty of death, which you owed for former sins and for your faithlessness before God" (*Quis div.* 22).

Thus, both the author of *2 Clement* and Clement of Alexandria appear to hold together (1) the declaration that salvation and atonement for sin come through the suffering and death of Jesus and (2) the affirmation that the practice of mercifully caring for the needy covers a multitude of sins for donors. These early Christian authors do pose a challenge to interpretative traditions and readings of 1 Pet 4:8 that find these two confessions inherently incompatible, for two convictions that modern readers have often felt the need to separate (especially after the Protestant Reformation) patristic writers were able comfortably to hold together. Perhaps the *Wirkungsgeschichte* of 1 Pet 4:8, then, offers an opportunity for modern readers, especially in the Protestant tradition, to think about the extent to which the allocation of resources within the community of faith has the potential to remove the sins of those who generously share their possessions with those in need. If, as the patristic evidence suggests, ἀγάπη in the phrase "love covers a multitude of sins" refers to human acts of love, including care for the poor, as capable of atoning for human sin, does this exercise in *Wirkungsgeschichte* suggest that early Christian advocates of the atoning power of almsgiving offer a faithful hermeneutical embodiment of the early church's inherited Scriptures? The issue cannot be decided on the basis of a study of a single statement from 1 Peter, and undoubtedly there will be some who regard patristic reception of 4:8 as entirely problematic, with the true "meaning" of the text recovered at some later time, perhaps during the Protestant Reformation, perhaps with the tools of the historical critic. But if the "meaning" of a text cannot be separated from its history of influence—with meaning emerging as the result of a conversation between a text, the influence of that text, and an interpreter or interpretive community—then the early Christian reception of 1 Pet 4:8 ought to play a key role answering the question of whether the efficacious, sacrificial love of Jesus Christ can be affirmed along with the idea that cruciform love shown by believers has the power to atone for the sins of those who demonstrate such love.

---

being" (*2 Clement*, 135 [emphasis in original]). In fact, the use of the noun ἀντιμισθία in 9.7 and 15.2 answers the questions, posed with the same noun, in 1.3, 5.

CHAPTER 7

MERCIFUL PRACTICE IS GOOD
AS REPENTANCE FOR SIN

Resurrection, Atonement, and Care for the Poor
in Second-Century Christianity

At some point in first half of the second century, Ignatius was arrested in
Syrian Antioch, where he served as bishop of the nascent Christian community. After his arrest, Ignatius was transported in chains by guards to Rome
in order to face his execution at the seat of imperial power. In the course of
his extended eastward journey, the bishop of Antioch wrote five letters to
churches in Asia Minor, one to the church awaiting his arrival in Rome, and
one to Polycarp in Smyrna, his fellow bishop.[1] In these dispatches, Ignatius is

---

[1] I assume the modern consensus, established by the work of J. B. Lightfoot (*The
Apostolic Fathers, Part 2: S. Ignatius; S. Polycarp* [3 vols.; London: Macmillan, 1885]) and
Theodor Zahn (*Ignatius von Antiochien* [Gotha: Perthes, 1873]), that the seven letters of
the so-called middle recension are authentic. Given recent discussions that have questioned the assumption that Ignatius' letters should be dated to the reign of Trajan (98–
117 CE; cf. Eusebius, *His. Eccl.* 3.36), I would posit a broad time frame for the letters
sometime in the first half of the second century. See Timothy D. Barnes, "The Date of
Ignatius," *ExpTim* 120 (2008): 119–30; Paul Foster, "The Epistles of Ignatius of Antioch,"
in *The Writings of the Apostolic Fathers* (ed. Paul Foster; London: T&T Clark, 2007), 81–
107; Thomas Lechner, *Ignatius Adversus Valentinianos? Chronologische und theologischichtliche Studien zu den Briefen des Ignatius von Antiochien* (VCSup 47; Leiden: Brill, 1999);
and the articles by Reinhard M. Hübner, Andreas Lindemann, Georg Schöllgen, and
M. J. Edwards in vols. 1 and 2 of *ZAC* (1997–1998).

particularly concerned with the danger of false teachers, a topic that provokes his ire in several of his letters.[2] When writing to the Smyrnaeans, for example, Ignatius levels an interesting and distinctive accusation against some false teachers in Smyrna. In addition to their abstention from the Eucharist and prayer (*Smyrn.* 7.1), these opponents, Ignatius alleges, neglect practices of caring for the needy:

> Observe well those who hold divisive views about the gracious gift of Jesus Christ that has come to us, and see how they are opposed to the purpose of God. They do not have any care for love (περὶ ἀγάπης οὐ μέλει αὐτοῖς), none for the widow, none for the orphan, none for the oppressed, none for the one who is in chains or the one released, none the one who is hungry or the one who is thirsty. (Ign. *Smyrn.* 6.2)

Key to Ignatius' critique of his Docetic opponents here is the connection between love for the poor, the flesh of Jesus Christ, and the reality of resurrection. Ignatius immediately follows his censure of his opponents' lack of love by condemning their abstinence from the Eucharist and prayer. The Docetists in Smyrna desist from these Christian practices, according to Ignatius, "because they do not confess that the Eucharist is the flesh of our savior, Jesus Christ, flesh that suffered for our sins and flesh that the Father raised up in his kindness" (6.2).[3] Then, after stating that those who deny God's gift will perish in their contentiousness, Ignatius suggests that practice of love (ἀγαπᾶν) leads to resurrection. Of his opponents Ignatius says, "It would be better for them to love, in order that they might also rise up" (ἵνα καὶ ἀναστῶσιν [7.1]). Since Ignatius has defined "love" (ἀγάπη) in the preceding statements in 6.2 as showing concern for widows, orphans, the oppressed,

---

[2] The nature of the false teaching identified and confronted by Ignatius is still very much debated. See Matti Myllykoski, "Wild Beasts and Rabid Dogs: The Riddle of the Heretics in the Letters of Ignatius," in *The Formation of the Early Church* (ed. Jostein Ådna; WUNT I/183; Tübingen: Mohr Siebeck, 2005), 341–77; John W. Marshall, "The Objects of Ignatius' Wrath and Jewish Angelic Mediators," *JEH* 56 (2005): 1–23; Christine Trevett, "Prophecy and Anti-Episcopal Activity: A Third Error Combatted by Ignatius?" *JEH* 34 (1983): 1–18. I think it is reasonable to label the false teachers in Smyrna "Docetists"; see Paul Trebilco, *The Early Christians in Ephesus from Paul to Ignatius* (WUNT I/166; Tübingen: Mohr Siebeck, 2004).

[3] The noun σάρξ occurs only in the phrase translated "the flesh of our savior"; the following two instances in which I have provided the word "flesh" represent the article τὴν and the relative pronoun ἥν, both of which I have translated "flesh." The emphasis on Jesus' embodied existence is important, since Ignatius is ostensibly contending against those who deny any salvific importance to the σάρξ of Jesus. The section numbering here reflects Michael W. Holmes' *The Apostolic Fathers: Greek Texts and English Translations* (3rd ed.; Grand Rapids: Baker, 2007); some editions include this material in 7.1.

prisoners, freed prisoners,[4] the hungry, and the thirsty, the implication is that those who do not care for the needy will not share in the resurrection of Christ. In these comments, Ignatius forges a close connection between almsgiving and soteriology: resurrection is the future of those who love, and love is the practice of caring for the needy. Moreover, Ignatius ascribes a theological motivation for his opponents' failure to show love to the destitute—namely, a rejection of the flesh (σάρξ) of Jesus Christ. These Docetists in Smyrna, according to Ignatius, explicitly reject the confession that the flesh of Jesus Christ suffered for the deliverance of sins and that the flesh of Jesus Christ was raised by God from the dead (6.2; cf. 1.1–2; 3.1–3; 5.2; 12.2). Ignatius implies that a lack of love—that is, caring for the needy—and a denial of the salvific importance of the flesh of Jesus Christ are tied together.

Ignatius' comments evocatively suggest that, among the competing visions of salvation in Smyrna, divergent views about the importance of embodied existence entailed not merely abstract christological debates about the *past* of the Christ event. These anthropological and christological differences were also intimately related to *present* practices of almsgiving, Eucharist, and prayer among Christians in Asia Minor. Ignatius implies that he and the ideal readers of his letter care about the bodies of the poor and powerless because of the soteriological importance of the embodied Jesus. For Ignatius, the body of Jesus Christ—both in suffering flesh and in resurrected flesh—matters for Christian practices of love. Conversely, Ignatius intimates that his opponents neglect love for the bodies of the destitute because they neglect the soteriological importance of the body of Christ.[5]

[4] The phrase οὐ περὶ δεδεμένου ἢ λελυμένου probably refers to those imprisoned and those recently released from prison, the latter group possibly including "Christian 'confessors' who on being released from prison continued to be supported by the church until they had established themselves again" (William R. Schoedel, *Ignatius of Antioch: A Commentary on the Letters of Ignatius of Antioch* [Hermeneia; Philadelphia: Fortress, 1985], 239). It is at least possible, however, that those "set free" are Christian martyrs "set free" by death, for whom the Docetists did not care while the martyrs were alive (cf. Ign. *Rom.* 4.1–5.3). Alexander N. Kirk has argued that the language of "freedom" in Ign. *Rom.* 4.3 refers to freedom obtained at death, including the martyrdoms of Peter and Paul (cf. Ign. *Pol.* 4.3); Kirk, "Paul's Approach to His Death in His Letters and in Early Pauline Effective History" (D.Phil. diss., Oxford University, 2013), 91–94. Elsewhere in Ignatius' letters, the verb λύω contrasts the bishops' chains with the freedom of his readers (Ign. *Magn.* 12.1), however.

[5] Ignatius regularly images the church as the corporate embodiment of Christ: *Smyrn.* 1.2; *Eph.* 4.2; *Trall.* 11.1–2; cf. Ign. *Eph.* 9.1, 15.3; Ign. *Magn.* 7.2. It might be objected that Ignatius' critique of his opponents' failure to love the poor is an exaggeration or untruth. Indeed, separating reality from fiction in early Christian polemic is notoriously difficult. Yet the fact that Ignatius is writing to a church that knows well and may

Ignatius' implication that his opponents' denial of the value of embodied existence of the earthly and resurrected Christ translates into disregard for the needy raises the question of whether this relationship between soteriology and charity can be discerned in other early Christian discourses about poverty and almsgiving. An examination of four second-century Christian texts—the *Gospel of Thomas*, the *Acts of Thomas*, *2 Clement*, and Polycarp's *To the Philippians*—will show how different visions of soteriology, including themes such as the value of embodied existence and the expectation of a final judgment, not only correspond to but also shape different views about and practices of care for the poor.

The *Gospel of Thomas*

If the approbation of care for the poor was common in the early Christian movement, it was not universal. Given the numerous first- and second-century Christian literary sources that commend merciful action on behalf of the needy, the *Gospel of Thomas* is notable for its rejection of almsgiving, along with other practices such as fasting and prayer (Gos. Thom. 6, 14; cf. *Gos. Thom.* 27, 104). A literary analysis of the presentation of almsgiving in the *Gospel of Thomas* shows not merely the dismissal but the disparagement of care for the poor in this second-century text.[6] Almsgiving is mentioned

---

even be tempted to welcome those whom Ignatius calls "wild beasts in human form" (Ign. *Smryn.* 4.1) suggests that Ignatius' assessment of his opponents' practices cannot be too off-target, or else his criticism of his opponents' lack of charity would be exposed as a lie and his hope for the repentance of these Docetists thwarted (Ign. *Smryn.* 4.1).

[6] For a model literary-critical approach to the *Gospel of Thomas*, see Richard Valantasis, *The Gospel of Thomas* (New Testament Readings; London: Routledge, 1997); cf. Michael Fieger, *Das Thomasevangelium: Einleitung, Kommentar, und Systematik* (NF 22; Münster: Aschendorff, 1991). Philip Sellew was one of the first to call for a shift from compositional and historical to literary approaches to the *Gospel of Thomas*; see his article "The *Gospel of Thomas*: Prospects for Future Research," in *The Nag Hammadi Library after Fifty Years: Proceedings of the 1995 Society of Biblical Literature Commemoration* (ed. John D. Turner and Anne McGuire; NHMS 44; Leiden: Brill, 1997), 327–46. The literary-critical approach adopted here differs from the form-critical method of April D. DeConick, *The Original Gospel of Thomas in Translation: With a Commentary and New English Translation of the Complete Gospel* (LNTS 287; London: T&T Clark, 2006). On the problems associated with DeConick's methodology, see Stephen J. Patterson, "Apocalypticism or Prophecy and the Problem of Polyvalence: Lessons from the Gospel of Thomas," *JBL* 130 (2011): 795–817. For a detailed discussion of the date of the *Gospel of Thomas*, including an argument for dating the text between 135–200 CE (which is the position adopted here), see Simon Gathercole, *The Gospel of Thomas: Introduction and Commentary* (TENTS 11; Leiden: Brill, 2014), 112–27.

twice in the *Gospel of Thomas*, both times in connection with the practices of fasting and prayer:

> [1]His disciples questioned him and said to him, "Do you want us to fast? How shall we pray? Shall we give alms? What diet should we observe?" [2]Jesus said, "Do not tell lies, [3]and do not do what you hate, [4]for all things are plain in the sight of heaven. [5]For nothing hidden will not become manifest, [6]and nothing covered will remain without being uncovered." (*Gos. Thom.* 6.1–6)[7]

> [1]Jesus said to them, "If you fast, you will give rise to sin for yourselves; [2]and if you pray, you will be condemned; and if you give alms, you will do harm to your spirits. [4]When you go into any land and walk about in the districts, if they receive you, eat what they will set before you, and heal the sick among them. [5]For what goes into your mouth will not defile you, but that which issues from your mouth—it is that which will defile you." (*Gos. Thom.* 14.1–5)

In the first instance, Jesus does not respond directly to the question posed by the disciples in 6.1. That 14.1–2 seems to provide a suitable answer to the inquiry has led to speculation that perhaps Jesus' reply has been displaced by deliberate redaction, by scribal error, or even by an accidental shuffling of pages.[8] If *Gos. Thom.* 6 and 14 were originally located together, such separation must have occurred relatively early in the manuscript tradition, for the Greek version of *Gos. Thom.* 6 contains similar material, though in fragmentary form (*P.Oxy.* 654). From a literary perspective that focuses on the Coptic version in its present form, however, such questions are secondary.

The saying that precedes *Gos. Thom.* 6 highlights the fact that Jesus' revelation is disclosed in his present teaching, a major theme of the document: "[1]Jesus said, 'Understand what is in front of you, and what is hidden from you will be revealed to you. [2]For there is nothing hidden that will not be manifested'" (*Gos. Thom.* 5; cf. *Gos. Thom.* 1, 59, 37, 62). When the disciples ask whether they should fast and how they should pray, give alms, and eat in *Gos. Thom.* 6, Jesus responds with a statement that essentially ignores the question and redirects attention to the disclosure of things hidden and covered. Thus, in response to a query about pious actions, Jesus offers a moral injunction ("Do not tell lies, and do not do what you hate") grounded in the

---

[7] Unless otherwise noted, all translations of the *Gospel of Thomas* come from Thomas O. Lambdin, "The Gospel According to Thomas," in *Nag Hammadi Codex II,2–7 together with XIII,2*, Brit. Lib. Or.4926(1), and P.Oxy. 1, 654, 655*, vol. 1 (ed. Bentley Layton; NHS 20; Leiden: Brill, 1989), 52–93.

[8] See the discussion in DeConick, *Original Gospel of Thomas*, 87–88.

visibility of all things. It seems that the performance of these visible acts of piety is ignored because it is, in fact, hidden motivations and attitudes that will be seen.[9]

Regardless of any theory of redaction or textual corruption, the answer to the disciples' question is eventually offered in ~~Gos. Thom.~~ 14. The mysterious Jesus has ignored the question about fasting, prayer, almsgiving, and diet in 6.1. Yet Jesus returns in 14.1–3 to the very issues raised by the earlier query. Here the practices of fasting, prayer, and almsgiving are not merely dismissed, however. ~~Fasting, prayer, and almsgiving are characterized as harmful: fasting occasions sin; prayer brings condemnation; and almsgiving results in personal harm.~~ With regard to the second part of the saying in 14.4–5, the claim that food does not defile seems to connect with the last part of the disciples' question in 6.1: "What diet should we observe?"

It is necessary to locate the disparagement of almsgiving in *Gos. Thom.* 14 in the larger context of the document's pervasive rejection of traditional Jewish religious practices.[10] If fasting, prayer, almsgiving, and dietary observances form a quadrumvirate of praxis in 6 and 14, these customs are also either rejected or redefined elsewhere in the *Gospel of Thomas*. Fasting, prayer, and sin, for example, are similarly associated in *Gos. Thom.* 104:

> [1]They said to Jesus, "Come, let us pray today and let us fast." [2]Jesus said, "What is the sin that I have committed, or wherein have I been defeated? [3]But when the bridegroom leaves the bridal chamber, then let them fast and pray." (*Gos. Thom.* 104.1–3)

At first glance, it would seem that Jesus allows fasting in *Gos. Thom.* 104, although only after the bridegroom has departed from the bridal chamber. This, in fact, is precisely how the parallel saying is interpreted in the Synoptic Gospels. In Mark 2:18-20, for instance, Jesus is asked why the Pharisees and the disciples of John fast but his disciples do not. Jesus responds, "The wedding guests cannot fast while the bridegroom is with them, can they? As long as they have the bridegroom with them, they cannot fast. The days will come when the bridegroom is taken away from them, and then they will fast on that day" (Mark 2:19-20; cf. Matt 9:14-15; Luke 5:33-35). According to synoptic tradition, Jesus is the bridegroom and his disciples will indeed fast after his death.

---

[9] Valantasis, *Gospel of Thomas*, 63–64.

[10] This point is developed in an insightful essay by Antti Marjanen, "Thomas and Jewish Religious Practices," in *Thomas at the Crossroads: Essays on the Gospel of Thomas* (ed. Risto Uro; Studies of the New Testament and Its World; Edinburgh: T&T Clark, 1998), 163–82.

Yet, in *Gos. Thom.* 104, Jesus does not indicate that his followers will pray and fast. In fact, the identity of those who ask Jesus to join them in prayer and fasting is not revealed, and it should not be assumed that those who extend the invitation are Jesus' disciples (cf. *Gos. Thom.* 91 and 100, where the precise identity of those who engage Jesus in conversation is not revealed). The meaning of 104 for the readers of *Thomas* hinges on the question of when the bridegroom will leave the bridal chamber. In *Gos. Thom.* 75.1, the image of the bridal chamber is employed to draw a distinction between "the many" and "the solitary": "Many are standing at the door, but it is the solitary who will enter the bridal chamber." From the perspective of the *Gospel of Thomas*, the bridal chamber is an image of salvation. The statement about prayer and fasting in 104, therefore, is likely ironic: there is no need to fast and pray because the bridegroom has not left, and will not leave, the bridal chamber.[11]

The only other place in the *Gospel of Thomas* where fasting is explicitly mentioned is 27.1-2: "<Jesus said>, 'If you do not fast as regards the world, you will not find the kingdom. If you do not observe the Sabbath as a Sabbath, you will not see the father.'" Again, it might appear that the text is advocating the practices of fasting and Sabbath observance. Yet the Greek νηστεύειν κόσμον and the Coptic ⲛ̄ⲣⲱⲧⲉⲩⲉ ⲉⲡⲕⲟⲥⲙⲟⲱ should been seen as accusatives of respect, showing "that the verb is not utilized in its concrete meaning of 'to fast from food' but figuratively as 'to abstain from something which is related to the world.'"[12] The same would be true with respect to the parallel clause that follows: what is being advocated is not observance of the Sabbath but taking a Sabbath with respect to the Sabbath—that is, nonobservance of the Sabbath. In this logion, then, fasting and Sabbath observance

---

[11] So also Marjanen, "*Thomas* and Jewish Religious Practices," 171–72; cf. Richard Valantasis, "The Nuptial Chamber Revisited: The *Acts of Thomas* and Cultural Intertextuality," *Semeia* 80 (1997): 261–76. April DeConick sees *Gos. Thom.* 104 as standing in tension with *Gos. Thom.* 6, 14, 27. She posits that 104 represents the earlier practice of obligatory fasting among earlier Thomasine Christians, a practice that was modified and critiqued by the later Thomasine community; see DeConick, *Original Gospel of Thomas*, 281–82; cf. Gathercole, *Gospel of Thomas*, 270. As Richard Valantasis comments on *Gos. Thom.* 75, "This bridal chamber metaphorizes the unity and merging of subjectivities which these saying promulgate, so that the solitary, by entering into the bridal chamber, joins the many others who have also become spiritual beings. The bridal chamber, in this sense, occupies a communal place similar to the language of the Kingdom of God or the Father's domain in the rest of the sayings: it is the place that mediates salvation, union, spiritualization, and life, but it remains a place for very few, because only the solitaries may enter it" (*Gospel of Thomas*, 153–54).

[12] Marjanen, "*Thomas* and Jewish Religious Practices," 173.

are redefined and the literal practices rejected. This interpretation accords
well with the world-denying values of the *Gospel of Thomas*.[13]

Together with this rejection of fasting, prayer, and Sabbath observance
should also be included as elements of a larger critique of Jewish practice in
the *Gospel of Thomas* (1) the polemic against the Pharisees and the scribes,
(2) the disparagement of Israel's written prophetic traditions, (3) the spiritualization of circumcision, (4) and the rejection of dietary laws found in the
Gospel of Thomas:

> [1]Jesus said, "The Pharisees and the scribes have taken the keys of knowl-
> edge (ⲛ-ⲅⲱⲱⲓⲱ) and hidden them. [2]They themselves have not entered,
> nor have they allowed to enter those who wish to. [3]You, however, be as
> wise as serpents and as innocent as doves." (*Gos. Thom.* 39.1-3; cf. *Gos.
> Thom.* 102)

> [1]His disciples said to him, "Twenty-four prophets spoke in Israel, and
> all of them spoke in you." [2]He said to them, "You have omitted the one
> living in your presence and have spoken [only] of the dead." (*Gos. Thom.*
> 52.1-2)[14]

> [1]His disciples said to him, "Is circumcision beneficial or not?" [2]He said
> to them, "If it were beneficial, their father would beget them already
> circumcised from their mother. [3]Rather, the true circumcision in spirit
> has become completely profitable." (*Gos. Thom.* 53.1-3)

---

[13] Stephan Witetschek ("Going Hungry for a Purpose: On *Gos. Thom.* 69.2 and a
Neglected Parallel in Origen," *JSNT* 32 [2010]: 379–93) has suggested that *Gos. Thom.*
69.2 ("Blessed are the hungry, for the belly of him who desires will be filled") alludes to the
practice of fasting and using the surplus resources that have been saved from abstention
for the benefit of others (cf. Gathercole, *Gospel of Thomas*, 270, 472–74.). Witetschek cites
a parallel in Origen's *Homilies on Leviticus*: "But there is another [i.e., practice of fasting]
that is even more religious, the praise of which is even pronounced in the writings of certain Apostles. For in a certain book we find it said by the Apostles, 'Blessed is he who also
fasts in order that he may feed the poor one'" (10.2). The parallel between *Gos. Thom.* 69.2
and Origen is intriguing, but even Witetschek admits that such a profound expression of
social concern would be "unusual" in *Thomas*. Given the other passages that disapprove of
fasting in the *Gospel of Thomas* and the lack of concern in the document for issues of social
ethics, Witetschek's reading is unconvincing. It seems most likely the two sayings in *Gos.
Thom.* 69.1–2 spiritualize and internalize persecution and hunger; so Valantasis, *Gospel
of Thomas*, 148–49.

[14] On this logion see Milton Moreland, "The Twenty-Four Prophets of Israel Are
Dead: *Gospel of Thomas* 52 as a Critique of Early Christian Hermeneutics," in *Thomas
Traditions in Antiquity: The Social and Cultural World of the Gospel of Thomas* (ed. Jon Ma.
Asgeirsson, April D. DeConick, and Risto Uro; NHMS 59; Leiden: Brill, 2006), 75–91.

Jesus said, "Why do you wash the outside of the cup? Do you not realize that he who made the inside is the same one who made the outside?"
(*Gos. Thom.* 89.1)

Thus, the identification of almsgiving as harmful in the *Gospel of Thomas*
should be interpreted in the wider context of the document's prevalent dismissal of Jewish religious practices—customs that are either denied or radically reinterpreted.[15] The polemic of *Thomas* against Judaism, or perhaps
against Christ-followers who identify with Judaism and its practices, is one
reason that the document can plausibly be dated to the early to middle part
of the second century, at a time when some strands of the Christian movement were advocating for the separation of Christianity and Judaism.[16]

Yet almsgiving in the *Gospel of Thomas* is perhaps characterized as injurious not merely because it is associated with Jewish religious ritual. The Gospel of Thomas also displays very little concern for socially embodied ethics,
including care for the poor. Of course, it is difficult to maintain that the *Gospel of Thomas* communicates a clear, consistent ethical agenda. It is important
to note, for example, that *Gos. Thom.* 25 does encourage brotherly love: "Jesus
said, 'Love your brother like your soul, guard him like the pupil of your eye.'"[17]

---

[15] So also David William Kim, "What Shall We Do? The Community Rules of
Thomas in the 'Fifth Gospel,'" *Bib* 88 (2007): 393–414 [399–406]. Marjanen locates this
thematic emphasis in the *Gospel of Thomas* in the context of emerging debates about the
relationship between followers of Jesus and Judaism: "Therefore the logia dealing with
Jewish religious practices are utilized to confront and to instruct [readers who are bound
to their Jewish heritage] in order that they might abandon that form of Christianity (or
Judaism) which is characterized by pious observance of various religious obligations, and
that they might assume the Thomasine version of Christianity with its emphasis on self-
knowledge and rejection of worldly values" ("*Thomas* and Jewish Religious Practices,"
181). Simon J. Gathercole also contends that *Gos. Thom.* 40, 68, and 71 reflect anti-Jewish
polemics centered on "the destruction of Judaism as an institution," including the destruction of the Jewish people and the Jewish temple ("'The Heavens and the Earth Will Be
Rolled Up': The Eschatology of the Gospel of Thomas," in *Eschatologie-Eschatology: The
Sixth Durham-Tübingen Research Symposium; Eschatology in Old Testament, Ancient Judaism, and Early Christianity* (ed. Hans-Joachim Eckstein et al.; WUNT I/272; Tübingen:
Mohr Siebeck, 2011), 280–302 [290].

[16] See Joshua W. Jipp and Michael J. Thate, "Dating Thomas: Logion 53 as a Test
Case for Dating the Gospel of Thomas within an Early Christian Trajectory," *BBR* 20
(2010): 237–55; Gathercole, *Gospel of Thomas*, 121–23.

[17] Yet even when it is acknowledged that this one text encourages brotherly love, it is
interesting that the injunction is phrased with reference to love of the soul. The canonical
command to "love your *neighbor* as *yourself*" (Lev 19:18; Mark 12:31; Luke 10:27; Matt
19:19; 22:39; Rom 13:9; Gal 5:14; Jas 2:8) seems to leave more room for an open, embodied love that considers the material needs of both insider and outsider.

Even if this is the only text that advocates social concern for the other in the entire document, the theme is at least nominally present here. On the whole, however, the *Gospel of Thomas* emphasizes an individualized soteriology with minimal concern for communally embodied existence. Logion 87 may, in fact, issue a warning against mutual dependence: "Jesus said, 'Wretched is the body that is dependent upon a body, and wretched is the soul that is dependent on these two.'"[18] That is, wretched is the individual human body that depends upon a social body. The individualism of the *Gospel of Thomas* does stand out when compared with other early Christian texts that advocate almsgiving, including those that stress the atoning value of the practice (e.g., *2 Clem.* 16.1–4). Perhaps almsgiving is harmful in the *Gospel of Thomas* not only because it constitutes a pious, Jewish observance that must be abandoned but also because the very nature of that pious observance diverts one from the soteriological vision revealed to the individual throughout the document. If one's primary goal is the interpretation of the secret sayings spoken by the living Jesus, then tangible manifestations of love and financial assistance for the impoverished other are distracting and, therefore, harmful.

Related to the individualized soteriology of *Thomas* is the document's framing of eschatology without reference to the future appearance of the kingdom of God or the future resurrection of the dead, the latter of which is probably explicitly rejected in *Gos. Thom.* 51. It is not quite accurate to say that the *Gospel of Thomas* is non-eschatological, for the document opens with the promise that "he who shall find the interpretation of these words shall not taste death" (*Gos. Thom.* 1).[19] Avoidance of death is mentioned several times in *Thomas* (cf. *Gos. Thom.* 18; 19; 111), and *Gos. Thom.* 50 appears to offer a path for the enlightened soul to ascend past the archontic powers into the bridal chamber (cf. *Gos. Thom.* 75).[20] The *Gospel of Thomas*, however, rejects notions of bodily resurrection, new creation, and a future kingdom, particularly through dialogues in which the disciples ask eschatological questions in which their assumptions about these realities are corrected by Jesus (*Gos. Thom.* 18, 51, 113).[21] There is in the *Gospel of Thomas*, therefore, no apparent

---

[18] See the discussion in Risto Uro, *Thomas: Seeking the Historical Context of the Gospel of Thomas* (JSPSup 1; London: T&T Clark, 2003), 58–62.

[19] Translation from Wilhelm Schneemelcher, ed., *New Testament Apocrypha*, vol. 1, *Gospels and Related Writings* [rev. ed.; trans. and ed. by R. McL. Wilson; Louisville, Ky.: Westminster John Knox, 1991], 117.

[20] Gathercole, "Heavens and the Earth," 286–87.

[21] Gathercole, "Heavens and the Earth," 291–93; Stephen J. Patterson, *The Gospel of Thomas and Christian Origins: Essays on the Fifth Gospel* (NHMS 84; Leiden: Brill, 2013), 61–92; Joshua W. Jipp, "Death and the Human Predicament, Salvation as Transformation, and Bodily Practices in 1 Corinthians and the Gospel of Thomas," in *Paul and the*

connection between deeds done in the body and eschatological reward or punishment, and almsgiving is neither meritorious nor atoning but injurious.

Almsgiving in the *Acts of Thomas*[22]

In sharp contrast to the negative assessment of almsgiving in the *Gospel of Thomas* stands the presentation of meritorious almsgiving in the *Acts of Thomas*, an early third-century writing that has no obvious literary or communal relationship to the earlier *Gospel of Thomas*.[23] The second act of the

---

Gospels: Christologies, Conflicts, Convergences (ed. Michael F. Bird and Joel Willitts; LNTS 412; London: T&T Clark, 2011), 242–66; pace Andrew Crislip, "Lion and Human in Gospel of Thomas Logion 7," *JBL* 126 (2007): 595–613; cf. Gathercole, *Gospel of Thomas,* 229–32.

[22] Translations of the *Acts of Thomas* are revised from Han J. W. Drijvers, "The Acts of Thomas," in *New Testament Apocrypha*, vol. 2, *Writings Relating to the Apostles; Apocalypses and Related Subjects* (rev. ed.; ed. Wilhelm Schneemelcher; trans. R. McL. Wilson; Louisville, Ky.: Westminster John Knox, 1992), 322–411. I work with the Greek text of *Acts of Thomas*, which is generally believed to preserve an older version; the Greek text is found in Maximilianus Bonnet, ed., *Acta Apostolorum Apocrypha* (Darmstadt: Wissenschaftliche Buchgesellschaft, 1959), 2:99–291. The *Acts of Thomas* should be provisionally dated to the beginning of the third century (so Albertus Frederik Johannes Klijn, *The Acts of Thomas: Introduction, Text, and Commentary* [rev. ed.; NovTSup 108; Leiden: Brill, 2003], 15), with a Syrian provenance, even if it is possible that the document originated in the late second century. For a recent discussion, see Susan E. Myers, *Spirit Epicleses in the Acts of Thomas* (WUNT II/281; Tübingen: Mohr Siebeck, 2010), 44–56. For a helpful overview of themes of wealth and poverty in this document, see Helen Rhee, "Wealth and Poverty in Acts of Thomas," in *Prayer and Spirituality in the Early Church*, vol. 5, *Poverty and Riches* (ed. Geoffrey D. Dunn et al.; Strathfield: St. Paul's, 2009), 111–18; Helen Rhee, *Loving the Poor, Saving the Rich: Wealth, Poverty, and Early Christian Formation* (Grand Rapids: Baker, 2012), 67–70.

[23] Christopher M. Hays has disputed the view that the *Gospel of Thomas* rejects almsgiving. Hays argues that—while Gos. Thom. 6 and 14 appear to repudiate fasting, prayer, and, almsgiving—practices of "fasting and prayer figure significantly in other Thomasine texts" and in Gos. Thom. 104 ("Resumptions of Radicalism: Christian Wealth Ethics in the Second and Third Centuries," *ZNW* 102 [2011]: 274; on Gos. Thom. 104, see above). Hays' reasoning, however, rests on the problematic assumption that it is possible to identify a unified "Thomasine Christianity" behind the *Gospel of Thomas*, the *Acts of Thomas*, and the *Book of Thomas the Contender*. On this point, see David J. Downs, "The Rhetoric of Almsgiving in 'Thomasine Christianity'" (paper presented at the annual meeting of the North American Patristics Society, Chicago, May 29, 2010). The term "community" is notoriously difficult to define. As anthropologist Anthony P. Cohen observes, "'Community' is one of those words—like 'culture,' 'myth,' 'ritual,' and 'symbol'—bandied about in ordinary, everyday speech, apparently intelligible to speaker and listener, which, when imported into the discourse of social science, however, causes immense difficulty. Over the years it has proved to be highly resistant to satisfactory definition in anthropology

Acts of Thomas contains a vignette that establishes a framework for the value of merciful care for the poor throughout the remainder of the narrative. In this second act, the apostle Thomas and Abban, the merchant to whom ~~Thomas is sold as a slave by Jesus in the first act,~~ arrive in India (17). Abban had come to Jerusalem on the orders of the Indian king Gundaphorus, with instructions to purchase a carpenter, and he acquires Thomas as a slave (2). When Thomas is presented to Gundaphorus, the king, who is impressed with Thomas' qualifications as a carpenter and builder, commissions Thomas to build him a palace, a task that Thomas willingly accepts (17). They discuss plans for the location and design of the building. The only unusual feature of their first meeting, which foreshadows the surprising development in the narrative, is Thomas' insistence that he undertake the construction during the winter season, in contrast to the customary practice of building in summer (18).

The king leaves Thomas with a considerable amount of money and continues to send funds to the apostle at appointed times. Thomas does not use the money to build the king a palace on earth, however. Instead, he distributes the funds to the poor and afflicted throughout the towns and villages, saying, "The king knows that he will receive a royal recompense, but the poor must

---

and sociology, perhaps for the simple reason that all definitions contain or imply theories, and the theory of community has been highly contentious" (*The Symbolic Construction of Community* [Chichester: Ellis Horwood, 1985], 11; Cohen's work is cited in Stephen C. Barton's instructive chapter, "Can We Identify the Gospel Audiences," in *The Gospels for All Christians: Rethinking the Gospel Audiences* [ed. Richard Bauckham; Grand Rapids: Eerdmans, 1998], 173–94 [174–76]). Yet to speak of a "~~community~~," one must at the very least account for shared values and practices. Derek Phillips offers the following helpful definition that highlights these two elements: "~~a group of people who live in a common territory, have a common history and shared values,~~ participate together ~~in various activities, and have a high degree of solidarity~~" (*Looking Backward: A Critical Appraisal of Communitarian Thought* [Princeton: Princeton University Press, 1993], 14). ~~It is, of course, always possible for a community to change its values and practices over the course of time.~~ If, according to the conventional dating of the documents, the *Gospel of Thomas* and the *Acts of Thomas* were written within about fifty to one hundred years of one another, it is certainly possible that a "community" of "Thomasine Christians" altered its position on almsgiving, perhaps to bring the group more in line with the larger orthodox church, a group for which almsgiving was an increasingly important endeavor. The problem is that such a hypothesis would require a rather dramatic alteration in the basic ethos, values, and practices advocated in the *Gospel of Thomas*, making the assumption of a stable "community" unworkable. Moreover, Hays' claim that the "later Coptic version of the Gospel marginalizes the qualified acceptance of almsgiving implied in the more original Greek version" rests on far too little evidence, not least because only a few letters survive from the Greek version of *Gos. Thom.* 14 and the extant portions of the Greek version of *Gos. Thom.* 6 are too badly preserved to bear the weight of Hays' suggestion.

for the present be refreshed" (19). When Gundaphorus asks for an update on the construction project, Thomas reports that the place is built, save for the roof. This results in more money from the king, which Thomas promptly redistributes to the afflicted, orphans, and widows (19). After Gundaphorus comes to the city to visit the palace, he learns from his friends that Thomas has built nothing but has instead given away everything to the poor (20). Outraged, the king meets with Thomas, who again insists that he has completed the building. When finally asked by Gundaphorus to see the palace, Thomas responds, "Now you cannot see it, but when you depart this life you will see it." The king is infuriated, and he throws Thomas into prison (21).

While Gundaphorus is contemplating the means of Thomas' execution, the king's brother, Gad, becomes severely ill, in part because of the shame that the king has endured (21). Gad quickly dies, whereupon he is taken to heaven. Angels show Gad a number of houses that he might inhabit, and his attention is captured by one building in particular. When he asks for permission to live in one of the lower rooms of the palace, the angels tell him, "You cannot live in this building. . . . This palace is the one which that Christian built for your brother" (22). Gad pleads for the opportunity to revisit his brother so that he might convince Gundaphorus to sell him the building, and he is allowed to return to the king (22–23). After some initial confusion, the king listens to his brother, although Gundaphorus decides to keep his palace for himself, sending Gad to Thomas so that the apostle can build Gad an even better palace (23–24). Thomas is released from prison, and both brothers turn to the worship of God. Their conversion is marked by an anointing of oil, a celebration of the Eucharist, and their own adoption of the practice of almsgiving, "supplying those who were in need, giving to and refreshing all" (26).

The concentration on the activity of almsgiving in this important episode at the beginning of the narrative has at least three functions in the larger context of the *Acts of Thomas*.[24] First, the story establishes the apostle Thomas as a trustworthy character who assists the needy and is committed to a life of simplicity. On the one hand, Thomas' actions emphasize the Christian virtue of care for the poor. Thomas says of his benefactions: "The Lord has dispensed this to you, and himself provides to each his food. For he

---

[24] Aside from Rhee's work, the only detailed study of this episode of which I am aware is A. Hilhorst, "The Heavenly Palace in the *Acts of Thomas*," in *The Apocryphal Acts of Thomas* (ed. Jan N. Bremmer; Studies on Early Christian Apocrypha 6; Leuven: Peeters, 2001), 53–64. Hilhorst focuses on parallels to this story in other ancient literature, however, and does not consider the function of the passage in its present literary context.

is the nourisher and the supporter of the widows, and to all that are afflicted he is relief and rest" (19).[25] In the apostle's speeches, God's concern for the destitute is an occasional theme: God is "the refuge and rest of the oppressed, the hope of the poor and redeemer of the captives" (10); God gives healing to day-laborers (60); God nourishes and supplies the needs of his impoverished servant Thomas (149). Jesus, too, is on the side of the poor, quite literally in at least one instance. In Act 5 Thomas' assistance is sought by a beautiful woman who, in spite of her commitment to chastity, has been raped by a demon for five years. When Thomas confronts the enemy, the demon is confused because Thomas looks like Jesus. What was true of the Son of God is true of Thomas: "For we knew him not; but he deceived us by his form most unsightly and by his poverty and need" (τῇ πενίᾳ αὐτοῦ καὶ τῇ ἐνδείᾳ [45]).[26] In Thomas' prayer after he exorcizes the demon, the apostle addresses Jesus as a "poor man" who went in need during his earthly ministry (47; cf. 143). This corresponds to Thomas' prayer to Jesus near the end of his life: "Companion and ally, hope of the weak and confidence of the poor. . . . You who has filled creation with your riches; the poor one who was in need and hungered forty days. . . . Be the physician of their bodies and souls" (156). In the *Acts of Thomas*, God, Jesus, and their agent Thomas all demonstrate a strong commitment to care for the destitute.

On the other hand, Thomas gives away all the money that he receives from the king because he himself is devoted to a life of simplicity. The act of giving away possessions can signal one's compassion for the poor—as almsgiving does in the *Acts of Thomas*—but dispossession can also indicate one's voluntary renunciation of wealth in the pursuit of an ascetic ideal.[27] Thomas' asceticism, too, is an important function of almsgiving in the narrative. When Gundaphorus' friends report the behavior of Thomas to the king, for

[25] On the emergence of care for the poor as a public virtue in Late Antiquity, see Peter Brown, *Poverty and Leadership in the Later Roman Empire: The Menahem Stern Jerusalem Lectures* (Hanover, N.H.: University Press of New England, 2002); Christel Freu, *Les Figures du pauvre dans le sources italiennes de l'antiquité tardive* (Collections de l'Université Marc Bloch-Strasbourg / Études d'Archéologie et d'Histoire Ancienne; Paris: De Boccard, 2007); cf. Paul M. Blowers, "Pity, Empathy, and the Tragic Spectacle of Human Suffering: Exploring the Emotional Culture of Compassion in Late Ancient Christianity," *JECS* 18 (2010): 1–27.

[26] The visual confusion here is an aspect of the polymorphic Christology in the *Acts of Thomas*. In *Acts Thom.* 48, Jesus is called "the polymorphic one" (ὁ πολύμορφος), and Judas Thomas and Jesus are frequently confused with one another in the narrative (31, 39, 54–55, 151–52). On this motif, see Paul Foster, "Polymorphic Christology: Its Origins and Development in Early Christianity," *JTS* 58 (2007): 66–99 [93–96].

[27] Hays, "Resumptions of Radicalism," 274–77.

example, they highlight his willing abandonment of property, expecting no return from those who benefit from his almsgiving:

> If he has anything he gives it all to the poor, and he teaches a new God and heals the sick and drives out demons and does many other wonderful things; and we think he is a magician. But his works of compassion, and the healings which are wrought by him without reward, and moreover his simplicity and kindness and the quality of his faith, show that he is righteous or an apostle of the new God whom he preaches. For continually he fasts and prays, and eats only bread and salt, and his drink is water, and he wears one garment whether in fine weather or in foul (winter), and takes nothing from anyone, and what he has gives to others. (20)

As Thomas continues his missionary endeavors throughout India, he is consistently portrayed as a wandering stranger who rejects material possessions.[28] Thomas' preaching and prayers are replete with appeals for voluntary poverty (61; 139; 144), and Thomas achieves renown for his rejection of worldly goods and his care for the poor. At the beginning of Act 7, for example, the wealthy general of an Indian king comes to Thomas and declares, "I have heard concerning you that you do not take reward of any man, but whatever you have you give to the needy" (62; cf. 104). For his suffering, Thomas receives the blessing of the humble (107). Thomas' description of himself in Act 11 is most fitting: "What have you come to see? A stranger, poor and contemptible and beggarly, who has neither wealth nor possession?" (136; cf. 145: "I have become poor and needy and a stranger and a slave, despised and a prisoner and hungry and thirsty and naked and weary"). Thomas goes on to assert that, although he is destitute, he has one possession that no one can take away and that will not perish—namely, "Jesus, the Savior of all humankind, the Son of the living God, who has given life to all who believe in him and take refuge with him, and is known in the number of his servants" (136).

This emphasis on simplicity is, of course, part of the broader motif of asceticism that can be seen throughout the document, particularly in Thomas' preaching of sexual renunciation. The converse of Thomas' embrace of voluntary poverty is found in his critique of material wealth and its pleasures. Material riches exist in this world only, and, since wealth threatens moral corruption, wealth can prevent a person from entering the kingdom of heaven (36; 144). Material possessions are transitory (37; 53; 117; 124);

---

[28] On this motif in the *Acts of Thomas*, see Daniel Caner, *Wandering, Begging Monks: Spiritual Authority and the Promotion of Monasticism in Late Antiquity* (The Transformation of the Classical Heritage 33; Berkeley: University of California Press, 2002), 57–65.

fine clothing profits nothing (88). As Thomas characteristically announces in Act 7, "Neither have I riches such as are found with some, which convict their possessors since they are utterly useless, and are abandoned upon the earth from which they came. But the transgressions which come upon men because of them, and the stains of sins, <they carry away> with them. But seldom are rich men found in acts of mercy" (σπανίως δὲ πλούσιοι εὑρίσκονται ἐν ἐλεημοσύναις [66]). Indeed, Thomas' renunciation of material possessions and his ascetic conduct are keys to his spiritual power, and these virtuous practices are what distinguish him from a magician or a sorcerer and identify him as someone whose preaching can be trusted.[29] Thus, the episode of the heavenly palace in *Acts of Thomas* 2 introduces the apostle as a reliable character who cares for the poor and embraces a lifestyle of asceticism.

A second function of the episode of the heavenly building in Act 2 is that Thomas' almsgiving becomes paradigmatic for several of those whom he encounters. In Act 2, for example, after Gundaphorus and Gad receive Thomas' proclamation, they follow him and imitate his concern for the poor, "themselves supplying those who were in need, giving to all and refreshing all" (26).[30] Similarly, in Act 6, a young man who had been convicted by Thomas' preaching about chastity kills his lover because she will not join him in his newfound commitment to celibacy. Thomas heals the young man's hands, which had been withered up when he attempted to participate in the Eucharist, and empowers the man to raise his paramour from the dead (51–54). After the woman recounts a tale of her journey to hell, Thomas exhorts the crowd to believe in Christ Jesus, the one who forgives sins (58). The people's response demonstrates a close connection between conversion and almsgiving: "So all the people believed, and yielded their souls obedient to the living God and to Christ Jesus, rejoicing in the blessed works of the Most High and in his holy service. And they brought much money for the service of the widows; for he had them gathered together in the cities, and to them all he

---

[29] Note that in *Acts Thom.* 20, the friends of Gundaphorus think that Thomas might be a μάγος, except that Thomas' deeds of compassion and his simplistic lifestyle show that he is, in fact, an "apostle of the new God whom he preaches" (cf. *Acts Thom.* 96); see Caner, *Wandering, Begging Monks*, 63–64; so also Peter Brown, *The Making of Late Antiquity* (Cambridge, Mass.: Harvard University Press, 1978), 22; Richard D. Finn, *Almsgiving in the Later Roman Empire: Christian Promotion and Practice (313–450)* (Oxford Classical Monographs; Oxford: Oxford University Press, 2006), 130–31. Negatively, Thomas' poverty is criticized by Charisius, who believes that Thomas is a charlatan and a magician (*Acts Thom.* 96).

[30] Cf. *Acts Thom.* 24, where Gundaphorus falls at Thomas' feet and asks, "I ask you and implore you before God, that I may become worthy of this ministry and service" (διακονίας καὶ ὑπηρεσίας).

sent what was necessary by his deacons, both clothing and provision for their nourishment" (59). At the conclusion of this episode, Thomas offers a prayer to God that highlights the fact that "we" have abandoned possessions for the sake of the Lord (60). Here, it seems, those converted by Thomas' preaching join him in his renunciation of worldly goods and in his ministry to the poor. To the extent that the *Acts of Thomas* consistently emphasizes Thomas' voluntary poverty and his criticism of material possessions, there appears to be an implicit invitation for readers of the text to adopt practices of almsgiving, as do several of those converted through Thomas' ministry.

A third and final function of the episode of the heavenly palace in Act 2 is that this narrative demonstrates a close connection between proper behavior in this life—particularly with regard to the sharing of material goods—and future blessing in the next. The implicit logic of the narrative is that almsgiving has the power to secure heavenly reward: with the funds that Thomas distributes to the destitute in India, he constructs a building for Gundaphorus in heaven. The notion that almsgiving is meritorious is certainly not unique to the *Acts of Thomas*. The interesting twist in this story, however, is that Thomas' beneficence accumulates reward for another, although, to the extent that Gundaphorus supplies the money that Thomas distributes to the poor, perhaps the king can be seen as indirectly (and certainly unintentionally) engaged in the practice of ἐλεημοσύνη. The king recognizes this dynamic when he says of the heavenly palace, "May I become a worthy inhabitant of that dwelling for which I did not labor at all, but you did build it for me laboring alone, the grace of your God working with you" (24).

Gundaphorus' affirmation of Thomas' labor and God's grace nicely captures a tension found throughout the *Acts of Thomas*. On the one hand, the narrative highlights the grace of God in Thomas' ministry and in the experience of salvation. At the very beginning of the story, Jesus declares, "Fear not, Thomas, go to India and preach the word there, for my grace is with you" (1; cf. 13). Grace is given by God (28; 34), and the narrative regularly portrays salvation and forgiveness of sin as the result of divine mercy and compassion (39; 48; 70; 80; 141).[31] On the other, there is clearly a sense in which divine recompense comes according to one's deeds. Just as almsgiving can lead to heavenly reward, acts such as adultery, slander, shamelessness, theft, and

[31] In this context, I find quite puzzling this statement in Han J. W. Drijvers' introduction to his translation of the *Acts of Thomas*: "The ATh thus have no soteriology in the strict sense of a doctrine of a redeemer. Terms like sin and grace do not occur. The incarnation, crucifixion, resurrection and ascension of Christ are not mentioned. Every man can freely achieve his own redemption, in so far as he appropriates to himself the knowledge of the truth and renounces sexuality" ("Acts of Thomas," 329).

failing to visit the sick and dying bring eternal torment (56). As a demon says to Thomas in Act 8, "As to you [your father] gives eternal life as reward for your working, so for me [my father] provides in requital for my works eternal destruction" (76). And as Thomas himself declares—with a possible allusion to Rom 2:6 and its own intertext, LXX Ps 61:13—at the end of the episode of the heavenly palace, "For he is the judge of the living and dead, and he gives to each one according to his works. . . . Come to him who is truly good, that you may receive grace from him and lay up his sign in your souls" (28). Unlike the *Gospel of Thomas*, in which there is no eschatological judgment for the deeds done in the body, the *Acts of Thomas* parallels texts from the canonical New Testament in imagining a final assize in which human actions, including practices of care for the needy, will be judged.

In one additional passage in the *Acts of Thomas*, almsgiving is declared to be worthy of eternal reward. When Thomas addresses the slaves of the wealthy woman Mygdonia, the apostle lists vices that should be avoided by those who do not want to incur God's judgment. Not surprisingly, adultery is placed first ("the beginning of all evils"), followed by murder, theft, intemperance, avarice, ostentation, and sexual intercourse. After this catalog of vices is a list of virtues, the last of which is "stretching out of the hand to the poor, and supplying the want of the needy, and distributing to them that are in necessity, especially them that walk in holiness. For this is chosen before God and leads to eternal life" (85).[32] In this scene, too, there is a correlation of almsgiving and eternal reward, although support of the poor in this context is part of a larger appeal to holiness.

With the passages that establish heavenly reward and the avoidance of divine judgment as the fruit of almsgiving, the *Acts of Thomas* is properly located within a wider stream of early Christian tradition that emphasized the meritorious nature of giving alms to the poor. Unlike other texts that image almsgiving as atoning in the sense that alms reckon with sin in some way, the *Acts of Thomas* does not directly coordinate almsgiving with atonement for sin. After he learns of the "royal recompense" that he has received because of Thomas' almsgiving, Gundaphorus, along with his brother Gad, repents of his mistreatment of the apostle and asks to become a servant of God (24). Thomas prays that Gundaphorus and Gad would be cleansed with "thy washing" and anointed "with thy oil from the error which surrounds them" (25), a prayer that precedes Thomas' sealing them with oil and welcoming them to receive the Eucharist (26).[33] The document does, however,

---

[32] Here I follow the translation of the Greek by Klijn, *Acts of Thomas*, 164.

[33] Anointing is featured more prominently in the conversion scenes in the *Acts of Thomas* than baptism (but see *Acts Thom.* 121, 132, 157). It is clear that Gundaphorus

encourage the practice of almsgiving as part of a holy life and as a means of securing heavenly reward.[34]

There are profoundly different perspectives on the practice of almsgiving in the *Gospel of Thomas* and the *Acts of Thomas*. The prohibition and promotion of almsgiving in these two documents appear to be rooted in disparate theological commitments. In the *Gospel of Thomas*, almsgiving is not merely rejected; it is described as personally harmful and is linked with other sinful and injurious practices. This disparagement of almsgiving in the *Gospel of Thomas* is likely the result of a rejection of Jewish religious praxis and of a soteriological perspective that emphasizes the concerns of the individual. Conversely, the practice of almsgiving in the *Acts of Thomas* is consistent with God's concern for the poor and Thomas' critique of wealth; it is paradigmatic for those who embrace Thomas' preaching; and it has the potential to secure heavenly reward. It would be difficult to find two more dissimilar perspectives on the practice of giving alms to the poor. These differences with regard to practices of care for the poor in the *Gospel of Thomas* and the *Acts of Thomas* do not necessarily reflect a literary relationship, and still less any sense of a "Thomasine community."

2 Clement

In contrast to the denigration of almsgiving in the *Gospel of Thomas* stands the elevation of ἐλεημοσύνη ("merciful practice" or "almsgiving") above fasting and prayer in the second-century homily called *2 Clement*. In the context of a call to repentance, the anonymous author of *2 Clement* constructs a hierarchy of praxis that ranks fasting better than prayer but identifies ἐλεημοσύνη as better than both: "Therefore, merciful practice (ἐλεημοσύνη)

---

and Gad are cleansed by God's washing of them, a reality sealed by their anointing. On the theme of anointing in *Acts Thom.*, see Myers, *Spirit Epicleses in the Acts of Thomas*, 109–44.

[34] The *Acts of Thomas* also does not explicitly frame Thomas' practice of almsgiving as the embodiment of scriptural traditions, in spite of the fact that the document evidences a deep reliance on Christian Scriptures. Possible allusions to scriptural intertexts regarding almsgiving in the story of Thomas and Gundaphorus can be found (cf. *Acts Thom.* 19//Matt 6:1-4 and 25:35-27; *Acts Thom.* 20//Matt 6:19-21 and Luke 18:22), but it is only in *Acts Thom.* 28, after Thomas has anointed Gundaphorus and Gad with oil, that he offers a sermon rich with scriptural resonance (cf. Matt 6:26, 34; 11:30; Luke 12:24; Acts 10:42; Rom 2:6; Titus 4:14; John 8:12; 12:35-36), and in this sermon the focus is sexual purity, not almsgiving. On the citation and use of Scripture in the *Acts of Thomas*, see Harold W. Attridge, "Intertextuality in the *Acts of Thomas*," *Semeia* 80 (1997): 87–124; Christopher R. Matthews, "Apocryphal Intertextual Activities: A Response to Harold W. Attridge's 'Intertextuality in the *Acts of Thomas*,'" *Semeia* 80 (1997): 125–35.

is good as repentance for sin. Fasting is better than prayer, but merciful practice (ἐλεημοσύνη) is better than both, and *love covers a multitude of sins* (1 Pet
4:8). Prayer from a good conscience delivers from death. Blessed is everyone
who is found full of these things, for merciful practice (ἐλεημοσύνη) lightens
the burden of sin (Tob 12:8)" (16:4). For the author of 2 Clement, merciful
practice is better than fasting and prayer because care for the needy clearly
demonstrates repentance.[35] Moreover, drawing on both 1 Pet 4:8 and Tob
12:8, 2 Clem. 16.4 stresses the atoning value of ἐλεημοσύνη: merciful practice demonstrates repentance for sin, covers a multitude of sins, and lightens
the burden of sin.

The Gospel of Matthew (6:1-18), 2 Clem. 16.1–4, and Gos. Thom. 6
and 14 are notable for their explicit combination of the language of fasting,
prayer, and almsgiving in such concentrated fashion.[36] Moreover, 2 Clement
and Thomas reflect wholly contradictory perspectives on fasting, prayer, and
almsgiving. Whereas prayer with a good conscience delivers from death and
almsgiving lightens the burden of sin in 2 Clement, prayer leads to condemnation and almsgiving to personal harm in the Gospel of Thomas (14.1–3). Given
this striking overlap, it is possible that either the author of 2 Clement or the
author of the Gospel of Thomas uses the discussion of almsgiving to critique
divergent notions among certain Christians. Without necessarily suggesting
any direct literary relationship between 2 Clement and the Gospel of Thomas,
in contrast to an individualized spirituality that regards the kingdom of God
as an entirely present reality and denies a final judgment (cf. Gos. Thom. 3,
113), 2 Clem. 16.1–4 challenges readers to consider almsgiving as a sign of
repentance in light of the impending appearance of Christ. The author of
2 Clement might be read as countering the rejection of almsgiving among
some Christian groups not merely by advocating the practice of almsgiving
for those who share in the mercy of Jesus but also by insisting that almsgiving
is better than both fasting and prayer.[37] It might also be observed that, like
Ignatius and Polycarp, the author of 2 Clement emphatically insists upon the

---

[35] See the earlier discussion of 2 Clem. 16 in chap. 6.

[36] It is possible that Herm. Sim. 5 (esp. 5.3.7–8) should be added to this list, since in
that parable the combination of almsgiving and fasting is portrayed as the key to effective
prayer. See the discussion in Richard D. Finn, "Almsgiving for the Pure of Heart: Continuity and Change in Early Christian Teaching," in Severan Culture (ed. Simon Swain, Stephen Harrison, and Jaś Elsner; Cambridge: Cambridge University Press, 2007), 419–29.

[37] Among those who have argued that 2 Clem. 16 is responding to the senti-
ments expressed in Gos. Thom. 6, 14, see Tashio Aono, Die Entwicklung des paulinischen
Gerichtsgedankens bei den apostolischen Vätern (EHS 23; Bern: Peter Lang, 1979), 120;
Karl Donfried, The Setting of Second Clement in Early Christianity (NovTSup 38; Leiden:
Brill, 1974). Christopher M. Tuckett, however, thinks that a direct link between these

enfleshment of Jesus and the fleshly resurrection of those who repent and keep the flesh pure (8.4–6):

> [1] And let none of you say that this flesh is not judged and does not rise again. [2] Think about this: In what state were you saved? In what state did you receive your sight, if it was not while you were in this flesh? [3] We must, therefore, guard the flesh as a temple of God. [4] For just as you were called in the flesh, so you will come in the flesh. [5] If Christ, the Lord who saved us, became flesh (even though he was originally spirit), and in that state called us, so also we will receive our reward in this flesh. (2 Clem. 9.1–5)[38]

Interestingly, the author of 2 Clement immediately follows this short discourse on resurrection with a call to mutual love: "Therefore, let us love one another, so we might all enter into the kingdom of God" (9.6). Clearly, for the author of 2 Clement there exists a close connection between hope for bodily resurrection and mutual love among the family gathered in the name of Christ.

Moreover, hierarchy of piety that includes and ranks merciful practice, fasting, and prayer suggests that all believers, from the perspective of the author of 2 Clement, should engage in merciful practices, just as all should pray (2.2; 16.4).[39] The practice of ἐλεημοσύνη in 2 Clement represents an embodied spirituality that does not separate confessions of faith or knowledge about God from required acts of righteousness. In fact, with language that parallels (but may not be drawn from) the Gospel of Matthew, this connection between belief and action is explicitly drawn in 2 Clem. 4.1–3:

---

texts is unlikely (2 Clement: Introduction, Text, and Commentary [Oxford Apostolic Fathers; Oxford: Oxford University Press, 2012], 273).

[38] The translation here is from Holmes, Apostolic Fathers, 149. The discussion of resurrection in 2 Clem. 9.1–5 is not as explicitly polemical as the teaching on resurrection in Ignatius' Smyrn. and Polycarp's Phil. Tuckett, however, suggests that 2 Clem. 9.1–5 may be directed at those who reject bodily resurrection: "The dangers of mirror-reading any (mildly) polemical text are well known. However, it would appear that, if the response given by the author to the (perceived) problem is apposite, the issue is not so much that some are denying the very idea of resurrection, nor necessarily claiming that resurrection is already present. Rather, the issue seems to be more specific: how far the 'flesh' participates in the (presumed future) resurrection. What seems to be regarded as dangerous here is any denial that the present physical body ('flesh') has any place in the future resurrection life. The author here insists passionately on the full participation of the 'flesh' in the future resurrection life" (2 Clement, 203 [emphasis in original]).

[39] Full weight should be given to πᾶς in 2 Clem. 16.4: "Blessed is everyone who is found full of these things, for merciful practice lightens the burden of sin."

¹For this reason we should not merely call him Lord; for this will not save us. ²For he says, "Not everyone who says to me, 'Lord, Lord' will be saved, but only the one who practices righteousness (ἀλλ' ὁ ποιῶν τὴν δικαιοσύνην)." ³So then, brothers and sisters, we should acknowledge him by what we do, by loving one another, by not committing adultery or slandering one another or showing envy. Instead, we should be self-controlled, practitioners of mercy (ἐλεήμονας), benevolent. And we should suffer together with one another and not love money (μὴ φιλαργυρεῖν).[40]

It is also significant that the author of 2 *Clement* roots the claim regarding the atoning power of merciful practice in 16.4 in appeals to both 1 Pet 4:8 and Tob 12:8-9.[41] In Raphael's final exhortation to Tobit and Tobias, the angel commends merciful practice (ἐλεημοσύνη) as a means of delivering from death and cleansing sin. Like Raphael in Tob 12:8, the author of 2 *Clement* asserts the superiority of merciful practice over prayer, a notable claim since 2 *Clem.* 16.4 also indicates that prayer from a good conscience delivers from death.[42] Yet the author of 2 *Clement* goes beyond Tobit by declaring that merciful practice is better than *both* fasting and prayer.[43] Without denying the essential goodness of any of these practices (cf. 2 *Clem.* 2.2, where readers are encouraged "to offer up prayers to God sincerely"), the author constructs a hierarchy of praxis that ranks ἐλεημοσύνη highest on the list.

That the author of 2 *Clement* advocates atoning almsgiving with a citation from 1 Pet 4:8 (or at least a saying also included in 1 Pet 4:8) and an allusion to Tob 12:8-9 does not necessarily indicate that the author considers these sources to be "scriptural" texts, since there is no clear marker of the author's drawing upon these materials, let alone an introductory clause such

---

[40] On the relationship between 2 *Clement* and the Gospel of Matthew, see Stephen E. Young, *Jesus Tradition in the Apostolic Fathers: Their Explicit Appeals to the Words of Jesus in Light of Orality Studies* (WUNT II/311; Tübingen: Mohr Siebeck, 2011), 239–77.

[41] On the relationship between 2 *Clem.* 16 and various textual traditions of Tobit, see the finely detailed study by Christopher M. Tuckett, "Tobit 12,8 and 2 Clement 16,4," *ETL* 88 (2012): 129–44.

[42] Tuckett, "Tobit 12,8 and 2 Clement 16,4," 141–42.

[43] Tuckett, however, points out that the G[III] tradition (found in MSS 106, 107) of Tob 12:8 indicates that ἐλεημοσύνη is "better than both" (i.e., prayer and fasting; cf. the Old Latin, which reads *super utrumque autem melius est modicum cum iustitia quam plurimum cum iniquitate*). Tuckett, "Tobit 12,8 and 2 Clement 16,4," 137–41. After a careful comparison of the text of 2 *Clem.* 16.4 with several various manuscript traditions of Tob 12:8-9, Tuckett concludes, "Clearly the 'parallels' are not close enough to label this a 'quotation' in any strict sense; but there is enough similarity between the texts, in the content and the general sequence of the sayings, to suggest that some allusion to (at least one version of) the text of Tobit is present here" (2 *Clement*, 268).

as "it is written." A measured conclusion would maintain that "Tobit was accepted as a book whose words could be used and exploited in the same way as the words of other scriptural books were used."[44] To the extent that 1 Peter and Tobit came to be regarded as "Scripture" by at least some segments of the early church, however, it might be said that the promotion of atoning almsgiving in 2 Clem. 16.4 emerges, in part, on the basis of scriptural exegesis, even if this scriptural warrant is not explicit in 2 Clement itself.[45]

Polycarp

A number of years after Ignatius traveled to Rome to face his death, Ignatius' friend and colleague, Polycarp of Smyrna, wrote a letter to the church at Philippi.[46] Polycarp was the bishop of Smyrna, both at the time he penned his missive to the Philippians and earlier when Ignatius wrote to him and

---

[44] Tuckett, 2 Clement, 268.

[45] Tobit is regarded as Scripture by Cyprian (Fort. 11–12), Clement of Alexandria (Strom. 2.139.3; 6.102.2), Dionysus of Alexandria, Hilary, Ambrose, and Augustine (see Fitzmyer, Tobit, 55–57). Origen notes its use in churches (Ep. Afr. 19), and Tobit was included in the biblical canon of the Council of Carthage in 397 CE (Shanzer, "Jerome," 88); but cf. Eusebius, Hist. Eccl. 4.26.14; Athanasius, Ep. 39. With regard to the clause ἐλεημοσύνη γὰρ κούφισμα ἁμαρτίας γίνεται ("for merciful practice lightens the burden of sin"), Susan Docherty claims, "The word 'for' introducing the final clause suggests that the author was citing a scriptural proof-text here in support of his argument, especially as similar wording is found in Polycarp's Letter to the Philippians: '. . . giving to charity frees a person from death . . .' (Pol. Phil. 10:2)" ("The Reception of Tobit in the New Testament and Early Christian Literature, with Special Reference to Luke–Acts," in The Scriptures of Israel in Jewish and Christian Tradition: Essays in Honour of Maarten J. J. Menken [ed. Bart J. Koet, Steve Moyise, and Joseph Verheyden; NovTSup 148; Leiden: Brill, 2013], 93–94). Docherty's assertion is puzzling, however. Docherty appears to think the γάρ in the final clause of 2 Clem. 16.4 is the equivalent of the quia in Pol. Phil. 10.2 (although she does not cite this word in her translation of Pol. Phil. 10.2), making the further unexplained assumption that Polycarp's quia is a scriptural citation formula (see chap. 9 for a discussion of this point). Yet it is not at all clear what evidence would support Docherty's claim that the mere presence of the word γάρ indicates the introduction of a scriptural proof-text. (see, e.g., Christopher D. Stanley, Paul and the Language of Scripture: Citation Technique in the Pauline Epistles and Contemporary Literature [SNTSMS 74; Cambridge: Cambridge University Press, 1992]). Moreover, Docherty's statement that "similar wording" is found in Pol. Phil. 10.2 is confusing because the wording is not similar, even though both texts draw on different portions of Tob 12.

[46] Assuming the literary unity of Pol. Phil., the letter was probably written between 100 and 140 CE, although the range could be more strictly limited to 100–117 CE (see Paul Hartog, Polycarp's Epistle to the Philippians and the Martyrdom of Polycarp: Introduction, Text, and Commentary [Oxford Apostolic Fathers; Oxford: Oxford University Press, 2013], 40–44).

to the church of the Smyrnaeans. Among the primary concerns reflected in Polycarp's letter to the Philippians are the bishop's moral exhortation about the avoidance of avarice (2.2 [φιλαργυρία]; 4.1, 3; 5.2 [ἀφιλάργυρος]; 6.1; 11.1, 2 [avaritia]) and his condemnation of false teaching (7.1–2).[47] These two central themes in Pol. *Phil.* have often not been understood in relation to one another, but avarice and heresy are closely connected in the logical progression of Polycarp's letter, and quite possibly this connection is forged for some of the very same reasons Ignatius had earlier criticized heresy in Polycarp's own city of Smyrna—namely, that certain false teachers denied a future resurrection and a future judgment of behavior, with the result that those who denied these eschatological realities also failed to care for the poor.

Much of Polycarp's paraenesis in his letter to the Philippians, and particularly Polycarp's instruction regarding the sin of "love of money" (φιλαργυρία/ *avaritia*), is rooted in his conviction regarding God's future judgment, a judgment Polycarp believes is denied by certain false teachers.[48] In Pol. *Phil.* 2.2, for example, Polycarp insists that "the one who raised [our Lord Jesus Christ] from the dead will raise us also, if we do his will and follow his commandments and love the things that he loved, while avoiding all unrighteousness, greed, *love of money*, evil speech, false testimony." This assertion is typical of Polycarp's presentation of the relationship between eschatology and ethics. The connection between eschatology and ethics is also emphasized with reference to "love of money" in 4.1–3, which begins, in a statement that echoes 1 Tim 6:10, with a declaration that readers should "follow the commandment of the Lord" (i.e., give alms) because of the belief that those who brought nothing into the world can take nothing out of it (i.e., when they stand before the judgment seat of Christ [6.2]).[49] Similarly, Polycarp teaches that deacons are to be blameless in the presence of God's righteousness—a blamelessness that includes not being lovers of money (ἀφιλάργυροι)—with the promise

---

[47] My understanding of these issues in Pol. *Phil.* is indebted to Hartog, *Polycarp's Epistle*, 76–78. For a more detailed articulation of Paul Hartog's thesis, see "The Relationship between *Paraenesis* and Polemic in Polycarp, *Philippians*," *StPatr* 65 (2013): 27–37. Michael Holmes has indicated that "a major interpretive question is the relationship (or lack thereof) between" the "Philippians' request for a discussion of 'righteousness' (3.1–10.3) and the problem of Valens, an avaricious presbyter (11.1–4)" (*Apostolic Fathers*, 274).

[48] Hartog, "Relationship between *Paraenesis*," 30. Polycarp mentions or alludes to future judgment in 2.1–3; 4.1; 5.2–3; 6.2; 7.1–2; 8.1; 10.2; 11.2; and 12.2; cf. the example and the reward of Ignatius, Zosimus, and Rufus in 9.1–2.

[49] For the argument that "the commandment of the Lord" in Pol. *Phil.* 4.1 refers to the practice of almsgiving, see David J. Downs and Wil Rogan, "'Let Us Teach Ourselves First to Follow the Commandment of the Lord' [Pol. *Phil.* 4.1]: An Additional Note on Almsgiving as 'The Commandment,'" article in preparation.

that those who please God in the present world and prove to be worthy citizens of God will receive the world to come and will be raised from the dead (5.2–3). According to Polycarp, the avoidance of avarice rests in the conviction that there will be a future judgment and resurrection, two eschatological realities denied by those whom Polycarp identifies as false teachers.

The connection between eschewing "love of money" (and the opposite of φιλαργυρία—namely, care for the poor), future judgment, and the non-eschatological nature of the false teaching Polycarp wishes to combat is seen most clearly in the logical progression of Pol. *Phil.* 6–7. In 6.1 Polycarp concludes the *Haustafeln* that runs from 4.1 to 6.1 with instructions for "presbyters" (οἱ πρεσβύτεροι) to practice almsgiving:

> The presbyters also should be compassionate, showing mercy to all (εἰς πάντας ἐλεήμονες), turning back those who have gone astray, looking after all the sick, not neglecting a widow (χήρας), or an orphan (ὀρφανοῦ), or a poor person (πένητος), but always considering the good before God and before people, abstaining from all anger, partiality, unjust judgment, being far from all love of money (μακρὰν ὄντες πάσης φιλαργυρίας), not being quick to believe the things spoken against someone, not harsh in judgment, knowing that we are all debtors of sins (πάντες ὀφειλέται ἐσμὲν ἁμαρτίας).

Polycarp then follows this instruction for presbyters to care for the needy while also avoiding avarice (among other transgressions) with a discussion of forgiveness and judgment: "Therefore, if we ask the Lord to forgive us, we ourselves also should forgive, for we are before the eyes of the Lord and of God, and everyone must stand before the judgment seat of Christ, and each one must render an account of himself or herself" (6.2).[50] It does not appear that Polycarp refers to forgiveness and judgment in 6.2 because he believes that the practices of almsgiving discussed in 6.1 are a means to obtain the former and fare well with respect to the latter. Yet the notion that all the Philippians (and not merely the presbyters mentioned in 6.1) are observed by God and will be judged by Christ on the basis of their actions, including for

---

[50] On the relationship between Pol. *Phil.* 6.2 and materials from the New Testament (esp. Matt 6:12-15; Mark 11:25; Luke 6:37; 11:4; Rom 14:10, 12; 2 Cor 5:10), see Michael W. Holmes, "Polycarp's *Letter to the Philippians* and the Writings that Later Formed the New Testament," in *The Reception of the New Testament in the Apostolic Fathers* (ed. Andrew Gregory and Christopher Tuckett; NTAF 1; Oxford: Oxford University Press, 2005), 187–227; Kenneth Berding, *Polycarp and Paul: An Analysis of Their Literary and Theological Relationship in Light of Polycarp's Use of Biblical and Extra-biblical Literature* (VCSup 62; Leiden: Brill, 2002).

their care for the needy and avoidance of avarice, clearly sets the instruction regarding almsgiving within an eschatological framework.

It is precisely this connection between ethics and eschatology that Polycarp's opponents fail to grasp, however. Pol. *Phil.* 6.3 "serves as a bridge between the moral *paraenesis* extending from 6.1 and the polemic against false teaching extending into 7.1":[51]

> And so let us serve him [i.e., Christ] with fear and reverence, just as he himself has commanded, as did the apostles who proclaimed the gospel to us, and the prophets who announced in advance the coming of the Lord. Let us be zealots regarding the good, and let us avoid those who tempt others to sin, and false brothers, and those who bear the name of the Lord in hypocrisy, who lead foolish people astray.

The Philippians are to serve Christ with fear and reverence, as was commanded by Christ himself, by apostles, and by prophets.[52] In the context of the letter, the exhortation to be "zealots regarding the good" (ζηλωταὶ περὶ τὸ καλόν) in 6.3 refers to practices of charity, for the phrase "always considering the good" (προνοοῦντες ἀεὶ τοῦ καλοῦ) is used in 6.1 as a way to designate what it means to show mercy to all, including the sick, widows, orphans, and the poor. Moreover, in 10.2, the Latin *benefacere* ("to do good") stands in a parallel relationship with *eleemosyna* ("merciful practice") in an exhortation to charitable action.

If Polycarp's appeal in 6.3 to be "zealots regarding the good" points back the discussion of almsgiving in 6.1, his warning against those who tempt others to sin, against false brothers, and against hypocrites points forward to the discourse against false teachers in 7.1–2. According to Polycarp in 7.1, a false teacher—polemically labeled (probably in language drawn from the Johannine epistles) an antichrist, of the devil, and the firstborn of Satan—is someone who (1) "does not confess that Jesus has come in the flesh" (cf. 1 John 4:2-4; 2 John 7; Ign. *Smyrn.* 1.1, 2; 3.1–2; 7.1; 12.2); (2) "does not acknowledge the testimony of the cross" (cf. Ign. *Smyrn.* 1.1; *Eph.* 18.1; *Trall.* 11.2; *Phld.* 8.2); and (3) distorts the sayings of the Lord in order to claim "that there is neither resurrection nor judgment."[53] In particular, the false

---

[51] Hartog, "Relationship between *Paraenesis*," 33.

[52] For the argument that the antecedent of the pronoun αὐτῷ in Pol. *Phil.* 6.1 is Christ instead of God and that the "prophets who announced in advanced the coming of our Lord" refers to Old Testament prophets, see Hartog, "Relationship between *Paraenesis*," 32–33.

[53] Hartog raises the possibility that, while Polycarp's words are addressed to the church in Philippi, the nature of the false teaching with which he is concerned is also

teacher "twists the sayings of the Lord to suit his own sinful desires" (7.1). Polycarp, therefore, appears to be disturbed by a denial of future judgment and resurrection that is tied to a distortion of Jesus' teaching that leads to sinful practice.

Interestingly, Polycarp's immediate solution to the problem of false teaching in Philippi in 7.2 involves an exhortation to "return to the word handed on to us from the beginning, being self-controlled with respect to prayer and being persistent with respect to fasting" (ἐπὶ τὸν ἐξ ἀρχῆς ἡμῖν παραδοθέντα λόγον ἐπιστρέψωμεν νήφοντες πρὸς τὰς εὐχὰς καὶ προσκαρτεροῦντες νηστείαις). Presumably, the content of "the word handed on to us from the beginning" alludes back to the instruction commanded by Jesus, the apostles, and the prophets in 6.3. If this commandment from Jesus in 6.3 is related to "the commandment of the Lord" to give alms in Pol. *Phil.* 4.1, then Pol. *Phil.* 7.2 would present practices of almsgiving, prayer, and fasting as ways of countering the false teaching in Philippi, the very tryptic of praxis highlighted in 2 *Clem.* 16.4 and two of the three practices (i.e., charity and prayer) that Ignatius indicates are rejected by Docetists in Smyrna. Regardless of the content of "the word handed on to us from the beginning," Polycarp stresses the close connection between ethics and eschatology: "The targeted opponents denied any future resurrection and judgment, and Polycarp feared the ethical ramifications of this denial."[54]

Such an understanding of the logical progression from the exhortation to almsgiving in 6.1 to the critique of false teachers in 7.1 also sheds light on Polycarp's discussion of the sin of the presbyter Valens near the end of the letter (11.1–4), for Valens failed in the office entrusted to him precisely because of avarice.[55] With reference to Valens, Polycarp indicates that the

---

present in Smyrna ("Relationship between Paraenesis," 36). Given the overlaps between the descriptions of false teaching in Pol. *Phil.* 7.1 and Ign. *Smyrn.* 6.2–7.2, it may be the case that Polycarp's concerns about false teaching in Philippi reflect his own experience in Smyrna.

[54] Hartog, "Relationship between *Paraenesis*," 37.

[55] The exact nature of Valens' offense is not specified by Polycarp. It has been suggested that perhaps Valens pilfered money from the congregation's communal fund or "compromised his Christianity to escape economic suffering" (Peter Oakes, "Leadership and Suffering in the Letters of Polycarp and Paul to the Philippians," in *Trajectories through the New Testament and Apostolic Fathers* [ed. Andrew Gregory and Christopher Tuckett; NTAF 2; Oxford: Oxford University Press,2007], 369). Given Valens' identity as a presbyter (11.1) and Polycarp's instruction for presbyters to care for the needy (6.1), it is likely that Valens' avarice involved some failure to practice almsgiving, either because he misappropriated funds marked for the poor or because his life was marked by failure to understand the importance of almsgiving and lack of avarice for those holding the position of presbyter.

fallen presbyter is, in fact, ignorant of the Lord's judgments: "But how can someone who is unable to exercise self-control in these matters preach self-control to anyone else? Anyone who does not avoid love of money (*avaritia*) will be polluted by idolatry and will be judged as one of the Gentiles, *who are ignorant of the Lord's judgment*. Or do we not know that the saints will judge the world, as Paul teaches" (11.2).[56] Drawing on 1 Cor 6:2, Polycarp reminds his readers in Philippi of their participation in the eschatological judgment of the cosmos, while also suggesting that either the cause or the result of Valens' fall into the sin of avarice is ignorance with regard to the final judgment. Valens, then, fills the profile of the false teacher described in 7.1; he is one who "twists the sayings of the Lord to suit his own sinful desires and claims that there is neither resurrection nor judgment." To be sure, Polycarp hopes for restoration for Valens and his wife (11.4). But until this couple repents, they are to be avoided and treated as sick and wayward members of the Philippian body.

In chapter 11, Polycarp does not articulate a precise remedy for the sin of Valens and his wife, aside from the bishop's wish that the transgressors be granted "true repentance" (*poenitentiam veram* [11.4]). It may be that the antidote to Valens' sin is proposed earlier in chapter 10, however. The final verse in chapter 10 issues a woe against "the one through whom the name of the Lord is blasphemed" and calls for all to be taught self-control (10.3). Valens is explicitly said to lack the virtue of self-control, a fact that disqualifies Valens from teaching about the topic (11.2). The offense of Valens is clearly in mind, then, in Pol. *Phil.* 10.3.[57] In the verse that immediately precedes this turn to Valens—after an exhortation to endurance and mutual love, concern, unity, and gentleness in 10.1—Polycarp cites a verse from Tobit in order to commend the practice of almsgiving: "When you are able to do good (*benefacere*), do not put it off, because charity delivers one from death (*quia eleemosyna de morte liberat*)" (10.2).[58] The phrase "charity delivers one from

---

[56] Translations from the Latin sections of Pol. *Phil.* 10–14 are from Holmes, *Apostolic Fathers*.

[57] So Hartog, *Polycarp's Epistle to the Philippians*, 140–41. The case of Valens is probably also targeted in Polycarp's command in 10.2 to "maintain an irreproachable standard of conduct among the Gentiles," lest God's name be blasphemed.

[58] As Hartog points out, "The phrase 'do good' can be used synonymously with charity" (cf. Mark 14:7; Luke 6:33-35; 1 Tim 6:18; Heb 13:16; Clement of Alexandria, *Quis div.* 33; *Paed.* 3.7; Herm. *Vis.* 3.9.2–6; *Mand.* 2.4), and in this context the equivalence seems justified (*Polycarp's Epistle to the Philippians*, 140).

death" is a quotation of either Tob 4:10 (διότι ἐλεημοσύνη ἐκ θανάτου ῥύεται) or Tob 12:9 (ἐλεημοσύνη γὰρ ἐκ θανάτου ῥύεται).[59]

If Polycarp's citation of the phrase "because charity delivers one from death" from Tobit is directed at the Valens situation, perhaps the bishop envisions merciful practice on behalf of the needy as a way to counter the sin of avarice and to restore "sick and wayward" believers like Valens and his wife (cf. the connection between bribery and atoning almsgiving in LXX Prov 15:27). In this sense, Polycarp might imply that almsgiving is atoning because charity provides a remedy for "love of money." There is little doubt that Polycarp maintains a vibrant belief in the atoning nature of Jesus' death. The letter opens with Polycarp's report that the bishop rejoices that the faith of the Philippians, "renowned from the earliest times, still endures and bears fruit to our Lord Jesus Christ, who endured *for our sins even to the point of death*" (1.2). Moreover, Pol. *Phil.* 8.1 reads, "Therefore, let us hold steadfastly and unfailingly to our hope and the guarantee of our righteousness, who is Jesus Christ, *who bore our sins in his own body upon the tree, who committed no sin*, and no deceit was found in his mouth; instead, for our sakes he endured all things, in order that we might live in him."

The allusions to 1 Pet 2:22-24 in Pol. *Phil.* 8.1 locate Polycarp in a stream of early Christian tradition that understands Jesus' death as a uniquely vicarious sacrifice that atones for sin. At the same time, after reminding the Philippians of the importance of the Pauline triad of faith, hope, and love, Polycarp earlier affirms that "the one who has love is far from all sin" (3.3). While Polycarp does not invoke Tobit explicitly to support the notion of atoning almsgiving, his pastoral response to Valens' avarice appears to be an encouragement that almsgiving can alleviate sin, for "charity delivers one from death." In order to heed this wisdom from Tobit mediated by the

---

[59] Berding, *Polycarp and Paul*, 105; Hartog, *Polycarp's Epistle to the Philippians*, 140. The claim for a direct citation of Tobit in *Pol. Phil.* 10.2 depends on the assumption that the Latin translator has accurately rendered Polycarp's phrasing. It has been suggested that the Latin *quia* is an abbreviated form of the scriptural citation formula "it is written"; so Roger T. Beckwith, *The Old Testament Canon of the New Testament Church and Its Background in Early Judaism* (Grand Rapids: Eerdmans, 1984), 336; Ken M. Penner, "Citation Formulae as Indices to Canonicity in Early Jewish and Early Christian Literature," in *Jewish and Christian Scriptures: The Function of "Canonical" and "Non-canonical" Religious Texts* (ed. James H. Charlesworth and Lee Martin McDonald; Jewish and Christian Texts in Contexts and Related Studies 7; London: T&T Clark, 2010), 62–84 [76, 84]. If Polycarp's (or his Latin translator's) *quia* is shorthand for "it is written," this would indicate that Polycarp considers Tobit to be a scriptural text. It is more likely, however, that *quia* is simply a translation of either διότι in Tob 4:10 or γάρ in Tob 12:9 (so Berding, *Polycarp and Paul*, 105; Hartog, *Polycarp's Epistle to the Philippians*, 140).

Smyrnaean bishop, however, Valens must forsake his ignorance regarding the Lord's judgment and recognize that care for the poor and the avoidance of avarice, two sides of the same ethical coin, are to be motivated by the expectation of the future judgment and future resurrection.[60]

Conclusion

Practices of gift-exchange, including care for the poor, have the power to engender, solidify, and occasionally threaten communal solidarity. For this reason, almsgiving, when it is practiced, is crucial to the formation and maintenance of communal identity. Practices of giving and receiving assistance "communicate a distinctive self-image of the community," both to insiders and to outsiders.[61]

In various but similar ways, Ignatius, the *Acts of Thomas*, 2 *Clement*, and Polycarp narrate a vision of Christian identity in which care for the poor is not only central but integrated into an eschatological hope that emphasizes bodily resurrection and God's judgment of deeds done in the body. This vision is forged in conversation and contrast with constructions of Christian identity in which, at least it is sometimes alleged, future resurrection and almsgiving are both rejected, either implicitly or explicitly. The advocacy of the meritorious (*Acts of Thomas*) and atoning (2 *Clement*, Polycarp) value of merciful deeds in these early Christian texts is forged in contrast with those who disregarded the body, including the bodies of the poor. To judge from these representative texts, then, practices of and discourses about almsgiving appear to have stood at the center of competing conceptions of Christian identity, solidarity, and community in the second and early third centuries.

---

[60] In this sense, I would offer a qualified agreement with Roman Garrison's claim that Polycarp advocates, in Garrison's terms, "redemptive almsgiving"; see Garrison, "The Love of Money in Polycarp's Letter to the Philippians," in *The Graeco-Roman Context of Early Christian Literature* (JSNTSup 137; Sheffield: Sheffield Academic, 1997), 74–79.

[61] Brown, *Poverty and Leadership*, 3. Rhee (*Loving the Poor*, 159–89) explores the issue of economics and early Christian identity with reference to a larger set of concerns, including business activities, the denunciation of avarice and luxury, almsgiving, and public service.

Chapter 8

BY ALMS AND FAITH SINS ARE
PURGED AWAY
Almsgiving and Atonement in Early Christian Scriptural Exegesis

Cyprian of Carthage was unquestionably one of the most influential ecclesiastical leaders of Latin Christianity in the third century. Perhaps no figure did more to guide the North African church through a tumultuous period of external persecution and internal conflict than Cyprian, who served as bishop of Carthage from 248 until his martyrdom in 258. Moreover, Cyprian's literary corpus continued to shape the development of North African Christianity in the centuries after his death. Appeals to Cyprian's writings on the role of the episcopate and the structure of the church were made, in diverse ways, by both parties of the Donatist controversy in the fourth and fifth centuries.[1] Perhaps most notably, however, Cyprian's treatise *De opere et eleemosynis* represents a seminal contribution to the emerging early Christian discourse about the atoning value of almsgiving.[2] Throughout the treatise, Cyprian offers scriptural support for his claim that almsgiving (*eleemosyna*) serves to purge the post-baptismal sins of the donor.[3]

---

[1] On Cyprian's legacy in North Africa, see J. Patout Burns, *Cyprian the Bishop* (Routledge Early Church Monographs; London: Routledge, 2002), 166–76.

[2] So, e.g., Jerome, *Epist.* 66.5, who recommends the text to Pammachius.

[3] I am inclined to place the composition of *Eleem.* in the short period after Cyprian's election as bishop of Carthage in 248 but prior to the outbreak of persecution under

233

Cyprian's *De opere et eleemosynis* appears to be the first "separate, formal, and independent treatise on *eleemosyna*" and its atoning value.[4] Yet as
much as Cyprian may be credited with an innovative discussion of the topic
of atoning almsgiving in *Eleem.*, the bishop's concentrated scriptural exegesis
in the work shows Cyprian's position to be coherent with, even if not directly
dependent upon, other earlier articulations of atoning almsgiving that also
reflect influence of scriptural traditions. The previous two chapters have
already suggested that the interpretation of texts or traditions from 1 Peter
and Tobit played an important role in the development of early Christian
advocacy of the atoning power of almsgiving.[5] Before considering Cyprian's
Eleem., it is worth examining the role of Scripture in two additional articulations of atoning almsgiving in the second century (the *Didache* and the *Epistle of Barnabas*), while also pausing to consider one document that obliquely
promotes atoning almsgiving, yet without any direct appeal to scriptural
antecedents—namely, the *Shepherd of Hermas*. With the *Shepherd of Hermas*
as a significant exception, it will be shown that second- and third-century

---

Decius in the winter of 249–250. The dating of this text does not greatly affect my interpretation of it, although I do not see Cyprian's advocacy of atoning almsgiving as a solution
developed in response to the problem of lapsed Christians during the Decian persecution. Hence, I follow the view of Edward V. Rebenack, *Thasci Caecili Cypriani: De opere
et eleemosynis; A Translation with an Introduction and a Commentary* (Patristic Studies
94; Washington, D.C.: Catholic University of America Press, 1962), 1–17; cf. Michael
Andrew Fahey, *Cyprian and the Bible: A Study in Third-Century Exegesis* (BGBH 9; Tübingen: J. C. B. Mohr, 1971), 20. In his important volume, Michel Poirier cautiously suggests
that the work was composed sometime between 253–256 (*Cyprien de Carthage: La bienfaisance et les aumônes; Introduction, texte critique, traduction, notes et index* [Sources Chrétiennes 440; Paris: Le Cerf, 1999], 19–21). For recent discussions that date the treatise to
the outbreak of plague in 252–253, see Geoffrey D. Dunn, "Cyprian's Care for the Poor:
The Evidence of *De opere et eleemosynis*," *StPatr* 42 (2006): 363–68; Helen Rhee, *Loving
the Poor, Saving the Rich: Wealth, Poverty, and Early Christian Formation* (Grand Rapids:
Baker, 2012), 66, 99–101. Although certainty in the matter is impossible, the severity of
the sin that can be redeemed through almsgiving in *Laps.* 35, a text written after the persecution, seems to me to reflect a very different, and far more serious, situation than the one
envisioned in *Eleem.* Moreover, atoning almsgiving was clearly not a strategy that Cyprian
developed in response to the failure of Christians during the Decian persecution (pace
William L. Countryman, *The Rich Christian in the Church of the Early Empire: Contradictions and Accommodations* [New York: Edwin Mellen, 1980], 195). Cyprian's selection of
biblical texts (e.g., Tob 4:5-11; Prov 16:6; Sir 3:30; Luke 11:40-41) in the section on the
benefit of works and alms in *Test.* 3.1 already shows his implicit advocacy of the concept of
atoning almsgiving before the persecution under Decius.
   [4] Rebenack, *Thasci Caecili Cypriani*, 17.
   [5] See also the allusions to LXX Prov 19:17 and LXX Prov 10:2 in *Sib. Or.* 2.78–89.

Christian advocacy of the atoning power of almsgiving emerges in part from engagement with scriptural traditions.

The *Didache* and the *Epistle of Barnabas*

The *Didache* is a second-century (or possibly first-century) text in which the promotion of the atoning power of merciful practice is supported by an allusion to Scripture. Although impossible to date with precision because of its composite nature and anonymous authorship, the *Didache* is a paraenetic document that addresses personal ethical formation, communal life, and the development of authority in the early church.[6] The text begins with instruction about "two ways, one of life and one of death" (1.1), and this "Two Ways" section covers *Did.* 1.1–6.2. Part of the instruction of the way of life includes teaching about the value of sharing generously:

> [5]Do not be someone who holds out the hands for receiving but who clenches the fists for giving. [6]If you have [something] through [the work of] your hands, give a redemption for your sins. [7]You shall not hesitate to give, nor shall you grumble when giving, for you know who is the good recompenser of the reward. [8]You shall not turn away from the one who has need. But you shall share all things with your brother, and you shall not say [that something is] your own. For if you are sharers in that which is immortal, how much more in that which is mortal? (*Did.* 4.5–8)

The passage employs themes of divine recompense (4.7), common ownership of possessions (4.8b), and mutual solidarity in spiritual and material matters (4.8c) in order to encourage among baptismal candidates unhesitant giving to and welcoming of those in need. This instruction appears to envision a scenario in which impoverished (or relatively impoverished) members of the church (cf. 4.14; 9.4; 10.5; 11.11) are not merely objects but also agents of almsgiving.[7] The command to hold out the hands both as a recipient and

---

[6] See Nancy Pardee, *The Genre and Development of the Didache: A Text-Linguistic Analysis* (WUNT II/231; Tübingen; Mohr Siebeck, 2012).

[7] See Denise Kimber Buell, "'Be Not One Who Stretches Out Hands to Recieve but Shuts Them When It Comes to Giving': Envisioning Christian Charity When Both Donors and Recipients Are Poor," in *Wealth and Poverty in Early Church and Society* (ed. Susan R. Holman; Holy Cross Studies in Patristic Theology and History; Grand Rapids: Baker, 2008), 37–47. Buell writes, "Though the rhetoric about charity creates an apparently mutually exclusive pairing—donor/recipient—some contexts allow for the possibility that the same person might in some instances be a donor and in other instances the recipient of charity. This cross-grained reading of the rhetoric offers one way to imagine

as a giver in verse 5—combined with the rhetoric of fictive kinship, which exhorts sharing everything with a brother or sister (4.8)—implies that someone might hold out hands for receiving but clench his or her fists when asked to give. This image implies that the objects of this pre-baptismal instruction may receive at times but should also give at times. Thus, the exhortation to merciful practice in the *Didache* does not assume a social setting in which material support is funneled from wealthy donors to poor recipients. Instead, in line with the fluidity of resource stratification and conjunctural poverty in Greco-Roman antiquity, the same individual might be a donor and a recipient at various points. In this context, "almsgiving" represents a mutual sharing of resources.

Particularly striking is the Didachist's exhortation—"If you have [something] through [the work of] your hands, give a redemption for your sins" (4.6)—for this statement reflects an early expression of the concept of atoning almsgiving. In this case, the term "redemptive almsgiving" would be appropriate because the metaphor suggests that sins are redeemed through giving away the fruit of one's manual labor. The verb δίδωμι ("give") is used four times in *Did.* 4.5–8, and the participle τὸν ἐνδεόμενον ("the one who has need") in verse 8 indicates that the object of one's giving is a brother or sister in material need. Thus, according to the logic of 4.6, the act of giving to a disadvantaged brother or sister is "a redemption for your sins." The construction δώσεις λύτρωσιν ἁμαρτιῶν σου is unusual, however, since the noun λύτρωσις in redemption imagery typically denotes the *experience* or *act* of being released from bondage, not the thing or price given to secure redemption.[8] In the LXX and other early Jewish literature, it is the noun λύτρον that

---

the economically marginal of antiquity as active agents. . . . In a context where resources are scarce the imperative to share what one has (again, interpreted as gifts from God) could also mean that many in the community could reasonably view themselves as in need; the onus is placed on the individual to strive to be a giver rather than a receiver— reinforcing the likelihood that the same person could potentially occupy both positions" (39, 45). Such a reading of this passage in the *Didache* is not without difficulties, not least because later in the document there is an explicit injunction to give the firstfruits of the community to those labeled "the poor" (δότε τοῖς πτωχοῖς) when there is no prophet present to receive the offering (13.4). Moreover, the vice-list of 5.1–2 critiques those who "show no mercy to the poor" (οὐκ ἐλεοῦντες πτωχόν) and those who "turn their backs on the needy, oppress the afflicted, and support the wealthy" (ἀποστρεφόμενοι τὸν ἐνδεόμενον καταπονοῦντες τὸν θλιβόμενον πλουσίων παράκλητοι). That the *Didache* can employ this binary rhetoric of "rich-poor" does not necessarily imperil the claim that the (relatively) impoverished were themselves agents of almsgiving, but these texts do challenge Buell's reading of *Did.* 4.5–8.

[8] So BDAG 4635: "experience of being liberated from an oppressive situation, transf. sense of commercial usage 'redemption of someth. for a price': ransoming, releasing,

usually designates the price or payment of the ransom, and thus it might be expected that the direct object of the verb δίδωμι would be λύτρον instead of λύτρωσις.[9] The entire phrase δώσεις λύτρωσιν ἁμαρτιῶν σου in ~~Did. 4~~.6 is also atypical because, depending on how the genitive ἁμαρτιῶν σου is understood, ~~the passage either implies that a redemption-price is to be given for the sake of one's sins or, perhaps more likely, that sins themselves are redeemed.~~[10]

For these reasons, Th Dan 4:27 suggests itself as an intriguing intertexual parallel to the phrase δώσεις λύτρωσιν ἁμαρτιῶν σου in *Did.* 4.6.[11] In Th Dan 4:27 the λυτρ- word is the verb λυτρόω, and the dual objects of λυτρόω are τὰς ἁμαρτίας σου ("your sins") and τὰς ἀδικίας σου ("your injustices"):

διὰ τοῦτο βασιλεῦ ἡ βουλή μου ἀρεσάτω σοι καὶ <u>τὰς ἁμαρτίας σου ἐν ἐλεημοσύναις λύτρωσαι καὶ τὰς ἀδικίας σου</u> ἐν οἰκτιρμοῖς πενήτων.

Therefore, O king, may my counsel be acceptable to you, and redeem your sins with acts of mercy and your injustices with compassion to the poor.

---

redemption." The notable exception to the usage of λύτρωσις as the experience of redemption is LXX Judg 1:15A, where λύτρωσις is also the object of the verb δίδωμι: καὶ εἶπεν αὐτῷ Ασχα δός μοι εὐλογίαν, ὅτι εἰς γῆν νότου ἐκδέδοσαί με, καὶ δώσεις μοι λύτρωσιν ὕδατος. καὶ ἔδωκεν αὐτῇ Χαλεβ κατὰ τὴν καρδίαν αὐτῆς τὴν λύτρωσιν μετεώρων καὶ τὴν λύτρωσιν ταπεινῶν ("And Ascha said to him, 'Give me a blessing, since you have given me away into the land of the south, you shall also give me the redemption of water.' And, according to her desire, Chaleb gave her the redemption of the upper and the redemption of the lower" [NETS]). The reading δώσεις in *Did.* 4.6 is found in Codex Hierosolymitanus (ca. 1056) and the early Georgian translation, but the *Const. Ap.* reads δὸς εἰς. The former reading is adopted by Holmes; the latter, by Ehrman. As Kurt Niederwimmer comments, the reading δώσεις λύτρωσιν "is indeed hard, but comprehensible" (*The Didache: A Commentary* [Hermeneia; Minneapolis: Fortress, 1998], 108).

[9] For this reason, BDAG offers a second gloss on λύτρωσις, one that includes *only* the usage of the noun in *Did.* 4.6 and *Barn.* 19.10: "2. abstr. for concr. ransom(-money) δώσεις λ. ἁμαρτιῶν σου you must give a ransom for your sins D 4:6; cp. B 19:10." For λύτρον as the ransom price, see Exod 21:30; 30:12; Lev 19:20; 25:51-52, 24-26; 27:31; Num 3:12, 46, 48-49, 51; 18:15; 35:31-32; Prov 6:35; 13:8; Isa 45:13. Obviously, the understanding λύτρον as a ransom/redemption price or payment in the LXX is important for the interpretation of the two instances in which the noun occurs in the NT—namely, in the "ransom sayings" of Mark 10:45 and Matt 20:28. For a discussion of λύτρον as a ransom price paid to liberate a captive and its significance for the Gospel of Matthew, see Nathan Eubank, *Wages of Cross-Bearing Sin: The Economy of Heaven in Matthew's Gospel* (BZNW 196; Berlin: De Gruyter, 2013), 148–62.

[10] That is, λύτρωσις in *Did.* 4.6 functions as ransom price paid (λύτρον) to bring release for sins, hence the translation "redemption for your sins."

[11] In OG Dan 4:27, it is injustices, not sins, that are redeemed with acts of mercy.

The phrasing in Th Dan 4:27 is itself unusual because, according to the normal biblical image of redemption, the verb λυτρόω typically refers to the redemption of some person(s) or thing(s) in bondage, not to the redemption of an abstract noun like "sin."[12] With the exception of Th Dan 4:27, when the biblical image of redemption is used as a soteriological metaphor in connection with sins or transgressions, it is sinners who are redeemed, not sins (cf. Isa 44:22; Col 1:14). This dynamic is nicely captured in LXX Ps 129:8: "[God] will redeem Israel from all his [i.e., Israel's] iniquities" (αὐτὸς λυτρώσεται τὸν Ισραηλ ἐκ πασῶν τῶν ἀνομιῶν αὐτοῦ). In fact, Th Dan 4:27, Did. 4.6, and Barn. 19.10 (see below) represent a rare combination of texts in early Jewish and/or Christian literature in which ἁμαρτίαι ("sins") are "redeemed."[13]

The language and metaphors in Th Dan 4:27 and Did. 4.6 are, therefore, distinctly similar: in Th Dan 4:27, Nebuchadnezzar is instructed to redeem his sins by means of merciful acts, and in Did. 4.6 giving to the needy is a redemption payment for sins. In both passages it is sins themselves that are redeemed by merciful practice on behalf of the needy and not, as the image of redemption would typically be used, sinners. In neither passage is there any indication of what might be holding sins in bondage and in need of redemption, but the image of redeeming sins (as opposed to sinners) is so unusual

---

[12] In the LXX, objects of λυτρόω include Israel or some other designation for the people of God (Exod 6:6; 15:13; Deut 7:8; 9:26; 13:6; 15:15; 21:8; 24:18; 2 Sam 7:23; 1 Chr 17:21; Neh 1:10; 1 Macc 4:11; Pss 24:22; 73:2; 76:16; 77:42; 105:10; 106:2; 129:8; 135:24; Sir 48:20; 49:10; 50:24; Isa 43:1, 14; 44:22-23; 51:11; 52:3; 62:12; 63:9; Jer 15:21; 38:11; Lam 5:8; Zeph 3:15); animals (Exod 13:13; 34:20; Lev 27:13; 27:27; Num 18:15, 17; Hos 7:13; 13:14; Mic 6:4; Zech 10:8; Isa 35:9); firstborn sons (Exod 13:13, 15); slaves (Lev 19:20; 25:48, 49, 54); possessions, houses, or fields (Lev 25:25, 30, 33; 27:15; 27:19-20); orphans (Prov 23:11); humans devoted to destruction (Lev 27:29); tithes (Lev 27:31, 33); and the life of an individual (2 Sam 4:9; 1 Kgs 1:29; Pss 7:3; 25:11; 30:6; 31:7; 33:23; 43:27; 48:8, 16; 54:19; 58:2; 68:19; 70:23; 71:14; 102:4; 118:134, 154; 143:10; Sir 51:2; Lam 3:58; Dan 3:88; 6:28).

[13] Doctrina apostolorum 4.5–8 should be included as well, but the tradition preserved in the Doctrina apostolorum is likely dependent upon the Didache, even if the Doctrina is not merely a Latin translation of the Didache; cf. Edgar Johnson Goodspeed, "The Didache, Barnabas and the Doctrina," AThR 27 (1945): 228–47; Berthold Altaner, "Zum Problem der lateinischen Doctrina Apostolorum," VC 6 (1952): 160–67; Roman Garrison, Redemptive Almsgiving in Early Christianity (JSNTSup 77; Sheffield: JSOT Press, 1993), 143–52. Conceptually, one might compare the phrase ἀντίψυχον γεγονότας τῆς τοῦ ἔθνους ἁμαρτίας in 4 Macc 17:21, but there the noun is ἀντίψυχος.

that it is highly likely that Th Dan 4:27 underlies the tradition preserved in *Did.* 4.6.[14]

It is necessary to speak of the underlying *tradition* preserved in *Did.* 4.6 because the exhortation "give a redemption for your sins" is part of the so-called "Two Ways" section in *Didache* 1–6, material that is paralleled in the *Epistle of Barnabas* 18–20.[15] *Barn.* 19.8–11 contains a series of instructions regarding practices of giving and receiving that correspond closely to the directives in *Did.* 4.5–8, including the statement in *Barn.* 19.10 that "you shall work with your hands for a redemption of your sins" (διὰ τῶν χειρῶν σου ἐργάσῃ εἰς λύτρον ἁμαρτιῶν σου):

> [8]You shall share in all things with your neighbor, and you shall not say [that something is] your own thing. For if you are sharers in the imperishable, how much more [should you share] in perishable things? Do not be talkative, for the mouth is a snare of death. Insofar as you are able, you shall be pure for the sake of your soul. [9]Do not be someone who holds out the hands for receiving but who clenches the fists for giving. You shall love as a pupil of your eye everyone who speaks to you the word of the Lord. [10]Remember the day of judgment night and day, and you shall seek out each day the faces of the saints, either laboring through the word and going out to encourage, and endeavoring to save a soul by the word, or you shall work with your hands for a redemption of your sins. [11]You shall not hesitate to give, nor shall you grumble when giving, but you will know who is the good recompenser of the reward. You shall guard what you have received, neither adding

---

[14] The possibility of an intertextual connection between Dan 4:27 and *Did.* 4.6 is not common in secondary literature (e.g., it is not mentioned in William Varner, "The Didache's Use of the Old and New Testaments," *MSJ* 16 [2005]: 127–51), but the suggestion is not entirely novel. Eubank asserts that *Did.* 4.5–7 "echoes Sirach 4:31 and Daniel 4:24"; see Eubank, *Wages of Cross-Bearing Sin*, 45; so also Gary A. Anderson, *Sin: A History* (New Haven: Yale University Press, 2010), 150. Eubank is surely correct that *Did.* 4.5 echoes Sir 4:31. That Sir 3:30 also advocates atoning almsgiving is suggestive when considering the scriptural influences upon atoning almsgiving in *Did.* 4.5–8, but the influence of Th Dan 4:27 is far more evident.

[15] The general consensus is that there is no direct literary relationship between the *Didache* and *Barnabas*; rather, both the *Didache* and *Barnabas* share a common Two Ways source that informs each text independently. See Goodspeed, "Didache, Barnabas and the Doctrina"; John S. Kloppenborg, "The Transformation of Moral Exhortation in Didache 1–5," in *Didache in Context: Essays on Its Text, History, and Transmission* (ed. Clayton N. Jefford; NovTSup 77; Leiden: Brill, 1995), 88–109; James N. Rhodes, "The Two Ways Tradition in the Epistle of Barnabas: Revisiting an Old Question," *CBQ* 73 (2011): 797–816.

nor subtracting. You shall completely hate the evil one. You shall judge righteously.

The command in *Barn*. 19.10 to "work with your hands for a redemption of your sins" is set explicitly within an eschatological framework. The earlier injunction to "remember the day of judgment, night and day" (19.10) serves as a warrant for the exhortation to care for the saints, either spiritually through encouraging speech or materially through sharing the proceeds of manual labor.[16] Moreover, the exhortation to give unhesitatingly and without grumbling in 19.11 is rooted in the knowledge that God is "the good recompenser of the reward." Charity, therefore, is to be practiced with God's judgment and the hope of divine reward in mind. As in *Did*. 4.6, so also in *Barn*. 19.10 the idea that daily seeking out the faces of the saints in order to offer provision represents work with one's hands "for a redemption of your sins" (εἰς λύτρον ἁμαρτιῶν σου) suggests the influence of Th Dan 4:27 on the tradition preserved in *Barnabas'* version of the Two Ways material.

That the *Didache* and *Barnabas* both draw upon the Two Ways tradition to claim that sins can be ransomed through almsgiving has sometimes been interpreted as an indication that these texts have abandoned or compromised the early Christian doctrine of grace.[17] Yet locating the affirmation of atoning almsgiving in the *Didache* and *Barnabas* in the genre and literary context of these documents mitigates this objection.

---

[16] The phrase "you shall work with your hands for a redemption of your sins" in *Barn*. 19.10 is perhaps a bit more ambiguous than the *Didache*'s phrasing: "If you have [something] through [the work of] your hands, give a redemption for your sins" (4.6). The verb δώσεις ("you shall give") in *Did*. 4.6 more clearly indicates that what is gained through labor should be given to a needy brother or sister. Yet the instruction about not being reticent or peevish when giving in *Barn*. 19.11 clarifies that one cares for the saints in 19.10 either through encouraging speech or through the provision of material support.

[17] Thomas F. Torrance, for example, says of the *Didache*: "There seems to be little doubt that deity is ascribed to Christ, but there is wanting here the warm joyous relation to Jesus such as we would expect from sinners who had been graciously forgiven and redeemed by Christ. . . . The person of Christ is not central, and there is very little apprehension of the amazing love of God in salvation and election. On the contrary, God is viewed almost exclusively as the Lawgiver and Judge who will reward the righteous, and as Master and Almighty" (*The Doctrine of Grace in the Apostolic Fathers* [Grand Rapids: Eerdmans, 1959], 39–40). On *Barnabas*, Torrance writes, "No doubt in an age characterised by such wanton lawlessness and libertinism as was the Graeco-Roman world in the second century, there was some excuse for presenting the Christian message under the form of law, but the result of this tended to be a thoroughgoing formalism and legalism, and the development of a doctrine of salvation by works. There is no doubt that this stage is reached in Barnabas. There could be nothing more crass than the words, 'By thy hands thou shalt work for the redemption of thy sins'" (108).

Barnabas appears to represent an attempt to encourage "covenant fidelity and eschatological perseverance" among those who already identify as followers of Jesus.[18] Assuming that the Two Ways material in *Barnabas* 18–20 is not merely a secondary appendix awkwardly added to the polemical material in chapters 1 to 16 but instead is deeply integrated into the literary and theological structure of the document, it is striking how regularly God's gracious initiative is emphasized elsewhere in *Barnabas*.[19] The letter opens, for example, with a reminder of divine love, righteousness, and grace:

[1]Greetings, sons and daughters, in the name of the Lord who has loved us, in peace. [2]Seeing that God's righteous acts toward you are so great and rich, I rejoice with an unbounded and overflowing joy over your blessed and glorious spirits; so deeply implanted is the grace of the spiritual gift that you have received! (*Barn.* 1.1–2)[20]

[18] So James N. Rhodes, *The Epistle of Barnabas and the Deuteronomic Tradition: Polemics, Paraenesis, and the Legacy of the Golden-Calf Incident* (WUNT II/188; Tübingen: Mohr Siebeck, 2004), 180–81.

[19] My reading of *Barnabas* is influenced by James Rhodes' argument that "the author's recourse to [the Two Ways] tradition is both too broad to be dismissed as incidental and too deep to be regarded as merely rhetorical; it is integral to Barnabas's mode of thinking" ("Two Ways Tradition," 800). As Rhodes demonstrates, there are particularly strong conceptual and linguistic links between the Two Ways material in *Barn.* 18–20 and *Barn.* 4 and 10. Thus, I treat *Barnabas* (chs. 1–21) as a coherent whole and do not seek to resolve tensions by appealing to an awkward stitching together of conflicting sources or perspectives.

[20] Translation from Michael W. Holmes, *The Apostolic Fathers: Greek Texts and English Translations* (3rd ed.; Grand Rapids: Baker, 2007), 381; unless otherwise noted, translations from *Barnabas* in the following section are also from Holmes. Tracing the theme of divine initiative in the entirety of *Barnabas* would be a tedious task. A sampling from merely the first four chapters would include the following: readers are said to have received "the Spirit [that] has been poured out upon you from the riches of the Lord's fountain" (1.3); readers are marked by great faith and love "though the hope of his [i.e., the Lord's] life (1.4)," and it is this hope of life that is both the first doctrine of the Lord and the beginning and end of faith (1.6); knowledge of things past and present has come from God through the prophets (1.7; cf. 2.4); the "new law of our Lord Jesus Christ" is "free from the yoke of compulsion" (2.6); the "gracious intention of our Father" (τὴν γνώμην τῆς ἀγαθωσύνης τοῦ πατρὸς ἡμῶν) speaks to readers and reminds them that God need not be approached through animal sacrifices (2.9); God, who is patient, "revealed everything to us in advance" (3.6); the "covenant of the beloved Jesus" is sealed in readers' hearts "by his faithfulness" (4.8; my translation of ἐν ἐλπίδι τῆς πίστεως αὐτοῦ, which I take as a subjective genitive; see Michael R. Whitenton, "After Pistis Christou: Evidence from the Apostolic Fathers," *JTS* 61 [2010]: 82–109 [101–2]); and the author employs the language of justification and election with the implication God is the actor (4.10–14; cf. 6.1).

With regard to the theme of atonement, Barnabas clearly emphasizes the death of Jesus as an atoning sacrifice that accomplishes forgiveness of sin. This view is first and perhaps most emphatically introduced in chapter 5. After warning readers not to become like the Israelites who fell asleep in their sins because of their confidence in their election as God's people (4.13–14), the author writes, "For it was for this reason that the Lord endured the deliverance of his flesh to corruption, so that we might be cleansed by the forgiveness of sins, that is, sprinkled by his blood" (5.1). The author then glosses this soteriological confession with a citation of LXX Isa 53:5, 7, reading the suffering of Yahweh's Servant in Isaiah 53 as a figure who "relates partly to Israel and partly to us" (5.2).[21] In this chapter, too, the purpose of the incarnation itself is depicted as dealing with the sins of those who persecuted God's spokespersons: "Therefore the Son of God came in the flesh for this reason, so that he might complete the full measure of the sins of those who persecuted his prophets to death" (5.11).

Later, the author of Barnabas interprets Jesus' death as a typological fulfillment of the sacrificial offering of Isaac by Abraham. The Lord (Jesus), the author states, "was planning to offer the vessel of his spirit as a sacrifice for our sins" (7.3). The nature of Jesus' sacrificial death for the sins of his people is then revealed in a figural reading of an unknown prophetic statement that is ostensibly fulfilled in Jesus' consumption of drink mixed with gall and vinegar upon the cross (7.4–5). The commandment in Leviticus 16 to identify two goats—one sacrificed as a sin offering, one offered as a cursed scapegoat—is read as a "type" (τύπος) of Jesus (7.6–8), as is the atoning slaughter of the red heifer in 8.1–7, an Old Testament figure interpreted allegorically such that the calf represents Jesus and "the children who sprinkle are those who preached to us the good news about the forgiveness of sins and the purification of the heart" (8.2). Clearly, for the author of Barnabas, atonement for sin comes through the Christ-event.

While the death of Jesus is an atoning sacrifice, the ritual of baptism, too, washes away sins in connection with the cross. Barnabas 11, for instance, offers a reflection on whether the Lord foreshadowed "the water and the cross" in Israel's Scriptures (11.1). The Israelites are accused of refusing to accept "the baptism that brings forgiveness of sins," since they choose instead to create a substitute for themselves.[22] The author cites a string of scriptural texts to make this point (11.2–7), punctuated by a quotation of LXX Ps 1:3-6, presumably because the psalmist's claim that "the one who does these things

---

[21] Barn. 5.5 also emphasizes the vicarious suffering of Jesus, characterizing him as the one who "submitted to suffer for our souls."

[22] The precise nature of the substitute is not specified.

will be like the tree that is planted by the streams of water" brings together imagery of a tree (= the cross) and water (= baptism). As the author of *Barnabas* glosses this citation, "Notice how he [i.e., the psalmist] pointed out the water and the cross together. For this is what he means: blessed are those who, having set their hope on the cross, descended into the water" (11.8). The author of *Barnabas* then attempts to clarify the connection between the cross and baptism at the end of this section with an interpretation of an unknown citation, or possibly with a loose paraphrase of the image of a life-giving river that flows from the temple in Ezek 47:1-12. Here the author affirms that baptism cleanses and effects new life:

> [10]Then what does he say? "And there was a river flowing on the right hand, and beautiful trees were rising from it, and whoever eats from them will live forever." [11]By this he means that while we descend into the water laden with sins and dirt, we rise up bearing fruit in our heart and with fear and hope in Jesus in our spirits. "And whoever eats from these will live forever" means this: whoever, he says, hears these things spoken and believes them will live forever. (*Barn.* 11.10–11)

If *Barn.* 11.10–11 does draw upon imagery from Ezekiel 47 to frame Jesus' death and baptism as twin events that atone for sin and bring eternal life, the temple imagery in chapter 11 would also correspond to the author's discussion of the temple in chapter 16.[23] In *Barnabas* 16, the author condemns "those wretched people" who desire, in the past and in the author's present, to localize God's presence in a building (16.1–6); instead, the author of *Barnabas* maintains that there is a temple of God in the hearts of those who call upon God.[24] The Lord's true temple is gloriously constructed "by receiving the forgiveness of sins and setting our hope upon the Name" (16.8): "For those who long to be saved look not to the human speaker but to the one who dwells and speaks in that person, and are amazed by the fact that they had never before heard such words from the mouth of the speaker not had they themselves ever desired to hear them. This is the spiritual temple that is being built for the Lord" (16.10).

---

[23] But see the cautions in Rhodes, *Epistle of Barnabas*, 63–64.

[24] *Barn.* 16.4–5 has figured significantly in proposals regarding the historical context of the document, including the view that *Barnabas* is written in the context of concern about plans either to rebuild the temple in Jerusalem or to build a temple to Jupiter on the site of the destroyed temple; see James Carleton Paget, *The Epistle of Barnabas: Outlook and Background* (WUNT II/64; Tübingen: Mohr Siebeck, 1994), 17–30; Rhodes, *Epistle of Barnabas*, 86–87.

There is little doubt that, according to the theological perspective of *Barnabas*, forgiveness of sin comes through the sacrificial death of Jesus and the act of baptism, a ritual that is closely connected to the cross. How, then, can the author of *Barnabas* state, "You shall work with your hands for a redemption of your sins" (19.10)? The answer is probably found in the author's use of the imagery of redemption elsewhere in the letter. In chapter 14, the author draws upon the Mount Sinai narrative in order to make a distinction between the Israelites, who were given God's covenant but "were not worthy to receive it because of their sins" (14.1; cf. 14.4), and the author and his readers: "Moses received [the covenant] as a servant, but the Lord himself gave it to us, so that we might become people of inheritance, by suffering for us" (14.4). Following this assertion that he and his readers have become people of inheritance through the Lord's vicarious suffering is an extended reflection on the redemption available in the covenant for the true people of inheritance. The concentrated appearance of the language of redemption in this section seemingly derives from the preceding memory of the Exodus:

> [5]And [the Lord] was made manifest in order that they might fill up the measure of their sins and we might receive the covenant through the Lord Jesus who inherited it, who was prepared for this purpose, in order that by appearing in person and *redeeming from darkness* (λυτρωσάμενος ἐκ τοῦ σκότους) our hearts, which had already been paid over to death and given over to lawlessness of error, he might establish a covenant in us by his word. [6]For it is written how the Father commands him to *redeem us from darkness* (ἐντέλλεται λυτρωσάμενον ἡμᾶς ἐκ τοῦ σκότους) and to prepare a holy people for himself. [7]Therefore the prophet says, "I, the Lord your God, have called you in righteousness, and I will grasp your hand and strengthen you; and I have given you as a covenant to the peple, a light to the nations, to open the eyes of the blind, and to release from their shackles those who are bound and from the prison house those who sit in darkness" (LXX Isa 42:6-7). *We understand, therefore, from what we have been redeemed* (γινώσκομεν οὖν πόθεν ἐλυτρώθημεν). [8]Again the prophet says, "Behold, I have established you as a light to the nations, so that you may be the means of salvation to the ends of the earth; *thus says the Lord God who redeemed you* (οὕτως λέγει κύριος ὁ λυτρωσάμενός σε θεός)" (cf. LXX 49:6-7). (*Barn.* 14.5–8)

In this reframing of the Exodus narrative, Moses is replaced by Jesus, and the Israelites are replaced by the author and his readers. But "redemption" is still a divine initiative and activity.

Interestingly, outside of chapter 14, the only other place in *Barnabas* where the language of "redemption" is used is in chapter 19, where it occurs twice.[25] The first instance is 19.2, which is the opening articulation of the content of the "Two Ways" material, providing the knowledge given to readers so that they might walk in the way of light (19.1): "You shall love the one who made you; you shall fear the one who created you; you shall glorify the one who redeemed you from death" (δοξάσεις τόν σε λυτρωσάμενον ἐκ θανάτου). This statement both hearkens back to the language of redemption in chapter 14 and provides the context in which to understand the command in 19.10: "You shall work with your hands for a redemption of your sins." The entirety of the Two Ways instruction in chapters 18 to 20 is preceded by the affirmation, highlighted especially by the language of redemption in chapter 14, that readers of the letter are recipients of God's covenant because God is the one who has redeemed them from darkness and death. The first command of the Two Ways in 19.2, then, functions as both a mandate and a reminder: it is a rule that encourages readers to remember the one responsible for their existence and redemption. The author of *Barnabas* sees no contradiction in affirming both the identity of God as redeemer and the notion that alms can be given as a redemption for sins, perhaps because those who practice "the way of light" (19.12) do so only because they have been redeemed from darkness. God's redemption of his covenant people represents the theological context in which the people of God are able to work with their hands for a redemption of their sins.

It is more difficult to locate the affirmation of atoning (or, more specifically, "redemptive") almsgiving in *Did.* 4.6 in the larger theological context of the *Didache* because, on the whole, the *Didache* offers very little in the way of soteriological reflection. Transgressions are to be confessed in the congregation (ἐκκλησία [4.14]), in part to keep pure the communal meal celebrated on the Lord's Day (14.1). *Didache* 8.2 cites a prayer from Jesus tradition that employs the language of forgiveness and debt ("forgive us our debt, as we also forgive our debtors"), but there is no discussion of any mechanism by which forgiveness is granted. The instruction regarding the celebration of the eucharistic meal in *Did.* 9.1–10.7 makes no obvious reference to Jesus' death, let alone to Jesus' death as an atoning sacrifice.

Perhaps the only soteriological statement with reference to the cross is found in *Did.* 16.5: "Then the creation of humans will come to the fire of testing, and many will fall away and perish, but those who endure in their

---

[25] One difference is that in 14.6–8 readers are consistently said to have been redeemed from "darkness" (cf. 18.1), not death.

faith will be saved by him who was cursed" (ὑπ' αὐτοῦ τοῦ καταθέματος). Yet it is not clear that *Did.* 16.5 should read as a reference to the crucified Jesus in the sense that Paul understands the crucifixion as a curse (Gal 3:13), particularly since the phrase ὑπ' αὐτοῦ τοῦ καταθέματος might alternatively be translated "by the curse itself" and also since the *Didache* nowhere else mentions the saving significance of the cross.[26] That the *Didache* does not develop or even reflect a soteriology of the Christ-event should not be ascribed to any theological deficiency, however. The purpose of the *Didache* appears to be to teach new converts about the ways of life appropriate for participation in a community that baptizes in the name of the Father, Son, and Holy Spirit (7.1), while also providing instruction regarding various aspects of community organization and practice (6.3–15.4).[27] Since the *Didache* is not a theological, and certainly not a soteriological, treatise, it should not be criticized for not offering a "theology of the cross."

At the same time, it is likely that the community or individual responsible for the *Didache* understood atoning almsgiving to be entirely consistent with known proto-Orthodox Christian belief, a point suggested by the fact that discussions of ἐλεημοσύνη ("merciful practice") at the beginning (1.5–6) and end (15.3–4) of the *Didache* frame merciful practice with reference to other early Christian traditions about "almsgiving."

The more obvious connection between early Christian tradition and the *Didache*'s encouragement of almsgiving is found at the end of the document, just before the final eschatological discourse in 16.1–8, where readers are instructed to act in ways that cohere with "the gospel":

> [3]Correct one another, not in anger, but in peace, *as you have [it] in the gospel* (ὡς ἔχετε ἐν τῷ εὐαγγελίῳ); and to everyone who commits a wrong against another person, let no one speak, nor let the wrongdoer hear a word from you, until he repents. [4]And with regard to your prayers and merciful practices (τὰς ἐλεημοσύνας) and all your deeds, do them in this way, *as you have [it] in the gospel of our Lord* (ἐν τῷ εὐαγγελίῳ τοῦ κυρίου ἡμῶν). (*Did.* 15.3–4)

That prayers and merciful deeds are mentioned together immediately after a directive regarding repentance is not an indication that merciful deeds

---

[26] For different perspectives, see Aaron Milavec, "The Saving Efficacy of the Burning Process in Didache 16.5," in *Didache in Context: Essays on Its Text, History, and Transmission* (ed. Clayton N. Jefford; NovTSup 77; Leiden: Brill, 1995), 131–55; Nancy Pardee, "The Curse That Saves (Didache 16.5)," in *Didache in Context: Essays on Its Text, History, and Transmission* (ed. Clayton N. Jefford; NovTSup 77; Leiden: Brill, 1995), 156–76.

[27] Pardee, *Genre and Development of the Didache.*

symbolize or effect repentance, for the commands in verses 3 and 4 do not appear to be logically or thematically connected.[28] The author of the *Didache* does maintain, however, that instruction about merciful practices (ἐλεημοσύναι) is provided "in the gospel of our Lord." Whether this "gospel" is a written text, such as the Gospel of Matthew, or a reference to oral tradition familiar to readers of the *Didache* is sharply debated.[29] It is clear, however, that the Didachist assumes that "the gospel of our Lord" provides some guidance about prayers, "merciful practices," and other deeds. Thus, either oral tradition or a written gospel ostensibly supplements the *Didache's* teaching about almsgiving.

More allusive but perhaps more intriguing is the discussion of giving and receiving in *Did.* 1.5–6, a passage that confirms that the language of ἐλεημοσύνη in *Did.* 15.4 refers to the merciful practice of almsgiving:

> [5]Give to everyone who asks you, and do not ask for anything back, for the Father wishes [people] to give to everyone from the gifts that have been graciously given to them. Blessed is the one who gives according to the commandment, for that person is innocent. Woe to the one who receives. For, on the one hand, if someone who has a need receives, that person will be innocent. But, on the other hand, the one who does not have a need will give an account [of] why he or she received and for what reason, and when that person is in prison he or she will be questioned about that which he or she did and he or she will not be free from there until which [time] he or she pays back the last penny. [6]But then about such a thing is it is said, "Let your merciful gift[30] (ἡ ἐλεημοσύνη σου) sweat in your hands until you know to whom you give."

This passage offers two potential points of contact with other early Christian traditions regarding almsgiving. In *Did.* 1.6, there is an explicit quotation of

---

[28] Niederwimmer, *Didache*, 204–5.

[29] See, e.g., James A. Kelhoffer, "'How Soon a Book' Revisited: Euangelion as a Reference to 'Gospel' Materials in the First Half of the Second Century," *ZNW* 95 (2004): 1–34; Christopher M. Tuckett, "The *Didache* and the Writings That Later Formed the New Testament," in *The Reception of the New Testament in the Apostolic Fathers* (ed. Andrew Gregory and Christopher Tuckett; NTAF 1; Oxford: Oxford University Press, 2005), 83–127; Young, *Jesus Tradition in the Apostolic Fathers*, 201–25.

[30] In this instance, it is appropriate to translate ἡ ἐλεημοσύνη σου as "your merciful gift" because the proverbial image of holding ἡ ἐλεημοσύνη σου in one's hand implies that this is a material distribution and not a merciful deed more generally; pace Steven L. Bridge ("To Give or Not to Give? Deciphering the Saying of Didache 1.6," *JECS* 5 [1997]: 555–68 [562–63]), who draws an unnecessary distinction between "alms" and "almsgiving."

a saying, the origin of which is impossible to identify with certainty.[31] The introductory phrase "But then about such a thing is it is said" (ἀλλὰ καὶ περὶ τούτου δὲ εἴρηται), however, has been interpreted as an indication that the Didachist understands the source of this saying to be scriptural.[32] Interestingly, numerous "Latin writers from Augustine onward know the saying in a form closely related to the *Didache* version; moreover, they frequently cite it as 'Scripture.'"[33] That much of the reception history of this saying in the Latin Church identifies the maxim as scriptural is not proof that the author of the Didache also considered the saying to be Scripture. It may be the case that Augustine, who several times cites the saying as Scripture, decisively influenced the Western tradition on this point. At the same time, the introductory formula itself should probably be interpreted as an indication that the saying, whatever its origin, was viewed as an authoritative scriptural source by the author of the *Didache*.[34]

The other connection between *Did.* 1.5–6 and early Christian tradition is an intriguing parallel between 1.5 and the *Shepherd of Hermas*. In Herm. *Mand.* 2.4–7, the Shepherd says to Hermas:

> [4]Clothe yourself with reverence, in which there is no wicked cause for offense, but everything is smooth and joyful. Work at what is good, and from your labors, which God gives you, give generously to all who are in need, not debating to whom you should give and to whom you

---

[31] Suggestions have included Sir 12:1 and *Sib. Or.* 2.79. Bridge argues that *Did.* 1.6 should be rendered, "Let your almsgiving bring sweat to your hands, until you know that it is to God to whom you are giving" ("To Give or Not to Give?"). Bridge's reread-ing is unconvincing, however, because he places too much weight on an alleged tension between the directive to give to everyone who asks in 1.5 and (according to the traditional reading of the passage) the exhortation to exercise discernment about the recipient of one's alms in 1.6.

[32] So Niederwimmer, *Didache*, 83: "At this point, I believe, the Didachist intro-duces a quotation from Sacred Scripture (which of course meant the 'Old' Testament) to serve as a warning against too-hasty giving and also as a scriptural foundation for such a warning (v. 6)."

[33] Niederwimmer, *Didache*, 84. Niederwimmer lists Augustine, *Enarrat Ps.* 102:12 (CCSL 40.1462); *Enarrat Ps.* 103 *Hom.* 3.10 (CCSL 40.1509); *Enarrat Ps.* 146:17 (CCSL 40.2135); Cassiodorus, *Expositiones in Psalterium* 40 (PL 70.295D); *Expositiones in Psal-terium* 103 (PL 70.733B); Gregory the Great, *Regula Pastoralis* 3.20 (PL 77.84CD); *Vita Chrodegangi episcopi Mettensium* 11.27; Abelard, *De Eleemosyna Sermo* 1.552; Bernard of Clairvaux, *Ep.* 95 (PL 182.228C); Peter Comestor, *Historia Scholastica, Liber Deuter-onomii* 5 (PL 198.1251C); Piers Plowman, B, *Passus* 7.75; Peter Cantor, *Verbum abbrevia-tum* 47 (PL 205.105B); Guntherus Cisterciensis, *De Oratione, Ieiunio et Eleemosyna*13.1 (PL 212.211BC); Innocent III, *De Eleemos* 5 (PL 217.756B); and Hugh of St. Cher, 3.194.

[34] So also Clayton N. Jefford, "Locating the Didache," *Forum* 3 (2014): 39–68 [47].

should not give. Give to everyone, for God wishes everyone to be given [something] from his own gifts (πᾶσιν δίδου· πᾶσιν γὰρ ὁ θεὸς δίδοσθαι θέλει ἐκ τῶν ἰδίων δωρημάτων). Therefore, those who receive will give back an account to God, about why they received and to what end. For distressed persons who receive will not be judged, but those who receive out of hypocrisy will pay a penalty. Therefore, the one who gives is innocent (ὁ οὖν διδοὺς ἀθῷός ἐστιν), for as he was given from the Lord a service to undertake, he undertook it generously, not thinking about to whom to give or not to give. This service, therefore, when generously undertaken, becomes glorious in God's sight. Therefore, the one who serves generously in this way will live to God. Therefore, keep this commandment, as I have spoken it to you (φύλασσε οὖν τὴν ἐντολὴν ταύτην ὥς σοι λελάληκα), in order that your repentance and the repentance of your household may be found in generosity and [your repentance] be pure and innocent and blameless.

More will be said about this passage from the *Shepherd of Hermas* below. Here it is sufficient to note that, assuming that there is no literary relationship between the *Didache* and the *Shepherd of Hermas*, both texts appear to be drawing upon a shared source, either written or oral.[35] Much as in the allusion to Th Dan 4:27 in *Did.* 4.6, there is an allusion to tradition in order to bolster ethical instruction, yet that tradition is not cited or identified. Additionally, the *Didache*'s macarism "Blessed is the one who gives according to the commandment" (1.5; cf. Herm. *Mand.* 2.6, 7) appears to be redactional, since the reference to "this commandment" (τὴν ἐντολὴν ταύτην) in Herm. *Mand.* 2.7 represents a commonly used construction in the narrative of *Hermas*.[36] Since the imperative "give according to the commandment" occurs twice later in the *Didache* (13.5, 7), both times with reference to the merciful provision of material support (i.e., food, money, clothing, and other possessions) to the poor, the *Didache* provides compelling evidence that giving "according to the commandment" served as a locution for almsgiving.[37]

---

[35] It is almost certain that the overlapping material stems from two independent uses of common tradition and not from any literary relationship between the *Didache* and the *Shepherd of Hermas*; see Osiek, *Shepherd of Hermas: A Commentary* (Hermeneia; Minneapolis: Fortress, 1999), 26–27; Niederwimmer, *Didache*, 68–72; Anthony Giambrone, "'According to the Commandment' [*Did.* 1.5]: Lexical Reflections on Almsgiving as 'The Commandment,'" *NTS* 60 (2014): 458–59. Herm. *Vis.* 5.7 does offer instruction that parallels the Two Ways tradition in several respects.

[36] Cf. *Mand.* 1.2; 3.2; 5.8; 8.12; *Sim.* 5.2, 7; 56.3; on this point, see Giambrone, "According to the Commandment," 458–59.

[37] Giambrone, "According to the Commandment."

The *Didache* and *Barnabas* both encourage not only merciful care for the poor but also almsgiving as a means of "redeeming" sins. Support for atoning almsgiving in the *Didache* and *Barnabas* comes from the Two Ways tradition, which itself alludes to Th Dan 4:27. Yet while both the *Didache* and *Barnabas* assert that sins can be redeemed by giving to those in need, in neither text is there any indication that this conviction stands in tension with the belief that atonement for sin comes through the death of Jesus, although the point is clearer in *Barnabas* than in the *Didache*.

Shepherd of Hermas

Any study of meritorious and atoning almsgiving in second-century Christianity must address the parable of the vine and the elm in Herm. *Sim.* 2. In this parable, Hermas observes an elm tree and a vine while walking in the countryside. As Hermas is reflecting on the complementarity of the elm and the vine (2.1: εὐπρεπέστατί εἰσιν ἀλλήλαις), the Shepherd appears and interprets the two plants as "a symbol (τύπος) of the servants of God" (2.2). According to the Shepherd's interpretation, the viticultural symbiosis between the vine, which bears fruit but cannot support itself, and the elm, which supports the vine but is fruitless on its own, reflects the synergetic relationship between the rich and the poor among God's servants:

> [5]The rich have much wealth, but are poor in the things of the Lord, being distracted by their wealth, and they have very little confession and prayer with the Lord, and what they do have is small and weak and has no power above. So whenever the rich go up to the poor and supply them their needs, they believe that what they do for the poor will be able to find a reward from God (δυνήσεται τὸν μισθὸν εὑρεῖν παρὰ τῷ θεῷ), because the poor are rich in intercession and confession, and their intercession has great power with God. The rich, therefore, unhesitatingly provide the poor with everything. [6]And the poor, being provided for by the rich, pray for them, thanking God for those who share with them. And the rich in turn are all the more zealous on behalf of the poor, in order that they may lack nothing in their life, for the rich know that the intercession of the poor is acceptable and rich before God. [7]They both, then, complete their work: the poor work with prayer, in which they are rich, which they received from the Lord; and this they return to the Lord who supplies them with it. And the rich likewise unhesitatingly share with the poor the wealth that they received from the Lord. And this work is great and acceptable to God, because the

rich understand about their wealth and work for the poor by using the gifts of the Lord, and correctly fulfill their ministry. (*Sim.* 2.5–7)[38]

The rhetoric of "rich/poor" in *Sim.* 2 does reflect a binary construct that allows these two groups to exist in symbiosis, and the nature of that complementary relationship limits the active agency of the poor to their spiritual act of prayer.[39] In this sense, a critical reading of the parable might suggest that *Hermas* assumes and legitimates maintenance of the status quo, for the economic vision of the parable allows the rich to maintain their wealth and keeps the poor in poverty.[40] Perhaps *Sim.* 2 even reinforces the notion of the "pious poor," who are called to serve the rich with their prayers while being held in a parasitic economic relationship overseen by their wealthy patrons.

Several elements of the *Shepherd of Hermas* resist such a critical reading of the parable of the vine and the elm, however. The story of the main character in the narrative, for example, the freedman Hermas (*Vis.* 1.1.1), suggests that the categories of "rich" and "poor" are more fluid than fixed, for Hermas himself, though a former slave, was once rich, presumably through some business enterprise (*Vis.* 3.6.7). But because of economic misfortune Hermas finds himself able to farm only one field (*Vis.* 3.1.2; 3.6.7; cf. *Mand.* 3.5). Something of the instability of the categories of "rich" and "poor" might also be indicated by the fact that, while the parable of the vine and the elm appears to be an allegory of some sort, it is never actually clear whether the elm represents the rich and the vine represents the poor, or vice versa.[41] This parabolic ambiguity complicates an easy identification of one group as supportive yet fruitless and the other group as fruit-bearing yet needing support, and the ambiguity surrounding the identity of the vine and the elm enhances

[38] Translation from Holmes, *Apostolic Fathers*, 561–63. A similar dynamic of exchange between the rich and the poor is also reflected in *1 Clem.* 38.2.

[39] See Carolyn A. Osiek, *Rich and Poor in the Shepherd of Hermas: An Exegetical-Social Investigation* (CBQMS 15; Washington, D.C: Catholic Biblical Association of America, 1983), 78–90; Buell, "Be Not One," 37–38. Herm. *Vis.* 3.9.5–6 offers something of an inverted picture: the warning is that the hungry and needy might groan to God, and, as a result of their pleas being heard by God, the wealthy will be shut out of the tower.

[40] So Susan R. Holman, *The Hungry Are Dying: Beggars and Bishops in Roman Cappadocia* (Oxford Studies in Historical Theology; Oxford: Oxford University Press, 2001), 124.

[41] As Osiek writes, "Different parts of the chapter lend themselves better to one interpretation than to the other, and probably neither was intended to be the only one. Exact correspondence is not the point of the teaching, but mutual help and dependence" (*Shepherd of Hermas*, 163). Osiek also argues effectively that the wealthy in Hermas are not members of the urban elite but rather relatively well-off among the nonelite; they might be plotted as PS4 on Friesen's seven-tiered poverty scale (see *Rich and Poor*, 136–37).

the motif of their mutuality.[42] Poor believers are granted agency in this exchange because they intercede on behalf of rich believers before God. In a cultural and religious context in which spiritual power matters, the agency of the poor should not be underestimated.

Additionally, the parable of the vine and the elm in Herm. *Sim.* 2 is an example of *meritorious* but not *atoning* almsgiving. Rich Christians are initially promised "reward from God" for their material support of poor Christians (2.5), but in the context of the parable that "reward" (μισθός) consists of intercessory prayers from the poor on behalf of the rich (2.5–8). God heeds not the merciful practices of the rich themselves but only the prayers of the poor prompted by the material support of the rich, indicating that meritorious almsgiving in *Sim.* 2 is only indirectly credited to the rich.[43] The work of rich Christians (i.e., sharing with poor Christians wealth given to them by the Lord) does become "great and acceptable to God," but only to the extent that the rich understand that their wealth comes from God and that they give to the poor (2.7).

It might be objected that the parable does endorse atoning (if not salvific) almsgiving because *Sim.* 2.9 indicates that, through their mutual exchange of material and spiritual goods, both the poor person and the rich person become "partners in the righteous work" (ἀμφότεροι κοινωνοὶ τοῦ ἔργου τοῦ δικαίου). As a result of this partnership in the work of righteousness, the Shepherd affirms, according to the translation of Michael Holmes, that "the one who does these things will not be abandoned by God, but will be enrolled in the books of the living" (ταῦτα οὖν ὁ ποιῶν οὐκ ἐγκαταλειφθήσεται ὑπὸ τοῦ θεοῦ, ἀλλὰ ἔσται γεγραμμένος εἰς τὰς βίβλους τῶν ζώντων).[44] At first glance, it would seem that enrollment of the individual Christian, whether poor or rich, "in the books of the living" is synonymous with salvation and based on partnership in "the righteous work."[45]

The book imagery in *Sim.* 2 is not soteriological, however. For this reason, the phrase ἔσται γεγραμμένος εἰς τὰς βίβλους τῶν ζώντων should not be identified with salvation. Early in the narrative, after the opening scene in which Hermas observes Rhoda bathing in the Tiber River, Hermas is accused by

---

[42] See Osiek, *Rich and Poor*, 86.

[43] I owe this insight to Christopher M. Hays.

[44] The translation is from Holmes, *Apostolic Fathers*, 563. Ehrman offers this translation: "And the one who does these things will not be abandoned by God, but will be recorded in the books of the living" (*Apostolic Fathers*, 2:313–15).

[45] This is implied in Osiek, *Shepherd of Hermas*, 164; cf. Markus Vinzent, *Christ's Resurrection in Early Christianity and the Making of the New Testament* (Farnham, UK: Ashgate, 2011), 64.

Rhoda of sinful desire for her (*Vis.* 1.1.5–9).[46] In the next scene, Hermas ponders this accusation, asking himself, "If this sin is recorded against me (Εἰ αὕτη μοι ἡ ἁμαρτία ἀναγράφεται), how will I be saved?" (1.2.1). With this question, Hermas alludes to a heavenly book of deeds in which is inscribed an account of people's works (cf. Isa 43:25; 65:6). The narrative of *Hermas* is full of references to different kinds of heavenly books, and the nature of these various books should be carefully distinguished.[47] In her first manifestation to Hermas, for example, the Woman Church states that, if Hermas' children repent with all their heart, "they will be inscribed in the books of life with the saints" (ἐγγραφήσονται εἰς τὰς βίβλους τῆς ζωῆς μετὰ τῶν ἁγίων [1.3.2]). According to the Woman Church, it is Hermas' children themselves, not their deeds, who might be written into these heavenly books, indicating that these are heavenly books of life that reveal inclusion in heavenly and/or eternal life (or exclusion, if one's name is blotted out; cf. *Mand.* 8.6; *Sim.* 9.24.4). Yet in the Shepherd's commentary on fasting in the parable of the vineyard, the Shepherd says, "Therefore, if you complete the fast in this way, as I have commanded you, your sacrifice will be acceptable to God, and *this fast will be recorded* (ἔγγραφος ἔσται ἡ νηστεία αὕτη), and the service performed in this way is beautiful and cheerful and acceptable to the Lord" (*Sim.* 5.3.8). In this instance, it is the act of fasting that is recorded in a book of deeds.

The heavenly book in *Sim.* 2.9 is similar to the heavenly book in *Sim.* 5.3.8 in that the phrase ἔσται γεγραμμένος εἰς τὰς βίβλους τῶν ζώντων in 2.9 refers to the writing of the *actions* of rich and poor, who become partners in the "righteous work," in a heavenly book of deeds. Not only does the phrase τοῦ ἔργου τοῦ δικαίου ("righteous work") in 2.9a employ the language of work, but also the clause ταῦτα οὖν ὁ ποιῶν in 2.9b emphasizes these deeds by framing the subject who will not be abandoned by God as *"the one who does these things."* For this reason, the subject of the future verb ἔσται in 2.9c is ταῦτα (not ὁ ποιῶν), and the clause should be translated, "The one who does these things will not be abandoned by God, but they [i.e., the things

---

[46] On the encounter between Hermas and Rhoda and the motif of desire in the *Shepherd of Hermas*, see B. Diane Lipsett, *Desiring Conversion: Hermas, Thecla, Aseneth* (Oxford: Oxford University Press, 2010), 19–53.

[47] For a thorough discussion, see Leslie Baynes, *The Heavenly Book Motif in Judeo-Christian Apocalypses 200 BCE–200 CE* (JSJSup 152; Leiden: Brill, 2001), 71–80. The terminology used in my discussion is adopted from Baynes, who defines heavenly books as "a form of writing stored in heaven that is restricted almost entirely to heavenly use" (18). Baynes lists four categories of heavenly books: (1) the heavenly book of life, (2) the heavenly book of deeds, (3) the heavenly book of fate, and (4) the heavenly book of action.

done] will be written[48] in the books of the living." Thus, 2.9 affirms that the righteous prayers of the poor and the righteous charity of the rich will be inscribed in a heavenly book of deeds. The rich Christian may be able "to do some good work" (2.10), but the rich believer is not promised atonement or salvation on the basis of material support of the poor. Indeed, given that Herm. *Vis.* 3 and *Sim.* 9 call for the *removal* of wealth, it may be the case that salvation for the rich (or, in imagery taken from *Hermas*, inclusion in the tower) is dependent upon dispossession of goods. In any case, almsgiving in *Sim. 2 is meritorious* but not *atoning* (or salvific).[49]

If there is a passage in the *Shepherd of Hermas* that indirectly advocates atoning almsgiving, it may be *Mand.* 2.4–7, seen earlier as the text that parallels *Did.* 1.5–6. Hermas is instructed by the Shepherd to "give generously to all who are in need" from the fruit of his labor, rendering support to all who ask without debating who is worthy and who is unworthy to receive (*Mand.* 2.4). After indicating that those who receive assistance are accountable to God (2.5), the Shepherd asserts that "the one who gives is innocent (ὁ οὖν διδοὺς ἀθῷός ἐστιν)" (2.6). On its own, this statement might be taken

---

[48] There are differences in the manuscript tradition: Codex Athous (fourteenth to fifteenth century) reads επιγεγραμμενος; Michigan Papyrus 129 (ca. second century) reads ενγεγραμμενος (so also the "Palatine" Latin translation, the Ethiopic translation, and the Sahidic Coptic version); and the Berlin Papyri (third to sixth century) and P.Oxy 1172[vid.] read γεγραμμενος. The differences are not substantive, however.

[49] Likewise, the Shepherd's exhortation to rescue someone who is in need and suffers great distress in *Sim.* 10.4 is an example of meritorious but not atoning almsgiving: "So whoever rescues such a person from misery *wins great joy for himself*," even while failing to help someone in such suffering is a "great sin" that implicates the one who failed to act in the suffering person's death (10.4.3). Here the reward is joy. Failure to provide assistance implicates someone in sin, but rendering help is not said to atone for sin. The notion that *joy* is the result of care for the needy is also reflected in *Sim.* 1. The Shepherd tells the parable in order to enjoin Hermas to think of God's servants as those who live in a foreign country, for their true (heavenly) home is elsewhere. The Shepherd exhorts Hermas, "So instead of fields, buy souls that are in distress, as anyone is able, and visit widows and orphans, and do not neglect them; and spend your wealth and all your possessions, which you received from God, on fields and houses of this kind. For this is why the Master made you rich, so that you might perform these ministries for him. It is much better to purchase fields and possessions and houses of this kind, which you will find in your own city when you go home to it. This lavish expenditure is beautiful and joyous; it does not bring grief or fear, but joy" (1.8–10). Practices such as purchasing freedom for Christian slaves (i.e., the language of "buying souls that are in distress" may refer to the literal emancipation of Christian slaves) and caring for widows and orphans brings *joy* to those who extravagantly participate in this divine economy. On issues of identity and economics in *Sim.* 1, see Benjamin H. Dunning, *Aliens and Sojourners: Self as Other in Early Christianity* (Divinations; Philadelphia: University of Pennsylvania Press, 2009), 78–90.

to imply that donors are rendered morally pure through almsgiving. In the context of the Shepherd's previously expressed concern regarding those who properly and improperly receive gifts, however, the affirmation of the innocence of those who provide charity indiscriminately means that generous donors are not implicated if some receive their assistance under false pretenses, a point clarified by the end of the sentence: "For as [the one who gives] was given from the Lord a service to undertake, he undertook it generously, not thinking about to whom to give or not to give." The one who performs this generous service does something glorious in God's sight, and it is promised that he "will live to God."[50]

The final line of *Mand.* 2 may, however, intimate a connection between almsgiving and the forgiveness of sin by signaling that pure repentance is the purpose of following the Shepherd's commandment to give generously: "Therefore, keep this commandment, as I have spoken it to you, in order that your repentance (ἡ μετάνοιά σου) and the repentance of your household may be found in generosity and [your repentance] may be pure and innocent and blameless" (2.7). As in *2 Clem.* 16.4 and Origen's *Hom. Lev.* 2.4.5, almsgiving in *Herm. Mand.* 2.7 would be atoning in the sense that giving generously to those in need is a sign of repentance, and sins can be forgiven through repentance (Herm. *Vis.* 1.3.1–3; 2.2.2–5; 5.7; *Mand.* 4.1.5, 8–11; *Sim.* 7.2–6; 8.11.1–5).[51]

Repentance (μετάνοιά) is a central and complex theme in *Hermas*.[52] Although *Vis.* 2.2.4–5 and *Mand.* 4.3 affirm one repentance for the saints

[50] The dative τῷ θεῷ is the indirect object of the verb ζήσεται, not the object of the participle διακονῶν (so Ehrman, *Apostolic Fathers*, 2:241; pace Holmes, *Apostolic Fathers*, 507: "Therefore the one who serves God sincerely in this manner will live"). The clause τῷ θεῷ ζήσεται is paralleled by the preceding παρὰ τῷ θεῷ, and the notion that those who keep God's commandments will "live to God" (i.e., will live in a godly manner) is common in *Mand.* (3.5: "And whoever hears this commandment and has nothing to do with that great wickedness, falsehood, will live to God" [ζήσεται τῷ θεῷ]; 4.2.4: "And whoever hears these commandments and keeps them will live to God" [ζήσεται τῷ θεῷ]; 12.3.1: "All who serve the good desire will live to God" [ζήσεται τῷ θεῷ]).

[51] Repentance is not the only means for the alleviation of sin in *Hermas*, however. In the Shepherd's explanation of the parable of the vineyard, for example, it is "the Son himself [who] cleansed their sins with great labor and enduring much toil" (*Sim.* 5.6.2–3). Elsewhere sin is said to be forgiven on account of the great mercy and compassion of God (*Vis.* 1.3.2), by not bearing a grudge (*Vis.* 2.3.1; cf. *Mand.* 2.2), by believing in God and turning to him and practicing righteousness (*Mand.* 12.6.2), and by suffering for the name of the Son of God (*Sim.* 9.28). Of course, sins are also cleansed at baptism (*Mand.* 4.3).

[52] See Alexis Torrance, *Repentance in Late Antiquity: Eastern Asceticism and the Framing of the Christian Life c.400–650 CE* (Oxford Theology and Religion Monographs; Oxford: Oxford University Press, 2012), 71–73; Alexis Torrance, "The Angel and the

after baptism (cf. *Mand.* 4.1.8), Hermas prays for and confesses his own sins on multiple occasions (*Vis.* 1.1.3; 2.1.2–3; 3.1.5–6; cf. *Mand* 4.2.3). This narrative tension might be interpreted as an indication that the one-time forgiveness of post-baptismal sins advocated in *Vis.* 2.2.4–5 and *Mand.* 4.3 reflects a different kind of repentance than the more mundane repentance exhibited by Hermas the character, perhaps a one-time repentance available to particularly grievous sinners.[53] Or perhaps the noun μετάνοιά in *Hermas* is not restricted to the act of confession and forgiveness—still less to the early development of a ritual of penance—but instead refers to a profound "personal and corporate transformation through the power of the good spirit, which necessitates new commitments for the future, not only the eschatological future but the immediate historical future as well."[54] In this sense, keeping the Shepherd's "commandment" to give generously to all who are in need is to be a sign of Hermas' and his family's transformation and a marker of true repentance.

Unlike *2 Clement*, Polycarp's *Letter to the Philippians*, the *Didache*, and the *Epistle of Barnabas*, the *Shepherd of Hermas* is a second-century Christian text that does not root its advocacy of meritorious and/or atoning almsgiving in appeals or allusions to Scripture. Given its parallels with *Did.* 1.5–6, *Mand.* 2.4–7 probably does draw upon early Christian tradition in the discussion of almsgiving, but there is no marking of this material in *Hermas* as tradition and no indication that the material is viewed as scriptural. The lack of clear scriptural influence on *Hermas'* teaching about almsgiving is hardly surprising, however, since it is notoriously difficult to identify any specific literary influences within the *Shepherd of Hermas*, either from the Old Testament or from other early Christian sources.[55]

Cyprian of Carthage[56]

~~While several second-century Christian texts promote atoning almsgiving on the basis of brief and sometimes allusive appeals to scriptural traditions,~~ ~~Cyprian's treatise *De opere et eleemosynis* is a tour de force scriptural exegesis.~~

Spirit of Repentance: Hermas and the Early Monastic Concept of Metanoia," *StPatr* 64 (2013): 15–20.

[53] So Torrance, *Repentance in Late Antiquity*, 72.

[54] Osiek, *Shepherd of Hermas*, 130.

[55] See Osiek, *Shepherd of Hermas*, 24–28. Dale C. Allison Jr. calls the citation of the book of Eldad and Modad in Herm. *Vis.* 2.3.4 "the only formal citation of anything in all of *Hermas*" ("Eldad and Modad," *JSP* 21 [2011]: 99–131 [101]).

[56] Some parts of this section on Cyprian are revised from David J. Downs, "Prosopological Exegesis in Cyprian's *De opera et eleemosynis*," *JTI* 6 (2012): 279–94.

With respect to the emergence of atoning almsgiving in the early church, Cyprian is a Janus-like figure, both facing the earliest articulations of the concept in the second century and anticipating the increased role of episcopal power, the rise of Christian wealth, and the development of rituals of penance that solidified practices of atoning almsgiving in the fourth century and beyond.[57] Two features of Cyprian's advocacy of atoning almsgiving in *Eleem.* stand out as particularly important and innovative. First, both the extent and the depth of Cyprian's engagement with Scripture in order to support his view that almsgiving atones for post-baptismal sins is striking. Second, Cyprian creatively articulates what might be called a "chronology of atoning almsgiving" that attempts to solve any tension between the belief that sins are atoned for by the Christ-event, on one hand, and the conviction that atonement for sins comes through almsgiving, on the other.

Cyprian's Interpretation of Scripture in De opere et eleemosynis

While there is little doubt regarding Cyprian's impact on the development of North African ecclesiology and the esteem with which Cyprian's intellectual contributions were held among many of his contemporaries and immediate successors, his theological acumen has often been judged lacking by modern interpreters.[58] Cyprian has been called "the most untheological" of the church fathers;[59] his work has been noted for its absence of "speculative theology," given that "his theology is intensely practical";[60] and his letters have been said to "prevent us from forgetting that we are studying not a theologian

---

[57] See, e.g., Peter Brown, *Through the Eye of a Needle: Wealth, the Fall of Rome, and the Making of Christianity in the West, 350–550* AD (Princeton: Princeton University Press, 2012), 72–90; idem, *The Ransom of the Soul: Afterlife and Wealth in Early Western Christianity* (Cambridge, Mass.: Harvard University Press, 2015), kindle 263–309.

[58] For estimations of Cyprian in antiquity, see Jerome, *Ep.* 22.22; 84.2; Augustine, *Ep.* 93.4.15; *Serm.* 310.4. On Jerome's high regard for Cyprian, see Simone Deléani, "Présence de Cyprien dans les œuvres de Jérôme sur la virginité," in *Jérôme entre l'occident et l'orient* (ed. Yves-Marie Duval; Paris: Études Augustiniennes, 1988), 61–82.

[59] Paul Parvis, "The Teaching of the Fathers: Cyprian and the Hours of Prayer," *Clergy* 69 (1984): 206–8 [206].

[60] Ronald E. Heine, "Cyprian and Novatian," in *The Cambridge History of Early Christian Literature* (ed. Frances Young, Lewis Ayres, and Andrew Louth; Cambridge: Cambridge University Press, 2004), 156. In similar terms, Roger E. Olson offers this backhanded accolade: "While Cyprian of Carthage may not have been one of Christian theology's great original thinkers or a genius of speculative or polemical theology—and thus not to be compared with Origen or Tertullian—his role in the development of organized Christianity is paramount" (*The Story of Christian Theology: Twenty Centuries of Tradition and Reform* [Downers Grove, Ill.: InterVarsity, 1999], 114).

but a pastoralist who had to deal by force of circumstances, with theological problems embedded in the practical decisions of his administration."[61] More positive assessments of Cyprian the theologian—which do not presuppose that all theology must be speculative or systematic—do exist, of course, including several contributions that are particularly sensitive to the contextual and pastoral nature of Cyprian's theology.[62]

It is impossible to separate Cyprian's theology from his interpretation of Scripture, for Cyprian's theological method is profoundly exegetical.[63] Yet if Cyprian has sometimes been disregarded as a theologian, the Bishop of Carthage has often not fared much better in assessments of his abilities as an interpreter of Scripture. Although not many interpreters today would go as far as one mid-twentieth-century voice, who opined that in Cyprian's selective use of scriptural texts the bishop left a good deal of the Bible on a "kind of exegetical scrap heap,"[64] Cyprian is often viewed as a second-rate exegete.[65] In particular, Cyprian's interpretation of Scripture has occasionally

[61] Graeme W. Clarke, ed., *The Letters of St. Cyprian of Carthage* (ACW 43; Ramsey, N.J.: Paulist, 1984), 4:19. About Cyprian's treatise *Unit. eccl.*, Geoffrey Bromiley asserts that Cyprian's "logical and rhetorical skill" is not matched by "theological discernment," and Bromiley consistently levels the charge of "oversimplification" against the document (*Historical Theology: An Introduction* [Grand Rapids: Eerdmans, 1978], 59–61). In the judgment of Stanley Greenslade, most of Cyprian's treatises are "of little importance," although Greenslade does allow that, although "moral exhortations are not often thrilling reading to later generations, they can be of much practical importance in their own day, and in this respect Cyprian was a good bishop" (*Early Latin Theology* [LCC 5; Philadelphia: Westminster, 1956], 117–18).

[62] I think especially of J. Jayakiran Sebastian, "Listening to the Speaking Bible: Interpreting the Use of the Bible in a Letter of Cyprian of Carthage," in *The Bible Speaks Today: Essays in Honour of Gnana Robinson* (ed. Daniel Jones Muthunayagom; Delhi: SPCK, 2000), 71–81; Burns, *Cyprian the Bishop*, passim; and Rolf Noormann, *Ad salutem consulere: Die Paränese Cyprians im Kontext antiken und frühchristlichen Denkens* (FKD 99; Göttingen: Vandenhoeck & Ruprecht, 2009).

[63] Hans von Campenhausen saw clearly the connection between theology and Scripture in the writings of Cyprian, declaring that "for Cyprian theology consists basically in the exposition of Scripture" (*The Fathers of the Latin Church* [Palo Alto, Calif.: Stanford University Press, 1969], 39).

[64] H. E. W. Turner, *The Pattern of Christian Truth: A Study in Relations between Orthodoxy and Heresy in the Early Church* (London: Mowbray, 1954), 277; cited in E. Fasholé-Luke, "Who Is the Bridegroom? An Excursion into St. Cyprian's Use of Scripture," *StPatr* 12 (1975): 294–98.

[65] E.g., Michael Andrew Fahey, the author of the most extensive and still-authoritative treatment of Cyprian's use of Scripture, offers the following observations at the conclusion of his study: "From these pages it should be clear first that Cyprian was not a profound or creative theologian gifted with rich and original insights.... From a modern viewpoint it is easy to criticize Cyprian's use of Scripture. He clearly lacks a coherent biblical theology

been critiqued for his practice of "proof-texting." It has been suggested, for example, that—in *Eleem.*—Cyprian appeals to a diverse array of scriptural "proof-texts" in order to demonstrate the validity of his assertion regarding the atoning value of merciful practice.[66]

There is no doubt that, in this treatise and elsewhere, Cyprian frequently presents ethical exhortation on the basis of scriptural proofs. Much of Cyprian's biblical exegesis was rooted in the Christian production and use of collections of scriptural proofs. Cyprian himself compiled two of these *testimonia* collections, *Ad Quirinum* and *Ad Fortunatum.*[67] Whether used in apologetic or catechetical contexts, this interpretative practice of appealing to "proof-texts" is often held to be naïve and unrefined, especially when compared with modern, historical-critical methods.[68] Cyprian—and along with

which knits together the various strands of Scriptural revelation. He consistently fails to appreciate the distinctive theological viewpoints of different biblical writers. Although he occasionally admits the superiority of NT revelation over its preliminary stage in the OT, in practice he generally ignores that insight by reading specifically NT teachings into the OT. Also, in his testimonial collections, Cyprian's Scriptural proof-texts are often tenuous, based on incidental verbal similarities and resonances. He sees significance in details which in fact are insignificant. Further, he never checks the accuracy of his existing Latin translation by comparing it with the Greek text. He realizes that interpretation could be correct or false (possibly even heretical), but never develops a consistent theory of hermeneutics. He approaches Scripture with a naive optimism and a disconcerting confidence, convinced that its orthodox meaning would be clear simply by the exercise of common sense (*ratio*)" (*Cyprian and the Bible: A Study in Third-Century Exegesis* [BGBH 9; Tübingen: Mohr Siebeck, 1971], 624–25). To be fair, Fahey's full assessment is not entirely negative. Fahey goes on to praise Cyprian's appreciation for the unity of the Bible, and earlier he notes that Cyprian's lack of originality as an interpreter of Scripture is a boon for the historian interested in the interpretation of the Bible among third-century North African Christians, since Cyprian's exegesis represents prevalent views and not the bishop's idiosyncratic perspective.

[66] Richard D. Finn, *Almsgiving in the Later Roman Empire: Christian Promotion and Practice (313–450)* (Oxford Classical Monographs; Oxford: Oxford University Press, 2006), 125; Fahey, *Cyprian and the Bible*, 179; Rowan A. Greer, *Broken Light and Mended Lives: Theology and Common Life in the Early Church* (University Park: Pennsylvania State University Press, 1986), 126–27; cf. Garrison (*Redemptive Almsgiving*, 66), who cites *Eleem.* 2 for its use of Luke 11:41 "as a proof-text to support the doctrine that almsgiving redeems sin."

[67] On Cyprian's *testimonia* in the context of other patristic scriptural collections, see Martin C. Albl, *And Scripture Cannot Be Broken: The Form and Function of the Early Christian Testimonia Collections* (NovTSup 96; Leiden: Brill, 1999), 132–33; cf. Pierre Monat, "Les testimonia bibliques, de Cyprien à Lactance," in *Le monde latin antique et la Bible* (ed. J. Fontaine and C. Pietri; BTT 2; Paris: Beauchesne, 1985), 499–507.

[68] On the modern origins of the term and practice of "proof-texting," see the discussion in Daniel J. Treier, "Proof Text," in *Dictionary for Theological Interpretation of the*

him a host of premodern biblical interpreters—has been criticized, therefore, for ignoring the literary contexts of the scriptural texts he cites, for failing "to appreciate the distinctive theological viewpoints of different biblical
writers," and for producing "proof-texts [that] are often tenuous, based on
incidental verbal similarities and resonances."[69]

Yet such a thoroughly negative assessment of this interpretative practice
runs the risk of imposing modern standards of critical exegesis on ancient
writers without also evaluating those interpreters in their own contexts.[70]
Moreover, the creativity and subtlety with which Cyprian engages Scripture
has often been underappreciated. Labeling Cyprian's scriptural exegesis as
"proof-texting," which can be perceived as a pejorative categorization, unfortunately oversimplifies Cyprian's interpretative and rhetorical strategies, for
in his treatise *De opera et eleemosynis* Cyprian offers a nuanced reading of
Scripture that goes beyond mere proof-texting.[71]

Bible (ed. Kevin Vanhoozer; Grand Rapids: Baker, 2005), 622–24. Unfortunately, Treier's essay does not engage precritical biblical interpretation. On this topic in the patristic
period, see especially Oskar Skarsaune, "The Development of Scriptural Interpretation in
the Second and Third Centuries," in *Hebrew Bible/Old Testament: The History of Its Interpretation*, vol. 1 (ed. Magne Saebø; Göttingen: Vandenhoeck & Ruprecht, 1996), 373–
442; and idem, *The Proof from Prophecy: A Study in Justin Martyr's Proof-Text Tradition:
Text-Type, Provenance, Theological Profile* (NovTSup 56; Leiden: Brill, 1987).

[69] Fahey, *Cyprian and the Bible*, 624 25.

[70] There is now a vast literature devoted to the topic, and sometimes the recovery,
of biblical interpretation in the patristic period. For a helpful introduction, see Charles
Kannengiesser, "The Bible as Read in the Early Church: Patristic Exegesis and Its Presup-
positions," in *The Bible and Its Readers* (ed. W. Beuken, S. Freyne, and A. Weiler; London:
SCM Press, 1991), 29–36; cf. also Frances M. Young, *Biblical Exegesis and the Formation of
Christian Culture* (Cambridge: Cambridge University Press, 1997); John David Dawson,
Christian Figural Reading and the Fashioning of Identity (Berkeley: University of California
Press, 2001); and now especially Charles Kannengiesser, *Handbook of Patristic Exegesis:
The Bible in Ancient Christianity* (BAC 1; Leiden: Brill, 2006).

[71] A recent exception is David E. Wilhite, "Cyprian's Scriptural Hermeneutic of
Identity: The Laxist 'Heresy,'" *HBT* 32 (2010): 58–98. Wilhite's insightful article exam-
ines Cyprian's employment of Scripture in the early letters and treatises written by the
bishop during the laxist controversy. Wilhite's primary concern is "Cyprian's use of scripture in identity construction and Cyprian's identity construction as a hermeneutic of
scripture," and Wilhite draws on insights from cultural anthropology in order to show
how Cyprian employs scriptural citations as boundary markers in the definition of his
group and the laxist "Other" that opposes Cyprian's ecclesiological and theological vision
(60). In describing Cyprian's appeals to the Old and New Testaments in *Ep.* 1–4, Wilhite
identifies two categories of scriptural invocation, categories that will recur throughout
Cyprian's early writings: (1) "*scriptum*-type" citations and (2) elucidative references. The
former, according to Wilhite, are introduced with the formulaic clause *scriptum est* ("it
is written") and are "quoted to speak directly to a certain situation, and in so doing no

One aspect of Cyprian's hermeneutical strategy in the treatise is the bishop's employment of "prosopological exegesis," an interpretative technique that allows Cyprian to identify the Holy Spirit as the "speaker" of certain biblical texts. This is seen in the citation of both Prov 15:27 (LXX) and Sir 3:30 in the introduction of the work (*Eleem.* 2), although the interpretative practice is found elsewhere in the document (e.g., *Eleem.* 4, 5, 9).[72] These two texts, along with Luke 11:40-41, provide the foundational scriptural warrant for Cyprian's theological claim that almsgiving removes post-baptismal sin. Thus, Cyprian's appeal for Christians to participate in the ministry of almsgiving and his critique of pagan euergetism is supported by a hermeneutical

---

commentary or interpretation is offered" (66); for examples of *scriptum*-type citations in *Eleem.*, see 3.6–8 (*cum scriptum sit*); 11.3–4 (*cum scriptum sit*); 18.13–17 (*Probat scriptura, dicens*); and 19.9–13 (*secundum fidem scripturae sanctae, dicentis*). This type of citation corresponds to Fahey's category of "proof-text." The latter, on the other hand, are found when Cyprian invokes Scripture in the context of an argument, "but in order to do so he gives a brief explanation of the human speaker and the context of the quotation" (67); for examples of elucidative references in *Eleem.*, see 3.8–10; 4.5–8; 5.3–7, 12–16, 19–22; 6.2–24; 9.10–14; 10.6–13; 14.1–7; 16.8–11, 12–17; 20.1–18; 24.8–11; 25.8–13). Wilhite posits that the difference in these two types of scriptural citation could possibly reflect Cyprian's awareness of the recipient's knowledge (or lack thereof) of the biblical tradition being invoked, making the necessity of providing more information dependent on the context and the reader's assumed knowledge. The data in *Ep.* 1–4 is not conclusively supportive of this hypothesis, however, as Wilhite himself observes. More pertinently, Wilhite points out that these categories offer an alternative to the category "proof-text" for three reasons: (1) the "term [proof-text] is inherently derogatory and only perpetuates the notion that Cyprian and others like him held a simplistic hermeneutic of scripture, while the later patristic writers of the formative ecumenical councils read the Bible in a more sophisticated and historically/theologically appropriate manner, a notion now known to be problematic"; (2) "Cyprian's penchant for introducing a citation with elaborate historical contextualization should supplement Fahey's conclusion that Cyprian viewed 'the Bible as a collection of divine sayings'"; and (3) the "distinction between these two types of scriptural citation "becomes accentuated when seen through the lens of identity: Cyprian's construction of social identity via his portrayal of a person's or group's relationship to the scriptures" (69–70). Wilhite's two categories of scriptural invocation—i.e., *scriptum*-type citations and elucidative references—can be supplemented by adding a third, which I will call a "prosopological-type citation," since in this type of reference Cyprian employs the early Christian practice of "prosopological exegesis"—namely, the assignment of a different πρόσωπα to the speaker of a divinely inspired text.

[72] Cyprian also employs prosopological exegesis in many of his other writings. A representative sampling would include *Ep.* 55.6; 61.1; 62.4; 62.11; 69.2; 75.2; *Unit. eccl.* 4, 8; *Hab. virg.*1, 13; *Laps.* 7, 10, 27; *Dom.* 35. Cyprian's citation of a Latin version of LXX Prov 15:27 (as opposed to Prov 16:6 in the MT) is an indication that his version of the Old Latin text derives from the LXX (Timothy Michael Law, *When God Spoke Greek: The Septuagint and the Making of the Christian Bible* [Oxford: Oxford University Press, 2013], 133).

strategy that identifies a divine speaker of the scriptural texts. Rather than simply assembling a list of biblical "proof-texts," Cyprian's *De opere et elee-mosynis* presents the whole of Scripture as a witness to "the strain and exhortation of the Holy Spirit," who speaks a word of command that all who hope in the heavenly kingdom should be instructed to give alms and perform other works of mercy (*Eleem.* 4).

The term "prosopological exegesis" has its origins in modern scholarly discussions about the emergence of Trinitarian theology in ancient interpretation of Scripture.[73] Briefly defined, prosopological exegesis is a literary and grammatical method of interpretation that discerns the identity of speakers, or πρόσωπα, in inspired texts. Or a more expansive definition of this phenomenon holds: "Prosopological exegesis is a reading technique whereby an interpreter seeks to overcome a real or perceived ambiguity regarding the identity of the speakers or addressees (or both) in the divinely inspired source text by assigning nontrivial prosopa (i.e., nontrivial vis-à-vis the 'plain sense' of the text) to the speakers or addressees (or both) in order to make sense of the text."[74] With origins in ancient notions of divine inspiration of literary texts, the dialogical nature of drama in antiquity, and discussions of προσωποποιΐα among classical rhetoricians, this interpretative practice became especially prominent among Christian authors in the second through the fourth centuries, including Justin Martyr, Tertullian, Athanasius, and Cyprian.[75] The classic early Christian discussion of this practice comes from Justin Martyr's *First Apology*:

> But whenever you hear the sayings of the prophets spoken as from a person (ὡς ἀπο προσώπου), do not assume [the sayings] to be spoken from the inspired persons themselves, but from the divine Word

[73] The seminal contribution was Carl Andresen, "Zur Entstehung und Geschichte des trinitarischen Personbegriffes," *ZNW* 52 (1961): 1–39; see also Basil Studer, "Zur Entwicklung der patristischen Trinitätslehre," *TGl* 74 (1984): 81–93; Marie-Josèphe Rondeau, *Les commentaires patristiques du Psautier (3e–5e siecles): 1. Les travaux des Pères grecs et latins sur le Psautier. Recherces et bilan; 2. Exégèse prosopologique et théologie* (2 vols.; OCA 220; Rome: Institutum Studiorum Orientalium, 1982–1985), esp. vol. 2; Michael Slusser, "The Exegetical Roots of Trinitarian Theology," *TS* 49 (1988): 461–76; and Matthew W. Bates, "Prosopographic Exegesis and Narrative Logic: Paul, Origen, and Theodoret of Cyrus on Ps 69:22-23," in *Greek Patristic and Eastern Orthodox Interpretations of Romans* (ed. Daniel Patte and Vasile Mihoc; Romans through History and Cultures 9; London: T&T Clark, 2013).

[74] Matthew W. Bates, *The Hermeneutics of Apostolic Proclamation: The Center of Paul's Method of Scriptural Interpretation* (Waco, Tex.: Baylor University Press, 2012), 218.

[75] On the context of early Christian use of prosopological exegesis, see Bates, *Hermeneutics*, 183–221; Slusser, "Exegetical Roots," 468–70.

(θείου Λόγου) who moves them. For sometimes the Word speaks as one announcing things that are going to come about; sometimes he utters as from the person of God, the Master and Father of all; sometimes as from the person of Christ; sometimes as from the people who are replying to the Lord and his Father—just as is seen in your own writers, one person being the writer of the whole, but many persons being brought forward as participating in discourse. (*1 Apol.* 36.1–2)[76]

Justin's statement reflects an assertion of the divine authorship of the prophetic writings, which leads to the conviction that this one divine author may employ many participants in the recorded dialogues, including the divine Logos itself, God the Father, Christ, and human agents. Moreover, these diverse πρόσωποι can be utilized by the Logos in speech that ostensibly represents the words of the (human) prophets. Indeed, in the next several sections of the *First Apology*, Justin provides examples of prophetic utterances by the Father (37, 44), Christ (38), and the Spirit (39–42, 44). Interestingly, Justin also reminds his interlocutor, the Roman emperor Antoninus, that this literary device has parallels in pagan literature (i.e., "just as is seen in your own writers").[77]

[76] My translation. See also Irenaeus, *Epid.* 49–50; Tertullian, *Prax.* 11; Origen, *Rom. Comm.* 2.11.2; Athanasius, *C. Ar.* 1.54.

[77] Bates has recently offered a fourfold methodology for the identification of prosopological exegesis in ancient texts (*Hermeneutics*, 219–20). First, since prosopological exegesis has to do with the identification of the true speaker of an earlier text, the pre-text must depict persons who are speaking or engaged in dialogue, regardless of the literary genre represented by the pre-text. This is the most important of the four criteria, according to Bates, since prosopological exegesis formally excludes texts that do not record speech or discourse. Second, the identity of the speaker supplied by the exegete in order to explain the earlier text must be a "non-trivial" person vis-à-vis the earlier text. That is, "if there is no real or perceived ambiguity in the identity of the prosopon which can be presupposed, the exegesis is in accordance with the 'plain sense' of the pre-text and does not warrant special comment or the prosopological label" (219). Related to this, the ancient interpreter must consider his or her pre-text in some way inspired or given by divine authorship. Third, when ancient authors explicitly mark their use of prosopological exegesis with a formulaic expression (e.g., ἀπὸ προσώπου, ἐκ προσώπου, τὸ λέγον προσώπου, etc.) or with the obvious introduction of a character-in-speech (e.g., "the Righteousness by Faith says . . ." in Rom 10:6), recognition of the interpretative practice is relatively straightforward. The former of these strategies Bates calls "explicitly introduced prosopological exegesis"; the latter, "marked prosopological exegesis"; both of these techniques are contrasted with "unmarked prosopological exegesis," which occurs when the interpretative practice might explain the author's hermeneutical approach, but no clear signal is given by the author (218). Fourth, and finally, "early Christian co-texts, post-texts, and proximate inter-texts can be useful in determining whether or not the author of a text may have exegeted a pre-text prosopologically, especially in cases of unmarked prosopological exegesis" (220).

The introduction of *De opere et eleemosynis* contains two important instances of prosopological exegesis.[78] At the end of an opening section in which he praises the benefactions and mercies of God and Christ, including the Lord's healing of the wounds born by Adam, Cyprian declares that divine love has come to assist frail humans a second time, following baptism, "so that whatever uncleanliness we afterwards contract [i.e., after baptism] we may wash away with corporal acts of mercy (*eleemosynis*)."[79] In the next section, Cyprian expands this last assertion by introducing the main thesis of the treatise with reference to three scriptural passages that support his claim.[80] First, in citing LXX Prov 15:27 ("By alms and faith sins are purged away"), Cyprian clarifies that this text does not refer to pre-baptismal sins, which are "cleansed by the blood and sanctification of Christ" (*Eleem.* 2.3–4). Second, Cyprian quotes Sir 3:30 ("As water will quench fire, so alms will quench sin") in order to demonstrate and prove (*ostenditur et probatur*) that the flame of post-baptismal sin is extinguished by *eleemosyna* (2.4–8). Although remission of sins is granted only once in baptism, the continual observance of *eleemosyna* imitates baptism in bestowing afresh the indulgence (*indulgentiam*) of God (2.9–11). The third scriptural text, from Luke 11:40–41 ("He that made that which is within

---

On this fourth criterion, if it is true that instances of prosopological exegesis are a priori more likely when the technique can be shown among proximate intertexts, then it is worth considering Cyprian's relationship with one of the clearest and most influential advocates of prosopological exegesis—namely, Tertullian, Cyprian's predecessor in Carthage. For a discussion of this point, see Downs, "Prosopological Exegesis," 287–88.

[78] In terms of the structure of the treatise, I follow Poirier's thematic division: introduction (1–3); exhortation (4–8); response to a first objection (9–15); response to a variation of the same objection (16–20); an appeal to do better (21–23); conclusion (24–26) (*La bienfaisance et les aumônes*, 27–28). For a more rhetorical approach, see Dunn, "Cyprian's Care for the Poor," 364.

[79] Although the English locution "corporal works of mercy" is somewhat clumsy, Rebenack's translation of *eleemosyna* should be retained. Cyprian does include financial contributions to the poor (i.e., "alms") in his use of *eleemosyna* (so *Eleem.* 2.13; 7.5–6; cf. 7.12–14; 8.1–13; 9.5–6). The term has a broader semantic range, however, one that also includes noneconomic acts of justice and mercy, including the provision of food, shelter, and clothing (4.14–16; 6.8–11; 23.11–35; 12.1–2; cf. 15.1–6) and works of compassion (5.14–16; 16.15–17; 17.1–24). Thus, the technical term "almsgiving," if understood to refer only to monetary contributions, does not suit Cyprian's more expansive definition of *eleemosyna*, which has close parallels in the treatise with terms such as *iustitia, iustus,* and *misericordiae* (see Rebenack, *Thasci Caecili Cypriani*, 32–56). Thus, Cyprian's employment of the loan word *eleemosyna* parallels the semantics of ἐλεημοσύνη in early Jewish and Christian literature (see chaps. 2 and 3).

[80] All three biblical references are also featured in *Test.* 3.1. Clearly, this scriptural triad was important for Cyprian.

made also that which is without. But give alms, and behold all things are clean unto you"), seems to indicate how exactly almsgiving is related to baptism: since Jesus speaks of giving alms as an activity that makes things clean for the donor (*vobis munda [sunt] omina*), both practices have to do with washing and cleaning (2.12–22).

The introduction of the citations of LXX Prov 15:27 and Sir 3:30 in *Eleem.* 2.1 is *Loquitur in scripturis Spiritus sanctus et dicit* ("In the Scriptures, the Holy Spirit speaks and says").[81] This introductory formula and the scriptural citations that follow are classic examples of "prosopological exegesis." First, the text highlights the issue of *speech*, including an emphasis on the declarative nature of the text cited (i.e., *Loquitur . . . et dicit*). Second, the citation identifies a "non-trivial" person as the speaker of the earlier text. Cyprian was well aware of the traditional ascription of the book of Proverbs to "Solomon, son of David, king of Israel" (Prov 1:1; cf. 10:1; 25:1). Later in the same treatise (*Eleem.* 5.4), Cyprian will quote Prov 21:13 with the following introduction: "And moreover, in Solomon, we read" (*Et aput Salomonen legimus*). The other mention of Solomon in *Eleem.* comes in a reference to Prov 28:27 in 9.6–8 where, interestingly, Cyprian writes, *Loquitur per Salomonem Spiritus sanctus et dicit* ("The Holy Spirit speaks through Solomon and says"). Such a claim of the Holy Spirit speaking *through* Solomon as human agent is not altogether uncommon in Cyprian's citations of Proverbs.[82] Given that Cyprian identifies only the Holy Spirit as the speaker of Prov 15:27 in *Eleem.* 2.1, however, the case for identifying this as a prosopological-type citation is secure. Third, Cyprian's naming of the Holy Spirit signals this as an example of "marked prosopological exegesis." The same logic governs the following citation of Sir 3:30 in *Eleem.* 2.4–5: there is an indication of speech (*Item denuo dicit*), and there is an implicit marking of a divine speaker, since the Holy Spirit is still the subject of the verb *dicit*.[83]

The impact of these two prosopological-type citations at the beginning of the treatise is best discussed with reference to two additional examples

---

[81] Technically, there is a second introduction to the quotation of Sir 3:30: *Item denuo dicit* ("Likewise, he says again"). This statement, however, clearly indicates that the same subject—namely, the Holy Spirit—is the "speaker" of both texts.

[82] So, e.g., *Ep.* 54.21; 62.5; 64.2; *Mort.* 23; *Fort.* 12.

[83] Elsewhere, Cyprian regularly identifies Solomon as the author of Ecclesiasticus (*Test.* 3.6, 12, 35, 51, 53, 97, 109, 110, 113; *Ep.* 3.2). In *Test.* 3.1, Cyprian incorrectly attributes Sir 3:30 to Solomon in Proverbs. That Cyprian is ostensibly unaware of Ben Sira's authorship of Sirach (Sir 50:27) does not mitigate the point. Although he is confused about the historical authorship of Sirach, Cyprian assumes the text was written by a human being—namely, Solomon. In *Eleem.* 2.2–3, however, Cyprian identifies a divine speaker of Sir 3:30.

of prosopological exegesis in *De opere et eleemosynis* (not including the Holy Spirit's speech *through* Solomon in 9.6–8). First, in *Eleem.* 5.9–12, Cyprian introduces a quotation of Ps 41:1 with an emphasis on the assertive speech of the Holy Spirit: "Likewise in the Psalms, the Holy Spirit declares and confirms this, saying (*Quod item in psalmis Spiritus sanctus declarat et probat, dicens*), 'Blessed is he that understands concerning the needy and the poor: the Lord will deliver him in the evil day.'" Given that the ascription of the psalm identifies the text as a psalm of David, this is another example of Cyprian interpreting the Holy Spirit as the speaker in place of a human author. Second, in *Eleem.* 4.1–6, Cyprian does not cite a specific scriptural text, but he does refer to the declarative action of the Holy Spirit in Scripture:

> Never in fine, my dearest brethren, has the divine admonition ceased and refrained from urging the people of God, in the holy Scriptures both the old and the new, always and everywhere to works of mercy, the Holy Spirit both declaring and exhorting that everyone who is instructed unto hope of the kingdom of heaven should be ordered to perform corporal works of mercy.

Like others before him, Cyprian believed that the speakers of certain scriptural passages could be assigned different, divine *prosopa*, and he employed a hermeneutical method that allowed him to identify the Holy Spirit as the true speaker of LXX Prov 15:27 and Sir 3:30, two of the three biblical texts that introduce the bishop's claim that *eleemosyna* cleanses post-baptismal sin. One effect of this interpretative strategy is to ground the ensuing ethical exhortation in divine speech. If these are "proof-texts," what they "prove" is that Cyprian's conviction regarding the ability of *eleemosyna* to purge sin is supported, not merely by the testimony of Scripture and its human authors, but by the direct speech of the Holy Spirit.

In *Eleem.* 4.1–6, moreover, readers are given an additional indication of the function of the Holy Spirit's speech in the promotion of redemptive almsgiving. Cyprian states that in the "holy Scriptures both old and new" the Holy Spirit has consistently participated in divine encouragement of almsgiving and acts of mercy, "declaring and exhorting (*canente adque exhortante*) that everyone who is instructed unto hope of the kingdom of heaven should be ordered to perform corporal works of mercy." It is the Holy Spirit who has been engaged in this activity of "declaring and exhorting." In terms taken from the field of speech act theory, Cyprian frames the Holy Spirit as delivering, through Scripture, illocutionary utterances that are both assertive (as in the proverbial expressions of *Eleem.* 2.1–2, 4–5) and directive (as in the exhortation represented in *Eleem.* 4.1–6).[84] Furthermore, what the Holy Spirit declares throughout Scripture is that "everyone who is instructed unto hope of the kingdom of heaven *should be ordered to perform corporal works of mercy*" (*Eleem.* 4.4–5). This illocutionary speech act is not only directive; it is also declarative.[85] In his own obedience to the command of the Holy Spirit, Cyprian himself—in his writing of this treatise and in his exposition of the Scriptures—is evidence of the fact that the Spirit's successful performance of this speech act has resulted in the "propositional content correspond[ing] to the world." Cyprian has been moved by the Spirit's declaration to fulfill the very command of entreating (*iuberetur*) those trained in the hope of the kingdom of heaven to commit themselves to *eleemosyna*. In this way, the Spirit's speech supports both Cyprian's theological assertion that almsgiving and acts of mercy alleviate post-baptismal sin and Cyprian's paraenetic activity of encouraging *eleemosyna*. The speech of the Holy Spirit authorizes both the message and the messenger.

Modern research on the ancient hermeneutical practice of prosopological exegesis has shed important light on the development of Trinitarian theology and, more recently, on the narrative substructure of Paul's gospel and Christology. In *De opere et eleemosynis*, Cyprian offers his readers neither speculative theology nor sustained christological reflection. Instead, the Bishop of Carthage is engaged in the task of pastoral paraenesis as he attempts to convince his readers of the purifying power of *eleemosyna*. Throughout the treatise, Cyprian draws deeply on the language of Scripture in order to develop his claim that almsgiving can purge the post-baptismal sins of the donor. Although it has been suggested that Cyprian merely cites a variety of "proof-texts" in order to substantiate his assertion, his reading of the Scripture is more complex than this image implies. One important aspect of Cyprian's hermeneutical approach is his use of prosopological exegesis, a hermeneutical technique that allows Cyprian to root his ethical exhortation and his authority as an expositor of Scripture in the speech of the Holy Spirit. In his use of this interpretative strategy, Cyprian stands in

---

[84] See John R. Searle, "A Taxonomy of Illocutionary Acts," in *Expression and Meaning: Studies in the Theory of Speech Acts* (Cambridge: Cambridge University Press, 1979), 1–29. Searle defines assertive/representative speech acts as those that "commit the speaker (in varying degrees) to something's being the case, to the truth of the proposition expressed" (354). Directive speech acts, on the other hand, "are attempts . . . by the speaker to get the hearer to do something" (355).

[85] John Searle writes of declarative speech acts: "It is the defining characteristic of this class that the successful performance of one of its members brings about the correspondence between propositional content and reality; successful performance guarantees that the propositional content corresponds to the world" ("Taxonomy," 358).

line with other early Christian advocates and practitioners of prosopological exegesis, including Justin, Tertullian, and Athanasius. Moreover, in applying this hermeneutical approach in the context of his ethical exhortation in *De opere et eleemosynis*, Cyprian also proves himself to be a creative interpreter of Scripture.

Cyprian's Chronology of Atoning Almsgiving

Christian authors and texts before Cyprian who drew upon scriptural traditions to promote atoning almsgiving do not appear to have seen any tension between the conviction that salvation and atonement for sin are possible because of the Christ-event and the view that merciful care for the needy is a means of canceling, cleansing, covering, extinguishing, lightening, or in some way atoning for human sin. In most second-century texts that advocate atoning almsgiving, these two confessions are held together with no direct attempt to harmonize or systematize beliefs that later interpreters have often viewed as mutually exclusive. Cyprian does not find any conflict between his belief that sins are cleansed by the blood of Christ and his opinion that merciful deeds have cleansing power. Cyprian's substantial move in *Eleem.*, however, is his clear articulation of a chronology of atoning almsgiving, one that locates atonement of pre-baptismal sins in the cross of Jesus, while allowing that "corporal works of mercy" (*eleemosyna*) offer a "remedy for sin" after baptism (*Eleem.* 26.4: *medulla peccati*). As Cyprian states directly in the introduction to *Eleem.*, the statement in LXX Prov 15:27 that sins are purged by alms and faith does not refer to "those sins which had been contracted before [baptism], for they are cleansed by the blood and sanctification of Christ" (2.1–4).[86]

Cyprian opens the treatise with an exaltation of the voluminous benefactions of God:

---

[86] A few lines later, Cyprian writes, "And since only once in baptism is the remission of sins given, the continuous and perpetual performance of corporal works of mercy, having imitated the likeness of baptism, may bestow the indulgence of God anew" (2.8–10). Then, as an interpretation of Luke 11:40-41, Cyprian states, "In His mercy, He [i.e., the Lord Jesus] admonishes that mercy be done, and, since He seeks to save those whom He has redeemed with a great price, He teaches that they, who after the grace of baptism have been defiled, can be cleansed again" (2.19–22). Cyprian makes the same point regarding alms and post-baptismal sin in *Ep.* 55.22: "Alms do deliver from death, and not, assuredly, from that death which once the blood of Christ extinguished, and from which the saving grace of baptism and of our Redeemer has delivered us, but from that which subsequently creeps in through sins (*sed ab ea quae per delicta posmodum serpit*)."

Many and great, my dearest brethren, are the divine benefactions, in which the bountiful and copious mercy of God the Father and of Christ, not only has been engaged, but also is forever engaged for our salvation, since, for preserving us and giving us life, the Father sent His Son that He might be able to restore us, and since the Son who had been sent wished to be and to be called the Son of man, that He might make us sons of God. (*Eleem.* 1.1–6)

The opening statement expresses Cyprian's conviction that God's work for human salvation is an ongoing act, for the mercy of God and of Christ is "forever engaged for our salvation." Thus, while Cyprian will go on in the opening section to emphasize the soteriological benefits of Christ's atoning death (1.6–9), Cyprian also notes that God preserves the one who has been redeemed (1.11–12). Cyprian's two-stage chronology of atonement does not, therefore, portray the forgiveness of sins before baptism as a divine endeavor and the cleansing of sins after baptism through merciful deeds as a human one disconnected from God's power and mercy. Instead, Cyprian frames the washing away of human sin by *eleemosyna* as a divine mercy. Commenting on the inability of humans entirely to avoid sin even after they have been healed, Cyprian writes:

We had been confined, and we had been closely hemmed in by the precept of sinlessness, and the weakness and impotence of human frailty would have nothing it might do, if divine love, coming to our aid a second time, by showing us works of justice and mercy, did not open up a way of preserving our salvation, so that whatever uncleanliness we afterwards [i.e., after baptism] contract we may wash away with corporal works of mercy. (1.15–21)

That it is possible to cleanse and remove sins through merciful deeds is, for Cyprian, a salutary gift of God's kindness and mercy (3.1–14).

To be sure, Cyprian's *Eleem.* is not merely a reflection on atoning almsgiving. Cyprian also touches on numerous biblical texts that promise some reward for those who care for the needy—as well as texts that portend divine judgment for the greedy and those who fail to show justice—in order to encourage his readers to lay claim to the heavenly rewards and divine favor available to Christians whose faith is marked by charity. The performance of *eleemosyna*, for Cyprian, brings present joy and eternal reward to the people of God (26.1). As Cyprian writes at the end of the treatise:

The salutary performance of corporal works of mercy, my dearest brethren, is a magnificent and divine thing, a great comfort for those who believe, a beneficial protection of our security, a defense of hope, a safeguard of faith, a remedy of sin, a thing placed in the power of the doer, a thing both great and easy, a crown of peace without the peril of persecution, a true and very great gift of god—a gift necessary for the weak, glorious to the strong, by the aid of which the Christian perseveres in spiritual grace, gains the favor of Christ the Judge, counts God his debtor.

Yet one of the key benefits of merciful practice is that almsgiving is "a remedy of sin." With this affirmation of the atoning power of *eleemosyna*, Cyprian both recapitulates an early Christian tradition and provides an important expansion of it.

Conclusion

Cyprian's construction of a timeline that allows for post-baptismal sins to be forgiven by works of mercy was not novel.[87] Perhaps one decade earlier, Origen had suggested a very similar position in his sermons on Leviticus, although Origen identifies six remissions of sin apart from baptism, one of which is almsgiving (*Hom. Lev.* 2.4.4–5). Origen initially hedges his position, first insisting, "Among us, there is only one pardon of sins, which is given in the beginning through the grace of baptism. After this, no mercy nor any indulgence is granted to the sinner" (2.4.4). Origen then concedes that there are numerous means of remitting sin for the Christian for whom God's son died: "And yet, lest these things not so much build up your souls for virtue as cast them down to despair, you heard how many sacrifices there were in the Law for sins. Now hear how many remissions of sins in the gospel" (2.4.4). Thus, by the middle of the third century, both Origen and Cyprian

---

[87] Half a generation before Cyprian, the Alexandrian presbyter Clement had discussed the forgiveness of post-baptismal sin in *Quis div.* Clement considers the wealthy believer who "has happened either because of ignorance or of weakness or of circumstances not of his own choice to fall after the baptismal seal and redemption into certain sins or transgressions so as to have become completely subject to them" (*Quis div.* 39; trans. Butterworth, LCL). Genuine repentance, according to Clement, will result in God's forgiveness, even after baptism, "for God alone can grant remission of sins and not reckon trespasses, though even we are exhorted by the Lord each day to forgive our brothers when they repent" (39). In his discourse on post-baptismal repentance in *Quis div.* 39–42, however, Clement does not specifically identify almsgiving or merciful deeds for the needy as a means to atone for post-baptismal sins. Instead, Clement insists that forgiveness for post-baptismal sin is procured by repentance, which he defines as "to condemn the deeds that are past and to ask forgetfulness of them from the Father, who alone of all is able to make undone what has been done, by wiping out former sins with mercy that comes from Him and with the dew of the Spirit" (40). Such repentance is illustrated by Clement in the dramatic story of St. John and the robber (42).

had located atoning almsgiving within a chronological framework that allowed forgiveness of sins through merciful deeds for believers who sinned after baptism.[88] The solutions to the problem of post-baptismal sin posed by Origen and Cyprian are worked out in the context of scriptural exegesis and pastoral paraenesis. These third-century writers may be more direct in their use of Scripture to support the concept of atoning almsgiving than their earlier predecessors. But Christian advocacy of atoning almsgiving in the second century, too, was shaped by the influence of scriptural traditions.

[88] On this development, see Bernard Poschmann, *Paenitentia secunda: Die kirchliche Busse im ältesten Christentum bis Cyprian und Origen; Eine dogmengeschichtliche Untersuchung* (Theophania 1; Bonn: P. Hanstein, 1940).

CONCLUSION

This book has attempted to tell the story of the emergence of atoning alms-giving in the first two centuries or so of the Christian movement, from the writings of the New Testament to Cyprian's *De opere et eleemosynis*. By and large, the earliest Christians, shaped as they were by a scriptural imagination that valued practices of charity, cared for the poor among their communities. Christian commitment to merciful deeds on behalf of the needy was particularly supported by scriptural traditions that promised recompense for an individual's or a community's treatment of the poor. The concept of atoning almsgiving developed in large part as a result of early Christian engagement with scriptural traditions that present care for the poor as having the potential to secure future reward, and even the cleansing of sin, for those who practice mercy. Chief among these scriptural witnesses are a cluster of passages from Greek translations of Daniel (Th 4:27) and Proverbs (15:27), from Tobit (12:8-10) and Sirach (3:30), and from the Gospel of Luke (11:41) and First Peter (4:8) that support, or were interpreted to support, the idea that sins could be redeemed, cleansed, purged, expiated, or covered by merciful deeds.

Nascent Christian endorsement of merciful deeds as a means of atoning for sin should be viewed as part of the larger tapestry of meritorious

almsgiving in early Jewish and early Christian literature. The idea that provision of material assistance to the needy serves as means of accumulating
some reward or treasure for donors is well represented in the Hebrew Bible,
the Septuagint, and other early Jewish sources. In both the New Testament
and postapostolic literature, appeals for charity are frequently rooted in the
conviction that beneficence will be rewarded, either in this life or in the next.

To be sure, expectation of recompense and self-interest are far from
the only motivating features found among exhortations for merciful deeds
or practices of justice within the New Testament and other early Christian
literature. It would be problematic not to recognize that the anticipation of
reward is but one ethical warrant among many represented in early Christian
appeals for material assistance for the needy. Within the New Testament,
for example, other ethical warrants for charity and justice include (1) warnings about God's judgment upon those who defraud and even murder the
poor (Jas 5:1-6; cf. 1 Cor 11:27-34) or who greedily cling to possessions
(Luke 12:15-21; 16:19-31);[1] (2) the contention that authentic faith is shown
through acts like clothing or feeding a brother or sister in need (Jas 2:14-26);
(3) the notion that caring for the hungry, the thirsty, the stranger, the naked,
the sick, and the prisoner is a ministry to Christ himself (Matt 25:31-49);[2]
(4) the idea that care for the poor in the Greco-Roman world is a countercul-
tural practice that establishes solidarity between the largely Gentile churches
of Paul's mission and Christ-believing Jews, on the one hand, and that marks
communities of Jesus' followers, regardless of their ethnicity, as participants
in Israel's story, a story unimaginable without a deep commitment to justice,
given this emphasis in Torah (Gal 2:10; Rom 15:25-31); or (5) the conviction
that in sharing the world's goods with a brother or sister in need believers
imitate the self-giving love of Christ (1 John 3:16-17; cf. 2 Cor 8:9).[3] That the
saying "love covers a multitude of sins" (1 Pet 4:8) was frequently interpreted
by patristic authors as a maxim about the atoning power of almsgiving is an
indication of the extent to which love served as an ethical warrant in many
early Christian exhortations to merciful practice. In his letter to the church
at Smyrna, for example, Ignatius critiques his Docetic opponents because
they do not concern themselves with love, which Ignatius defines as caring

---

[1] The threat of eschatological judgment for those who neglect the poor is also a reg-
ular feature of patristic paraenesis; see Herm. *Vis.* 3.9.5; *Sim.* 10.4.1–5; *2 Clem.* 16.1–4;
Cyprian, *Eleem.* 15, 21–23, 26; cf. Hays, "By Almsgiving and Faith," 275–76.

[2] Cf. Clement of Alexandria, *Quis div.* 30; Cyprian, *Eleem.* 23.

[3] See the section "Other Stimuli to Almsgiving: An Encomium," in Hays, "By
Almsgiving and Faith," 277–78. I am indebted to Hays' insightful essay at various points
in this epilogue.

for the widow, the orphan, the oppressed, the one who is in chains, the one who is released, the one who is hungry, and the one who is thirsty (*Smryn.* 6.2). It is perhaps not surprising that Christian charitable paraenesis would often be grounded in love, for Jesus himself reshaped Israel's scriptural traditions to articulate the double-love command for God and neighbor as the greatest commandment (Matt 22:37-39//Mark 12:30//Luke 10:27; cf. Deut 6:5 and Lev 19:18).[4]

In addition to love, numerous appeals for the sharing of resources reflect the aim of creating, strengthening, or demonstrating communal solidarity through practices of mutual assistance.[5] Both the *Didache* and the *Epistle of Barnabas*, for instance, insist that members of the same family of God who are sharers (κοινωνοί) in imperishable things should be sharers in perishable things (*Did.* 4.8; *Barn.* 19.8; cf. Rom 15:26-27). Cyprian brings together the ethical warrants of love and solidarity when he introduces a citation of Acts 4:32 by stating, "Then, the full measure of their [i.e., the earliest believers and apostles in Jerusalem] performance of corporal works of mercy corresponded to their *unanimity in love*, as we read in the Acts of the Apostles: And the multitude of them that had believed acted with one soul and mind, and there was no difference among them: neither did they judge that aught of the goods which they possessed, was their own; but all things were common unto them" (*Eleem.* 25.9–13). Practices of almsgiving were central to the formation and maintenance of early Christian identity, particularly in the cultural context of the early Roman Empire in which care for the poor was not a prominent social value. Self- or communal-interest, therefore, was far from the only warrant for merciful deeds in early Christianity. Indeed, the very fact that "almsgiving" in early Christian literature was regularly denoted by the Greek word ἐλεημοσύνη (or the Latin loanword *eleemosyna*)—a term that emphasizes not merely the provision of assistance but the *merciful* provision

---

[4]   In addition to citations of the saying "love covers a multitude of sins" with reference to charity, Christian texts that ground merciful deeds or almsgiving in the practice of love include *2 Clem.* 4.3; *Did.* 1.2–6; Tertullian, *Apol.* 39; Clement of Alexandria, *Strom.* 2.18; 4.18; *Quis div.* 38; Cyprian, *Eleem.* 18, 25. Christopher M. Hays points out that Jesus' love command was frequently interpreted with reference to charitable giving (Clement of Alexandria, *Strom.* 2.15; 3.6; *Paed.* 2.13; Tertullian, *Marc.* 4.28; Irenaeus, *Haer.* 4.12.2–5; cited in Hays, "By Almsgiving and Faith," 261).

[5]   E.g., *Did.* 4.8; *Barn.* 19.8; Herm. *Vis.* 3.9.3–4; Clement of Alexandria, *Paed.* 2.13; 3.7; *Strom.* 3.7; *Quis div.* 31; Cyprian, *Eleem.* 25; *Sent. Sext.* 82b; 227–28; 295–96; 377; Justin, *1 Apol.* 14, 67; Tertullian, *Apol.* 39.

of assistance—might also be taken as an indication that genuine compassion for the needy was at least ideally understood as a motivation for charity.[6]

Yet it is impossible to avoid the frequency with which discussions of and appeals to merciful care for the poor in both the New Testament and Christian literature of the second and third centuries indicate that those who show mercy to the needy will be rewarded for their compassion. The provision of alms in early Christianity was often framed as an "interested" exchange in the sense that donors would receive a return on their investment. There is variation in the nature of this return and the identity of the source from whence it comes. In some passages, it is the recipients of material assistance themselves who reciprocate donors, either through the implied or potential return of material assistance at a future time when the initial givers require economic support themselves (2 Cor 8:13-14; *Did.* 4.5) or through the prayers of needy beneficiaries on behalf of their relatively wealthier Christian benefactors (Herm. *Sim.* 2; cf. *1 Clem.* 38). Both the ever-present threat of conjunctural poverty faced by most Christians in the first three centuries of the Common Era and scriptural passages that envisioned storing up a treasure through almsgiving for a "day of necessity" encouraged mutual interdependence through the sharing of material goods. Almsgiving could literally rescue from death (Tob 14:10-11), for the one who shared with a needy brother or sister in Christ might not only alleviate the privation of a fellow follower of Jesus but also make an investment to be returned when the original donor required material assistance. Christian rhetoric of solidarity also fostered the formation of reciprocal relationships in which material blessings were exchanged for spiritual ones, allowing both (relatively) wealthy and (relatively) poor believers to become active agents in this material-spiritual interchange (Rom 15:26-27; Phil 4:14-20; Herm. *Sim.* 2).

In other texts, God is imagined as the actor who ensures the return for merciful deeds.[7] Most often in the writings of the New Testament, divine recompense for charity—or, in some cases, abandonment of possessions, which is not the same as almsgiving—is envisioned as an eschatological reward, a return to be recouped at the final judgment (Mark 9:41; 10:17-22;

---

[6] For an illuminating analysis of the rhetoric of compassion in later Christian preaching about almsgiving, see Paul M. Blowers, "Pity, Empathy, and the Tragic Spectacle of Human Suffering: Exploring the Emotional Culture of Compassion in Late Ancient Christianity," *JECS* 18 (2010): 1–27.

[7] In some contexts, belief in God's active participation in the exchange may have been stimulated by the idea that giving to the poor is a loan to God (Prov 19:17; cf. Cyprian, *Eleem.* 16; *Sib. Or.* 2.80); see Gary A. Anderson, *Charity: The Place of the Poor in the Biblical Tradition* (New Haven: Yale University Press, 2013), 35–52.

Matt 6:1-21; 10:40-42; 19:21, 28-30; 25:31-46; Luke 12:32-34; 14:7-14;
16:1-9; 18:22, 29-30; 2 Cor 9:6-12; Phil 1:9-11; 4:17-19; 1 Tim 6:17-19; cf.
Sib. Or. 2.78–89; *Acts Thom.* 17–29).[8] In frequently locating the return for
almsgiving within an eschatological framework, early Christian texts move
beyond earlier scriptural antecedents that conceived of recompense primarily in this-worldly terms, even as contemporary Jewish writings from
the Tannaitic period also begin to situate the recompense for charity in the
eschatological future (*Mekhilta de-Rabbi Ishmael Nezikin* 10; *Tosefta Pe'ah*
4). Early Christian writings do, of course, depict divine reward for merciful deeds as something received in the present. In the New Testament, for
instance, participation in the present reality of God's kingdom and God's
family (Mark 10:29-31; Luke 18:30; 19:1-10) and the present experience of
joy and blessedness are presented as rewards for those who give away or share
their possessions (Acts 20:35; Gal 4:12-15; 1 Tim 6:17-19; cf. Herm. *Sim.*
1.8–9; 10.4). Several patristic writers, engaged as they were in the project of
articulating the Christian faith in light of contemporary philosophical traditions, emphasize almsgiving as a means of taming the passions, a benefit
for the believer seeking virtue and avoiding vice.[9] Yet while present reward
for practices of caring for the poor is an important feature of early Christian
discourse about almsgiving, the majority of texts frame the return in terms
of eschatological recompense.

Atoning almsgiving is an aspect of meritorious almsgiving. That is, the
idea that merciful deeds can serve as a means of canceling, cleansing, covering, extinguishing, lightening, or in some way atoning for human sin and/

---

[8]   One strand of Protestant interpretation discounts the notion that believers will be
rewarded at the final judgment for good deeds performed in the present life (so, e.g., Craig
Blomberg, "Degrees of Reward in the Kingdom of Heaven," *JETS* 35 [1992]: 159–72;
cf. Emma Disley, "Degrees of Glory: Protestant Doctrine and the Concept of Rewards
Hereafter," *JTS* 42 [1991]: 77–105). It is difficult, however, to avoid the implication—not
merely with regard to the New Testament's teaching about charity but also with regard to
the larger issue of judgment according to deeds—that the New Testament supports the
idea that believers will receive varying degrees of this-worldly blessedness or eschatological reward or judgment based on their care for the poor. As even Melancthon parses the
issue, "We teach that good works are meritorious, not for the remission of sins, nor for
grace and justification (for we obtain this by faith alone), but for other bodily and spiritual
rewards, both in this life and after this life, as Paul says" (*Apology, IV*: 194; cited in Christopher J. Malloy, *Engrafted into Christ: A Critique of the Joint Declaration* [New York: Peter
Lang, 2005], 47).
[9]   See the discussion in Hays, "By Almsgiving and Faith," 265–66. Hays cites Irenaeus, *Haer.* 4.12.5; Herm. *Sim.* 10.1.3; *Sent. Sextus*, 70–72; Clement of Alexandria, *Paed.*
2.1; *Quis div.* 11–12, 14–18; *Strom.* 3.5; 4.6, 18; *Ps-Clementine Homilies* 15.9; Origen, *Cels.*
7.18, 21; Cyprian, *Laps.* 11.

or its consequences is a facet of the larger connection between charity and divine recompense in early Jewish and early Christian literature. Christian advocates of atoning almsgiving in the second and third centuries of the Common Era developed this concept on the basis of engagement with earlier scriptural texts that supported the connection between almsgiving and atonement. It is one of the main contentions of this book that early Christian advocacy of atoning almsgiving emerges as a result of Christian interpretation of scriptural traditions.[10]

In order to reflect upon the importance of Scripture in the construction of Christian views about atoning almsgiving, it may be helpful to highlight the primary thesis of the only other book devoted solely to the subject, Roman Garrison's *Redemptive Almsgiving in Early Christianity*.[11] Garrison's oft-cited account of the development of this tradition maintains that atoning almsgiving is "seemingly incompatible with the fundamental soteriology of the community, namely, that Jesus died for our sins once and for all."[12] According to Garrison, conflicting views about wealth among the earliest traditions and followers of Jesus created an awkward social problem. Some strands of the Jesus tradition display harsh denunciations of wealth and the wealthy (e.g., Luke 6:24-26; 12:15-21; 14:33; 16:19-31; Matt 19:23-24// Mark 10:23-25//Luke 18:24-25). Other aspects of the Jesus tradition and other early Christian scriptural texts, however, accommodate the wealthy by "[compromising] the demand of renunciation and [promoting] the virtues of hospitality and charity, the good deeds of the rich" (e.g., Matt 6:1-4; 25:31-46; Mark 14:7; 15:43; Luke 12:33; Acts 20:35; 1 Tim 6:17-19). Moreover, the Jesus movement was initially characterized by wandering charismatic teachers who believed in the imminent end of the world and who disparaged wealth and worldly possessions in light of their eschatological convictions. Yet when the Jesus movement moved beyond Palestine and established residential communities in urban centers throughout the Mediterranean region,

---

[10] The same could be said for the development of atoning almsgiving in Rabbinic literature; see chap. 4.

[11] Roman Garrison does not ignore the role of Scripture in the formation of "redemptive almsgiving" in early Christianity, but he tends to depict Scripture as a proof employed to validate a doctrine formulated on other grounds. For example, at the conclusion of his chapter entitled "The Jewish Background of Redemptive Almsgiving," Garrison writes, "Early Christianity has its own crisis that stimulates the growth of the doctrine of redemptive almsgiving. And the church looked to her Scripture to 'authenticate' the emerging tradition. The Jewish background of this doctrine offers a fascinating parallel to its emergence in early Christianity" (*Redemptive Almsgiving in Early Christianity* [JSNT-Sup 77; Sheffield: JSOT Press, 1993], 59).

[12] Garrison, *Redemptive Almsgiving*, 109.

wealthy believers "were able to join these congregations without needing to sever their ties to the world. As time passed and communities became well-established, the prospect of an imminent Parousia grew more and more remote and upper-class Christians invested more time and wealth in this life."[13] Garrison maintains that the development among Pauline churches of "love-patriarchalism"—an ideology that calls the poor and marginalized to submit to the wealthy, who are in turn called to love the needy by providing them material support—allowed early Christian communities to integrate both poor and wealthy members.[14] In contexts in which there existed conflict between rich and poor believers—such as Rome and Corinth, in Garrison's view—there was an even greater need to incentivize charity among wealthy Christians. This social context prepared for the development of what Garrison calls "redemptive almsgiving":

> Under the umbrella of love-patriarchalism, wealth and labour were honoured inasmuch as they served to relieve the poverty of fellow believers. The social crisis of the needy made almsgiving a necessity. Theological concerns elevated the status of almsgiving to the place where it was regarded as a redemptive act of love. At some state in the development of these ideas, the distribution to the poor of one's earned wages was considered a ransom for sin. . . . The natural reluctance of the affluent to provide for those who could not make a reciprocal gift was in some cases reinforced by the knowledge of the abuse of charity on the part of those who were not truly in need of assistance. Inevitably, several Christian communities, the most notable being Corinth and Rome, experienced deep social divisions in their fellowship. Redemptive almsgiving offered incentive to the wealthy to distribute part of their abundance. They would be rewarded. At some point it was claimed that the poor could return a benefit to the one who had supplied their need: the poor could (and should) intercede for the rich. Redemptive almsgiving clearly has roots in the social conflicts within early Christianity.[15]

In addition to the social crisis that prompted the necessity of providing wealthy believers additional incentive to aid the poor, Garrison points to the problem of post-baptismal sin as a second significant feature in the emergence of the doctrine of redemptive almsgiving. Garrison contends that wealthy

[13] Garrison, *Redemptive Almsgiving*, 113.
[14] Garrison adopts the term "love-patriarchalism" from the influential writings of Gerd Theissen; see, e.g., Thesissen, *The Social Setting of Pauline Christianity: Essays on Corinth* (ed. and trans. John H. Schütz; Philadelphia: Fortress, 1982).
[15] Garrison, *Redemptive Almsgiving*, 115, 119.

Christians in the first and second centuries increasingly "abandoned the hope/fear of an imminent Parousia."[16] Without fear of God's imminent judgment, rich believers were particularly prone to devote themselves to worldly passions, including drunkenness, gluttony, and greed. Yet if post-baptismal sin deserves divine punishment, "redemptive almsgiving" offers a solution to the moral laxity of the rich: "As early Christianity wrestled with numerous issues, including support for the needy and the crisis of post-baptismal sin, redemptive almsgiving emerged as the critical doctrine that would prompt the rich to provide for the needy and to offer a means of redeeming sins committed after being washed of former sins."[17]

There are doubtless elements of the picture painted by Garrison that ring true. By the early to middle part of the third century, for instance, the external threat of persecution and internal conflict over how to respond to the lapsed created a vexing question for the church regarding the possibility of forgiveness for post-baptismal sin. Both Origen and Cyprian formulated their positions on atoning almsgiving in light of this crisis surrounding a *paenitentia secunda*. Additionally, the existence of a yawning divide between "the rich" and "the poor" that Garrison contends was characteristic of the Jesus movement almost from the beginning does seem to be a more apt description of the socioeconomic realities of the Christian communities in Clement's Alexandria or Cyprian's Carthage in the early to middle third century than of believers in the first century. The evidence suggests that in the first and second centuries of the Common Era, however, the Christian movement was not characterized by such a drastic economic split between "the rich" and "the poor." Practices of merciful care for the needy in nascent Christianity of the first and second centuries were often, and almost always potentially, reciprocal, and "almsgiving" was a survival strategy that involved the mutual exchange of goods and services along a more or less horizontal axis of those whose lives were characterized by conjunctural poverty. It is not at all evident that the earliest Christian exponents of atoning almsgiving—including the authors of the *Didache*, the *Epistle of Barnabas*, *2 Clement*, and Polycarp of Smyrna—inhabited worlds in which Christian affluence was a problem that necessitated the creation of atoning almsgiving.

Perhaps most significantly, nowhere is it clear that early Christian advocates of atoning almsgiving wrestled with a concern that the idea that sins could be cleansed or covered through merciful deeds might be "incompatible

[16] Garrison, *Redemptive Almsgiving*, 120.
[17] Garrison, *Redemptive Almsgiving*, 133.

with the earliest soteriology of Christianity."[18] Nor is it obvious why, if atoning almsgiving contradicted "the earliest soteriology of Christianity," it should have become so popular in the second and third centuries and beyond.[19] Garrison accounts for the "widespread acceptance of the new doctrine and the fact that it is not criticized in any extant sources from the period" on the basis of the claim that "among those who first advocated redemptive almsgiving were some who held positions of considerable authority in the early church of the empire," including, particularly, the prominent role and influence of the church in Rome.[20] Putting aside Garrison's problematic thesis that the endorsement of atoning almsgiving in 2 Clement represents the perspective of "Roman Christianity" and the equally questionable assumption that the influence of the Roman church alone might have "legitimated the doctrine of redemptive almsgiving in early Christianity," the attempt to locate the emergence of atoning almsgiving as a feature of Roman Christianity simply fails to account for the diverse voices in support of the tradition.[21] Neither Polycarp, nor the *Epistle of Barnabas*, nor the *Didache*, nor, for that matter, 2 Clement displays any clear connection to the church in Rome, and the three most prominent third-century advocates of atoning almsgiving— Clement, Origen, Cyprian—are all products of North African Christianity. What these authors and texts do hold in common, however, is that their promotion of atoning almsgiving is rooted in an engagement with scriptural traditions. That none of the promoters of atoning almsgiving in the second and third centuries show any hint that the idea contradicts or undermines the confession that atonement for sin is found in the life, death, and resurrection of Jesus should not be viewed as a sign of the theological incoherence of these patristic voices. Instead, this fact should be taken as an indication that atoning almsgiving represents a measured and faithful hermeneutical embodiment of the early church's inherited Scriptures.

The earliest proponents of atoning almsgiving do not provide much evidence on the basis of which to understand how, exactly, some in the early

---

[18] Garrison, *Redemptive Almsgiving*, 134. Garrison's formulation appears to assume that there was an early, singular "soteriology of Christianity" from which "redemptive almsgiving" represented a departure.

[19] As noted, patristic proponents of atoning almsgiving include Clement of Alexandria, Origen, Cyprian, Basil of Caesarea, John Chrysostom, Ambrose, and Augustine.

[20] Garrison, *Redemptive Almsgiving*, 134.

[21] Garrison, *Redemptive Almsgiving*, 142.

church understood that merciful deeds cleanse or cover sins.[22] This lack of theological precision is not entirely surprising, however, for second-century advocates of atoning almsgiving were engaged in pastoral paraenesis and not systematic theologizing. Moreover, even when the early church turned its attention to the precise formulation of doctrinal positions (as it did with regard to the topic of the human and divine natures of Christ and the mystery of the Trinity, for example), it never articulated any one particular position on atonement, leading to instead a variety of metaphors, models, and theories, drawn from the diverse witness of Scripture itself, that attempt to explain the complex reality of the human (and cosmic) plight and the solution to it provided by God in Christ.[23] The four canonical gospels themselves narrate the story of Jesus in ways that locate forgiveness of sin variously in baptism, in the act of petitioning God for forgiveness and forgiving others, and in the sacrificial death of Jesus, often without any clear sense of how these different means of forgiveness relate to one another.

Perhaps the closest that second-century proponents of atoning almsgiving come to offering an answer to the question of how almsgiving atones for sin is found in several documents in which the practice of merciful deeds (ἐλεημοσύνη) is either linked with or depicted as a symbol of repentance (2 Clem. 16.4; Herm. Mand. 2.7; Clement of Alexandria, Quis div. 38; Origen, Hom. Lev. 2.4.5).[24] In the New Testament, forgiveness of sin is regularly

---

[22] Both Origen and Cyprian indicate that merciful deeds are not merely preventative, in the sense that almsgiving in some way averts future transgressions, but restorative, in the sense that post-baptismal sins already committed can be expiated by merciful practice.

[23] Emphasis on this diversity has been standard fare in recent discussion of the atonement; see, e.g., P. R. Eddy and J. Beilby, "Atonement," in Global Dictionary of Theology: A Resource for the Worldwide Church (ed. William A. Dyrness and Veli-Matti Kärkkäinen; Downers Grove, Ill.: InterVarsity, 2009), 84–92; Joel B. Green and Mark D. Baker, Recovering the Scandal of the Cross: Atonement in New Testament & Contemporary Contexts (2nd ed.; Downers Grove, Ill.: InterVarsity, 2011); Adam J. Johnson, Atonement: A Guide for the Perplexed (London: T&T Clark, 2015), 1–26.

[24] Here it might be appropriate to offer a brief response to one recent attempt to answer this question—namely, Gary A. Anderson's stimulating two volumes, Sin and Charity. Although I am sympathetic to some of Anderson's interpretations and aims, including his broader concern to emphasize the biblical connection between charity and reward and his stress on the necessity of divine grace in Jewish and Christian discourse about almsgiving and merit, I am generally unpersuaded by the grand metaphorical framework for sin and its redemption that Anderson develops in these books.

In short, Anderson argues that, during the Second Temple period, the "dominant metaphor for sin [in Jewish literature] becomes that of financial debt" (Charity, 122). The metaphorical shift from "sin as burden" in the preexilic period to "sin as debt" in the postexilic period introduced the related idea that virtuous activity, including "almsgiving,"

connected with repentance, often embodied in the act of baptism. Sometimes the connection between forgiveness and repentance is forged with no obvious relationship to the crucifixion and resurrection of Jesus.[25] As almsgiving came to be understood as a demonstrable and embodied sign of repentance, it is easy to see how a link between almsgiving and atonement for sin could be established, especially in conversation with scriptural traditions that had already connected merciful deeds and atonement. This connection between almsgiving and repentance would also anticipate and explain the importance

---

is viewed as "credit." This metaphorical development paves the way, according to Anderson, for the development of the idea that charity can become a merit stored up in a heavenly treasury: "[S]ins are debts that can be repaid by charitable deeds that have been stored in a heavenly treasury" (121).

The primary problem is that Anderson allows his metaphorical thesis to shape his interpretation of the evidence, resulting in the construction of a theological abstract (or a meta-metaphor) that exists in Anderson's mind (and which coheres with Anderson's theological tradition) but nowhere in the primary texts of early Judaism or early Christianity. Anderson, for example, regularly asserts that in passages like Prov 10:2, Sir 29:8-13, Tob 4:7-10, and Tob 12:8-9, almsgiving funds deposit in a "heavenly treasury," when, in fact, these passages use the language of "treasury" but say nothing about its heavenly location. The Synoptic Gospels do, of course, speak of almsgiving or the dispossession of goods as a means of storing up treasure with God in heaven (Matt 6:19-21; 19:21; Mark 10:21; Luke 12:33-34; 18:22), but never with the implication that the "funds" of this heavenly treasure are used to pay the debt of sin. (That is, the image of heavenly treasure in the Synoptic Gospels is meritorious but not atoning, a distinction lost in Anderson's work.) Similarly, a cluster of passages do use the economic metaphor of "redemption" with reference to merciful deeds "redeeming" sins or the "redemption" of sins (Th Dan 4:27; *Did.* 4.6; *Barn.* 19.10), but never with reference to the image of a (heavenly) treasury. On the other hand, many texts that explicitly advocate "atoning" almsgiving use an entirely different set of (noneconomic) metaphors to refer to the expiation (Sir 3:30), cleansing (Tob 12:9), purification (Luke 11:41), or covering (1 Pet 4:8; *2 Clem.* 16.4) of sin through merciful deeds.

That Anderson employs his grand metaphorical framework and the textual evidence forced into it in *Charity* to develop a theological abstract (e.g., "charity was construed as a loan to God, which was then converted into a form of spiritual currency and stored in an impregnable divine bank" [*Charity*, 182]) that he uses to justify Catholic teaching on purgatory, the treasury of merits, and indulgences is not necessarily a mark against his work, but it is a sign that the book should be appreciated as a kind of dogmatic theology from a Catholic confessional perspective rather than as a study of "the biblical teaching about the treasury of heaven" (10).

[25] Cf. Mark 1:4//Luke 3:3//Matt 3:11. The connection between repentance and forgiveness of sin is an especially important theme in the narrative of Luke–Acts (Luke 3:3; 5:32; 15:1-32; 17:3-4; 24:47; Acts 2:38; 3:19; 5:31; 8:22; 13:24; 19:4; cf. 17:30-31), but the trope of repentance and forgiveness is not absent from the Pauline Epistles (cf. Rom 6:4; 2 Cor 7:9-10; 12:21; Col 2:12-14; 2 Tim 2:25-26).

of almsgiving in emerging practices of penitence as they developed in the third and fourth centuries and beyond.[26]

No interpretation of Scripture occurs in a vacuum. If the question is further pressed why early Christian writers and texts were inclined to connect merciful deeds, repentance, and atonement, an intriguing, though by no means certain, possibility presents itself. Atoning almsgiving reflects an understanding of sin and its solution that is socially and ecclesiologically embodied, a vision that frequently contrasts with disregard for the social body, and the bodies of the poor, in Docetic and gnostic Christianity. Second-century writers and texts like Ignatius of Antioch, Polycarp, *2 Clement*, the *Didache*, the *Epistle of Barnabas*, and the *Shepherd of Hermas* narrate a vision of Christian identity in which care for the poor is a central aspect of practice and belief. A soteriology that maintains that sins are expiated through the Christ-event *and* through practices of care for the needy is only comprehensible among communities in which poor believers are both present and valued. The statement "love covers a multitude of sins" in 1 Pet 4:8 is particularly suggestive, for in the literary context of 1 Peter the love that covers a multitude of sins is mutual love within the community of believers, particularly as that love is demonstrated through practices of hospitality (1 Pet 4:9). In contrast to constructions of Christian identity in which future resurrection and almsgiving were allegedly rejected, and in which salvation was rooted in an individual's ability to obtain proper knowledge, proponents of atoning almsgiving emphasize the social nature of sin and its remedy.

Questions about the theological legitimacy of early Christian advocacy of atoning almsgiving and its legacy, particularly in Western Christianity, will doubtless be answered differently by various branches of the Christian faith, including Catholics and Protestants. Yet the story of the emergence of atoning almsgiving in nascent Christianity suggests that canonical questions should be considered alongside hermeneutical ones. Any critical assessment of early Christian promotion of atoning almsgiving must first recognize that several passages from the Septuagint (including LXX Prov 15:27; Th Dan 4:27; Tob 12:8-10; and Sir 3:30) played a crucial role in shaping the

---

[26] Near the end of the fourth century, the link between almsgiving and repentance is masterfully explored in a series of homilies delivered by John Chrysostom in Syrian Antioch; see Gus George Christo, trans., *St. John Chrysostom, On Repentance and Almsgiving* (The Fathers of the Church: A New Translation 96; Washington, D.C.: Catholic University of America Press, 1998). The historical development of practices of penance has attracted much scholarly attention; for a brief orientation to the literature, see Alexis Torrance, *Repentance in Late Antiquity: Eastern Asceticism and the Framing of the Christian Life c.400–650 CE* (Oxford Theology and Religion Monographs; Oxford: Oxford University Press, 2012), 10–26.

development of the tradition, for these documents, in Greek translation, were considered sources of scriptural authority by the authors and communities who interpreted them to support belief in and practice of atoning alms-giving.[27] While the importance of the reception history of prominent New Testament texts like Luke 11:41 and 1 Pet 4:8 cannot be denied, it might not be a stretch to say that the concept of atoning almsgiving would not exist without the Septuagint.

At the conclusion of his book on the Septuagint and the making of the Christian Bible, T. Michael Law asks, "What would modern Christian theology look like if its theologians returned the Septuagint to the place it occupied at the foundation of the church, or at least began to read it along-side the Hebrew Bible, as a witness to the story of the Bible and in acknowl-edgement of its role in shaping Christianity?"[28] Protestants, and particularly evangelical Protestants, have often held the Bible in high regard as a founda-tion of authority without paying sufficiently nuanced attention to the con-struction of the Bible in the history of the church.[29] Recently, voices within the Protestant fold have inquired about the possibility that the Septuagint might serve as a source of authority for Christian theology.[30] It is likely that the claim that the Septuagint be taken seriously as a norm for Christian faith and practice would need to gain more traction before most Protestants would be willing to embrace the "scriptural" warrants for the early Christian practice of atoning almsgiving. Absent a readiness to read the Septuagint as Christian Scripture, early Christian promotion of atoning almsgiving may still appear misguided for most Protestants. For those inclined to consider the theological implications of the Septuagint's role in the formulation of

---

[27] Significant, too, is Origen's allegorical interpretation of Leviticus.

[28] Timothy Michael Law, *When God Spoke Greek: The Septuagint and the Making of the Christian Bible* (Oxford: Oxford University Press, 2013), 171.

[29] For a sensitive assessment from an evangelical Protestant perspective, see Craig D. Allert, *A High View of Scripture?: The Authority of the Bible and the Formation of the New Testament Canon* (Evangelical Ressourcement; Grand Rapids: Baker, 2007).

[30] In addition to Law (*When God Spoke Greek*, 167–71), see Robert W. Wall, *1 & 2 Timothy and Titus* (THNTC; Grand Rapids: Eerdmans, 2012), 271–74; J. Ross Wag-ner, "The Septuagint and the 'Search for the Christian Bible,'" in *Scripture's Doctrine and Theology's Bible: How the New Testament Shapes Christian Dogmatics* (ed. Markus Bock-muehl and Alan J. Torrance; Grand Rapids: Baker, 2008), 17–28; Brevard Childs, *The Struggle to Understand Isaiah as Christian Scripture* (Grand Rapids: Eerdmans, 2004); Martin Hengel, *The Septuagint as Christian Scripture: Its Prehistory and the Problem of Its Canon* (Edinburgh: T&T Clark, 2002); Adrian Schenker, "L'Ecriture Sainte subsiste en plusieurs forms canoniques simultanées," in *L'interpretatione della Bibbia nelle chieas: Atti del Simposio promosso dalla Congregazione per la Dottrina della Fede* (Rome: Vatican, 2001), 178–86.

Christian belief and practice, however, the development of atoning almsgiving in early Christianity offers a fascinating test case, not least because of the associated questions this topic raises about issues such as the church as holder of a treasury of merits, the existence of purgatory, and the practice of selling indulgences, none of which were clearly developed in Christian literature before the middle of the third century but all of which are, at least indirectly, related to the topic of atoning almsgiving.[31] Even for those disinclined to view the Septuagint as a part of the church's authoritative canonical witness, there may yet be wisdom found among the many patristic witnesses who held together the conviction that salvation and atonement for sin come through the life, death, and resurrection of Jesus, on one hand, and the affirmation that the practice of mercifully caring for the needy cleanses or covers sin, on the other. At the very least, perhaps this study has shown how some early Christians, motivated in part by the promise of recompense, embodied a connection between care for the poor and atonement for sin. And perhaps the patristic testimony on the integration of charity, reward, and atonement has the potential to challenge contemporary theological traditions in which those spheres are separated.

---

[31] Anderson's defense of the Catholic doctrine of the church's *thesaurus meritorum*, purgatory, and indulgences is a case in point because, in his discussion of these topics, he relies heavily on texts from the Old Testament (though not in Greek translation, although at various points the Septuagint would support his claims) and Apocrypha. Among New Testament writings, he discusses only Matt 6:1-21; Mark 10:17-31; Matt 25:31-46; and Acts 9:36-40 in any detail, and with the exception of Acts 9:36-40, the New Testament passages are discussed with reference to heavenly treasure but not purgatory or indulgences (Anderson, *Charity*, 113–89).

BIBLIOGRAPHY

Achtemeier, Paul J. *1 Peter: A Commentary on 1 Peter*. Hermeneia. Minneapolis: Fortress, 1996.

Adams, Samuel L. "Poverty and Otherness in Second Temple Instructions." Pages 189–203 in *The "Other" in Second Temple Judaism: Essays in Honor of John J. Collins*. Edited by Daniel C. Harlow, Karina Martin Hogan, Matthew Goff, and Joel S. Kaminsky. Grand Rapids: Eerdmans, 2011.

———. *Wisdom in Transition: Act and Consequence in Second Temple Instructions*. Supplements to Journal for the Study of Judaism 125. Leiden: Brill, 2008.

Albl, Martin C. *And Scripture Cannot Be Broken: The Form and Function of the Early Christian Testimonia Collections*. Novum Testamentum Supplements 96. Leiden: Brill, 1999.

Allahyari, Rebecca Anne. *Visions of Charity: Volunteer Workers and Moral Community*. Berkeley: University of California Press, 2000.

Allen, Pauline, trans. *John Chrysostom, Homilies on Paul's Letter to the Philippians*. Society of Biblical Literature Writings from the Greco-Roman World 16. Atlanta: Society of Biblical Literature, 2013.

Allert, Craig D. *A High View of Scripture?: The Authority of the Bible and the Formation of the New Testament Canon*. Evangelical Ressourcement. Grand Rapids: Baker, 2007.

Allison, Dale C., Jr. "Eldad and Modad." *Journal for the Study of the Pseudepigrapha* 21 (2011): 99–131.

———. "The Structure of the Sermon on the Mount." *Journal of Biblical Literature* 106 (1987): 423–45.

Altaner, Berthold. "Zum Problem der lateinischen Doctrina Apostolorum." *Vigiliae Christianae* 6 (1952): 160–67.

Altmann, Peter. *Festive Meals in Ancient Israel: Deuteronomy's Identity Politics in Their Ancient Near Eastern Context.* Beihefte zur Zeitschrift für die alttestamentliche Wissenschaft 424. Berlin: De Gruyter, 2011.

Amit, Aaron. "A Rabbinic Satire on the Last Judgment." *Journal of Biblical Literature* 129 (2010): 679–97.

Anderson, Gary A. *Charity: The Place of the Poor in the Biblical Tradition.* New Haven: Yale University Press, 2013.

———. "How Does Almsgiving Purge Sins?" Pages 1–14 in *Hebrew in the Second Temple Period: The Hebrew of the Dead Sea Scrolls and of Other Contemporary Sources.* Edited by Steven E. Fassberg, Moshe Bar-Asher, and Ruth A. Clements. Studies on the Texts of the Desert of Judah 108. Leiden: Brill, 2013.

———. "Redeem Your Sins by the Giving of Alms: Sin, Debt, and the 'Treasury of Merit' in Early Jewish and Christian Tradition." *Letter & Spirit* 3 (2007): 39–69.

———. "Redeem Your Sins through Works of Charity." Pages 57–65 in *To Train His Soul in Books: Syriac Asceticism in Early Christianity.* Edited by Robin Darling Young and Monica Blanchard. Washington, D.C.: Catholic University of America Press, 2011.

———. *Sin: A History.* New Haven: Yale University Press, 2010.

Andresen, Carl. "Zur Entstehung und Geschichte des trinitarischen Personbegriffes." *Zeitschrift für die neutestamentliche Wissenschaft und die Kunde der älteren Kirche* 52 (1961): 1–39.

Ansberry, Christopher B. *Be Wise, My Son, and Make My Heart Glad: An Exploration of the Courtly Nature of the Book of Proverbs.* Beihefte zur Zeitschrift für die alttestamentliche Wissenschaft 422. Berlin: De Gruyter, 2011.

Aono, Tashio. *Die Entwicklung des paulinischen Gerichtsgedankens bei den apostolischen Vätern.* Europäische Hochschulschriften 23. Bern: Peter Lang, 1979.

Attanasi, Katherine, and Amos Yong, eds. *Pentecostalism and Prosperity: The Socio-economics of the Global Charismatic Movement.* New York: Palgrave Macmillan, 2012.

Attridge, Harold W. "Intertextuality in the *Acts of Thomas.*" *Semeia* 80 (1997): 87–124.

Baker, D. L. *Tight Fists or Open Hands? Wealth and Poverty in Old Testament Law*. Grand Rapids: Eerdmans, 2009.

Bakke, Odd Magne. *"Concord and Peace": A Rhetorical Analysis of the First Letter of Clement with an Emphasis on the Language of Unity and Sedition*. Wissenschaftliche Untersuchungen zum Neuen Testament. Second Series 141. Tübingen: Mohr Siebeck, 2001.

Balabanski, Vicky. *Eschatology in the Making: Mark, Matthew and the Didache*. Society for New Testament Studies Monograph Series. Cambridge: Cambridge University Press, 1997.

Barbarick, Clifford A. "The Pattern and the Power: The Example of Christ in 1 Peter." Ph.D. diss., Baylor University, 2011.

Barclay, John M. G. "Paul, the Gift and the Battle over Gentile Circumcision: Revisiting the Logic of Galatians." *Australian Biblical Review* 58 (2010): 36–56.

Barkley, Gary Wayne, trans. *The Fathers of the Church*. Vol. 83, *Origen*. Translation of *Homiliae in Leviticum*. Washington, D.C.: The Catholic University of America Press, 1990.

Barnes, Timothy D. "The Date of Ignatius." *Expository Times* 120 (2008): 119–30.

Barrera, Albino. *Market Complicity and Christian Ethics*. New Studies in Christian Ethics 29. Cambridge: Cambridge University Press, 2011.

Barton, Stephen C. "Can We Identify the Gospel Audiences." Pages 173–94 in *The Gospels for All Christians: Rethinking the Gospel Audiences*. Edited by Richard Bauckham. Grand Rapids: Eerdmans, 1998.

Bates, Matthew W. *The Hermeneutics of Apostolic Proclamation: The Center of Paul's Method of Scriptural Interpretation*. Waco, Tex.: Baylor University Press, 2012.

———. "Prosopographic Exegesis and Narrative Logic: Paul, Origen, and Theodoret of Cyrus on Ps 69:22-23." Pages 105–34 in *Greek Patristic and Eastern Orthodox Interpretations of Romans*. Edited by Daniel Patte and Vasile Mihoc. Romans through History and Cultures 9. London: T&T Clark, 2013.

Baynes, Leslie. *The Heavenly Book Motif in Judeo-Christian Apocalypses 200 BCE–200 CE*. Journal for the Study of Judaism Supplement Series 152. Leiden: Brill, 2001.

Beckwith, Roger T. *The Old Testament Canon of the New Testament Church and Its Background in Early Judaism*. Grand Rapids: Eerdmans, 1984.

Ben-Dov, Jonathan. "The Poor's Curse: Exodus XXII 20-26 and Curse Literature in the Ancient World." *Vetus Testamentum* 56 (2006): 431–51.

Bénétreau, Samuel. "La richesse selon 1 Timothée 6,6-10 et 6,17-19." *Etudes Theologiques et Religieuses* 83 (2008): 49–60.

Ben Shalom, Yael W. "Poverty, Charity and the Image of the Poor in Rabbinic Texts from the Land of Israel." Ph.D. diss., Duke University, 2011.

Berding, Kenneth. *Polycarp and Paul: An Analysis of Their Literary and Theological Relationship in Light of Polycarp's Use of Biblical and Extra-biblical Literature*. Vigiliae Christianae Supplements 62. Leiden: Brill, 2002.

Berger, Klaus. "Almosen für Israel." *New Testament Studies* 23 (1977): 180–204.

Beyerle, Stephan. "'Release Me to Go to My Everlasting Home . . .' [Tob 3:6]: A Belief in an Afterlife in Late Wisdom Literature?" Pages 71–88 in *The Book of Tobit: Text, Tradition, Theology: Papers of the First International Conference on the Deuterocanonical Books, Pápa, Hungary, 20–21 May 2004*. Edited by Geza G. Xeravits and József Zsengellér. Supplements to the Journal for the Study of Judaism 98. Leiden: Brill, 2005.

Bird, Michael F. *The Saving Righteousness of God: Studies on Paul, Justification, and the New Perspective*. Paternoster Biblical Monographs. Milton Keynes: Paternoster, 2007.

Blanton, Thomas R., IV. "The Benefactor's Account-Book: The Rhetoric of Gift Reciprocation according to Seneca and Paul." *New Testament Studies* 59 (2013): 396–414.

———. "Saved by Obedience: Matthew 1:21 in Light of Jesus' Teaching on the Torah." *Journal of Biblical Literature* 132 (2013): 393–413.

Block, Daniel I. *How I Love Your Torah, O LORD! Studies in the Book of Deuteronomy*. Eugene, Ore.: Cascade, 2011.

Blomberg, Craig. "Degrees of Reward in the Kingdom of Heaven." *Journal of the Evangelical Theological Society* 35 (1992): 159–72.

Blowers, Paul M. "Pity, Empathy, and the Tragic Spectacle of Human Suffering: Exploring the Emotional Culture of Compassion in Late Ancient Christianity." *Journal of Early Christian Studies* 18 (2010): 1–27.

Boda, Mark J. *A Severe Mercy: Sin and Its Remedy in the Old Testament*. Siphrut: Literature and Theology of the Hebrew Scriptures 1. Winona Lake, Ind.: Eisenbrauns, 2009.

Bonnet, Maximilianus, ed. *Acta Apostolorum Apocrypha*. Vol. 2. Darmstadt: Wissenschaftliche Buchgesellschaft, 1959.

Bons, Eberhard, ed. *"Car c'est l'amour qui me plaît, non le sacrifice . . .": Recherches sur Osée 6:6 & son interprétation juive & chrétienne*. Supplements to the Study of Judaism 88. Leiden: Brill, 2004.

Bovon, François. "Tradition et rédaction en Actes 10,1-11,18." *Theologische Zeitschrift* 26 (1970): 22–45.

Bowe, Barbara Ellen. "'Many Women Have Been Empowered through God's Grace . . .' (1 Clem 55.3): Feminist Contradictions and Curiosities in Clement of Rome." Pages 15–25 in *A Feminist Companion to Patristic*

Literature. Edited by Amy-Jill Levine and Maria Mayo Robbins. London: T&T Clark, 2008.

Bowler, Kate. *Blessed: A History of the American Prosperity Gospel*. Oxford: Oxford University Press, 2013.

Brackney, William H. *A Genetic History of Baptist Thought*. Macon, Ga.: Mercer University Press, 2004.

Brändle, Rudolf. "This Sweetest Passage: Matthew 25:31-46 and Assistance to the Poor in the Homilies of John Chrysostom." Pages 127–39 in *Wealth and Poverty in Early Church and Society*. Edited by Susan R. Holman. Holy Cross Studies in Patristic Theology and History. Grand Rapids: Baker, 2008.

Bredin, Mark, ed. *Studies in the Book of Tobit: A Multidisciplinary Approach*. Library of Second Temple Studies 55. London: T&T Clark, 2006.

Breytenbach, Cilliers. "Civic Concord and Cosmic Harmony: Sources of Metaphoric Mapping in *1 Clement* 20:3." Pages 182–96 in *Encounters with Hellenism: Studies on the First Letter of Clement*. Arbeiten zur Geschichte des antiken Judentums und des Urchristentums 53. Edited by Cilliers Breytenbach and Laurence L. Welborn. Leiden: Brill, 2004.

Bridge, Steven L. "To Give or Not to Give? Deciphering the Saying of Didache 1.6." *Journal of Early Christian Studies* 5 (1997): 555–68.

Briones, David E. *Paul's Financial Policy: A Socio-theological Approach*. Library of New Testament Studies 494. London: Bloomsbury, 2013.

Bromiley, Geoffrey. *Historical Theology: An Introduction*. Grand Rapids: Eerdmans, 1978.

Brondos, David A. *Paul on the Cross: Reconstructing the Story of Redemption*. Minneapolis: Fortress, 2006.

Brown, Jeannine K. "Matthew's 'Least of These' Theology and Subversion of 'Us/Other.'" Pages 287–301 in *Matthew: Texts @ Contexts*. Edited by James P. Grimshaw and Nicole Wilkinson Duran. Minneapolis: Fortress, 2013.

Brown, Peter. *The Making of Late Antiquity*. Cambridge, Mass.: Harvard University Press, 1978.

———. *Poverty and Leadership in the Later Roman Empire: The Menahem Stern Jerusalem Lectures*. Hanover, N.H.: University Press of New England, 2002.

———. *The Ransom of the Soul: Afterlife and Wealth in Early Western Christianity*. Cambridge, Mass.: Harvard University Press, 2015.

———. *Through the Eye of a Needle: Wealth, the Fall of Rome, and the Making of Christianity in the West, 350–550 AD*. Princeton: Princeton University Press, 2012.

Brox, Norbert. *Der erste Petrusbrief.* 4th ed. Evangelisch-katholischer Kommentar zum Neuen Testament 21. Zürich: Benziger, 1993.

Brueggemann, Walter. *Deuteronomy.* Abingdon Old Testament Commentaries. Nashville: Abingdon, 2001.

Büchner, Dirk. "Some Reflections on Writing a Commentary on the Septuagint of Leviticus." Pages 107–17 in *Translation Is Required.* Edited by Robert J. V. Hiebert. Society of Biblical Literature Septuagint and Cognate Studies Series 56. Atlanta: Society of Biblical Literature, 2010.

Buell, Denise Kimber. " 'Be Not One Who Stretches Out Hands to Receive but Shuts Them When It Comes to Giving': Envisioning Christian Charity When Both Donors and Recipients Are Poor." Pages 37–47 in *Wealth and Poverty in Early Church and Society.* Edited by Susan R. Holman. Holy Cross Studies in Patristic Theology and History. Grand Rapids: Baker, 2008.

Bultmann, Rudolf. *Theology of the New Testament.* Waco, Tex.: Baylor University Press, 2007. 2 vols. in 1. Reprint of *Theology of the New Testament.* Translated by Kendrick Grobel. 2 vols. New York: Scribner's, 1951, 1955.

Burns, J. Patout. *Cyprian the Bishop.* Routledge Early Church Monographs. London: Routledge, 2002.

Caillé, Alain. "Anti-utilitarianism, Economics, and the Gift-Paradigm." Online: http://www.revuedumauss.com.fr/media/ACstake.pdf.

Calvin, John. *Commentaries on the Epistles to Timothy, Titus, and Philemon.* Translated by William Pringle. Grand Rapids: Eerdmans, 1948.

———. *The Epistle of Paul the Apostle to the Hebrews and the First and Second Epistles of St. Peter.* Translated by William B. Johnston. Edited by David W. Torrance and Thomas F. Torrance. Calvin's Commentaries 12. Grand Rapids: Eerdmans, 1963.

———. *Institutes of the Christian Religion: The First English Version of the 1541 French Edition.* Translated by Elsie Anne McKee. Grand Rapids: Eerdmans, 2009.

Campbell, Constantine R. *Paul and Union with Christ: An Exegetical and Theological Study.* Grand Rapids: Zondervan, 2012.

Campbell, Douglas A. *Framing Paul: An Epistolary Biography.* Grand Rapids: Eerdmans, 2014.

Campenhausen, Hans von. *The Fathers of the Latin Church.* Palo Alto, Calif.: Stanford University Press, 1969.

Caner, Daniel. *Wandering, Begging Monks: Spiritual Authority and the Promotion of Monasticism in Late Antiquity.* The Transformation of the Classical Heritage 33. Berkeley: University of California Press, 2002.

Carroll, John T. "Luke's Portrayal of the Pharisees." *Catholic Biblical Quarterly* 50 (1988): 604–21.

Carter, Christopher L. *Great Sermon Tradition as a Fiscal Framework in 1 Corinthians: Towards a Pauline Theology of Material Possessions.* Library of New Testament Studies 403. London: T&T Clark, 2010.

Carter, Warren. "Evoking Isaiah: Matthean Soteriology and an Intertextual Reading of Isaiah 7–9 and Matthew 1:23 and 4:15-16." *Journal of Biblical Literature* 119 (2000): 503–20.

———. *Matthew and Empire: Initial Explorations.* Harrisburg, Pa.: Trinity International, 2001.

Chapman, Stephen B. "Reading the Bible as Witness: Divine Retribution in the Old Testament." *Perspectives in Religious Studies* 31 (2004): 171–90.

Charette, Blaine. *The Theme of Recompense in Matthew's Gospel.* Journal for the Study of the New Testament Supplement Series 79. Sheffield: JSOT Press, 1992.

Charlesworth, James H., ed. *The Old Testament Pseudepigrapha.* 2 vols. Garden City, N.Y.: Doubleday, 1983.

Childs, Brevard S. *The Struggle to Understand Isaiah as Christian Scripture.* Grand Rapids: Eerdmans, 2004.

Chilton, Bruce, and Jacob Neusner. *Types of Authority in Formative Christianity and Judaism.* London: Routledge, 1999.

Christo, Gus George, trans. *St. John Chrysostom, On Repentance and Almsgiving.* The Fathers of the Church: A New Translation 96. Washington, D.C.: Catholic University of America Press, 1998.

Clarke, Andrew D. "'Do Not Judge Who Is Worthy and Unworthy': Clement's Warning Not to Speculate about the Rich Young Man's Response (Mark 10.17-31)." *Journal for the Study of the New Testament* 31 (2009): 447–68.

Clarke, Graeme W., ed. *The Letters of St. Cyprian of Carthage.* Vol. 4. Ancient Christian Writings 43. Ramsey, N.J.: Paulist, 1984.

Cohen, Anthony P. *The Symbolic Construction of Community.* Chichester: Ellis Horwood, 1985.

Cohen, Mark R. *Poverty and Charity in the Jewish Community of Medieval Egypt.* Jews, Christians, and Muslims from the Ancient to the Modern World. Princeton: Princeton University Press, 2008.

Cohn, Naftali S. *The Memory of the Temple and the Making of the Rabbis.* Divinations: Rereading Late Ancient Religion. Philadelphia: University of Pennsylvania Press, 2012.

Collins, Adela Yarbro. *Mark: A Commentary.* Hermeneia. Minneapolis: Fortress, 2007.

Collins, C. John. "Proverbs and the Levitical System." *Presbyterion* 35 (2009): 9–34.

Cook, Edward. "Sin and Salvation, Aramaic Style: Reflections on the Aramaic Vocabulary of Sin in the Light of Gary Anderson's 'Sin: A

History.'" Paper presented at the annual meeting of the SBL. Atlanta, Georgia, 2010.

Cook, Johann. *The Septuagint of Proverbs: Jewish and/or Hellenistic Proverbs? Concerning the Hellenistic Colouring of LXX Proverbs.* Vetus Testamentum Supplement 69. Leiden: Brill, 1997.

———. "Septuagint Proverbs and Canonization." Pages 79–91 in *Canonization and Decanonization: Papers presented to the International Conference of the Leiden Institute for the Study of Religions (LISOR) held at Leiden 9–10 January 1997.* Edited by A. van der Kooij and K. van der Toorn. Numen 82. Leiden: Brill, 1998.

———. "The Translator(s) of the Septuagint of Proverbs." *TC: A Journal of Biblical Textual Criticism* 7 (2002): 1–50.

Copeland, Gloria. *God's Will Is Prosperity.* Tulsa, Okla.: Harrison House, 1978.

Corley, Jeremy, and Vincent Skemp. *Intertextual Studies in Ben Sira and Tobit: Essays in Honor of Alexander A Di Lella, O.F.M.* Catholic Biblical Quarterly Monograph Series 38. Washington, D.C.: Catholic Biblical Association of America, 2005.

Countryman, William L. *The Rich Christian in the Church of the Early Empire: Contradictions and Accommodations.* New York: Edwin Mellen, 1980.

Couser, Greg A. "God and Christian Existence in the Pastoral Epistles: Toward Theological Method and Meaning." *Novum Testamentum* 42 (2000): 262–83.

Cranfield, C. E. B. *I & II Peter and Jude: Introduction and Commentary.* Torch Bible Commentaries. London: SCM Press, 1960.

Crislip, Andrew. "Lion and Human in Gospel of Thomas Logion 7." *Journal of Biblical Literature* 126 (2007): 595–613.

Crowe, Brandon D. "'Oh, Sweet Exchange!' The Soteriological Significance of the Incarnation in the Epistle to Diognetus." *Zeitschrift für die Neutestamentliche Wissenschaft und die Kunde der Älteren Kirche* 102 (2011): 96–109.

Daly, Robert J. "Sacrificial Soteriology in Origen's Homilies on Leviticus." *Studia Patristica* 17, no. 2 (1982): 872–78.

Davids, Peter H. *The First Epistle of Peter.* New International Commentary on the New Testament. Grand Rapids: Eerdmans, 1990.

Dawson, John David. *Christian Figural Reading and the Fashioning of Identity.* Berkeley: University of California Press, 2001.

DeConick, April D. *The Original Gospel of Thomas in Translation: With a Commentary and New English Translation of the Complete Gospel.* Library of New Testament Studies 287. London: T&T Clark, 2006.

Deléani, Simone. "Présence de Cyprien dans les œuvres de Jérôme sur la virginité." Pages 61–82 in *Jérôme entre l'occident et l'orient*. Edited by Yves-Marie Duval. Paris: Études Augustiniennes, 1988.

Derrida, Jacques. *Given Time: 1. Counterfeit Money*. Translated by Peggy Kamuf. Chicago: University of Chicago Press, 1992.

deSilva, David A. *The Jewish Teachers of Jesus, James, and Jude: What Earliest Christianity Learned from the Apocrypha and Pseudepigrapha*. Oxford: Oxford University Press, 2012.

Dibelius, Martin, and Hans Conzelmann. *The Pastoral Epistles: A Commentary on the Pastoral Epistles*. Translated by Philip Buttolph and Adela Yarbro. Hermeneia. Philadelphia: Fortress, 1972.

Di Lella, Alexander A. "A Study of Tobit 14:10 and Its Intertextual Parallels." *Catholic Biblical Quarterly* 71 (2009): 497–506.

Disley, Emma. "Degrees of Glory: Protestant Doctrine and the Concept of Rewards Hereafter." *Journal of Theological Studies* 42 (1991): 77–105.

Doane, William, and Robert Lowry, eds. *Gospel Music*. New York: Biglow & Main, 1876.

Docherty, Susan. "The Reception of Tobit in the New Testament and Early Christian Literature, with Special Reference to Luke–Acts." Pages 81–94 in *The Scriptures of Israel in Jewish and Christian Tradition: Essays in Honour of Maarten J. J. Menken*. Edited by Bart J. Koet, Steve Moyise, and Joseph Verheyden. Novum Testamentum Supplements 148. Leiden: Brill, 2013.

Dodson, Joseph R. *The Powers of Personification: Rhetorical Purpose in the Book of Wisdom and the Letter to the Romans*. Beihefte zur Zeitschrift für die neutestamentliche Wissenschaft 161. Berlin: De Gruyter, 2008.

Donelson, Lewis R. *I & II Peter and Jude: A Commentary*. New Testament Library. Louisville, Ky.: Westminster John Knox, 2010.

Donfried, Karl. *The Setting of Second Clement in Early Christianity*. Supplements to Novum Testamentum 38. Leiden: Brill, 1974.

Downs, David J. "Economics." Pages 219–26 in *Dictionary of Jesus and the Gospels*. 2nd ed. Edited by Joel B. Green, Jeannine K. Brown, and Nicholas Perrin. Downers Grove, Ill.: InterVarsity, 2013.

———. "The God Who Gives Life That Is Truly Life: Meritorious Almsgiving and the Divine Economy in 1 Timothy 6." Pages 242–60 in *The Unrelenting God: God's Action in Scripture; Essays in Honor of Beverly Roberts Gaventa*. Edited by David J. Downs and Matthew L. Skinner. Grand Rapids: Eerdmans, 2013.

———. "Justification, Good Works, and Creation in Clement of Rome's Appropriation of Romans 5–6." *New Testament Studies* 59 (2013): 415–32.

———. "'Love Covers a Multitude of Sins': Redemptive Almsgiving in 1 Peter 4:8 and Its Early Christian Reception." *Journal of Theological Studies* 65 (2014): 489–514.

———. *The Offering of the Gentiles: Paul's Collection for Jerusalem in Its Chronological, Cultural, and Cultic Contexts.* Wissenschaftliche Untersuchungen zum Neuen Testament. Second Series 248. Tübingen: Mohr Siebeck, 2008.

———. "Paul's Collection and the Book of Acts Revisited." *New Testament Studies* 52 (2006): 50–70.

———. "Prosopological Exegesis in Cyprian's *De opere et eleemosynis.*" *Journal of Theological Interpretation* 6 (2012): 279–94.

———. "Redemptive Almsgiving and Economic Stratification in 2 Clement." *Journal of Early Christian Studies* 19 (2011): 493–517.

———. "The Rhetoric of Almsgiving in 'Thomasine Christianity.'" Paper presented at the annual meeting of the North American Patristics Society. Chicago, May 29, 2010.

Draper, Jonathan A. "Pure Sacrifice in Didache 14 as Jewish Christian Exegesis." *Neotestamentica* 42 (2008): 223–52.

Drijvers, Han J. W. "The Acts of Thomas." Pages 322–411 in *New Testament Apocrypha.* Vol. 2, *Writings Relating to the Apostles; Apocalypses and Related Subjects.* Rev. ed. Edited by Wilhelm Schneemelcher. Translated by R. McL. Wilson. Louisville, Ky.: Westminster John Knox, 1992.

Dryden, J. de Waal. *Theology and Ethics in 1 Peter.* Wissenschaftliche Untersuchungen zum Neuen Testament. Second Series 209. Tübingen: Mohr Siebeck, 2006.

Dschulnigg, Peter. "Warnung vor Reichtum und Ermahnung der Reichen: 1 Tim 6,6-10.17-19 im Rahmen des Schlußteils 6,3-21." *Biblische Zeitschrift* 37 (1993): 60–77.

Dunn, Geoffrey D. "Cyprian's Care for the Poor: The Evidence of *De opere et eleemosynis.*" StPatr 42 (2006): 363–68.

———. *Tertullian.* The Early Church Fathers. London: Routledge, 2004.

Dunn, James D. G. *The Theology of Paul the Apostle.* Grand Rapids: Eerdmans, 1998.

Dunning, Benjamin H. *Aliens and Sojourners: Self as Other in Early Christianity.* Divinations: Rereading Late Antique Religion. Philadelphia: University of Pennsylvania Press, 2009.

Ebner, Martin. "Symposion und Wassersucht, Reziprozitätsdenken und Umkehr: Sozialgeschichte und Theologie in Lk 14,1-24." Pages 115–35 in *Paulus und Die antike Welt: Beiträge zur zeit- und religionsgeschichtlichen Erforschung des paulinischen Christentums.* Edited by David C. Bienert, Joachim Jeska, and Thomas Witulski. Forschungen zur Religion und Literatur des Alten und Neuen Testaments 222. Göttingen: Vandenhoeck & Ruprecht, 2008.

Eddy, P. R., and J. Beilby. "Atonement." Pages 84–92 in *Global Dictionary of Theology: A Resource for the Worldwide Church*. Edited by William A. Dyrness and Veli-Matti Kärkkäinen. Downers Grove, Ill.: InterVarsity, 2009.

Edwards, J. Christopher. *The Ransom Logion in Mark and Matthew: Its Reception and Its Significance for the Study of the Gospels*. Wissenschaftliche Untersuchungen zum Neuen Testament. Second Series 237. Tübingen: Mohr Siebeck, 2012.

Ehrman, Bart D. *The Apostolic Fathers*. Vols. 1 and 2. Loeb Classical Library 24–25. Cambridge, Mass.: Harvard University Press, 2003.

Elliott, John H. *1 Peter: A New Translation with Introduction and Commentary*. Anchor Bible 37B. New York: Doubleday, 2000.

Engberg-Pedersen, Troels. "Giving and Doing: The Philosophical Coherence of the Sermon on the Plain." Pages 267–87 in *Jenseits von Indikativ und Imperativ: Kontexte und Normen neutestamentlicher Ethik / Contexts and Norms of New Testament Ethics*. Vol. 1. Edited by Friedrich Wilhelm Horn and Ruben Zimmermann. Wissenschaftliche Untersuchungen zum Neuen Testament 238. Tübingen: Mohr Siebeck, 2009.

Eubank, Nathan. "Almsgiving Is 'the Commandment': A Note on 1 Timothy 6.6-19." *New Testament Studies* 58 (2012): 144–50.

———. "Storing Up Treasure with God in the Heavens: Celestial Investments in Matthew 6:1-21." *Catholic Biblical Quarterly* 76 (2014): 77–92.

———. *Wages of Cross-Bearing and Debt of Sin: The Economy of Heaven in Matthew's Gospel*. Beihefte zur Zeitschrift für die neutestamentliche Wissenschaft 196. Berlin: De Gruyter, 2013.

Fahey, Michael Andrew. *Cyprian and the Bible: A Study in Third-Century Exegesis*. Beitrage zur Geschichte der biblischen Hermeneutik 9. Tübingen: J. C. B. Mohr, 1971.

Fairchild, Diane. "Don humanitaire, don pervers." *Revue du Mauss* 8 (1996): 294–300.

Fasholé-Luke, E. "Who Is the Bridegroom? An Excursion into St. Cyprian's Use of Scripture." *StPatr* 12 (1975): 294–98.

Feldmeier, Reinhard. *The First Letter of Peter*. Waco, Tex.: Baylor University Press, 2008.

Fewster, Gregory P. *Creation Language in Romans 8: A Study in Monosemy*. Linguistic Biblical Studies 8. Leiden: Brill, 2013.

Fieger, Michael. *Das Thomasevangelium: Einleitung, Kommentar, und Systematik*. Neutestamentliche Abhandlungen 22. Münster: Aschendorff, 1991.

Finley, Moses I. *The Ancient Economy.* 2nd ed. Sather Classical Lectures 43. Berkeley: University of California Press, 1999.

Finn, Richard D. "Almsgiving for the Pure of Heart: Continuity and Change in Early Christian Teaching." Pages 419–29 in *Severan Culture.* Edited by Simon Swain, Stephen Harrison, and Jaś Elsner. Cambridge: Cambridge University Press, 2007.

———. *Almsgiving in the Later Roman Empire: Christian Promotion and Practice (313–450).* Oxford Classical Monographs. Oxford: Oxford University Press, 2006.

Fiske, Alan Paige. *Structures of Social Life: The Four Elementary Forms of Human Relations.* New York: Free Press, 1991.

Fitzmyer, Joseph A. *Tobit.* Commentaries on Early Jewish Literature. Berlin: De Gruyter, 2003.

Forti, Tova. "The Concept of 'Reward' in Proverbs: A Diachronic of Synchronic Approach?" *Currents in Biblical Research* 12 (2014): 129–45.

Foster, Paul. "The Epistles of Ignatius of Antioch." Pages 81–107 in *The Writings of the Apostolic Fathers.* Edited by Paul Foster. London: T&T Clark, 2007.

———. "Polymorphic Christology: Its Origins and Development in Early Christianity." *Journal of Theological Studies* 58 (2007): 66–99.

———. "Who Wrote 2 Thessalonians? A Fresh Look at an Old Problem." *Journal for the Study of the New Testament* 35 (2012): 150–75.

Fowl, Stephen. "Effective History and the Cultivation of Wise Interpreters." *Journal of Theological Interpretation* 7 (2013): 153–61.

Fox, Michael V. *Proverbs 1–9: A New Translation with Introduction and Commentary.* Anchor Bible 18A. New York: Doubleday, 2000.

France, R. T. *The Gospel of Matthew.* New International Commentary on the New Testament. Grand Rapids: Eerdmans, 2007.

Franzmann, Majella. "Augustine's View of Manichaean Almsgiving and Almsgiving by the Manichaean Community at Kellis." *HTS Teologiese Studies* 69 (2013). http://www.hts.org.za/index.php/HTS/article/view/1356.

Fretheim, Thorstein. "In Defense of Monosemy." Pages 79–115 in *Pragmatics and the Flexibility of Word Meaning.* Edited by Németh T. Enikö and Károly Bibok. Current Research in the Semantics/Pragmatics Interface 8. Amsterdam: Elsevier, 2001.

Freu, Christel. *Les Figures du pauvre dans le sources italiennes de l'antiquité tardive.* Collections de l'Université Marc Bloch-Strasbourg / Études d'Archéologie et d'Histoire Ancienne. Paris: De Boccard, 2007.

Friesen, Steven J. "Injustice or God's Will? Early Christian Explanations of Poverty." Pages 17–36 in *Wealth and Poverty in Early Church and Society.*

Edited by Susan R. Holman. Holy Cross Studies in Patristic Theology and History. Grand Rapids: Baker, 2008.

———. "Poverty in Pauline Studies: Beyond the So-Called New Consensus." *Journal for the Study of the New Testament* 26 (2004): 323–61.

Gadamer, Hans-Georg. *Truth and Method.* 2nd rev. ed. Translated by Joel Weinsheimer and Donald G. Marshall. London: Continuum, 2004.

Gardner, Gregg E. "Charity Wounds." Pages 173–88 in *The Gift in Antiquity.* Edited by Michael L. Satlow. Oxford: Wiley-Blackwell, 2013.

———. "Competitive Giving in the Third Century CE: Early Rabbinic Approaches to Greco-Roman Civic Benefaction." Pages 81–92 in *Religious Competition in the Third Century CE: Jews, Christians, and the Greco-Roman World.* Edited by Jordan D. Rosenblum, Lily Vuong, and Nathaniel DesRosiers. Göttingen: Vandenhoeck & Ruprecht, 2014.

———. *The Origins of Organized Charity in Rabbinic Judaism.* Cambridge: Cambridge University Press, 2015.

———. "Who Is Rich? The Poor in Early Rabbinic Judaism." *Jewish Quarterly Review* 104 (2014): 515–36.

Garrison, Roman. "The Love of Money in Polycarp's Letter to the Philippians." Pages 74–79 in *The Graeco-Roman Context of Early Christian Literature.* Journal for the Study of the New Testament Supplement Series 137. Sheffield: Sheffield Academic, 1997.

———. *Redemptive Almsgiving in Early Christianity.* Journal for the Study of the New Testament Supplement Series 77. Sheffield: JSOT Press, 1993.

Gasché, Rodolphe. "Heliocentric Exchange." Pages 100–117 in *The Logic of the Gift: Toward an Ethic of Generosity.* Edited by Alan D. Schrift. London: Routledge, 1997.

Gathercole, Simon J. *Defending Substitution: An Essay on Atonement in Paul.* Acadia Studies in Bible and Theology. Grand Rapids: Baker, 2015.

———. *The Gospel of Thomas: Introduction and Commentary.* Texts and Editions for New Testament Study 11. Leiden: Brill, 2014.

———. "'The Heavens and the Earth Will Be Rolled Up': The Eschatology of the Gospel of Thomas." Pages 280–302 in *Eschatologie-Eschatology: The Sixth Durham-Tübingen Research Symposium; Eschatology in Old Testament, Ancient Judaism, and Early Christianity.* Edited by Hans-Joachim Eckstein, Christof Landmesser, and Hermann Lichtenberger. Wissenschaftliche Untersuchungen zum Neuen Testament 272. Tübingen: Mohr Siebeck, 2011.

Gaventa, Beverly Roberts. "Galatians 1 and 2: Autobiography as Paradigm." *Novum Testamentum* 28 (1986): 309–26.

———. "Theology and Ecclesiology in the Miletus Speech: Reflections on Content and Context." *New Testament Studies* 50 (2004): 36–52.

Gerdmar, Anders. *Roots of Theological Anti-Semitism: German Biblical Inter-pretation and the Jews, from Herder and Semler to Kittel and Bultmann.* Studies in Jewish History and Culture 20. Leiden: Brill, 2009.

Gerhardsson, Birger. "Geistiger Opferdienst nach Matth 6,1-6, 16-21." Pages 69–77 in *Neues Testament und Geschichte: Historisches Geschehen und Deutung im Neuen Testament.* Edited by Heinrich Baltensweiler and Bo Reiche. Zurich: Theologischer, 1972.

Giambrone, Anthony. "'According to the Commandment' [Did. 1.5]: Lexi-cal Reflections on Almsgiving as 'The Commandment.'" *New Testament Studies* 60 (2014): 448–65.

Giese, Ronald L., Jr. "Compassion for the Lowly in Septuagint Proverbs." *Journal for the Study of the Pseudepigrapha* 11 (1993): 109–17.

———. "Qualifying Wealth in the Septuagint of Proverbs." *Journal of Bibli-cal Literature* 111 (1992): 409–25.

Glancy, Jennifer A. *Slavery in Early Christianity.* Oxford: Oxford University Press, 2002.

Godbout, Jacques T., and Alain Caillé. *The World of the Gift.* Translated by Donald Winkler. Montreal: McGill-Queen's University Press, 1998.

Goldenberg, Robert. "Early Rabbinic Explanations of the Destruction of Jerusalem." *Journal of Jewish Studies* 33 (1982): 517–25.

Goldingay, John E. *Daniel.* Word Biblical Commentary 30. Dallas: Word, 1989.

Goodspeed, Edgar Johnson. "The Didache, Barnabas and the Doctrina." *Anglican Theological Review* 27 (1945): 228–47.

Goppelt, Leonhard. *Der erste Petrusbrief.* Kritisch-exegetischer Kom-mentar über das Neue Testament 12/1. Göttingen: Vandenhoeck & Ruprecht, 1978.

Gorman, Michael J. *The Death of the Messiah and the Birth of the New Covenant: A (Not So) New Model of the Atonement.* Eugene, Ore.: Cascade, 2014.

Graeber, David. *Toward an Anthropological Theory of Value: The False Coin of Our Own Dreams.* New York: Palgrave, 2001.

Gray, Alyssa M. "The Formerly Wealthy Poor: From Empathy to Ambiv-alence in Rabbinic Literature of Late Antiquity." *Association for Jewish Studies Review* 33 (2009): 101–33.

———. "Redemptive Almsgiving and the Rabbis of Late Antiquity." *Jewish Studies Quarterly* 18 (2011): 144–84.

Gray, Sherman W. *The Least of My Brothers: Matthew 25:31-46; A History of Interpretation.* Society of Biblical Literature Dissertation Series 114. Atlanta: Scholars Press, 1989.

Green, Joel B. *1 Peter.* Two Horizons New Testament Commentary. Grand Rapids: Eerdmans, 2007.

————. *The Gospel of Luke*. New International Commentary on the New Testament. Grand Rapids: Eerdmans 1997.

————. *The Theology of the Gospel of Luke*. New Testament Theology. Cambridge: Cambridge University Press, 1995.

Green, Joel B., Jacqueline E. Lapsley, Rebekah Miles, and Allen Verhey, eds. *Dictionary of Scripture and Ethics*. Grand Rapids: Baker, 2011.

Green, Joel B., and Mark D. Baker. *Recovering the Scandal of the Cross: Atonement in New Testament & Contemporary Contexts*. 2nd ed. Downers Grove, Ill.: InterVarsity, 2011.

Greenslade, Stanley, ed. *Early Latin Theology*. Library of Christian Classics 5. Philadelphia: Westminster, 1956.

Greer, Rowan A. *Broken Light and Mended Lives: Theology and Common Life in the Early Church*. University Park: Pennsylvania State University Press, 1986.

Gregory, Bradley C. *Like an Everlasting Signet Ring: Generosity in the Book of Sirach*. Deuterocanonical and Cognate Literature Studies 2. Berlin: De Gruyter, 2010.

Gregory, Chris A. *Gifts and Commodities*. London: Academic, 1982.

Griffin, Patrick J. "A Study of *Eleēmosynē* in the Bible with Emphasis upon Its Meaning and Usage in the Theology of Tobit and Ben Sira." M.A. thesis, The Catholic University of America, 1982.

Grimonprez-Damm, Benoît. "Le 'sacrifice' eucharistique dans la Didachè." *Revue des sciences religieuses* 64 (1990): 9–25.

Grindheim, Sigurd. "Ignorance Is Bliss: Attitudinal Aspects of the Judgment according to Works in Matthew 25:31-46." *Novum Testamentum* 50 (2008): 313–31.

Grondin, Jean. *Introduction à Hans-Georg Gadamer*. Paris: Le Cerf, 1999.

Groody, Daniel G. *Globalization, Spirituality, and Justice*. Maryknoll, N.Y.: Orbis, 2007.

Grudem, Wayne. *1 Peter*. Tyndale New Testament Commentaries. Grand Rapids: Eerdmans, 1988.

Gudeman, Stephen. "Postmodern Gifts." Pages 459–74 in *Postmodernism, Economics and Knowledge*. Edited by Stephen Cullenburg, Jack Amariglio, and David F. Ruccio. London: Routledge, 2001.

Gurtner, Daniel M. "The 'House of the Veil' in Sirach 50." *Journal for the Study of the Pseudepigrapha* 14 (2005): 187–200.

Hägg, Henny Fiskå. *Clement of Alexandria and the Beginnings of Christian Apophaticism*. Oxford: Oxford University Press, 2006.

Hagner, Donald A. *Matthew*. Word Biblical Commentary 33. 2 vols. Dallas: Word, 1993, 1995.

Hamm, Dennis. "Zacchaeus Revisited Once More: A Story of Vindication or Conversion?" *Biblica* 72 (1991): 248–52.

Hansen, G. Walter. *The Letter to the Philippians.* Pillar New Testament Commentary. Grand Rapids: Eerdmans, 2009.

Harink, Douglas. *1 & 2 Peter.* Brazos Theological Commentary on the Bible. Grand Rapids: Baker, 2009.

Harnisch, Wolfgang. "Der Paulinische Lohn: (I Kor 9,1-23)." *Zeitschrift für Theologie und Kirche* 104 (2007): 25–43.

Harrington, Daniel J. *Jesus Ben Sira of Jerusalem: A Biblical Guide to Living Wisely.* Collegeville, Minn.: Liturgical, 2005.

Harris, Murray J. *The Second Epistle to the Corinthians.* New International Greek Testament Commentary. Grand Rapids: Eerdmans, 2005.

Hartin, Patrick J. *James.* Sacra Pagina. Collegeville, Minn.: Liturgical, 2009.

Hartog, Paul. *Polycarp's Epistle to the Philippians and the Martyrdom of Polycarp: Introduction, Text, and Commentary.* Oxford Apostolic Fathers. Oxford: Oxford University Press, 2013.

———. "The Relationship between *Paraenesis* and Polemic in Polycarp, *Philippians.*" *Studia Patristica* 65 (2013): 27–37.

Hawthorne, Gerald F. *Philippians.* Word Biblical Commentary 43. Dallas: Word, 1983.

Hays, Christopher M. "Beyond Mint and Rue: The Implications of Luke's Interpretive Controversies for Modern Consumerism." *Political Theology* 11 (2010): 383–98.

———. "By Almsgiving and Faith Sins Are Purged? The Theological Underpinnings of Early Christian Care for the Poor." Pages 260–80 in *Engaging Economics: New Testament Scenarios and Early Christian Reception.* Edited by Bruce W. Longenecker and Kelly D. Liebengood. Grand Rapids: Eerdmans, 2009.

———. *Luke's Wealth Ethics: A Study in Their Coherence and Character.* Wissenschaftliche Untersuchungen zum Neuen Testament. Second Series 275. Tübingen: Mohr Siebeck, 2010.

———. "Resumptions of Radicalism: Christian Wealth Ethics in the Second and Third Centuries." *Zeitschrift für die neutestamentliche Wissenschaft und die Kunde der älteren Kirche* 102 (2011): 261–82.

Hays, Richard B. *The Moral Vision of the New Testament: A Contemporary Introduction to New Testament Ethics.* San Francisco: HarperSanFrancisco, 1996.

Hayward, Robert. "Sacrifice and World Order: Some Observations on Ben Sira's Attitude to the Temple Service." Pages 22–34 in *Sacrifice and Redemption: Durham Essays in Theology.* Edited by Stephen Sykes. Cambridge: Cambridge University Press, 1991.

Heiligenthal, Roman. "Werke der Barmherzigkeit oder Almosen: Zur Bedeutung von ἐλεημοσύνη." *Novum Testamentum* 25, no. 4 (1983): 289–301.

Heine, Ronald E. "Cyprian and Novatian." Pages 152–60 in *The Cambridge History of Early Christian Literature*. Edited by Frances Young, Lewis Ayres, and Andrew Louth. Cambridge: Cambridge University Press, 2004.

Hengel, Martin. *The Septuagint as Christian Scripture: Its Prehistory and the Problem of Its Canon*. Edinburgh: T&T Clark, 2002.

Herron, Thomas J. *Clement and the Early Church of Rome: On the Dating of Clement's First Epistle to the Corinthians*. Steubenville, Ohio: Emmaus Road, 2010

Hicks-Keeton, Jill. "Already/Not Yet: Eschatological Tension in the Book of Tobit." *Journal of Biblical Literature* 132 (2013): 97–117

Hilhorst, A. "The Heavenly Palace in the *Acts of Thomas*." Pages 53–64 in *The Apocryphal Acts of Thomas*. Edited by Jan N. Bremmer. Studies on Early Christian Apocrypha 6. Leuven: Peeters, 2001.

Hirshman, Marc. *The Stabilization of Rabbinic Culture, 100 C.E.–350 C.E.: Texts on Education and Their Late Antique Context*. Oxford: Oxford University Press, 2009.

Hoek, Annewies van den. "How Alexandrian Was Clement of Alexandria? Reflections on Clement and His Alexandrian Background." *Heythrop Journal* 31 (1990): 179–94.

Holman, Susan R. *The Hungry Are Dying: Beggars and Bishops in Roman Cappadocia*. Oxford Studies in Historical Theology. Oxford: Oxford University Press, 2001.

Holmes, Michael W. *The Apostolic Fathers: Greek Texts and English Translations*. 3rd ed. Grand Rapids: Baker, 2007.

———. "Polycarp's *Letter to the Philippians* and the Writings That Later Formed the New Testament." Pages 187–227 in *The Reception of the New Testament in the Apostolic Fathers*. Edited by Andrew F. Gregory and Christopher M. Tuckett. The New Testament and the Apostolic Fathers 1. Oxford: Oxford University Press, 2005.

Horrell, David G. "Disciplining Performance and 'Placing' the Church: Widows, Elders, and Slaves in the Household of God (1 Tim 5,1–6,2)." Pages 109–34 in *1 Timothy Reconsidered*. Edited by Karl P. Donfried. Colloquium Oecumenicum Paulinum 18. Leuven: Peeters, 2008.

———. "'The Lord Commanded . . . but I Have Not Used . . .': Exegetical and Hermeneutical Reflections on 1 Cor 9.14-15." *New Testament Studies* 43 (1997): 587–603.

Horsley, Richard A. *Hearing the Whole Story: The Politics of Plot in Mark's Gospel*. Louisville, Ky.: Westminster John Knox, 2001.

Houston, Walter J. "'You Shall Open Your Hand to Your Needy Brother': Ideology and Moral Formation in Deut 15:1-18." Pages 296–314 in *The Bible in Ethics: The Second Sheffield Colloquium*. Edited by John W.

Rogerson, Margaret Davies, and M. Daniel Carroll. Journal for the Study of the Old Testament Supplement Series 207. Sheffield: Sheffield Academic, 1995.

Hurtado, Larry W. "The Jerusalem Collection and the Book of Galatians." *Journal for the Study of the New Testament* (1979): 46–62.

Ilan, Ṭal. *Mine and Yours Are Hers: Retrieving Women's History from Rabbinic Literature*. Arbeiten zur Geschichte des antiken Judentums und des Urchristentums 41. Leiden: Brill, 1997.

Ingarden, Roman. *The Cognition of the Literary Work of Art*. Translated by Ruth Ann Crowley and Kenneth R. Olson. Evanston, Ill.: Northwestern University Press, 1973.

Itter, Andrew C. *Esoteric Teaching in the Stromateis of Clement of Alexandria*. Vigiliae Christianae Supplements 97. Leiden: Brill, 2009.

Jastrow, Marcus. *Dictionary of the Targumim, the Talmud Babli and Yerushalmi, and the Midrashic Literature*. 2 vols. New York: Pardes, 1950.

Jefford, Clayton N. "Locating the Didache." *Forum* 3 (2014): 39–68.

Jewett, Robert. *Romans: A Commentary*. Hermeneia. Minneapolis: Fortress, 2007.

Jipp, Joshua W. "Death and the Human Predicament, Salvation as Transformation, and Bodily Practices in 1 Corinthians and the Gospel of Thomas." Pages 242–66 in *Paul and the Gospels: Christologies, Conflicts and Convergences*. Edited by Michael F. Bird and Joel Willitts. Library of New Testament Studies 411. London: T&T Clark, 2011.

Jipp, Joshua W., and Michael J. Thate. "Dating Thomas: Logion 53 as a Test Case for Dating the Gospel of Thomas within an Early Christian Trajectory." *Bulletin for Biblical Research* 20 (2010): 237–55.

Jobes, Karen H. *1 Peter*. Baker Exegetical Commentary on the New Testament. Grand Rapids: Baker, 2005.

———. "The Septuagint Textual Tradition in 1 Peter." Pages 311–33 in *Septuagint Research: Issues and Challenges in the Study of the Greek Jewish Scriptures*. Edited by Wolfgang Kraus and R. Glenn Wooden. Atlanta: Society of Biblical Literature, 2006.

Johnson, Adam J. *Atonement: A Guide for the Perplexed*. London: T&T Clark, 2015.

Johnson, Luke Timothy. *The First and Second Letters to Timothy: A New Translation with Introduction and Commentary*. Anchor Bible 35A. New York: Doubleday, 2001.

Johnson, Steven R. *Seeking the Imperishable Treasure: Wealth, Wisdom, and a Jesus Saying*. Eugene, Ore.: Wipf & Stock, 2008.

Joosten, Jan. "חסד 'bienveillance' et *ELEOS* 'pitié': Réflexions sur une équivalence lexicale dans la Septante." Pages 25–42 in *"Car c'est l'amour qui me plaît, non le sacrifice . . .": Recherches sur Osée 6:6 & son interprétation*

juive & chrétienne. Edited by Eberhard Bons. Supplements to the Study of Judaism 88. Leiden: Brill, 2004.

———. *Collected Studies on the Septuagint: From Language to Interpretation and Beyond*. Forschungen zum Alten Testament 83. Tübingen: Mohr Siebeck, 2012.

Juel, Donald H. *The Gospel of Mark*. Interpreting Biblical Texts. Nashville: Abingdon, 2011.

Kannengiesser, Charles. "The Bible as Read in the Early Church: Patristic Exegesis and Its Presuppositions." Pages 29–36 in *The Bible and Its Readers*. Edited by W. Beuken, S. Freyne, and A. Weiler. London: SCM Press, 1991.

———, ed. *Handbook of Patristic Exegesis: The Bible in Ancient Christianity*. The Bible in Ancient Christianity 1. Leiden: Brill, 2006.

Käsemann, Ernst. "Das Formular einer neutestamentlichen Ordinationsparänese." Pages 261–68 in *Neutestamentliche Studien für Rudolf Bultmann: Zu seinem siebzigsten Geburtstag*. Edited by Walther Eltester. Beihefte zur Zeitschrift für die neutestamentliche Wissenschaft 21. Berlin: De Gruyter, 1954.

Keating, Daniel. *First and Second Peter, Jude*. Catholic Commentary on Sacred Scripture. Grand Rapids: Baker, 2011.

Keener, Craig S. *Acts: An Exegetical Commentary*. 4 vols. Grand Rapids: Baker, 2012–2015.

Kelhoffer, James A. "'How Soon a Book' Revisited: Euangelion as a Reference to 'Gospel' Materials in the First Half of the Second Century." *Zeitschrift für die neutestamentliche Wissenschaft und die Kunde der älteren Kirche* 95 (2004): 1–34.

———. "Reciprocity as Salvation: Christ as Salvific Patron and the Corresponding 'Payback' Expected of Christ's Earthly Clients according to the Second Letter of Clement." *New Testament Studies* 59 (2013): 433–56.

Kelly, J. N. D. *The Epistles of Jude and Peter*. Black's New Testament Commentaries. London: Harper, 1969.

Kiel, Micah D. "Tobit and Moses Redux." *Journal for the Study of the Pseudepigrapha* 17 (2008): 83–98.

———. "Tobit's Theological Blindness." *Catholic Biblical Quarterly* 73 (2011): 281–98.

———. *The "Whole Truth": Rethinking Retribution in the Book of Tobit*. Library of Second Temple Studies 82. London: T&T Clark, 2012.

Kim, David William. "What Shall We Do? The Community Rules of Thomas in the 'Fifth Gospel.'" *Biblica* 88 (2007): 393–414.

Kim, Kyoung-Shik. *God Will Judge Each One according to Works: Judgment according to Works and Psalm 62 in Early Judaism and the New Testament*.

Beihefte zur Zeitschrift für die neutestamentliche Wissenschaft 178. Berlin: De Gruyter, 2010.

Kirk, Alexander N. "Paul's Approach to His Death in His Letters and in Early Pauline Effective History." D.Phil. diss., University of Oxford, 2013.

Kittel, G., and G. Friedrich, eds. *Theological Dictionary of the New Testament*. Translated by G. W. Bromiley. 10 vols. Grand Rapids: Eerdmans, 1964–1976.

Klawans, Jonathan. *Impurity and Sin in Ancient Judaism*. Oxford: Oxford University Press, 2000.

———. *Purity, Sacrifice, and the Temple: Symbolism and Supersessionism in the Study of Ancient Judaism*. Oxford: Oxford University Press, 2006.

Klijn, Albertus Frederik Johannes. *The Acts of Thomas: Introduction, Text, and Commentary*. Rev. ed. Novum Testamentum Supplements 108. Leiden: Brill, 2003.

———. "The Question of the Rich Young Man in a Jewish-Christian Gospel." *Novum Testamentum* 8 (1966): 149–55.

Kline, Leslie. "Ethics for the End Time: An Exegesis of 1 Peter 4:7-11." *Restoration Quarterly* 7 (1963): 113–23.

Kloppenborg, John S. "Poverty and Piety in Matthew, James and the Didache." Pages 201–32 in *Matthew, James, and Didache: Three Related Documents in Their Jewish and Christian Settings*. Edited by Huub van de Sandt and Jürgen K. Zangenberg. Society of Biblical Literature Symposium Series 45. Atlanta: Society of Biblical Literature, 2008.

———. "The Transformation of Moral Exhortation in Didache 1–5." Pages 88–109 in *Didache in Context: Essays on Its Text, History, and Transmission*. Edited by Clayton N. Jefford. Novum Testamentum Supplements 77. Leiden: Brill, 1995.

Knibb, Michael A. "Temple and Cult in Apocryphal and Pseudepigraphal Writings from before the Common Era." Pages 401–16 in *Temple and Worship in Biblical Israel*. Edited by John Day. Library of Hebrew Bible/Old Testament Studies 422. London: T&T Clark, 2005.

Knight, Mark. "*Wirkungsgeschichte*, Reception History, and Reception Theory." *Journal for the Study of the New Testament* 33 (2010): 137–46.

Knust, Jennifer Wright, and Zsuzsanna Varhelyi, eds. *Ancient Mediterranean Sacrifice*. Oxford: Oxford University Press, 2011.

Koch, Dietrich-Alex. "The God-Fearers between Facts and Fiction: Two Theosebeis-Inscriptions from Aphrodisias and Their Bearing for the New Testament." *Studia Theologica* 60, no. 1 (2006): 62–90.

Koch, Klaus. "Der Schatz im Himmel." Pages 47–60 in *Leben Angesichts des Todes: Beiträge zum theologischen Problem des Todes; Helmut Thielicke zum 60 Geburtstag*. Edited by Berhard Lohse and H. P. Schmidt. Tübingen: Mohr, 1968.

———. "Stages in the Canonization of the Book of Daniel." Pages 421–46 in *The Book of Daniel: Composition and Reception*. Vol. 2. Edited by John J. Collins and Peter W. Flint. Supplements to Vetus Testamentum 83. Leiden: Brill, 2001.

Komter, Aafke. *Social Solidarity and the Gift*. Cambridge: Cambridge University Press, 2005.

Kottsieper, Ingo. "The Aramaic Tradition: Ahikar." Pages 109–24 in *Scribes, Sages, and Seers: The Sage in the Eastern Mediterranean World*. Edited by Leo G. Perdue. Göttingen: Vandenhoeck & Ruprecht, 2008.

Kovacs, Judith. "Divine Pedagogy and the Gnostic Teacher according to Clement of Alexandria." *Journal of Early Christian Studies* 9 (2001): 3–25.

Lambdin, Thomas O. "The Gospel according to Thomas." Pages 52–93 in *Nag Hammadi Codex II,2–7 together with XIII,2*, Brit. Lib. Or.4926(1), and P.Oxy. 1, 654, 655*. Vol. 1. Edited by Bentley Layton. Nag Hammadi Studies 20. Leiden: Brill, 1989

Lampe, G. W. H., ed. *A Patristic Greek Lexicon*. Oxford: Oxford University Press, 1969.

Lapin, Hayim. "The Origins and Development of the Rabbinic Movement in the Land of Israel." Pages 206–29 in *The Cambridge History of Judaism*. Vol. 4, *The Late Roman-Rabbinic Period*. Edited by Steven T. Katz. Cambridge: Cambridge University Press, 2006.

Laporte, Jean. "Forgiveness of Sins in Origen." *Worship* 60 (1986): 520–27.

Lappenga, Benjamin J. "Misdirected Emulation and Paradoxical Zeal: Paul's Redefinition of 'The Good' as Object of ζῆλος in Galatians 4:12-20." *Journal of Biblical Literature* 131 (2012): 775–96.

———. *Paul's Language of Ζῆλος: Monosemy and the Rhetoric of Identity and Practice*. Biblical Interpretation Series 137. Leiden: Brill, 2015.

Lauterbach, Jacob Z. *Mekilta de-Rabbi Ishmael*. Vol. 1. Philadelphia: Jewish Publication Society of America, 1976.

Law, Timothy Michael. *When God Spoke Greek: The Septuagint and the Making of the Christian Bible*. Oxford: Oxford University Press, 2013.

Lechner, Thomas. *Ignatius Adversus Valentinianos? Chronologische und theologischichtliche Studien zu den Briefen des Ignatius von Antiochien*. Vigiliae Christianae Supplements 47. Leiden: Brill, 1999.

Lee, John A. L. *A Lexical Study of the Septuagint Version of the Pentateuch*. Society of Biblical Literature Septuagint and Cognate Studies 14. Chico, Calif.: Scholars Press, 1983.

———. "Review of T. Muraoka, *A Greek-English Lexicon of the Septuagint*." *Bulletin of the International Organization of Septuagint and Cognate Studies* 43 (2010): 115–25.

Lehtipuu, Outi. "The Rich, the Poor, and the Promise of an Eschatological Reward in the Gospel of Luke." Pages 229–46 in *Other Worlds and Their*

Relation to This World. Edited by Tobias Nicklas, Joseph Verheyden, Erik M. M. Eynikel, and Florentino García Martínez. Supplements to the Journal for the Study of Judaism 143. Leiden: Brill, 2010.

Lieberman, Saul. "Two Lexicographical Notes." *Journal of Biblical Literature* 65 (1946): 67–72.

Lightfoot, J. B. *The Apostolic Fathers, Part 2: S. Ignatius; S. Polycarp.* 3 vols. London: Macmillan, 1885.

Lightfoot, J. L. *The Sibylline Oracles: With Introduction, Translation, and Commentary on the First and Second Books.* Oxford: Oxford University Press, 2007.

Lindeman, Andreas. *Die Clemensbriefe.* Handbuch zum Neuen Testament 17. Tübingen: J. C. B. Mohr, 1992.

Lipsett, B. Diane. *Desiring Conversion: Hermas, Thecla, Aseneth.* Oxford: Oxford University Press, 2010.

Littman, Robert J. *Tobit: The Book of Tobit in Codex Sinaiticus.* Septuagint Commentary Series 9. Leiden: Brill, 2008.

Lona, Horatio E. *Der erste Clemensbrief: Übersetzt und Erklärt.* Kommentar zu den Apostolischen Vätern 3. Göttingen: Vandenhoeck & Ruprecht, 1998.

Longenecker, Bruce W. "Exposing the Economic Middle: A Revised Economy Scale for the Study of Early Urban Christianity." *Journal for the Study of the New Testament* 31 (2009): 243–78.

———. *Remember the Poor: Paul, Poverty, and the Greco-Roman World.* Grand Rapids: Eerdmans, 2010.

———. "'Until Christ Is Formed in You': Suprahuman Forces and Moral Character in Galatians." *Catholic Biblical Quarterly* 61 (1999): 92–108.

Longman, Tremper. *Proverbs.* Baker Commentary on the Old Testament Wisdom and Psalms. Grand Rapids: Baker, 2006.

Lundbom, Jack R. *Deuteronomy: A Commentary.* Grand Rapids: Eerdmans, 2013.

Lundhaug, Hugo. *Images of Rebirth: Cognitive Poetics and Transformational Soteriology in the Gospel of Philip and the Exegesis of the Soul.* Nag Hammadi and Manichean Studies 73. Leiden: Brill, 2010.

Lusini, Gianfrancesco. "La citation d'Osée 6:6 dans les Oracles Sibyllins." Pages 43–55 in *"Car c'est l'amour qui me plaît, non le sacrifice . . .": Recherches sur Osée 6:6 & son interprétation juive & chrétienne.* Edited by Eberhard Bons. Supplements to the Study of Judaism 88. Leiden: Brill, 2004.

Lust, Johan. "Cult and Sacrifice in Daniel: The Tamid and the Abomination of Desolation." Pages 671–88 in *The Book of Daniel: Composition and Reception.* Vol. 2. Edited by John J. Collins and Peter W. Flint. Supplements to Vetus Testamentum 83. Leiden: Brill, 2001.

Luther, Martin. *Commentary on Peter and Jude.* Translated by John Nichols Lenker. Grand Rapids: Kregel Classics, 1990.

Lyonnet, Stanislas, and Léopold Sabourin. *Sin, Redemption, and Sacrifice: A Biblical and Patristic Study.* Rome: Biblical Institute, 1998.

Lyu, Sun Myung. *Righteousness in the Book of Proverbs.* Forschungen zum Alten Testament. Second Series 55. Tübingen: Mohr Siebeck, 2012.

Macatangay, Francis M. "Acts of Charity as Acts of Remembrance in the Book of Tobit." *Journal for the Study of the Pseudepigrapha* 23 (2013): 69–84.

———. *The Wisdom Instructions in the Book of Tobit.* Deuterocanonical and Cognate Literature Studies 12. Berlin: De Gruyter, 2011.

Macdonald, Nathan. "'Bread on the Grave of the Righteous' (Tob. 4.17)." Pages 99–103 in *Studies in the Book of Tobit: A Multidisciplinary Approach.* Edited by Mark Bredin. Library of Second Temple Studies 55. London: T&T Clark, 2006.

Malherbe, Abraham. "Godliness, Self-Sufficiency, Greed, and the Enjoyment of Wealth: 1 Timothy 6:3-19, Part I." *Novum Testamentum* 52 (2010): 376–405.

———. "Godliness, Self-Sufficiency, Greed, and the Enjoyment of Wealth: 1 Timothy 6:3-19, Part II." *Novum Testamentum* 53 (2011): 73–96.

Malloy, Christopher J. *Engrafted into Christ: A Critique of the Joint Declaration.* New York: Peter Lang, 2005.

Marcovich, M., ed. *Clemntis Alexandri Paedagogus.* Vigiliae Christianae Supplements 61. Leiden: Brill, 2002.

Marcus, Joel. *Mark 8–16: A New Translation with Introduction and Commentary.* Anchor Bible 27A. New Haven: Yale University Press, 2009

———. "The *Testaments of the Twelve Patriarchs* and the *Didascalia Apostolorum*: A Common Jewish Christian Milieu?" *JTS* 61 (2010): 596–626.

Marguerat, Daniel. *Le jugement dans l'Évangile de Matthieu.* 2nd ed. Geneva: Labor et Fides, 1995.

Marjanen, Antti. "Thomas and Jewish Religious Practices." Pages 163–82 in *Thomas at the Crossroads: Essays on the Gospel of Thomas.* Edited by Risto Uro. Studies of the New Testament and Its World. Edinburgh: T&T Clark, 1998.

Marshall, I. Howard. *A Critical and Exegetical Commentary on the Pastoral Epistles.* International Critical Commentary. London: T&T Clark, 1999.

———. *The Gospel of Luke.* New International Greek Testament Commentary. Grand Rapids: Eerdmans, 1978.

Marshall, John W. "The Objects of Ignatius' Wrath and Jewish Angelic Mediators." *Journal of Ecclesiastical History* 56 (2005): 1–23.

Martin, Dale B. "Review Essay: Justin J. Meggitt, *Paul, Poverty and Survival.*" *Journal for the Study of the New Testament* 24 (2001): 51–64.

Martin, Ralph P. *2 Corinthians.* Word Biblical Commentary 40. Dallas: Word, 2002.

Matera, Frank J. *God's Saving Grace: A Pauline Theology.* Grand Rapids: Eerdmans, 2012.

Matthews, Christopher R. "Apocryphal Intertextual Activities: A Response to Harold W. Attridge's 'Intertextuality in the *Acts of Thomas.*'" *Semeia* 80 (1997): 125–35.

Mauss, Marcel. *The Gift: Forms and Functions of Exchange in Archaic Societies.* Translated by Ian Cunnison. London: Cohen & West, 1966. Translation of "Essai sur le don: Forme et raison de l'échange dans les sociétés archaïques." *Annee sociologique* 1 (1925): 30–186.

McGuckin, John Anthony. *The Westminster Handbook to Patristic Theology.* Louisville, Ky.: Westminster John Knox, 2004.

McLay, R. Timothy. *The OG and Th Versions of Daniel.* Society of Biblical Literature Septuagint and Cognate Studies 43. Atlanta: Scholars Press, 1996.

———. "The Old Greek Translation of Daniel IV–VI and the Formation of the Book of Daniel." *Vetus Testamentum* 55 (2005): 304–23.

Meadowcroft, T. J. *Aramaic Daniel and Greek Daniel: A Literary Comparison.* Journal for the Study of the Old Testament Supplement Series 198. Sheffield: Sheffield Academic, 1995.

Meggitt, Justin J. *Paul, Poverty and Survival.* Studies of the New Testament and Its World. Edinburgh: T&T Clark, 1998.

———. "Response to Martin and Theissen." *Journal for the Study of the New Testament* 24 (2001): 85–94.

Mendelson, Alan. "Philo's Dialectic of Reward and Punishment." *Studia philonica* 9 (1997): 104–25.

———. *Secular Education in Philo of Alexandria.* Cincinnati, Ohio: Hebrew Union College Press, 1982.

Merkel, Helmut. *Die Pastoralbriefe.* Das Neue Testament Deutsch 9/1. Göttingen: Vandenhoeck & Ruprecht, 1991.

Michaels, J. Ramsey. *1 Peter.* Word Biblical Commentary 49. Waco, Tex.: Word, 1988.

———. "Almsgiving and the Kingdom Within: Tertullian on Luke 17:21." *Catholic Biblical Quarterly* 60 (1998): 475–83.

Mihoc, Vasile. "The Final Admonition to Timothy (1 Tim 6,3-21)." Pages 135–52 in *1 Timothy Reconsidered.* Edited by Karl P. Donfried. Colloquium Oecumenicum Paulinum 18. Leuven: Peeters, 2008.

Milavec, Aaron. *The Didache: Faith, Hope, and Life of the Earliest Christian Communities, 50–70 C.E.* Mahwah, N.J.: Paulist, 2003.

———. *The Didache: Text, Translation, Analysis, and Commentary.* Collegeville, Minn.: Liturgical, 2003.

————. "The Saving Efficacy of the Burning Process in Didache 16.5." Pages 131–55 in *Didache in Context: Essays on Its Text, History, and Transmission*. Edited by Clayton N. Jefford. Novum Testamentum Supplements 77. Leiden: Brill, 1995.

Miller, James David. *The Pastoral Letters as Composite Documents*. Society for New Testament Studies Monograph Series 93. Cambridge: Cambridge University Press, 1997.

Minear, Paul S. *And Great Shall Be Your Reward: The Origins of Christian Views of Salvation*. Yale Studies in Religion 12. New Haven: Yale University Press, 1941.

Monat, Pierre. "Les testimonia bibliques, de Cyprien à Lactance." Pages 499–507 in *Le monde latin antique et la Bible*. Edited by J. Fontaine and C. Pietri. Bible de tous les temps 2. Paris: Beauchesne, 1985.

Moore, Carey A. *Tobit: A New Translation with Introduction and Commentary*. Anchor Bible 40A. New York: Doubleday, 1996.

Moreland, Milton. "The Twenty-Four Prophets of Israel Are Dead: *Gospel of Thomas* 52 as a Critique of Early Christian Hermeneutics." Pages 75–91 in *Thomas Traditions in Antiquity: The Social and Cultural World of the Gospel of Thomas*. Edited by Jon Ma. Asgeirsson, April D. DeConick, and Risto Uro. Nag Hammadi and Manichean Studies 59. Leiden: Brill, 2006.

Morley, Neville. "The Poor in the City of Rome." Pages 21–39 in *Poverty in the Roman World*. Edited by Margaret Atkins and Robin Osborne. Cambridge: Cambridge University Press, 2006.

Mounce, William D. *Pastoral Epistles*. Word Biblical Commentary 46. Nashville: Thomas Nelson, 2000.

Muraoka, Takamitsu. *A Greek-English Lexicon of the Septuagint*. Louvain: Peeters, 2009.

Murphy, Roland E. *Proverbs*. Word Biblical Commentary 22. Nashville: Thomas Nelson, 1998.

————. "Sin, Repentance, and Forgiveness in Sirach." Pages 261–70 in *Der Einzelne und seine Gemeinschaft bei Ben Sira*. Edited by Ingrid Krammer and Renate Egger-Wenzel. Beihefte zur Zeitschrift für die alttestamentliche Wissenschaft 270. Berlin: De Gruyter, 1998.

Mybes, Fritz, ed. *Die Werke der Barmherzigkeit*. Dienst am Wort 81. Göttingen: Vandenhoeck & Ruprecht, 1998.

Myers, Susan E. *Spirit Epicleses in the Acts of Thomas*. Wissenschaftliche Untersuchungen zum Neuen Testament. Second Series 281. Tübingen: Mohr Siebeck, 2010.

Myllykoski, Matti. "Wild Beasts and Rabid Dogs: The Riddle of the Heretics in the Letters of Ignatius." Pages 341–77 in *The Formation of the*

Early Church. Edited by Jostein Ådna. Wissenschaftliche Untersuchungen zum Neuen Testament 183. Tübingen: Mohr Siebeck, 2005.

Nardoni, Enrique. *Rise Up, O Judge: A Study of Justice in the Biblical World*. Translated by Sean Martin. Grand Rapids: Baker, 2001.

Nave, Guy D., Jr. *The Role and Function of Repentance in Luke–Acts*. Society of Biblical Literature Academia Biblica 4. Atlanta: Society of Biblical Literature, 2002.

Neil, Bronwen. "Models of Gift Giving in the Preaching of Leo the Great." *Journal of Early Christian Studies* 18 (2010): 225–59.

Nelson, Derek R. *Sin: A Guide for the Perplexed*. London: Continuum, 2011.

Neusner, Jacob. *The Tosefta, Translated from the Hebrew: First Division; Zera'im*. Hoboken, N.J.: KTAV, 1986.

Neville, David J. "Toward a Teleology of Peace: Contesting Matthew's Violent Eschatology." *Journal for the Study of the New Testament* 30 (2007): 131–61.

Nguyen, vanThanh. *Peter and Cornelius: A Story of Conversion and Mission*. American Society of Missiology Monograph Series 15. Eugene, Ore.: Wipf & Stock, 2012.

Niederwimmer, Kurt. *The Didache: A Commentary*. Hermeneia. Minneapolis: Fortress, 1998.

Nolland, John. *The Gospel of Matthew: A Commentary on the Greek Text*. New International Greek Testament Commentary. Grand Rapids: Eerdmans, 2005.

———. *Luke 9:21–18:34*. Word Biblical Commentary 35B. Dallas: Word, 1993.

Noormann, Rolf. *Ad salutem consulere: Die Paränese Cyprians im Kontext antiken und frühchristlichen Denkens*. Forschungen zur Kirchen- und Dogmengeschichte 99. Göttingen: Vandenhoeck & Ruprecht, 2009.

Novick, Tzvi. "Wages from God: The Dynamics of a Biblical Metaphor." *Catholic Biblical Quarterly* 73 (2011): 708–22.

Oakes, Peter. "Leadership and Suffering in the Letters of Polycarp and Paul to the Philippians." Pages 353–74 in *Trajectories through the New Testament and Apostolic Fathers*. Edited by Andrew Gregory and Christopher Tuckett. The New Testament and the Apostolic Fathers. Oxford: Oxford University Press, 2007.

———. *Reading Romans in Pompeii: Paul's Letter at Ground Level*. Minneapolis: Fortress, 2009.

O'Brien, David P. "Rich Clients and Poor Patrons: Functions of Friendship in Clement of Alexandria's *Quis dives salvetur*." Ph.D. diss., University of Oxford, 2004.

O'Donnell, Tim. "Complementary Eschatologies in John 5:19-30." *Catholic Biblical Quarterly* 70 (2008): 750–65.

Ogereau, Julien M. "Paul's κοινωνία with the Philippians: *Societas* as a Missionary Funding Strategy." *New Testament Studies* 60 (2014): 360–78.

O'Leary, Joseph S. "Atonement." Pages 66–68 in *The Westminster Handbook to Origen*. Edited by John Anthony McGuckin. Louisville, Ky.: Westminster John Knox, 2004.

Olson, Roger E. *The Story of Christian Theology: Twenty Centuries of Tradition and Reform*. Downers Grove, Ill.: InterVarsity, 1999.

Olyan, Saul M. "Ben Sira's Relationship to the Priesthood." *Harvard Theological Review* 80 (1987): 261–86.

Osborn, Eric. *Clement of Alexandria*. Cambridge: Cambridge University Press, 2005.

Osiek, Carolyn A. *Rich and Poor in the Shepherd of Hermas: An Exegetical-Social Investigation*. Catholic Biblical Quarterly Monograph Series 15. Washington, D.C.: Catholic Biblical Association of America, 1983.

————. *Shepherd of Hermas: A Commentary*. Hermeneia. Minneapolis: Fortress, 1999.

Paget, James Carleton. *The Epistle of Barnabas: Outlook and Background*. Wissenschaftliche Untersuchungen zum Neuen Testament. Second Series 64. Tübingen: Mohr Siebeck, 1994.

Pardee, Nancy. "The Curse That Saves (Didache 16.5)." Pages 156–76 in *Didache in Context: Essays on Its Text, History, and Transmission*. Edited by Clayton N. Jefford. Novum Testamentum Supplements 77. Leiden: Brill, 1995.

———. *The Genre and Development of the Didache: A Text-Linguistic Analysis*. Wissenschaftliche Untersuchungen zum Neuen Testament. Second Series 231. Tübingen: Mohr Siebeck, 2012.

Parkin, Anneliese. "Poverty in the Early Roman Empire: Ancient and Modern Conceptions and Constructs." Ph.D. diss., University of Cambridge, 2001.

———. "'You Do Him No Service': An Exploration of Pagan Almsgiving." Pages 60–82 in *Poverty in the Roman World*. Edited by Margaret Atkins and Robin Osborne. Cambridge: Cambridge University Press, 2006.

Parry, Jonathan. "The Gift, the Indian Gift and the 'Indian Gift.'" *Man* 21 (1986): 453–73.

Parsons, Mikeal C. "'Nothing Defiled AND Unclean': The Conjunction's Function in Acts 10:14." *Perspectives in Religious Studies* 27 (2000): 263–74.

Parvis, Paul. "The Teaching of the Fathers: Cyprian and the Hours of Prayer." *Clergy* 69 (1984): 206–8.

Patlagean, Evelyne. *Pauvreté économique et pauvreté sociale à Byzance 4e–7e siècles*. Mouton: Paris, 1977.

Patterson, Stephen J. "Apocalypticism or Prophecy and the Problem of Poly-valence: Lessons from the Gospel of Thomas." *Journal of Biblical Literature* 130 (2011): 795–817.

———. *The Gospel of Thomas and Christian Origins: Essays on the Fifth Gospel.* Nag Hammadi and Manichean Studies 84. Leiden: Brill, 2013.

Pennacchio, Maria Cristina. "L'interpretation Patristique d'Osée 6:6." Pages 147–78 in *"Car c'est l'amour qui me plaît, non le sacrifice . . .": Recherches sur Osée 6:6 & son interprétation juive & chrétienne.* Edited by Eberhard Bons. Supplements to the Study of Judaism 88. Leiden: Brill, 2004.

Penner, Ken M. "Citation Formulae as Indices to Canonicity in Early Jewish and Early Christian Literature." Pages 62–84 in *Jewish and Christian Scriptures: The Function of "Canonical" and "Non-canonical" Religious Texts.* Edited by James H. Charlesworth and Lee Martin McDonald. Jewish and Christian Texts in Contexts and Related Studies 7. London: T&T Clark, 2010.

Pennington, Jonathan T. *Heaven and Earth in the Gospel of Matthew.* Novum Testamentum Supplements 126. Leiden: Brill, 2007.

Perdue, Leo G. *Wisdom and Cult: A Critical Analysis of the Views of Cult in Wisdom Literatures of Israel and the Ancient Near East.* Society of Biblical Literature Dissertation Series 30. Missoula, Mont.: Scholars Press, 1977.

Peterman, Gerald W. "Social Reciprocity and Gentile Debt to Jews in Romans 15:26-27." *Journal of the Evangelical Theological Society* 50 (2007): 735–46.

Phillips, Derek. *Looking Backward: A Critical Appraisal of Communitarian Thought.* Princeton: Princeton University Press, 1993.

Poirier, Michel. *Cyprien de Carthage: La bienfaisance et les aumônes; Introduction, texte critique, traduction, notes et index.* Sources Chrétiennes 440. Paris: Le Cerf, 1999.

Polanyi, Karl. *The Great Transformation: The Political and Economic Origins of Our Time.* Boston: Beacon, 1944.

Pope, Stephen J. "Aquinas on Almsgiving, Justice and Charity: An Interpretation and Reassessment." *Heythrop Journal* 32 (1991): 167–91.

Porter, Stanley. "Greek Linguistics and Lexicography." Pages 19–61 in *Understanding the Times: New Testament Studies in the 21st Century; Essays in Honor of D. A. Carson on the Occasion of His 65th Birthday.* Edited by Andreas J. Köstenberger and Robert W. Yarbrough. Wheaton, Ill.: Crossway, 2011.

Poschmann, Bernard. *Paenitentia secunda: Die kirchliche Busse im ältesten Christentum bis Cyprian und Origen; Eine dogmengeschichtliche Untersuchung.* Theophania 1. Bonn: P. Hanstein, 1940.

Pratscher, Wilhelm. *The Apostolic Fathers: An Introduction*. Waco, Tex.: Baylor University Press, 2010.

———. *Der zweite Clemensbrief*. Kommentar zu den Apostolischen Vätern 3. Göttingen: Vandenhoeck & Ruprecht, 2007.

Quarles, Charles L. "The New Perspective and Means of Atonement in Jewish Literature of the Second Temple Period." *Criswell Theological Review* 2 (2005): 39–56.

Quinn, Jerome D., and William C. Wacker. *The First and Second Letters to Timothy: A New Translation with Notes and Commentary*. Eerdmans Critical Commentary. Grand Rapids: Eerdmans, 2000.

Rabenau, Merten. *Studien zum Buch Tobit*. Beihefte zur Zeitschrift für die alttestamentliche Wissenschaft 220. Berlin: De Gruyter, 1994.

Raith, Charles, II. "Aquinas and Calvin on Merit, Part II: Condignity and Participation." *Pro ecclesia* 21 (2012): 195–209.

———. "Calvin's Critique of Merit, and Why Aquinas (Mostly) Agrees." *Pro ecclesia* 20 (2011): 135–66.

Ramsey, Boniface. "Almsgiving in the Latin Church: The Late Fourth and Early Fifth Centuries." *Theological Studies* 43 (1982): 226–59.

Rebenack, Edward V. *Thasci Caecili Cypriani: De opere et eleemosynis; A Translation with an Introduction and a Commentary*. Patristic Studies 94. Washington, D.C.: Catholic University of America Press, 1962.

Redalié, Yann. "'Travailler de ses mains': Un modèle, plusieurs modes d'emploi (Ac 20,33ss; 1 Tm 5,17s; 2 Th 3,7-10)." Pages 295–303 in *Reception of Paulinism in Acts*. Edited by Daniel Marguerat. Bibliotheca ephemeridum theologicarum lovaniensium 229. Leuven: Peeters, 2009.

Repschinski, Boris. "'For He Will Save His People from Their Sins' (Matthew 1:21): A Christology for Christian Jews." *Catholic Biblical Quarterly* 68 (2006): 248–67.

Rhee, Helen. *Loving the Poor, Saving the Rich: Wealth, Poverty, and Early Christian Formation*. Grand Rapids: Baker, 2012.

———. "Wealth and Poverty in Acts of Thomas." Pages 111–18 in *Prayer and Spirituality in the Early Church*. Vol. 5, *Poverty and Riches*. Edited by Geoffrey D. Dunn, David Luckensmeyer, and Lawrence Cross. Strathfield: St. Paul's, 2009.

Rhodes, James N. *The Epistle of Barnabas and the Deuteronomic Tradition: Polemics, Paraenesis, and the Legacy of the Golden-Calf Incident*. Wissenschaftliche Untersuchungen zum Neuen Testament. Second Series 188. Tübingen: Mohr Siebeck, 2004.

———. "The Two Ways Tradition in the Epistle of Barnabas: Revisiting an Old Question." *Catholic Biblical Quarterly* 73 (2011): 797–816.

Roberts, Jonathan, and Christopher Rowland. "Introduction." *Journal for the Study of the New Testament* 33 (2010): 131–36.

Roloff, Jürgen. *Der Erste Brief an Timotheus*. Evangelisch-katholischer Kommentar zum Neuen Testament 15. Zürich: Benziger & Neukirchener, 1988.

Rondeau, Marie-Josèphe. *Les commentaires patristiques du Psautier (3e–5e siecles): 1. Les travaux des Pères grecs et latins sur le Psautier. Recherces et bilan; 2. Exégèse prosopologique et théologie*. 2 vols. Orientalia Christiana Analeta 220. Rome: Institutum Studiorum Orientalium, 1982–1985.

Roose, Hanna. "Sharing in Christ's Rule: Tracing a Debate in Earliest Christianity." *Journal for the Study of the New Testament* 27 (2004): 123–48.

———. "Umkehr und Ausgleich bei Lukas: Die Gleichnisse vom verlorenen Sohn (Lk 15.11-32) und vom reichen Mann und armen Lazarus (Lk 16.19-31) als Schwestergeschichten." *New Testament Studies* 56 (2010): 1–21.

Root, Michael. "Aquinas, Merit, and Reformation Theology after the Joint Declaration on the Doctrine of Justification." *Modern Theology* 20 (2004): 5–22.

Rosenthal, Franz. "Sedaka, Charity." *Hebrew Union College Annual* 23 (1950–1951): 411–30.

Safrai, Shmuel, ed. *The Literature of the Sages, Part One: Oral Tora, Halakha, Mishna, Tosefta, Talmud, External Tractates*. Compendia Rerum Iudaicarum ad Novum Testamentum 2. Philadelphia: Fortress 1987.

Sahlins, Marshall. *Stone Age Economics*. Chicago: Aldine-Atherton, 1972.

Saldarini, Anthony J. *The Fathers according to Rabbi Nathan (Abot de Rabbi Nathan) Version B: A Translation and Commentary*. Studies in Judaism in Late Antiquity 11. Leiden: Brill, 1975.

Samely, Alexander. *Rabbinic Interpretation of Scripture in the Mishnah*. Oxford: Oxford University Press, 2002.

Sanders, E. P. *Paul and Palestinian Judaism: A Comparison of Patterns of Religion*. Philadelphia: Fortress, 1977.

Sandoval, Timothy J. *The Discourse of Wealth and Poverty in the Book of Proverbs*. Biblical Interpretation Series 77. Leiden: Brill, 2006.

———. "Revisiting the Prologue of Proverbs." *Journal of Biblical Literature* 126 (2007): 455–73.

Satlow, Michael L. "'Fruit and the Fruit of Fruit': Charity and Piety among Jews in Late Antique Palestine." *Jewish Quarterly Review* 100 (2010): 244–77.

———, ed. *The Gift in Antiquity*. Oxford: Wiley-Blackwell, 2013.

Sauer, Georg. *Jesus Sirach / Ben Sira*. Das Alte Testament Deutsch: Apokryphen 1. Göttingen: Vandenhoeck & Ruprecht, 2000.

Scheidel, Walter. "Stratification, Deprivation, and Quality of Life." Pages 40–59 in in *Poverty in the Roman World*. Edited by Margaret Atkins and Robin Osborne. Cambridge: Cambridge University Press, 2006.

Scheidel, Walter, and Steven J. Friesen. "The Size of the Economy and the Distribution of Income in the Roman Empire." *Journal of Roman Studies* 99 (2009): 61–91.

Schelkle, Karl H. *Die Petrusbriefe, der Judasbrief.* 5th ed. Herders theologischer Kommentar zum Neuen Testament 13/2. Freiburg: Herder, 1980.

Schenker, Adrian. "L'Ecriture Sainte subsiste en plusieurs forms canoniques simultanées." Pages 178–86 in *L'interpretatione della Bibbia nelle chieas: Atti del Simposio promosso dalla Congregazione per la Dottrina della Fede.* Rome: Vatican, 2001.

Schipper, Bernd U. "Das Proverbienbuch und die Toratradition." *Zeitschrift für Theologie und Kirche* 108 (2011): 381–404.

Schmidt, Thomas E. "Mark 10:29-30, Matthew 19:29: 'Leave Houses ... and Region'?" *New Testament Studies* 38 (1992): 617–20.

Schneemelcher, Wilhelm, ed. *New Testament Apocrypha.* Edited and translated by R. McL. Wilson. 2 vols. Rev. ed. Philadelphia: Westminster John Knox, 1991, 1992.

Schnelle, Udo. *Theology of the New Testament.* Translated by M. Eugene Boring. Grand Rapids: Baker, 2009.

Schoedel, William R. *Ignatius of Antioch: A Commentary on the Letters of Ignatius of Antioch.* Hermeneia. Philadelphia: Fortress, 1985.

Schreiner, Thomas R. *1, 2 Peter, Jude.* New American Commentary 37. Nashville: B & H, 2003.

Scoralick, Ruth. *Einzelspruch und Sammlung: Komposition im Buch der Sprichwörter Kapitel 10–15.* Beihefte zur Zeitschrift für die alttestamentliche Wissenschaft 233. Berlin: De Gruyter, 1995.

———. "Salomos griechische Gewänder—Beobachtungen zur Septuagintafassung des Sprichwörterbuches." Pages 43–75 in *Rettendes Wissen: Studien zum Fortgang weisheitlichen Denkens im Frühjudentum und im frühen Christentum.* Edited by Karl Löning and Martin Fassnacht. Alter Orient und Altes Testament 300. Winona Lake, Ind.: Eisenbrauns, 2002.

Scott, J. Julius, Jr. "The Cornelius Incident in the Light of Its Jewish Setting." *Journal of the Evangelical Theological Society* 34 (1991): 475–84.

Searle, John R. "A Taxonomy of Illocutionary Acts." Pages 1–29 in *Expression and Meaning: Studies in the Theory of Speech Acts.* Cambridge: Cambridge University Press, 1979.

Sebastian, J. Jayakiran. "Listening to the Speaking Bible: Interpreting the Use of the Bible in a Letter of Cyprian of Carthage." Pages 71–81 in *The Bible Speaks Today: Essays in Honour of Gnana Robinson.* Edited by Daniel Jones Muthunayagom. Delhi: SPCK, 2000.

Seiler, Stefan. "Die theologische Dimension von Armut und Reichtum im Horizont alttestamentlicher Prophetie und Weisheit." *Zeitschrift für Die Alttestamentliche Wissenschaft* 123 (2011): 580–95.

Seitz, Christopher R. "Prayer in the Old Testament or Hebrew Bible." Pages 3–22 in *Into God's Presence: Prayer in the New Testament*. Edited by Richard N. Longenecker. Grand Rapids: Eerdmans, 2001.

Sellew, Philip. "The *Gospel of Thomas*: Prospects for Future Research." Pages 327–46 in *The Nag Hammadi Library after Fifty Years: Proceedings of the 1995 Society of Biblical Literature Commemoration*. Edited by John D. Turner and Anne McGuire. Nag Hammadi and Manichaean Studies 44. Leiden: Brill, 1997.

Sénéchal, Vincent. *Rétribution et intercession dans le Deutéronome*. Beihefte zur Zeitschrift für die alttestamentliche Wissenschaft 408. Berlin: De Gruyter, 2009.

Senior, Donald. *The Passion of Jesus in the Gospel of Matthew*. Collegeville, Minn.: Liturgical, 1985.

Senior, Donald P., and Daniel J. Harrington. *1 Peter, Jude and 2 Peter*. Sacra Pagina 15. Collegeville, Minn.: Liturgical, 2008.

Seow, Choon Leong. *Daniel*. Westminster Bible Companion. Louisville, Ky.: Westminster John Knox, 2003.

Shalom, Yael Wilfand Ben. "Poverty, Charity and the Image of the Poor in Rabbinic Texts from the Land of Israel." Ph.D. diss., Duke University, 2011.

Shanzer, Danuta. "Jerome, Tobit, Alms, and the *Vita Aeterna*." Pages 87–103 in *Jerome of Stridon: His Life, Writings and Legacy*. Edited by Andrew Cain and Josef Lössl. Farnham, UK: Ashgate, 2009.

Sim, David C. *Apocalyptic Eschatology in the Gospel of Matthew*. Society for New Testament Studies Monograph Series 88. Cambridge: Cambridge University Press, 2005.

———. "The Meaning of Palingenesia in Matthew 19.28." *Journal for the Study of the New Testament* (1993): 3–12.

Skarsaune, Oskar. "The Development of Scriptural Interpretation in the Second and Third Centuries." Pages 373–442 in *Hebrew Bible/Old Testament: The History of Its Interpretation*. Vol. 1. Edited by Magne Saebø. Göttingen: Vandenhoeck & Ruprecht, 1996.

———. *The Proof from Prophecy: A Study in Justin Martyr's Proof-Text Tradition: Text-Type, Provenance, Theological Profile*. Novum Testamentum Supplements 56. Leiden: Brill, 1987.

Sklar, Jay. "Sin and Atonement: Lessons from the Pentateuch." *Bulletin for Biblical Research* 22 (2012): 467–91.

Slusser, Michael. "The Exegetical Roots of Trinitarian Theology." *Theological Studies* 49 (1988): 461–76.

Smith, Dennis E. *From Symposium to Eucharist: The Banquet in the Early Christian World*. Minneapolis: Augsburg Fortress, 2003.

Spicq, Ceslas. *Les Épîtres de Saint Pierre*. Sources bibliques. Paris: Gabalda, 1966.

Sprinkle, Preston M. *Law and Life: The Interpretation of Leviticus 18:5 in Early Judaism and in Paul*. Wissenschaftliche Untersuchungen zum Neuen Testament. Second Series 241. Tübingen: Mohr Siebeck, 2008.

Stanley, Christopher D. *Paul and the Language of Scripture: Citation Technique in the Pauline Epistles and Contemporary Literature*. Society for New Testament Studies Monograph Series 74. Cambridge: Cambridge University Press, 1992.

Starling, David. "Meditations on a Slippery Citation: Paul's Use of Psalm 112:9 in 2 Corinthians 9:9." *Journal of Theological Interpretation* 6 (2012): 241–55.

Stegemann, Ekkehard W., and Wolfgang Stegemann. *The Jesus Movement: A Social History of Its First Century*. Translated by O. C. Dean Jr. Minneapolis: Fortress, 1999.

Stein, Robert H. *Mark*. Baker Exegetical Commentary on the New Testament. Grand Rapids: Baker, 2008.

Stewart-Sykes, Alistar. *The Didascalia Apostolorum: An English Version with Introduction and Annotation*. Studia Traditionis Theologiae. Explorations in Early and Medieval Theology 1. Turnhout: Brepols, 2009.

Still, Todd D. "Did Paul Loathe Manual Labor? Revisiting the Work of Ronald F. Hock on the Apostle's Tentmaking and Social Class." *Journal of Biblical Literature* 125 (2006): 781–95.

Strack, Hermann Leberecht, and Günter Stemberger. *Introduction to the Talmud and Midrash*. Minneapolis: Fortress, 1992.

Studer, Basil. "Zur Entwicklung der patristischen Trinitätslehre." *Theologie und Glaube* 74 (1984): 81–93.

Suh, Joong Suk. "Das Weltgericht und die Matthäische Gemeinde." *Novum Testamentum* 48 (2006): 217–33.

Swanson, R. N., ed. *Promissory Notes on the Treasury of Merits: Indulgences in Late Medieval Europe*. Brill's Companions to the Christian Tradition 5. Leiden: Brill, 2006.

Swete, H. B. "Penitential Discipline in the First Three Centuries." *Journal of Theological Studies* 4 (1903): 249–65.

Taylor, Bernard A., John A. L. Lee, Peter R. Burton, and Richard E. Whitaker, eds. *Biblical Greek Language and Lexicography: Essays in Honor of Frederick W. Danker*. Grand Rapids: Eerdmans, 2004.

Tertullian. *Adversus Marcionem*. Translated by Ernest Evans. Oxford Early Christian Texts. Oxford: Clarendon, 1972.

Testart, Alain. "Uncertainties of the 'Obligation to Reciprocate': A Critique of Mauss." Pages 97–110 in *Marcel Mauss: A Centenary Tribute*. Edited by Wendy James and N. J. Allen. Oxford: Berghahn, 1998.

Theissen, Gerd. "Social Conflicts in the Corinthian Community: Further Remarks on J. J. Meggitt, *Paul, Poverty and Survival*." *Journal for the Study of the New Testament* 25 (2003): 371–91.

———. *The Social Setting of Pauline Christianity: Essays on Corinth*. Edited and translated by John H. Schütz. Philadelphia: Fortress, 1982.

———. "The Social Structure of Pauline Communities: Some Critical Remarks on J. J. Meggitt, *Paul, Poverty and Survival*." *Journal for the Study of the New Testament* 24 (2001): 65–84.

Thompson, Marianne Meye. *The God of the Gospel of John*. Grand Rapids: Eerdmans, 2001.

Toolan, Michael J. *Narrative: A Critical Linguistic Introduction*. 2nd ed. London: Routledge, 2001.

Torrance, Alexis. "The Angel and the Spirit of Repentance: Hermas and the Early Monastic Concept of Metanoia." *Studia patristica* 64 (2013): 15–20.

———. *Repentance in Late Antiquity: Eastern Asceticism and the Framing of the Christian Life c. 400–650 CE*. Oxford Theology and Religion Monographs. Oxford: Oxford University Press, 2012.

Torrance, Thomas F. *The Doctrine of Grace in the Apostolic Fathers*. Grand Rapids: Eerdmans, 1959.

Tov, Emanuel. *The Greek and Hebrew Bible: Collected Essays on the Septuagint*. Supplements to Vetus Testamentum 72. Leiden: Brill, 1999.

Towner, Philip H. *The Letters to Timothy and Titus*. New International Commentary on the New Testament. Grand Rapids: Eerdmans, 2006.

Trebilco, Paul. *The Early Christians in Ephesus from Paul to Ignatius*. Wissenschaftliche Untersuchungen zum Neuen Testament 166. Tübingen: Mohr Siebeck, 2004.

Treier, Daniel J. "Proof Text." Pages 622–24 in *Dictionary for Theological Interpretation of the Bible*. Edited by Kevin Vanhoozer. Grand Rapids: Baker, 2005.

———. *Proverbs & Ecclesiastes*. Brazos Theological Commentary on the Bible. Grand Rapids: Brazos, 2011.

Trevett, Christine. "Prophecy and Anti-Episcopal Activity: A Third Error Combatted by Ignatius?" *Journal of Ecclesiastical History* 34 (1983): 1–18.

Tucker, W. Dennis, Jr. "A Polysemiotic Approach to the Poor in the Psalms." *Perspectives in Religious Studies* 31 (2004): 425–39.

Tuckett, Christopher M. *2 Clement: Introduction, Text, and Commentary*. Oxford Apostolic Fathers. Oxford: Oxford University Press, 2012.

———. "Tobit 12,8 and 2 Clement 16,4." *Ephemerides theologicae lovanienses* 88, no. 1 (2012): 129–44.

Tuckett, Christopher M., and Andrew F. Gregory, eds. *The Reception of the New Testament in the Apostolic Fathers.* The New Testament and the Apostolic Fathers. Oxford: Oxford University Press, 2005.

———, eds. *Trajectories through the Apostolic Fathers.* The New Testament and the Apostolic Fathers. Oxford: Oxford University Press, 2007.

Turner, H. E. W. *The Pattern of Christian Truth: A Study in Relations between Orthodoxy and Heresy in the Early Church.* London: Mowbray, 1954.

Ullucci, Daniel C. *The Christian Rejection of Animal Sacrifice.* Oxford: Oxford University Press, 2011.

Ulmer, Rivka. *The Evil Eye in the Bible and in Rabbinic Literature.* Hoboken, N.J.: KTAV, 1994.

Unnik, W. C. van. "Teaching of Good Works in 1 Peter." *New Testament Studies* 1 (1954): 92–110.

Uro, Risto. *Thomas: Seeking the Historical Context of the Gospel of Thomas.* Journal for the Study of the Pseudepigrapha Supplement Series 1. London: T&T Clark, 2003.

Valantasis, Richard. *The Gospel of Thomas.* New Testament Readings. London: Routledge, 1997.

———. "The Nuptial Chamber Revisited: The *Acts of Thomas* and Cultural Intertextuality." *Semeia* 80 (1997): 261–76.

Vall, Gregory. *Learning Christ: Ignatius of Antioch & the Mystery of Redemption.* Washington, D.C.: Catholic University of America Press, 2013.

Van Aarde, Andries G. "'On Earth as It Is in Heaven': Matthew's Eschatology as the Kingdom of the Heavens That Has Come." Pages 35–63 in *Eschatology of the New Testament and Some Related Documents.* Edited by Jan G. van der Watt. Wissenschaftliche Untersuchungen zum Neuen Testament. Second Series 315. Tübingen: Mohr Siebeck, 2011.

Van Leeuwen, Raymond C. "Toward a Biblical Account of Sin?" *Journal of Theological Interpretation* 5 (2011): 133–44.

Varner, William. "The Didache's Use of the Old and New Testaments." *Master's Seminary Journal* 16 (2005): 127–51.

Verheyden, Joseph, Bart Koet, and Steve Moyise, eds. *The Scriptures of Israel in Jewish and Christian Tradition: Essays in Honour of Maarten J. Menken.* Novum Testamentum Supplements 148. Leiden: Brill, 2013.

Vinzent, Markus. *Christ's Resurrection in Early Christianity and the Making of the New Testament.* Farnham, UK: Ashgate, 2011.

Vogel, Winfried. *The Cultic Motif in the Book of Daniel.* New York: Peter Lang, 2010.

Vries, Johannes de, and Martin Karrer, eds. *Textual History and the Reception of Scripture in Early Christianity.* Society of Biblical Literature

Septuagint and Cognate Studies 60. Atlanta: Society of Biblical Literature, 2013.

Waard, Jan de. "Difference in Vorlage or Lexical Ignorance: A Dilemma in the Old Greek of Proverbs." *Journal for the Study of Judaism* 38 (2007): 1–8.

Wagner, J. Ross. *Reading the Sealed Book: Old Greek Isaiah and the Problem of Septuagint Hermeneutics.* Forschungen zum Alten Testament 88. Tübingen: Mohr Siebeck, 2013.

———. "The Septuagint and the 'Search for the Christian Bible.'" Pages 17–28 in *Scripture's Doctrine and Theology's Bible: How the New Testament Shapes Christian Dogmatics.* Edited by Markus Bockmuehl and Alan J. Torrance. Grand Rapids: Baker, 2008.

Wahlen, Clinton. "Peter's Vision and Conflicting Definitions of Purity." *New Testament Studies* 51 (2005): 505–18.

Wall, Robert W. *1 & 2 Timothy and Titus.* Two Horizons New Testament Commentary. Grand Rapids: Eerdmans, 2012.

———. "Peter, 'Son' of Jonah: The Conversion of Cornelius in the Context of Canon." *Journal for the Study of the New Testament* 29 (1987): 79–90.

Wallace, Daniel B. *Greek Grammar beyond the Basics: An Exegetical Syntax of the New Testament with Scripture, Subject, and Greek Word Indexes.* Grand Rapids: Zondervan, 1997.

Waltke, Bruce K. *The Book of Proverbs, Chapters 15–31.* New International Commentary on the Old Testament. Grand Rapids: Eerdmans, 2005.

Walton, Jonathan L. "Stop Worrying and Start Sowing! A Phenomenological Account of the Ethics of 'Divine Investment.'" Pages 107–29 in *Pentecostalism and Prosperity: The Socio-economics of the Global Charismatic Movement.* Edited by Katherine Attanasi and Amos Yong. New York: Palgrave Macmillan, 2012.

Watson, Duane F., and Terrance D. Callan. *First and Second Peter.* Paideia. Grand Rapids: Baker, 2012.

Watson, Francis. "Liberating the Reader: A Theological-Exegetical Study of the Parable of the Sheep and the Goats (Matt 25:31-46)." Pages 57–84 in *The Open Text: New Directions in Biblical Studies?* Edited by Francis Watson. London: SCM Press, 1993.

Weber, Kathleen. "The Image of Sheep and Goats in Matthew 25:31-46." *Catholic Biblical Quarterly* 59 (1997): 657–78.

Weinfeld, Moshe. "'Justice and Righteousness'—משפט וצדקה—the Expression and Its Meaning." Pages 228–46 in *Justice and Righteousness: Biblical Themes and Their Influence.* Edited by H. G. Reventlow and Y. Hoffman. Journal for the Study of the Old Testament Supplement Series 137. Sheffield: JSOT Press, 1992.

———. *Social Justice in Ancient Israel and in the Ancient Near East*. Minneapolis: Fortress, 1995.

Welborn, Laurence L. "On the Date of First Clement." *Biblical Research* 29 (1984): 35–54.

Wengst, Klaus. "Aspects of the Last Judgment in the Gospel according to Matthew." Pages 233–45 in *Eschatology in the Bible and in Jewish and Christian Tradition*. Edited by Henning Graf Reventlow. Journal for the Study of the Old Testament Supplement Series 243. Sheffield: Sheffield Academic, 1997.

Werline, Rodney Alan. "Prayer, Politics, and Social Vision in Daniel 9." Pages 17–32 in *Seeking the Favor of God*. Vol. 2, *The Development of Penitential Prayer in Second Temple Judaism*. Edited by Mark J. Boda, Daniel K. Falk, and Rodney A. Werline. Early Judaism and Its Literature 22. Atlanta: Society of Biblical Literature, 2007.

West, Gerald O. *The Academy of the Poor: Towards a Dialogical Reading of the Bible*. Pietermaritzburg: Cluster, 2003.

Wevers, John William. *Notes on the Greek Text of Deuteronomy*. Society of Biblical Literature Septuagint and Cognate Studies 39. Atlanta: Scholars Press, 1995.

Wheeler, Sondra Ely. *Wealth as Peril and Obligation: The New Testament on Possessions*. Grand Rapids: Eerdmans, 1995.

Whitenton, Michael R. "After Pistis Christou: Evidence from the Apostolic Fathers." *Journal of Theological Studies* 61 (2010): 82–109.

Whybray, R. Norman. *Wealth and Poverty in the Book of Proverbs*. Journal for the Study of the Old Testament Supplement Series 99. Sheffield: JSOT Press, 1990.

Widmer, Michael. *Moses, God, and the Dynamics of Intercessory Prayer: A Study of Exodus 32–34 and Numbers 13–14*. Forschungen zum Alten Testament. Second Series 8. Tübingen: Mohr Siebeck, 2004.

Wilhite, David E. "Cyprian's Scriptural Hermeneutic of Identity: The Laxist 'Heresy.'" *Horizons in Biblical Theology* 32 (2010): 58–98.

Williams, Francis E. "Is Almsgiving the Point of the 'Unjust Steward.'" *Journal of Biblical Literature* 83 (1964): 293–97.

Winter, Bruce W. *Seek the Welfare of the City: Christians as Benefactors and Citizens*. Grand Rapids: Eerdmans, 1994.

Winter, Michael M. "Interlopers Reunited: The Early Translators of Ben Sira." *Journal of Biblical Literature* 131 (2012): 251–69.

Witetschek, Stephan. "Going Hungry for a Purpose: On *Gos. Thom.* 69.2 and a Neglected Parallel in Origen." *Journal for the Study of the New Testament* 32 (2010): 379–93.

Witherington, Ben, III. *Letters and Homilies for Hellenized Christians*. Vol. 2, *A Socio-rhetorical Commentary on 1–2 Peter*. Downers Grove, Ill.: Inter-Varsity, 2007.

Wood, Susan K. "Catholic Reception of the Joint Declaration on the Doctrine of Justification." Pages 43–59 in *Rereading Paul Together: Protestant and Catholic Perspectives on Justification*. Edited by David E. Aune. Grand Rapids: Baker, 2006.

Woolf, Greg. "Writing Poverty in Rome." Pages 83–99 in *Poverty in the Roman World*. Edited by Margaret Atkins and Robin Osborne. Cambridge: Cambridge University Press, 2006.

Wright, Benjamin G., III. "'Fear the Lord and Honor the Priest': Ben Sira as Defender of the Jerusalem Priesthood." Pages 189–222 in *The Book of Ben Sira in Modern Research: Proceedings of the First International Ben Sira Conference, 28–31 July 1996, Soesterberg, Netherlands*. Edited by Pancratius Cornelis Beentjes. Beihefte zur Zeitschrift für die alttestamentliche Wissenschaft 255. Berlin: De Gruyter, 1997.

———. *Praise Israel for Wisdom and Instruction: Essays on Ben Sira and Wisdom, the Letter of Aristeas and the Septuagint*. Supplements to the Journal for the Study of Judaism 131. Leiden: Brill, 2008.

Yinger, Kent L. *Paul, Judaism, and Judgment according to Deeds*. Society for New Testament Studies Monograph Series 105. Cambridge: Cambridge University Press, 1999.

Yong, Amos. "A Typology of Prosperity Theology: A Religious Economy of Global Renewal or a Renewal Economics?" Pages 15–33 in *Pentecostalism and Prosperity: The Socio-economics of the Global Charismatic Movement*. Edited by Katherine Attanasi and Amos Yong. New York: Palgrave Macmillan, 2012.

Young, Frances M. *Biblical Exegesis and the Formation of Christian Culture*. Cambridge: Cambridge University Press, 1997.

Young, Stephen E. *Jesus Tradition in the Apostolic Fathers: Their Explicit Appeals to the Words of Jesus in Light of Orality Studies*. Wissenschaftliche Untersuchungen zum Neuen Testament. Second Series 311. Tübingen: Mohr Siebeck, 2011.

Young, Steve. "Being a Man: The Pursuit of Manliness in the *Shepherd of Hermas*." *Journal of Early Christian Studies* 2 (1994): 237–55.

Zahn, Theodor. *Ignatius von Antiochien*. Gotha: Perthes, 1873.

Zeller, Dieter. "The Life and Death of the Soul in Philo of Alexandria: The Use and Origin of a Metaphor." *SPhilo* 7 (1995): 19–55.

Ziegler, Joseph, Olivier Munich, and Detlef Fraenkel, eds. *Susanna, Daniel, Bel et Draco*. 2nd ed. Vetus Testamentum Graecum 16/2. Göttingen: Vandenhoeck & Ruprecht, 1999.

INDEX OF SCRIPTURE AND ANCIENT SOURCES

APOCRYPHA